Professional
Windows® Workflow Fc

Todd Kitta

Copyright © 2007 by Wiley Publishing, Inc., Indianapolis, Indiana

Published simultaneously in Canada

For general information on our other products and services please contact our Customer Care Department within the United States at (800) 762-2974, outside the United States at (317) 572-3993 or fax (317) 572-4002.

Trademarks: Wiley, the Wiley logo, Wrox, the Wrox logo, Programmer to Programmer, and related trade dress are trademarks or registered trademarks of John Wiley & Sons, Inc. and/or its affiliates, in the United States and other countries, and may not be used without written permission. Microsoft and Windows are registered trademarks of Microsoft Corporation in the United States and/or other countries. All other trademarks are the property of their respective owners. Wiley Publishing, Inc., is not associated with any product or vendor mentioned in this book.

Wiley also publishes its books in a variety of electronic formats. Some content that appears in print may not be available in electronic books.

Chapter 5: Workflow Hosting, Execution, and Communication

Professional
Windows® Workflow Fo

Todd Kitta

Wiley Publishing, Inc.

Professional Windows® Workflow Foundation

Published by
Wiley Publishing, Inc.
10475 Crosspoint Boulevard
Indianapolis, IN 46256
www.wiley.com

ISBN: 978-0-470-05386-7

Manufactured in the United States of America

10 9 8 7 6 5 4 3 2 1

Library of Congress Cataloging-in-Publication Data:
Kitta, Todd.
 Professional Windows Workflow Foundation / Todd Kitta.
   p. cm.
 ISBN-13: 978-0-470-05386-7 (paper/website)
 ISBN-10: 0-470-05386-0 (paper/website)
 1. Internet programming. 2. World Wide Web. I. Title.
 QA76.625.K57 2007
 005.2 76—dc22

                    2006102236

About the Author

Todd Kitta resides in the suburbs of St. Louis, Missouri, with his beautiful wife, beautiful new daughter, and smelly Boxer (dog, not shorts).

Todd has a background in .NET development, and he has worked with .NET since its initial release in 2002. More recently, Todd's involvement in business process software such as BizTalk led him to Windows Workflow Foundation, and the development of this book soon followed. Todd also writes articles for technical publications and speaks at local .NET User Group meetings. He is currently employed at a consulting firm in St. Louis called Covenant Technology Partners, which focuses on business intelligence and portal solutions that use Microsoft technologies.

Todd also enjoys playing his XBOX 360. You can find him by using gamer tag ZillaB2B2.

For Scarlett, my angel

Credits

Acquisitions Editor
Katie Mohr

Development Editor
John Sleeva

Technical Editor
Scott Spradlin

Production Editor
Kathryn Duggan

Copy Editor
Kathryn Duggan

Editorial Manager
Mary Beth Wakefield

Production Manager
Tim Tate

Vice President and Executive Group Publisher
Richard Swadley

Vice President and Executive Publisher
Joseph B. Wikert

Graphics and Production Specialists
Carrie A. Foster
Jennifer Mayberry
Barbara Moore
Heather Ryan
Alicia B. South

Quality Control Technicians
Laura Albert
John Greenough
Jessica Kramer
Brian H. Walls

Project Coordinator
Erin Smith

Proofreader
Kathy Simpson

Indexing
Valerie Haynes Perry

Anniversary Logo Design
Richard Pacifico

Acknowledgments

God—He makes anything and everything possible.

Shannon—Thank you for always believing in me and encouraging me. I love you now and forever. It isn't often a pregnant woman/new mother would support her husband when he's at various coffee shops working on a geeky project such as this book. I'm very lucky and blessed!

Mom and Dad—I wouldn't have been able to accomplish anything I have if it weren't for your support and guidance throughout the years. I'm blessed to have parents like you.

Joe—For being Joe. You rock!

Contents

Contents

Contents

Contents

Contents

Contents

Introduction

Windows Workflow Foundation is one of four major pillars of the recently released .NET Framework 3.0. Although workflow has appeared in Microsoft technologies in the past, it has generally been implemented as a one-off solution specific to a product such as BizTalk or Microsoft Content Management Server. With the release of Windows Workflow Foundation, Microsoft is providing a general use, extensible API for developing process- or workflow-based software solutions. You can think of Windows Workflow Foundation in the same way you think of the .NET Framework: as a general purpose API for building software applications from the ground up.

Windows Workflow Foundation was developed to fill a missing hole in the Microsoft offerings. Workflow-based applications have been developed for many years, but for the most part, the workflow infrastructure has been implemented by using custom code. This, of course, requires that more code be created and maintained over the long term. In addition, this plumbing code isn't solving any specific business problem. Therefore, frameworks like Windows Workflow Foundation provide the general-purpose infrastructure to enable developers to build workflow-based solutions without having to worry about constructing the underlying workflow logic.

This book gives developers and architects alike everything they need to know to start building Windows Workflow Foundation-based solutions in their organizations. Each major area of the technology is covered through examples and sample code. The goal was to provide a good mix of explanatory material covering what comes out of the box with Windows Workflow Foundation as well as examples of what can be built with the technology.

Because Windows Workflow Foundation is a brand new, version one, product, it remains to be seen how most people will use it. However, based on how Microsoft has positioned the product and how organizations have used workflow techniques in the past, certain assumptions can be made as to how people will use this great new technology. This book aims to provide practical instructions on how to develop workflow-based software as well as how to integrate this software into existing technology landscapes.

Whom This Book Is For

This book is for anyone who is interested in learning more about Windows Workflow Foundation. For the most part, if you have an interest in this technology, from a low-level developer perspective to a higher-level architectural perspective, this book has something for you. However, it helps if the reader is already familiar with the .NET Framework, because Windows Workflow Foundation is built directly on top of that technology.

The first few chapters cover the basics of workflow and Windows Workflow Foundation, and use simple code to show how to do some of the fundamental operations related to generic workflow applications. After that, each chapter delves into the different areas of the Windows Workflow Foundation architecture. Topics related to developing solutions using the out of the box functionality as well as extending the base APIs are included in this book.

What This Book Covers

Chapter 1 covers some high level information related to workflow and the .NET Framework 3.0. Chapter 2 is geared toward readers who want to jump right into the code and start developing. Chapter 3 is a great resource for those who want to get an overview of the different pieces of Windows Workflow Foundation. Chapters 5 though 12 are devoted to covering, in detail, specific areas of the framework. Chapters 13, 14, and 15 are related to Windows Workflow Foundation and other technologies such as web services, ASP.NET, and SharePoint, respectively.

How This Book Is Structured

The book has three logical sections: introductory text, detailed descriptions of the Windows Workflow Foundation components, and scenarios for using Windows Workflow Foundation with other technologies. Although it's best if you read the whole book front to back, you are free to browse the information based on your knowledge of the workflow framework. However, you should read the first three chapters before jumping around in Chapters 4 through 15.

What You Need to Use This Book

For those who want to follow along with the code in this book, which is not required, there are only a few prerequisites, the biggest of which is access to Visual Studio 2005. Although Visual Studio is not required to develop C# or other .NET code, it is the most common tool for developers to do so. Therefore, most of the code in this book assumes the reader has access to Visual Studio.

The remaining software needed to develop software using Windows Workflow Foundation is free and can easily be obtained on the Microsoft website. The first download needed is the .NET Frameworks 2.0 and 3.0. .NET 2.0 provides the base class library and common language runtime for .NET 3.0. However, .NET 3.0 contains the new code for Windows Workflow Foundation and the other pillars (which are introduced in Chapter 1).

The next downloadable piece of software is the Visual Studio 2005 extensions for .NET Framework 3.0. This software enables the development of Windows Workflow Foundation in Visual Studio by providing a visual workflow designer and general workflow project templates.

The final, and optional, download is the Microsoft Windows Software Development Kit (SDK) for Windows Vista and .NET Framework 3.0 Runtime Components. Don't be fooled by the name of this SDK—it works for Windows operating systems such as Windows 2003 and Windows XP SP2. This download provides you with documentation and samples to help get you started developing on the next-generation Windows development platform, the .NET Framework 3.0.

Conventions

To help you get the most from the text and keep track of what's happening, a number of conventions are used throughout the book.

> **Boxes like this one hold important, not-to-be forgotten information that is directly relevant to the surrounding text.**

Tips, hints, tricks, and asides to the current discussion are offset and placed in italics like this.

As for styles in the text:

- ❏ New terms and important words are *highlighted* when they are introduced.
- ❏ Keyboard strokes are shown like this: Ctrl+A.
- ❏ URLs and code within the text look like this: `persistence.properties`.
- ❏ Code listings are presented in two different ways:

```
In code examples, new and important code is highlighted with a gray background.
```

```
The gray highlighting is not used for code that's less important in the present
context, or has been shown before.
```

Source Code

As you work through the examples in this book, you may choose either to type in all the code manually or to use the source code files that accompany the book. All of the source code used in this book is available for download at `www.wrox.com`. On this site, simply locate the book's title (either by using the Search box or by using one of the title lists) and click the Download Code link on the book's detail page to obtain all the source code for the book.

Because many books have similar titles, you may find it easiest to search by ISBN; this book's ISBN is 978-0-470-05386-7.

After you download the code, just decompress it with your favorite compression tool. Alternately, you can go to the main Wrox code download page at `www.wrox.com/dynamic/books/download.aspx` to see the code available for this book and all other Wrox books.

Errata

We make every effort to ensure that there are no errors in the text or in the code. However, no one is perfect, and mistakes do occur. If you find an error in one of our books, like a spelling mistake or faulty piece of code, we would be very grateful for your feedback. By sending in errata you may save another reader hours of frustration and at the same time you will be helping us provide even higher quality information.

To find the errata page for this book, go to `http://www.wrox.com` and locate the title using the Search box or one of the title lists. Then, on the book details page, click the Book Errata link. On this page you can view all errata that has been submitted for this book and posted by Wrox editors. A complete book list including links to each book's errata is also available at `www.wrox.com/misc-pages/booklist.shtml`.

If you don't spot "your" error on the Book Errata page, go to www.wrox.com/contact/techsupport
.shtml and complete the form there to send us the error you have found. We'll check the information
and, if appropriate, post a message to the book's errata page and fix the problem in subsequent editions
of the book.

p2p.wrox.com

For author and peer discussion, join the P2P forums at p2p.wrox.com. The forums are a Web-based system for you to post messages relating to Wrox books and related technologies and interact with other
readers and technology users. The forums offer a subscription feature to e-mail you topics of interest of
your choosing when new posts are made to the forums. Wrox authors, editors, other industry experts,
and your fellow readers are present on these forums.

At http://p2p.wrox.com you will find a number of different forums that will help you not only as you
read this book, but also as you develop your own applications. To join the forums, just follow these steps:

1. Go to p2p.wrox.com and click the Register link.

2. Read the terms of use and click Agree.

3. Complete the required information to join as well as any optional information you wish to provide and click Submit.

4. You will receive an e-mail with information describing how to verify your account and complete the joining process.

   *You can read messages in the forums without joining P2P but in order to post your own messages, you
   must join.*

Once you join, you can post new messages and respond to messages other users post. You can read messages at any time on the Web. If you would like to have new messages from a particular forum e-mailed
to you, click the Subscribe to this Forum icon by the forum name in the forum listing.

For more information about how to use the Wrox P2P, be sure to read the P2P FAQs for answers to questions about how the forum software works as well as many common questions specific to P2P and Wrox
books. To read the FAQs, click the FAQ link on any P2P page.

An Introduction to Workflow and Windows Workflow Foundation

This chapter gives you an overview of how business applications were and are traditionally developed, as well as an introduction to workflow and the Windows Workflow Foundation platform.

A Little Background

Initially, computers were used at universities to solve mathematically complex problems. The use of computing power was limited to the world of academia for a period of time before the world realized computers could be applied to solve business problems. Thus began the era of business applications.

If you are reading this book, you likely have some involvement in the world of business applications. Maybe you write .NET code, C++, Java, SQL, or other language to help businesses achieve strategic or cost savings goals. If so, you play an important role in the success of modern business.

Traditionally, a business decides that a given project involving information technology is worth doing because it will give the organization a competitive advantage, trim operating costs, or automate a complex manual process. Generally, the project's software developers gather requirements from the business, perform system and software design, and create the source code. Of course, any software development process worth its salt is much more complicated than that, but you get the idea.

The software development process has evolved greatly in the 50-plus years that businesses have been using computers to help solve business processes. In the not-too-distant past, procedural code was the de facto method for implementing software solutions. Over the past 10–15 years, object-oriented code has given developers a great way to build reusable blocks of code that can be mapped to real-world objects. This building-block approach, when used correctly, can lend itself to helping developers build software solutions more efficiently and quickly.

Order processing, new employee processing, and insurance claim processing are just a few examples of the types of business processes that can be automated. These processes are modeled and documented, at which point a software developer creates his or her interpretation of the process with source code. It is very common in the stages before the actual coding begins for a business analyst to capture the steps in a process and represent the process graphically or with a list of tasks that must be completed and in what order. At this point, the perfectly nice list or visual representation is reduced to source code so that a machine is able to perform the process.

This approach might work in many instances, and in reality, it has been working for many years now. That doesn't mean there isn't a better way. Although this book is dedicated to conveying the technical aspects of Windows Workflow Foundation, understanding the problem domain of workflow and business processes can help you, as a developer, relate the technology to its business drivers.

What Is Workflow?

Workflow is a word that means different things to different people. As you may suspect by the name, workflow defines a process flow or a set of tasks that produces a result. Although this is a good general definition, workflow is also commonly discussed in the context of software systems.

Workflow systems are often associated with the domain of document management. In general, document-management systems handle the transfer of documents between people and other software systems according to a set of policies and procedures. Although document management may be the default concept that comes to mind, it is by no means the only area associated with workflow.

In addition, an archetypal feature of workflow is graphical representation. Workflows are frequently shown as a series of shapes and icons that represent discrete actions. Arrows are also commonly used to represent the flow of work from one step to the next. Although document management and visual representation may represent a large part of workflow, they are really so much more.

Before going too deep into workflow, you need to understand why it is important. One of the top priorities of IT organizations in recent years automating and supporting key business processes. Business process management (BPM) is the framework that describes how organizations can achieve these goals.

Business Process Management

BPM has gained a lot of attention in recent years. Essentially, it is a set of activities that organizations can follow to better understand, implement, and monitor business processes. There are many resources available to you that discuss BPM, its traits, and implementation methods. However, in the context of this book, you need only a good understanding of BPM's high-level qualities and how it relates to workflow.

BPM is commonly broken down into discrete phases that take an organization from one level of maturity to the next. You can find many different descriptions of what these phases are by searching online. However, the following phases are generally represented in one form or another:

1. Design
2. Execution/deployment
3. Management/monitoring
4. Optimization

During the design phase, an organization takes a good hard look at the processes that support the business. Emphasis is placed on fully understanding individual processes and the steps they entail. This might sound fairly obvious, but to fully understand a process and determine where there may be efficiency gains, this phase is crucial. The output of this phase is typically documentation that details the design discoveries.

Typically, the next phase in the BPM lifecycle is to implement the processes that were documented in the design phase. This happens by either making personnel behavior modifications or by implementing or updating technical solutions. There are commercial products available to assist in this phase of the BPM lifecycle from vendors such as Microsoft and TIBCO. These systems are specifically geared toward the problem domain of process development, execution, and management.

Process monitoring describes the step in the lifecycle in which processes are tracked and examined during normal day-to-day operations. For example, the business may be interested to know how many orders are currently in the shipping stage of an order fulfillment process. This is a very important quality of a BPM implementation because if you cannot monitor what is going on with business processes, the metrics that the processes generate cannot help an organization learn and improve.

Monitoring is crucial for the last phase: optimization. Monitoring, when implemented effectively, can help expose issues in processes that were not identified during the design and deployment phases. As you might imagine, these phases are not performed just once — this is an iterative cycle of refinement and improvement.

Of course, for an organization to consider implementing BPM, there have to be some benefits to doing so. If a company better understands its processes and process components, the most obvious advantage is a decline in errors related to performing processes throughout the organization. In addition, because processes implemented through the BPM lifecycle produce valuable business metrics, it is much easier to monitor this information with reports, alerts, and other types of human-consumable data. Better yet, this data can be made available in real time so that adjustments to the process can occur much quicker than in the past, saving precious time and money. Overall, BPM can provide organizations with a larger degree of understanding of its processes while lending itself to better decision making and a higher degree of agility.

Workflow Tenets

According to Microsoft, there are four major tenets that architects and developers can use when considering workflow-based applications. Furthermore, a workflow platform, which can be defined as a software framework to assist in the development of workflow-based applications, should embody these features. The tenets are as follows:

- ❏ Workflows coordinate work performed by people and software.
- ❏ Workflows are long running and stateful.
- ❏ Workflows are based on extensible models.
- ❏ Workflows are transparent and dynamic throughout their lifecycle.

Workflows Coordinate Work Performed by People and Software

This tenet tells us that people play a vital role in the world of software systems related to workflow and processes. Human interaction often occurs through e-mail, web pages, mobile devices, or other front ends. In some instances, the interface between people and software can be part of the normal flow of a process. For example, a workflow might require a human to approve every transaction that comes through an e-commerce website. Human interaction may also be necessary to handle exceptions that cannot be managed in an automated fashion. This scenario may arise when a piece of information necessary for workflow progression is missing.

Because of this requirement, a workflow platform should provide features and infrastructure to effectively handle human interaction and all the issues that come along with it. This includes sending and receiving messages in an untimely manner. People cannot always be relied upon to act quickly or consistently.

Workflows Are Long Running and Stateful

This tenet is important due in large part to the previous one. Because humans are inherently not reliable and tend to interact with software systems on an ad hoc basis, workflows need to be able to run for long periods of time. More specifically, they should be able to pause and wait for input. This could be for hours or months or even longer. Consider a vacation-request workflow at a company. If an employee's manager is out of town, and the employee is requesting a vacation occurring nine months from now, the manager may not respond for weeks.

In addition, a workflow that coordinates software services that are external to an organization cannot rely on instant responses from these peripheral systems. Because of these characteristics, workflows need to be able to run, or at least be waiting to run, for an undetermined amount of time.

The stateful requirement means that the context of a workflow instance should remain intact while the workflow is waiting for feedback. Consider the vacation workflow that goes on for many weeks. If the workflow is not able to save its state, it may be lost forever if the server it is running on is rebooted due to a power outage or other issue.

Workflows Are Based on Extensible Models

The purpose of workflow is to automate a business process, and because each type of business has a wide range of problems, a workflow platform should be extensible at its core. What works for one business problem domain may not apply to another. It is reasonable that a workflow platform cannot account for every kind of activity that needs to occur in every type of workflow. The great thing about a well-architected, extensible system is that developers are able to build the components that were not included out of the box.

To apply this idea to another area, the workflow management architecture should also be extensible. Most workflow platforms provide functionality for persistence, tracking, and dynamic modifications. These areas should be open for extension by developers so that an organization's needs that were not covered in the platform's base functionality can be achieved.

Workflows Are Transparent and Dynamic Throughout Their Lifecycle

This tenet is easier to understand when compared to the traditional software development paradigm. In conventional software, the code itself defines the behavior of the system. As you know, writing and understanding code are very specialized skills that a very small percentage of the business population possesses. Because of this fact, software systems are generally considered to be a black box. People in the business cannot look at a block of code and ascertain what is happening behind the scenes. This can even be difficult for a developer if the code was written by someone else. Workflows should provide the advantage of being able to quickly and easily determine functionality at design time — that is, when the workflow is not running.

Additionally, workflows should be transparent during runtime. This means that a workflow should be able to be queried so that progress can be monitored while it is running. If you take this transparent runtime concept a step further, a running workflow's steps that have not yet occurred should be modifiable. Compare this to traditional code, which, after it is compiled, cannot change itself. This notion of a workflow that can be changed during runtime is very powerful and can open a new set of possibilities related to process automation.

Types of Workflows

At the risk of being too general, there are two types of workflow: ordered and event-driven. Both types provide distinct functionality and would be used in different situations, depending on the requirements of a given system.

Ordered Workflows

When people think of workflow, the first thing that comes to mind is probably an ordered workflow. An *ordered workflow* represents a process that starts with a trigger and flows from one step to the next in a predefined order. The process likely contains control or decision-making logic that includes `if-then` statements and `while` loops.

The steps in an ordered workflow and the order in which they occur are non-negotiable based on the workflow's definition. For example, in an order processing scenario, a customer's credit check *always* occurs before the order is shipped. It wouldn't make much sense to swap those two tasks.

Event-Driven Workflows

Event-driven workflows, sometimes called *finite state machines (FSM),* are based on the idea that you start in one state and jump to another state based on a specific activity or event. For example, a light switch starts in the *off* state. When someone performs the *turn on light* action the light switch transitions to the *on* state.

Like ordered workflows, event-driven workflows have rules that describe which states can transition to other states based on some predefined events. It would not make sense for the light switch to transition to the *on* state if someone unscrewed the face plate.

Workflow Scenarios and Examples

Now that you have a good handle on what traits a workflow platform should possess and what types of workflows exist, the following sections discuss various workflow scenarios and illustrate a few supporting examples.

Human-to-System Interaction

The aforementioned workflow tenets mentioned that human-to-system interaction is vital in the context of workflow-based systems. The importance of this principle cannot be overemphasized.

System-to-System Interaction

As you now know, it is important for workflows to be able to interact with people. It is equally important that systems are able to interact with other systems through a defined workflow. This process of tying external systems together in one cohesive set of steps is sometimes referred to as *orchestration*. If you are familiar with Microsoft's server product BizTalk, you have probably heard this term.

This type of workflow is commonly associated with service-oriented architecture (SOA). SOA is a large topic that is discussed briefly later in this chapter and in subsequent chapters of the book.

Application Flow

A workflow does not have to be an interaction between entities that are external to each other. A common scenario is defining the order in which to display data entry forms or other interface to a user. Think about a college application website. The order in which pages are presented to the applicant is important and is probably based on the education program to which the user is applying.

Another scenario might be a system in which data is processed from a beginning state to an end, cleansed state. Along the way, the data is placed into different buckets that represent different states of being processed. If during a given state, the data cannot be processed because of an extraneous issue, an exception is raised so that a human is forced to inspect and manually fix the problem. This scenario could be applied to customer data coming in from multiple outside sources.

A Few Examples

To get you in the overall workflow mindset, the first example is not a model for a software system at all. It is a set of instructions for an IT recruiter to follow related to an employee hiring process. Figure 1-1 illustrates what this type of process might look like.

The steps could obviously go on from here, but this should give you an idea of what an *ordered workflow* might look like. The first step is always the receipt of an application and résumé, and the next step is always the review for job requirements. The order of the tasks is non-negotiable.

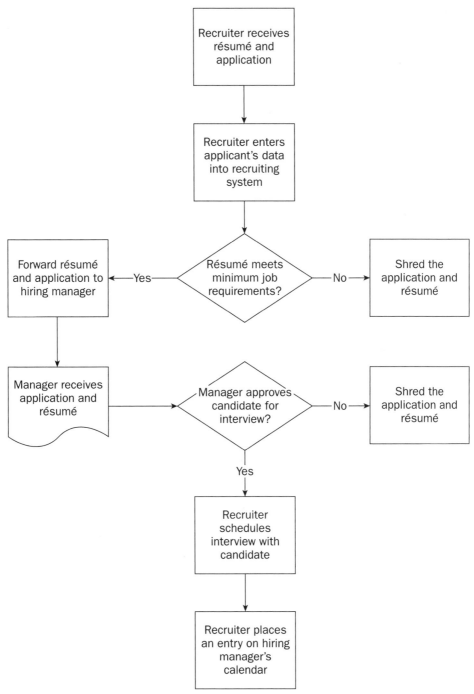

Figure 1-1

Conversely, a workflow does not have to be a set of ordered tasks. The *event-driven workflow* concept introduced previously still has discrete steps that occur to advance a process, but these steps take place based on some action or trigger. For example, a workflow that tracks software bugs may have states to represent bugs that are active, fixed, and irreproducible (see Figure 1-2). A developer is first assigned a bug by a tester, at which point the bug is active. After the code has been modified, the bug enters the fixed state, a tester verifies the fix, and the bug is closed. However, what if the bug was not really fixed by the developer? Instead of progress the bug to the closed state, the tester sends it back to the active state. This cycle could happen over and over until the bug is actually eradicated. Of course, this state-based workflow needs to jump logically from one state to another. It doesn't make sense for a bug to start in the closed state and then transition to the fixed state.

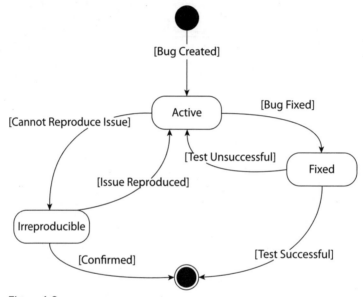

Figure 1-2

As previously mentioned, a workflow can define the interaction between people and systems. For example, an order processing software application might notify a consumer if his or her credit check fails, prompting him or her to provide an alternative form of payment. In addition, this same order processing workflow could call a remote inventory web service to make sure the desired item is available for shipment. Both examples describe a scenario in which the workflow hands off a portion of work to an external entity.

Workflow Implementation

You can implement a workflow in many different ways. The following sections describe a few examples and how each relates to software systems.

Conceptual Implementation

Throughout history, the most common implementation of workflows probably involved no code or software. Imagine all the process flow diagrams developed over the years that represent manual processes. Just because a process is not automated does not mean it is not a workflow.

These types of workflows were developed using a variety of tools, from paper and pencil to Microsoft Visio or other modeling medium. Imagine the court system over 100 years ago or some kind of medical procedure. They all involve a series of steps and a decision-making process.

Workflows with Code

Take a look at the following code listing:

```
public void ProcessOrder(Order order)
{
    if (order.Lines.Count > 0)
    {
        if (order.Customer.CreditCheck())
        {
            if (order.Lines.AllItemsInStock())
            {
                order.ShipOrder();
                return;
            }
        }
    }

    order.Cancel();
}
```

Although this is not a graphical diagram with shapes and arrows, it is a workflow. It uses specific information, in this case an `Order` object, to make decisions and produce an outcome. As long as the order has line items and all items are in stock, it will be shipped. Otherwise, the order will cancel itself, perhaps sending the customer an apology letter.

Object-oriented or procedural code is probably the most common way to implement workflows in modern software. Think about the projects you've worked on. Most likely you have automated some kind of business process.

Although this is probably the most popular way to implement workflows today, it comes with its own set of issues. One of the biggest problems with code is that the only people who can understand it are software developers. Although this may provide job security for some individuals, it doesn't make for a happy business community.

Line of Business Systems

A *line of business* (LOB) system helps a business do something it is probably already doing. LOB systems can range from the monstrous SAP and Oracle Financials to smaller, more specific applications that handle tasks such as customer relationship management, order processing, or human resource-related activities.

LOB systems can solve business problems common across many organizations, but they solve only very specific problems. Although you may be able to customize an out-of-the-box process, you would probably not develop a workflow from scratch inside an LOB. That is the kind of problem better left for workflow engines.

Workflow Engines

A *workflow engine* is a piece of software that provides a way to declare, modify, and monitor a workflow process. For example, you could create a workflow for an engine that defines a patient admittance process in a hospital emergency room. Then when the process changes due to a new privacy law, you could modify it accordingly. Also, because the hospital staff is interested in potential bottlenecks in the procedure, you could use metrics to report how many people are waiting to see the doctor.

Custom Workflow Engines

Because there has not been a widely accepted, compelling answer to the problem of workflow, many developers have approached the problem individually. You may have worked on a project where the concept of workflow was so prevalent that a custom engine was developed just for that initiative.

Commonly, these engines are data driven. For example, steps in a process may be represented by rows in a database table or nodes in an XML file. This makes changing a process relatively easy, and using this model does not require changes to code. Another advantage to developing a custom engine is that it is tailored to the exact needs of the project at hand.

Although developing a custom workflow engine has some benefits, such as ease of process definition and modification (depending on how well your engine is architected), there are a few problems with this approach. First and most obvious, developing a workflow engine takes time. This is time that could have been used for solving a business problem, which is what you're getting paid to do. Second, because you wrote the workflow engine, you have to maintain and support it. Again, this shifts the focus from solving a business problem to supporting a technology problem. Finally, a custom workflow engine probably cannot be all things to everyone. Off-the-shelf engines, which are discussed next, commonly contain functionality for tracking and visualization. It would be quite a task to develop such software when that is not your main business.

Off-the-Shelf Workflow Engines

The free-market system is a wonderful thing. When a need arises, invariably someone invents something to fill the void. Workflow technology is not exempt from this idea. Many vendors offer workflow products to solve the problems discussed in this chapter.

Generally, these products offer features such as workflow definition, management, tracking, persistence, and so on. Going with an off-the-shelf solution has many advantages. Aside from the advantages associated with workflow engines in general (mentioned previously), using a third-party vendor frees you from having to maintain an extra set of code. This relates to the classic buy-versus-build dilemma. In most cases, it is cheaper and more efficient to purchase a workflow product rather than build it yourself. Of course, there are exceptions to the rule, and you should evaluate the needs of your organization before making any decision.

A potential disadvantage of buying a workflow platform is the reliance on the vendor for support and updates. If the vendor goes out of business or decides to start manufacturing hats for small dogs, you are left with the responsibility of supporting an obsolete technology.

This book is not meant to be a commercial for any particular company; however, it is probably prudent to mention at least the most prevalent workflow products. K2.net (www.k2workflow.com) provides a platform to develop, run, monitor, and administer workflows. Skelta Workflow.NET (www.skelta.com)

provides similar functionality. Interestingly, since the announcement of Windows Workflow Foundation, both of these companies have stated that the next generation of their respective products will be built on top of the Microsoft workflow software.

Windows Workflow Foundation

Windows Workflow Foundation, sometimes called Windows WF, was developed by Microsoft to provide developers with a single platform on which to develop workflow- or process-based software solutions. Windows Workflow Foundation is built on top of .NET and is a major component of the .NET Framework 3.0.

An Introduction to .NET and the .NET Framework 3.0

Because Windows Workflow Foundation is built on .NET and is part of the .NET Framework 3.0, the following sections provide some background and context related to those technologies.

The .NET Framework

At its core, the .NET Framework is a platform that supports application development and the ability to run software built on the framework. The types of software that you can build on the .NET Framework include web applications with ASP.NET, smart client applications, and XML web services, to name a few. Figure 1-3 is a graphical representation of the .NET Framework stack.

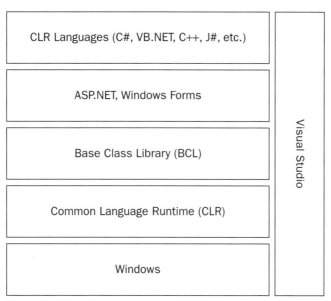

Figure 1-3

The .NET Framework also provides a managed runtime that allows developers to not worry about memory management as part of writing software. Source code is compiled into *Intermediate Language*

(IL), which is a just-in-time (JIT) compilation at runtime. This means that the IL is changed into machine language that the current operating system can understand and run. This concept enables you to develop software in virtually any language that compiles to IL. Microsoft provides several languages, such as C#, Visual Basic .NET, and managed C++.

Another main pillar of the .NET Framework is the Base Class Library (BCL). The BCL is an extremely large and rich set of classes that provide out-of-the-box functionality for developers. This includes classes for string and XML manipulation, ADO.NET classes for database interaction and structured data operations, and much more.

The .NET Framework 3.0

The .NET Framework 3.0 is a next-generation development platform that is available out of the box on Windows Vista and can also be downloaded for other versions of Windows, including Windows XP SP2 and Windows 2003 Server. Essentially, the .NET Framework 3.0 is an extension of .NET that provides developers with a library of managed APIs. The .NET Framework 3.0 components are as follows:

❑   Windows Presentation Foundation (WPF; formerly known as *Avalon*)

❑   Windows Communication Foundation (WCF; formerly known as *Indigo*)

❑   Windows CardSpace (WCS; formerly known as *InfoCard*)

❑   Windows Workflow Foundation (WF; formerly known as *WinOE*)

Figure 1-4 illustrates the .NET Framework 3.0 architecture.

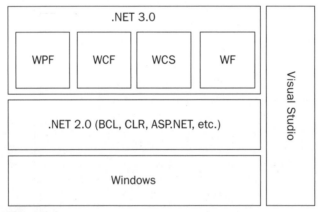

Figure 1-4

Windows Presentation Foundation

Windows Presentation Foundation (WPF), formerly known as Avalon, provides a framework for developing a rich user interface experience. Unlike Windows Forms, which is driven by code, WPF can be developed with a declarative markup model. This markup is called *XAML* (pronounced *zamel*), which stands for *Extensible Application Markup Language*.

XAML is XML based, which means that all you need to develop a user interface layout is your handy Notepad executable. Check out the following code listing for a simple example:

```
<Window x:Class="XamlSample.Window1"
 xmlns=http://schemas.microsoft.com/winfx/2006/xaml/presentation
 xmlns:x="http://schemas.microsoft.com/winfx/2006/xaml" Title="XAML Sample"
 Height="150" Width="200">
  <DockPanel>
    <Button Width="100" Height="50">I am a button!</Button>
  </DockPanel>
</Window>
```

This creates a form that looks like Figure 1-5.

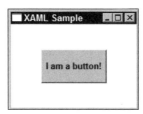

Figure 1-5

Although WPF and XAML are separate Windows Workflow Foundation components, XAML plays a role in the declarative model of workflow development (which you learn more about in later chapters).

Windows Communication Foundation

Windows Communication Foundation (WCF), formerly known as Indigo, is a framework on which you can create SOAs based on industry standards.

SOA is a buzzword of recent years that can cause a lot of controversy when people of the technical persuasion get together to discuss it. Essentially, SOA describes an architecture of loosely coupled services (usually web services) that expose a unique and discrete functionality. Usually, these services perform one very small task, but they perform it well.

Building an SOA at an enterprise is a lot different from building a singular application. SOA provides the foundation to build applications—it is not an application itself. Imagine a company that manufacturers and sells widgets at retail outlets. The organization might have services to submit a bill of materials, to order new widget glue, or to receive and process purchase orders.

Now back to Windows Communication Foundation. One of the biggest advantages of WCF is that it provides a unified platform on which you can develop distributed applications. In the past, if you wanted to develop a distributed application on the Microsoft platform, your options included ASP.NET Web Services (ASMX), .NET Remoting, Enterprise Services, WSE, and MSMQ, to name a few. That's a daunting list, isn't it?

WCF uses industry standards such as SOAP to bring all these technologies together. This enables applications built on the Microsoft stack to interact with technologies from other vendors, such as Java. Essentially, WCF is the replacement and glue for these technologies of yesteryear.

Chapter 14 discusses SOA and WCF in greater detail.

Windows CardSpace

Windows CardSpace is a next-generation identity platform. CardSpace is built on open standards and tries to succeed where Microsoft Passport failed. Passport was not able to live up to its grand promises basically because it required your personal information to be stored with Microsoft. CardSpace reverses the location of personal information to your local machine in *identity cards.* An easy analogy is to consider the cards carried in your wallet, such a driver's license or library card. Whenever you get pulled over, your license acts as proof of who you are. This is because the card was issued by the state you live in, and the friendly police officer trusts the state, not you.

CardSpace uses this same concept. An identity provider issues identities that are trusted by other sites on the Internet. For example, a credit card company could issue an identity to you that represents a physical card you already have. When you purchase something from an online store, you could present the issued card instead of signing in with a user name and password as you would traditionally. The benefits are twofold in a situation like this. First, you do not have to maintain a user name and password combination for every site you frequent. Second, there is an added layer of security because you are not actually entering credit card information. Rather, because the online store trusts the identity issued by the credit card company, it can use it to take care of the payment details.

In addition to the identity cards issues by third-party providers, you can create self-issued cards. This enables you to create a lightweight identity on a site that requires you to register to obtain access to content, such as a forum. Then the site, if it chose to implement CardSpace, could allow you to authenticate by presenting your self-issued card. This again has the benefit of not requiring multiple user names and passwords. In addition, you can create multiple self-issued cards. This enables you to have identities with varying levels of detail for different types of sites. Figure 1-6 shows an example of a self-issued card in Windows Vista.

Figure 1-6

Windows Workflow Foundation

Last but certainly not least, Windows Workflow Foundation rounds out the .NET Framework 3.0 platform and is the main topic of discussion in this book.

Why Windows Workflow Foundation?

After reviewing all this information about workflows and process-oriented software, you might be wondering why Windows Workflow Foundation matters. The following paragraphs relate Windows Workflow Foundation to the four tenets of workflow discussed earlier. This should help you determine whether to use Windows Workflow Foundation in your software development efforts.

❑ **Workflows coordinate work performed by people and software.** This tenet is a key piece of a workflow platform, and Windows Workflow Foundation provides several features that can help you achieve this goal. Workflows built on this framework allow human interaction with basically any interface imaginable — e-mail, web forms, windows forms, instant messaging, InfoPath — the list goes on and on.

The important thing to remember is that the workflow realizes when it is requesting feedback and waits until the required data has been received into the context of the application before progressing. With the Windows Workflow Foundation platform, the possibilities are limited only by your imagination.

❑ **Workflows are long running and stateful.** Windows Workflow Foundation provides a rich framework of runtime services. These services, which are discussed in detail in Chapter 7, offer you an extensible framework to, among other things, persist running workflows to a durable medium. This is important because workflows can run for long periods of time, and storing a workflow's context in live memory isn't practical for many reasons.

If every running workflow in an enterprise had to be stored in memory while waiting for something to happen, the scalability of the system would be nonexistent. The server would run out of memory in no time. In addition, if the server crashed, the volatile memory would be cleared and all data would be lost.

Workflows need to be reliably stateful. Out of the box, Windows Workflow Foundation provides a way for you to persist a workflow's state to a stable channel such as a database. You can extend these persistence services to store workflow state just about anywhere.

❑ **Workflows are based on extensible models.** This is a large part of Windows Workflow Foundation — just about every part of the platform is extensible. Workflows are made up of discrete actions called *activities*. Windows Workflow Foundation provides base activities as well as basic and generic workflow functions. You can extend these activities to meet the needs of essentially any requirement. You can also develop new activities from scratch.

There are many other parts of the platform that are extensible as well. Runtime services provide functionality related to tracking, management, and persistence — which are all extensible.

❑ **Workflows are transparent and dynamic throughout their lifecycle.** Windows Workflow Foundation meets this requirement in two areas: design time and runtime. Because Windows Workflow Foundation is based on a declarative and visual design-time model, processes are easier to understand. This means you can modify existing workflows without having to change source code.

During runtime, you can query the status and overall general health of workflows. The tracking features of Windows Workflow Foundation also enable you to log information to a persistent medium for later inspection. Finally, and very important, you can modify workflows built on this platform even during runtime. This provides for extremely flexible workflow scenarios.

Aside from the features related to workflow tenets, Windows Workflow Foundation supports both ordered and event-driven workflows. The ordered workflow is implemented as a *sequential* workflow (as depicted in Figure 1-7), and the event-driven workflow is implemented at a *state machine* (as depicted in Figure 1-8).

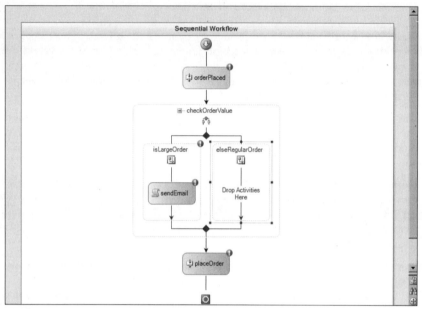

Figure 1-7

Who Should Care About Windows Workflow Foundation?

The following sections describe those who should consider using Windows Workflow Foundation and why. (This is by no means an exhaustive list.)

.NET Developers

The majority of people who can benefit from using Windows Workflow Foundation on a day-to-day basis are .NET developers. Just like it is a good idea to use the latest version of ASP.NET and SQL Server, boning up on workflow can add to your value as a software professional.

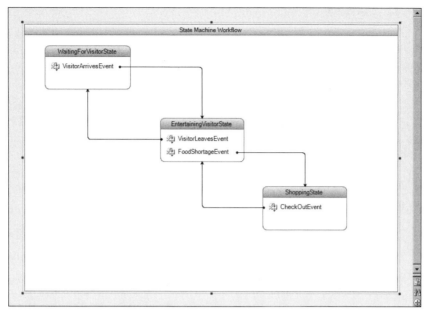

Figure 1-8

Think about some of the applications and projects you've worked on during your career as a developer. You can probably think of several instances where a workflow platform could have come in handy. Now think about workflow in the context of ongoing maintenance of a system that supports a business process. One of the biggest advantages workflow provides to developers is a more efficient maintenance model. Not only is it easier to work with a graphical representation of a process that you developed, but coming up to speed on a workflow someone else developed is also much simpler.

The tools that are part of the .NET Framework, such as ASP.NET, provide you with a rich development environment and enable you to focus on solving business problems rapidly. Windows Workflow Foundation is no exception. By using a platform explicitly geared toward the specific domain of business process, developers can garner a great deal of efficiency and focus.

Architects

It is the architect's never-ending job to evaluate what systems are going to look like from a macro and often a micro level. New technologies come along all the time, and it is up to the architect to determine how these technologies fit in the overall system landscape.

Architects can use workflow to add value to their development efforts and the makeup of a particular enterprise or individual project. They can also use workflows to interact with other pieces of technology. For example, a workflow could coexist and communicate with existing LOB systems.

Technology Leadership

Although most CIOs don't care about how Windows Workflow Foundation works or its technical architecture, they should care about some of the benefits such a tool can bring to an enterprise. For one, workflows provide a unified process-oriented development platform. The integration and consolidation of technologies is a key objective for many in technical leadership positions.

In addition, workflow helps bring process to the forefront of software projects. As anyone in a leadership position knows, recent legislation such as Sarbanes-Oxley requires organizations to have a good handle on their processes. Windows Workflow Foundation provides a framework for tracking and monitoring these processes.

ISVs and Service Providers

One thing Microsoft has been very good at, whether intentionally or not, is fostering a community of vendors that build software on and for Microsoft technologies. Even though Microsoft is the behemoth that it is, it cannot always build software that meets everyone's needs. This is where Independent Software Vendors (ISVs) and service partners come into play.

ISVs are great at catering to the needs of niche and even mainstream markets. For example, the web controls that come out of the box with ASP.NET, such as the GridView, are great and provide a nice foundation on which to create web applications. However, many industries require more robust controls with client-side capabilities and enhanced editing features. There are many grid controls on the market today that, for a relatively inexpensive price, provide developers with the flexibility and functionality they require.

No doubt it will be the same story with workflow. For example, Microsoft is including a few prebuilt workflows with Office and SharePoint 2007 for documentation and management. However, there may be complex scenarios for specific industries, perhaps healthcare, that will allow technology service providers and ISVs to meet a need not yet met by Microsoft.

Summary

This chapter gave you a little background on the history of software development and a crash course in workflow. You learned that because workflow is already a predominant function of traditional software development, it makes sense for workflow-specific platforms to exist.

There are several traits that a workflow platform should possess. Workflows should coordinate work performed by people and software, and should be long running and stateful, based on extensible models, and transparent and dynamic throughout their lifecycle.

You were also introduced to Windows Workflow Foundation, Microsoft's answer to the problem of workflow in software. Windows Workflow Foundation is part of the .NET Framework 3.0.

Finally, this chapter discussed who should consider using Windows Workflow Foundation and why.

2

Hello, Workflow!

This chapter introduces you to the Windows Workflow Foundation development environment that is Visual Studio 2005. You develop a simple Hello World application that highlights several core pieces of a workflow.

The topics included in this chapter are as follows:

- ❑ Developing workflows in Visual Studio 2005
- ❑ Calling a workflow from a console application
- ❑ Simple workflow communications with parameters

Hello World

The preceding chapter introduced you to workflows and Windows Workflow Foundation. In this chapter, you get your hands dirty and develop your first real workflow. What better way to get acclimated to Windows Workflow Foundation than through a Hello World example?

What You Need

To follow along with the examples throughout the book, you need the following installed on your system:

- ❑ **The .NET Framework 3.0** — Because Windows Workflow Foundation is built on top of this, you need the .NET Framework 3.0 installed for runtime functionality.

    Windows Vista comes with the .NET 3.0 Framework out of the box; however, you should ensure that this option is installed on your machine. If you are running an operating system other than Windows Vista, you need to install the .NET Framework 3.0. If you are running Windows XP Service Pack (SP2) or Windows 2003 Server, you are good to go; otherwise, you need to check the requirements for which operating systems the .NET 3.0 Framework supports.

❑ **Visual Studio 2005 (any edition)** — Required for workflow development.

❑ **Windows Workflow Foundation extensions for Visual Studio 2005** — Available for download from Microsoft.

Exercise Objectives

The main objective of this exercise is to provide a high-level view of developing workflows using Windows Workflow Foundation. The example focuses on a console application that passes someone's first name to a workflow, which in turn generates a personalized message. This message is passed back to the calling application and displayed.

This exercise also introduces you to the development environment for Windows Workflow Foundation in Visual Studio 2005.

Getting Started

To get going with the example, launch Visual Studio 2005. As with any other type of Visual Studio solution, the first step is to create a new, blank project. Just like the templates for ASP.NET websites and Windows Forms projects, Windows Workflow Foundation has its own set of project types.

To create the project for this example, select File ➪ New ➪ Project. In the New Project dialog box that appears is a Workflows section under Visual C#. Don't worry too much about studying this screen. The Visual Studio 2005 environment is discussed in detail in Chapter 4. Next, select Sequential Workflow Console Application, as shown in Figure 2-1, and name the project **HelloWorld**.

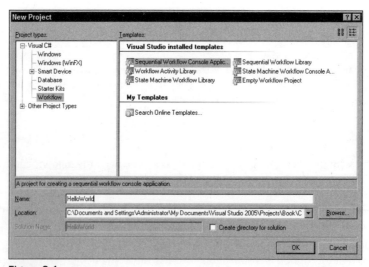

Figure 2-1

After you create the new project, your development environment should look similar to Figure 2-2.

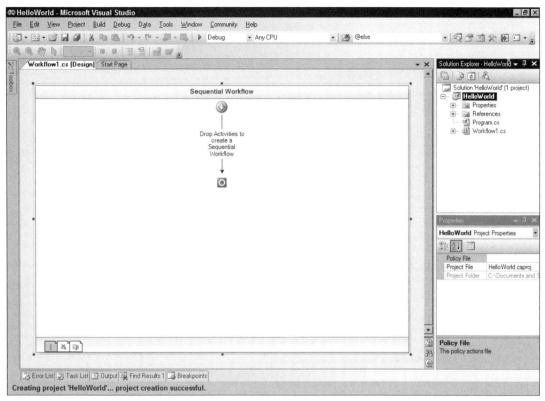

Figure 2-2

If the Solution Explorer is not displayed, select View ⇨ Solution Explorer so that you can examine the files within the project. The Workflow1.cs file is the workflow itself, and the Program.cs file contains the .NET code that starts the application. The following sections discuss both files.

The Workflow

Open the workflow by double-clicking Workflow1.cs in the Solution Explorer if it is not already open. The document is labeled Workflow1.cs [Design] in the document view area of Visual Studio.

Just as with ASP.NET web forms, you can use a code-beside model to create workflows. Code-beside is a way for developers to keep the presentation or design separate from code. The code-beside and other workflow-development models are covered in Chapter 4.

To see the .NET code that is behind the workflow, right-click Workflow1.cs in the Solution Explorer and select View Code. The following code is displayed:

```
using System;
using System.ComponentModel;
using System.ComponentModel.Design;
```

```
using System.Collections;
using System.Drawing;
using System.Workflow.ComponentModel.Compiler;
using System.Workflow.ComponentModel.Serialization;
using System.Workflow.ComponentModel;
using System.Workflow.ComponentModel.Design;
using System.Workflow.Runtime;
using System.Workflow.Activities;
using System.Workflow.Activities.Rules;

namespace HelloWorld
{
    public sealed partial class Workflow1: SequentialWorkflowActivity
    {
        public Workflow1()
        {
            InitializeComponent();
        }
    }
}
```

Because you are passing a string representation of someone's name to the workflow to create a personalized message, you need to add some fields and properties to this file. In the `Workflow1` class, modify the code to look like the following:

```
namespace HelloWorld
{
    public sealed partial class Workflow1: SequentialWorkflowActivity
    {
        private string firstName;
        private string message;

        public string FirstName
        {
            set { firstName = value; }
        }

        public string Message
        {
            get { return message; }
        }

        public Workflow1()
        {
            InitializeComponent();
        }
    }
}
```

These fields and properties pass data to and from the calling console application and the workflow itself. Notice that the `FirstName` property has only a `set` accessor. This is because you are passing the first name to the workflow. The opposite applies to the `Message` property; you are exposing this to the world outside the workflow, so it needs a `get` accessor.

Switch back to the design view for Workflow1. If the Toolbox is not currently displayed in Visual Studio, select View ⇨ Toolbox. Next, drag the Code component from the Windows Workflow section of the Toolbox (see Figure 2-3) onto the design surface of the workflow. Drag it between the green circle at the top and the red octagon at the bottom. (These components, called *activities,* are discussed in Chapter 6.)

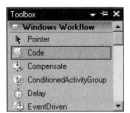

Figure 2-3

Next, rename the Code activity something more meaningful. Do this by selecting the Code activity with your mouse on the design surface and pressing F4 on your keyboard to display the properties available for the activity. Then change the (Name) property to createMessage. A red circle with an exclamation point in it appears in the upper-right corner of the Code activity. This indicates a problem. Click the red icon to display the Code activity error message and find out what's wrong (see Figure 2-4).

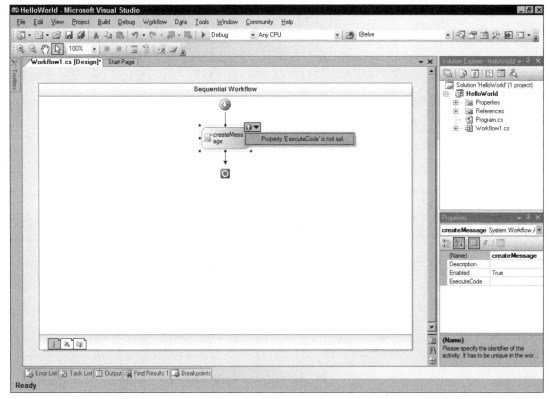

Figure 2-4

This message tells you that an action required for the Code activity has not yet been performed. In this case, the ExecuteCode property has not been set.

To remedy this, you need to wire a handler to the ExecuteCode event (the same way you wire an event handler in ASP.NET or Windows Forms with Visual Studio). Select the Code activity so that its properties are displayed in the Properties window. Next, switch to the events view in the Properties window by clicking the lightning-bolt icon. This displays the only event for the Code activity: ExecuteCode. To wire an event handler automatically, simply double-click the empty text area to the right of the ExecuteCode event label. This creates a method in the Workflow1.cs code-beside file and wires it to the event. The events view of the Properties window should now look like Figure 2-5.

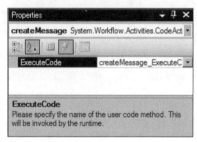

Figure 2-5

The next step is to create the message to be returned from the workflow. Modify the createMessage_ExecuteCode method to look like the following code:

```
private void createMessage_ExecuteCode(object sender, EventArgs e)
{
    message = "Hello " + firstName + "!";
}
```

This code simply sets the class field, message, with a personalized hello greeting. Remember, the message field is exposed through the public Message property. This allows the calling application to read the value set within the workflow.

The Console Application

The purpose of the console application is to act as a host for the workflow. Hosting, an essential part of Windows Workflow Foundation, is discussed in Chapter 5.

Open the Program.cs file by double-clicking it in the Solution Explorer. This file contains the following code, which kicks off the console application and then starts the workflow:

```
using System;
using System.Collections.Generic;
using System.Text;
using System.Threading;
using System.Workflow.Runtime;
using System.Workflow.Runtime.Hosting;
```

```
using WorkflowConsoleApplication1.Properties;

namespace HelloWorld
{
    class Program
    {
        static void Main(string[] args)
        {
            WorkflowRuntime workflowRuntime = new WorkflowRuntime();
            AutoResetEvent waitHandle = new AutoResetEvent(false);

            workflowRuntime.WorkflowCompleted += delegate(object sender,
                WorkflowCompletedEventArgs e) {waitHandle.Set();};

            workflowRuntime.WorkflowTerminated += delegate(object sender,
                WorkflowTerminatedEventArgs e)
            {
                Console.WriteLine(e.Exception.Message);
                waitHandle.Set();
            };

            WorkflowInstance instance =
                workflowRuntime.CreateWorkflow(typeof(HelloWorld.Workflow1));
            instance.Start();

            waitHandle.WaitOne();
        }
    }
}
```

You need to modify this code so that the personalized greeting that was generated in the workflow can be accessed and displayed. To do this, you create a string variable called message and then modify the WorkflowCompleted event handler to retrieve the message from the WorkflowCompletedEventArgs instance.

The event handler for WorkflowCompleted is an anonymous method. *Anonymous methods* are features of C# that enable developers to create inline code that typically exists in a method. This feature is usually used with small amounts of code.

To learn more about the features of C#, check out *Professional C# 2005* (available at www.wrox.com**).**

To retrieve the message from the workflow, you use the OutputParameters property in the Workflow CompletedEventArgs instance passed to the event handler. OutputParameters is a Dictionary <string, object> object, so you need to supply it with a string key. The OutputParameters property is called a *generic.* Like anonymous methods, generics are specific features of C# that are not covered in detail here. At a high level, generics provide a way for developers to use strong typing with collections and other types that may normally be loosely typed. This is a very powerful feature of C# 2.0.

To retrieve the message from the dictionary, use the name of the public property from the workflow as the key. In this case, the key string passed is `Message`. Because the dictionary returns an object, you need to cast it to a string when setting the `message` member, as shown in the following code:

```
static void Main(string[] args)
{
    WorkflowRuntime workflowRuntime = new WorkflowRuntime();
    AutoResetEvent waitHandle = new AutoResetEvent(false);

    // a variable to hold the message from the workflow
    string message = String.Empty;

    workflowRuntime.WorkflowCompleted += delegate(object sender,
        WorkflowCompletedEventArgs e)
    {
        // the workflow is done, get the message from
        // the output parameters dictionary
        message = (string)e.OutputParameters["Message"];
        waitHandle.Set();
    };
```

The next step is to write the code that passes a person's first name to the workflow. To do this, you use a `Dictionary<string, object>` collection, just as you did with the output parameters. After you create this input parameters object, you use the `Add` method to add the first name to the dictionary. Because the first-name parameter is set to the workflow's public `FirstName` property, you must use the same spelling and case for the key when you add it to the dictionary. Then you need to modify the line of code that creates the `WorkflowInstance` object to pass the parameters dictionary. Here's how all of this works:

```
...
workflowRuntime.WorkflowTerminated += delegate(object sender,
WorkflowTerminatedEventArgs e)
{
    Console.WriteLine(e.Exception.Message);
    waitHandle.Set();
};

// create a dictionary for input parameters
Dictionary<string, object> inParms = new Dictionary<string, object>();

// add a first name to the parms list
inParms.Add("FirstName", "Todd");

WorkflowInstance instance =
workflowRuntime.CreateWorkflow(typeof(HelloWorld.Workflow1), inParms);
instance.Start();
...
```

The final step for this first example is to display the message in the console's output. Add the `Console.WriteLine()` call, as follows:

```
...
instance.Start();

waitHandle.WaitOne();
```

```
// write the message to the console
Console.WriteLine(message);
```

The example is now ready to run. To test it, press F5. The code should compile, and a console window should appear with the output (see Figure 2-6).

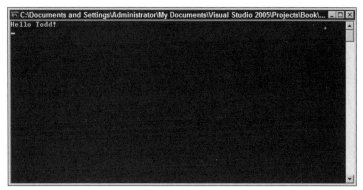

Figure 2-6

Congratulations — you've just developed your first Windows Workflow Foundation workflow!

Going a Step Further

Although the previous example may have been a nice crash course in developing with Windows Workflow Foundation, it was pretty boring. This section expands on the first example and lets you do something a little more complex.

In the first example, the calling application is forced to pass a name to the workflow to receive the message. To spice things up a bit, this example uses some decision-making logic to generate the message based on whether or not a name was passed in.

To achieve this functionality, you again tap the power of the Visual Studio Toolbox. This time, locate the IfElse activity (see Figure 2-7) and drag it on to the workflow surface above the existing Code activity.

Figure 2-7

The IfElse activity can have any number of *branches* that are executed based on an expression that returns either `true` or `false`. The final branch on an IfElse activity does not need an expression because it can act as the `else` case just as in traditional programming. Figure 2-8 shows what the IfElse activity looks like before configuration.

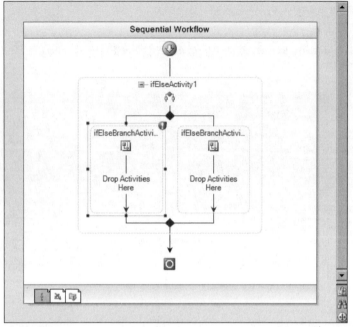

Figure 2-8

Just as with the Code activity in the previous example, the IfElse activity is warning the developer that something is not quite right and needs to be fixed before proceeding. Again, the error is indicated by the red exclamation point. In this case, the `Condition` property of the first IfElse branch activity has not been set.

To fix the issue, you need to supply a condition so the IfElse activity is able to make decisions. The IfElse activity is covered in detail in Chapter 6, so there is not a detailed discussion here about how it works. However, you need to have a basic understanding of this activity to follow this example.

To provide a condition for the IfElse activity, you first need to write a method with a predefined signature in the code-beside file. Here is the method skeleton:

```
private void HaveFirstName(object sender, ConditionalEventArgs e)
{
}
```

Notice the method's name is `HaveFirstName` because that is what the workflow checks for when making its decision.

Next, finish the `HaveFirstName` method by adding the following Boolean expression:

```
private void HaveFirstName(object sender, ConditionalEventArgs e)
{
```

```
    if (!String.IsNullOrEmpty(this.firstName))
    {
        e.Result = true;
    }
}
```

Here, the `Result` property of the `ConditionalEventArgs` instance is being set to `true` only when the `firstName` member contains a value. (The `Result` property is `false` by default.) The IfElse activity then uses the value set in this method to determine whether or not to execute a given conditional branch.

Now switch back to the workflow's design view. Select the first conditional branch, currently called `ifElseBranchActivity1`, on the left side of the IfElse activity so that its properties are displayed. Your current objective is to provide a condition to the branch. To do this, select the `Condition` property from the properties grid and select `System.Workflow.Activities.CodeCondition` from the drop-down list. Selecting this condition type enables you to provide a method with the same signature as the method you just created.

Expand the `Condition` property by clicking the plus symbol. A subproperty, also called `Condition`, displays a drop-down list from which you can select the `HaveFirstName` method. When this branch is evaluated during execution, it uses the logic that exists in `HaveFirstName`. Because this branch provides the same functionality as the first example, the existing Code activity needs to be placed in this branch. Drag and drop the `createMessage` Code activity from below the IfElse activity to the `Drop Activities Here` branch on the left.

Next, you need to place a new Code activity in the `ifElseBranchActivity2` branch on the right. This activity produces a message that doesn't depend on the existence of a name.

Rename the new Code activity to `createMessage2`, and wire a handler to its `ExecuteCode` event as you did in the previous example. The code in the event handler should look like the following:

```
private void createMessage2_ExecuteCode(object sender, EventArgs e)
{
    message = "Hello world!";
}
```

As you can see, the `message` member is simply set to a static Hello World! message.

Now switch to the workflow's design view. Performing a little cleanup on the activities' names might be a good idea at this point to make the workflow a little more readable. Make the following naming changes:

❑   `IfElseActivity1` — HaveName

❑   `IfElseBranchActivity1` — Yes

❑   `IfElseBranchActivity2` — No

The finished workflow should look like Figure 2-9.

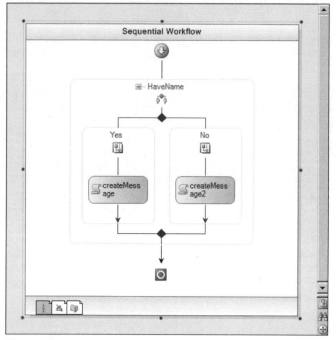

Figure 2-9

This workflow produces the same result as before: a personalized message. This is because the calling application is still passing in a name to the workflow. To test the new logic, comment the line of code in the console application that adds the `FirstName` parameter to the `inParms` object as follows:

```
// inParms.Add("FirstName", "Todd");
```

This produces a screen that looks like Figure 2-10.

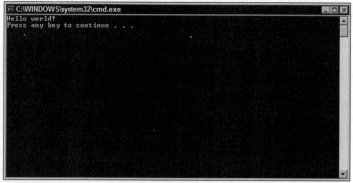

Figure 2-10

Summary

Even though the two examples in this chapter didn't do anything extremely exciting, both covered some key points, considering Windows Workflow Foundation is a new software development paradigm. First, you learned how to start a new workflow project in Visual Studio 2005. In this case, the workflow gets called from a standard .NET console application. This console application is referred to as a *host*. Workflow hosting is an important topic that is discussed further in Chapter 5.

In addition, you were introduced to a very important piece of the workflow framework: activities. Activities are the reusable building blocks for composing workflows. Chapter 6 covers them in detail.

3

Breaking It Down

This chapter introduces you to the individual components of Windows Workflow Foundation at a high level. (Subsequent chapters dig into further detail on each topic.) This chapter also discusses a few areas of interest related to the Windows Workflow Foundation platform, such as extensibility and other technologies that affect workflow — for example, BizTalk and SharePoint.

Topics covered in this chapter include the following:

❑ Workflow types

❑ Components of Windows Workflow Foundation

❑ Windows Workflow characteristics

❑ Windows Workflow and other technologies

Platform Overview

Chapter 1 gives you a high-level view of Windows Workflow Foundation and its architecture. This chapter delves deeper into what you were introduced to earlier. Figure 3-1 shows the workflow stack.

It's a Foundation

One of the most basic things to understand about Windows Workflow Foundation, but initially one of the biggest misconceptions, is that it is a framework for developing workflow-based systems. It is not a server- or client-based product (like Office or SharePoint is a product). Neither is it a language (like C# or VB.NET).

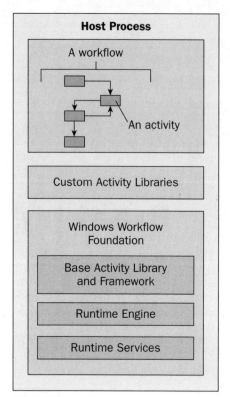

Figure 3-1

You do not just install, configure, and run Windows Workflow Foundation, and then you have work-flow. Just as with Windows Forms and ASP.NET, Windows Workflow Foundation provides a foundation on which to build workflow-based systems. All the pieces required to build workflows and manipulate the workflow infrastructure are provided. The rest is up to you.

Who Is It For?

Although there have been many predictions that software will someday be developed by business users, and certain products do indeed seem to be headed in that direction, Windows Workflow Foundation is still largely a tool for developers — at least during the development cycle. Even though workflows are developed largely with a visual and declarative model, there is still a lot to be done in the background.

Additionally, many of the common tasks performed during a workflow project include the development of .NET code. Obviously, these types of tasks need to be performed by traditional developers. The learning curve related to the tools is simply too high to expect workflows to be developed from scratch by anyone but developers.

Windows Workflow Foundation Components

The following sections outline the various pieces of the Windows Workflow Foundation framework. These high-level items represent the functionality that is provided out of the box.

Workflows

The most obvious piece of Windows Workflow Foundation is the workflow itself. This includes items such as workflow design functionality, the different types of workflows, the infrastructure available to run the workflows, and the workflow development tools.

Types of Workflows

Windows Workflow Foundation provides two workflow types: sequential and state-machine. Each of these has its own distinct traits and set of activities that you can execute within a workflow instance. Chapter 1 introduces these workflow types as ordered and event-driven workflows, respectively. Sequential and state-machine workflows are simply how these types are referenced in the domain of Windows Workflow Foundation.

Sequential Workflows

A sequential workflow is probably the most common type of workflow and the prime example of what most people think about related to this topic. This type of workflow describes a process that has a beginning point, performs any number of actions in a given order, and then arrives at an end state.

You can easily spot the sequential workflow in the designer; it has a green indicator icon at the top of the workflow and a red icon at the bottom (see Figure 3-2). This should tip you off that workflows run from top to bottom, meaning that activities farther up the design surface execute first.

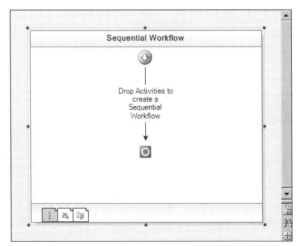

Figure 3-2

In sequential workflows, you can use several logic control constructs from traditional development, such as `if-then` statements and `while` loops. The difference is that these constructs are defined visually and declaratively rather than programmatically, as with C# or other programming languages.

State-Machine Workflows

State-machine workflows differ from sequential workflows in that they jump around in their execution rather than move in an ordered manner. These jumps are triggered by events, and each jump is to a defined *state*. State-machine workflows start in a beginning state; move to and from any number of interim states; and then arrive in an end state, at which point the workflow instance is complete.

When to Use What

You might opt to use the sequential workflow by default because it is such a common way of thinking about the flow of processes. However, here are some instances where using the state-machine workflow type is the best option:

- ❑ When events external to the workflow dictate the next step

- ❑ When the order of work activities is not always the same or predictable

- ❑ When human interaction is prevalent throughout the process

- ❑ When you're using a sequential workflow, and it becomes increasingly difficult to model all the possible execution paths (which may be a sign that you are using the wrong type of workflow)

Activities

Activities are the basic building blocks of workflows built on Windows Workflow Foundation. When a workflow instance is started, activities are executed as defined in the workflow definition until the last activity is executed, at which point the workflow is complete.

Activities are meant to be standalone pieces of functionality that can be reused multiple times within a workflow or across multiple workflows. Additionally, activities generally have some configurable properties.

Workflows Are Activities

Workflows themselves are actually implemented as activities. `SequentialWorkflowActivity` and `StateMachineWorkflowActivity`, the classes that represent the two workflow types introduced previously, both indirectly inherit from `System.Workflow.ComponentModel.Activity`. This means you can theoretically develop your own workflow types — however, you would probably not need to do this very often. In addition, because workflows are actually activities, they have the same behavior and properties as other activities.

The following code defines the `Activity` class. You can find this metadata by navigating to the `Activity` class definition in Visual Studio:

```
public class Activity : DependencyObject
{
    public static readonly DependencyProperty ActivityContextGuidProperty;
    public static readonly DependencyProperty CancelingEvent;
```

```
public static readonly DependencyProperty ClosedEvent;
public static readonly DependencyProperty CompensatingEvent;
public static readonly DependencyProperty ExecutingEvent;
public static readonly DependencyProperty FaultingEvent;
public static readonly DependencyProperty StatusChangedEvent;

public Activity();
public Activity(string name);

public string Description { get; set; }
public bool Enabled { get; set; }
public ActivityExecutionResult ExecutionResult { get; }
public ActivityExecutionStatus ExecutionStatus { get; }
public bool IsDynamicActivity { get; }
public string Name { get; set; }
public CompositeActivity Parent { get; }
public string QualifiedName { get; }
protected Guid WorkflowInstanceId { get; }

public event EventHandler<ActivityExecutionStatusChangedEventArgs> Canceling;
public event EventHandler<ActivityExecutionStatusChangedEventArgs> Closed;
public event EventHandler<ActivityExecutionStatusChangedEventArgs>
    Compensating;
public event EventHandler<ActivityExecutionStatusChangedEventArgs> Executing;
public event EventHandler<ActivityExecutionStatusChangedEventArgs> Faulting;
public event EventHandler<ActivityExecutionStatusChangedEventArgs>
    StatusChanged;

protected internal virtual ActivityExecutionStatus Cancel(
    ActivityExecutionContext executionContext);
public Activity Clone();
protected internal virtual ActivityExecutionStatus Execute(
    ActivityExecutionContext executionContext);
public Activity GetActivityByName(string activityQualifiedName);
public Activity GetActivityByName(string activityQualifiedName,
    bool withinThisActivityOnly);
protected internal virtual ActivityExecutionStatus HandleFault(
    ActivityExecutionContext executionContext, Exception exception);
protected internal virtual void Initialize(IServiceProvider provider);
public static Activity Load(Stream stream, Activity outerActivity);
public static Activity Load(Stream stream, Activity outerActivity,
    IFormatter formatter);
protected internal virtual void OnActivityExecutionContextLoad(
    IServiceProvider provider);
protected internal virtual void OnActivityExecutionContextUnload(
    IServiceProvider provider);
protected virtual void OnClosed(IServiceProvider provider);
protected internal void RaiseEvent(DependencyProperty dependencyEvent,
    object sender, EventArgs e);
public void RegisterForStatusChange(DependencyProperty dependencyProp,
    IActivityEventListener<ActivityExecutionStatusChangedEventArgs>
        activityStatusChangeListener);
public void Save(Stream stream);
public void Save(Stream stream, IFormatter formatter);
```

```
        public override string ToString();
        protected void TrackData(object userData);
        protected void TrackData(string userDataKey, object userData);
        protected internal virtual void Uninitialize(IServiceProvider provider);
        public void UnregisterForStatusChange(DependencyProperty dependencyProp,
            IActivityEventListener<ActivityExecutionStatusChangedEventArgs>
                activityStatusChangeListener);
    }
```

Base Activity Library

The Windows Workflow Foundation framework ships with more than 30 activities in the *base activity library* (BAL). The BAL contains activities from the most basic control logic to more complex activities, such as invoking remote web services. Figure 3-3 shows all the BAL activities within the Visual Studio Toolbox.

Figure 3-3

There are also some activities that are specific to the state-machine workflow type (see Table 3-1).

Table 3-1: State-Machine Activity Classes

Class	Description
EventDrivenActivity	Allows a workflow state to be executed based on the firing of an event external to the workflow instance.
SetStateActivity	Allows the explicit transition to a new workflow state.
StateActivity	Symbolizes a workflow state.
StateInitializationActivity	This activity can contain child activities that execute when a workflow state is entered.
StateFinalizationActivity	This activity can contain child activities that execute when a workflow state is ending.

Custom Activities

Because Windows Workflow Foundation is extensible to its core, you can easily create new activities to meet specific business needs. Custom activities could be something as generic as a SQL table-row insert or something very specific, such as creating an order within an existing line of business (LOB) system.

Chapter 6 describes the BAL and developing custom activities in greater detail.

Hosting

Because Windows Workflow Foundation is not a standalone product, it needs a host application in which to run. A *host* can be any type of .NET software, such as a Windows Forms, ASP.NET, console, Windows Service, or web service application.

Even though the workflow is where most of the interesting business logic takes place, the host plays a vital role in the lifecycle of workflow execution. The host is where the workflow is kicked off and, generally, where user interaction takes place.

The Runtime Engine

The Windows Workflow Foundation *runtime engine* is what makes workflows go, essentially. What it isn't, however, is a separate service or process. In fact, the workflow runtime engine runs in the same process as the host application.

The workflow runtime engine also exposes several events that let your application when a workflow instance is completed, aborted, or has gone idle. Another important piece of Windows Workflow Foundation is the concept of runtime services (discussed later in this chapter). The workflow runtime engine manages the addition, removal, and execution of these runtime services.

Communication with the Host

Workflows do not execute in a vacuum; hence, Windows Workflow Foundation provides facilities for back-and-forth communication between a workflow instance and its host. There are communication methods that enable you to quickly and easily pass data in and out of a workflow, and more customizable methods that can handle external events and call methods outside a workflow instance's context.

Parameters allow simplistic communication between a workflow instance and its host. When you start a workflow in a host application by calling the `CreateWorkflow` method of the `WorkflowRuntime` class, you can pass a `Dictionary<string, object>` instance that contains items of interest to a workflow. Conversely, you can obtain a `Dictionary<string, object>` instance in a `WorkflowCompleted` event handler. This instance can contain any number of variables from the workflow, which can then be used in the calling host application.

Another form of workflow communication is called *local communication services.* This type of communication is performed with classes through events and methods. The host can talk to the workflow by firing events, which are then handled internally by the workflow. The workflow can also communicate with the host by calling methods on the communication service class. This is an elegant form of communication because it uses concepts already familiar to developers.

Using local communication services is easy. First, you need to develop a .NET interface that defines the events and methods to be used for communicating back and forth between the host and a workflow instance. The following code shows an example interface:

```
[ExternalDataExchangeAttribute]
public interface ITalkWithMe
{
    void TellSomethingToTheHost(string message);
    event EventHandler<EventArgs> NotifyTheWorkflow;
}
```

The next step is to create a class that implements this interface, as follows:

```
public class TalkWithMeService : ITalkWithMe
{
    public void TellSomethingToTheHost(string message)
    {
        System.Windows.Forms.MessageBox("The workflow told me: " + message);
    }

    public event EventHandler<EventArgs> NotifyTheWorkflow;

    public void SendAnEventToTheWorkflow()
    {
        NotifyTheWorkflow(this,
            new ExternalDataEventArgs(WorkflowEnvironment.WorkflowInstanceId));
    }
}
```

A couple of interesting things are going on with the interface and the `TalkWithMeService` class. First, notice that the `ITalkWithMe` interface has an `ExternalDataExchange` attribute. This tells Windows Workflow Foundation that this is a local communication service. Next, take a look at the `TellSomethingToTheHost` implementation in the `TalkWithMeService` class. This method is called from within the workflow instance and a string message is passed. The `SendAnEventToTheWorkflow` method is provided so the host can raise the `NotifyTheWorkflow` event. The workflow should have a handler already wired up so that it can handle this event.

Chapter 5 discusses the concept of workflow hosting, which includes communication between workflows and the host. Workflow communication discussed in the previous context does not include communication using web services. However, this type of communication is very important and is supported on the Windows Workflow Foundation platform. Chapter 14 discusses workflows and web services.

Runtime Services

The following sections discuss the concept of *runtime services*. Runtime services consist of out-of-the-box and custom classes that essentially live in the workflow runtime engine during execution. These runtime services perform specific tasks related to workflow execution and maintenance.

Out-of-the-Box Services

There are several types of runtime services included with the base workflow framework. These classes provide functionality that is generic to a problem domain and commonly needed in many scenarios. The following sections describe the different classifications of out-of-the-box services.

Transaction Services

Transaction runtime services, or commit batch services, enable you to maintain integrity in workflow applications. Transactions are generally defined as a group of activities (not necessarily workflow-type activities) that must occur successfully as a whole. If one of the activities in a chain fails, the actions that have already occurred are undone — this is called a *rollback*. However, transactions that run over long periods of time cannot always be undone; rather, some logic is implemented to maintain a stable workflow state. This is called *compensation*.

The classic example is an ATM transaction. If a customer is performing a monetary transfer between accounts and an error occurs, the software needs to ensure that one account was not debited without the other account's being credited. From this simple example, you can see that transactions are extremely vital to software systems.

The transaction runtime service infrastructure included in Windows Workflow Foundation supports two types of transactions: ACID and long running.

ACID Transactions

ACID transactions refer to the types of transactions that are traditionally associated with a relational database. The driver behind transactions ensures that a system is left in a stable and valid state before and after an action or manipulation of data. The ACID acronym defines this particular classification of transactions, as follows:

- ❑ **Atomic** — This property states that either all or none of the activities included in the scope of the transaction are completed.

- ❑ **Consistent** — This means that a workflow must be in a valid state before and after a transaction is executed.

- ❑ **Isolated** — If a transaction is isolated, no entity outside the transaction can see what the workflow's state looks like before the transaction is committed or rolled back.

- ❑ **Durable** — This means that after a transaction is successfully implemented, its outcome is not lost.

Long-Running Transactions

Given the ACID properties, transactions that last over long periods of time do not meet the descriptions of every category. The only properties that long-running transactions meet are consistency and durability. They are not atomic because certain activities in this type of transaction cannot be undone. For example, if an e-mail is sent to a customer regarding a recent order and then the order fails for some reason, the e-mail cannot be unsent. Rather, the transaction should contain compensation logic that can attempt to smooth out any actions that previously occurred. The customer whose order failed could be sent a second e-mail informing him or her of the error, for example.

Long-running transactions are also not isolated. This makes sense because there might be a long period of time between steps, and a software system cannot hide the changes while waiting to continue, the way a database can during a transaction that lasts a matter of seconds.

Persistence Services

Think back to Chapter 1, where the four workflow tenets were introduced. One of these tenets stated that workflows needed to be long-running and stateful. This tenet is important because workflows that interact with external entities such as humans and exterior services should be able to sleep while outside parties are performing work.

Because it doesn't make sense for a workflow's state to be permanently stored in volatile memory, Windows Workflow Foundation provides an architecture conducive to persisting active workflows to a durable medium. Probably the most common scenario, and one that is supported natively, is persisting state to a relational database such as SQL Server.

The `SqlWorkflowPersistenceService` class, provided out of the box, provides developers with an easy and transparent way to maintain workflow state over long periods of time. When a workflow instance becomes idle while waiting for some kind of outside input, the runtime engine recognizes this, and any active persistence service writes the workflow's state to its respective data store.

Tracking Services

Tracking services enable you to monitor and record the execution of workflows. If you remember the workflow tenets introduced in Chapter 1, tracking covers allowing workflows to be transparent throughout their lifecycle.

Tracking services use the concepts of *tracking profiles* and *tracking channels* to specify which activities are reported and to what kind of medium. The `TrackingProfile` and `TrackingChannel` classes are used to represent these concepts, respectively. The abstract `TrackingService` class is responsible for managing these profiles and channels for the workflow runtime.

Out of the box, Windows Workflow Foundation provides the `SqlTrackingService` class, which allows you to persist workflow execution data to a SQL Server database. In addition to tracking data, you can store and maintain tracking profiles in the database.

Aside from defining tracking profiles in the aforementioned `TrackingProfile` class, you can define profiles in XML. The following code shows an example of what an XML-defined tracking profile might look like:

```xml
<?xml version="1.0" encoding="utf-16" standalone="yes"?>
<TrackingProfile
    xmlns="http://www.microsoft.com/WFTrackingProfile" version="3.0.0">
    <TrackPoints>
        <WorkflowTrackPoint>
            <MatchingLocation>
                <WorkflowTrackingLocation>
                    <TrackingWorkflowEvents>
                        <TrackingWorkflowEvent>Created</TrackingWorkflowEvent>
                        <TrackingWorkflowEvent>Completed</TrackingWorkflowEvent>
                    </TrackingWorkflowEvents>
                </WorkflowTrackingLocation>
            </MatchingLocation>
        </WorkflowTrackPoint>
        <ActivityTrackPoint>
            <MatchingLocations>
                <ActivityTrackingLocation>
                    <Activity>
                        <Type>System.Workflow.ComponentModel.Activity,
                            System.Workflow.ComponentModel, Version=3.0.0.0,
                            Culture=neutral, PublicKeyToken=31bf3856ad364e35
                        </Type>
                        <MatchDerivedTypes>true</MatchDerivedTypes>
                    </Activity>
                    <ExecutionStatusEvents>
                        <ExecutionStatus>Executing</ExecutionStatus>
                        <ExecutionStatus>Faulting</ExecutionStatus>
                    </ExecutionStatusEvents>
                </ActivityTrackingLocation>
            </MatchingLocations>
        </ActivityTrackPoint>
    </TrackPoints>
</TrackingProfile>
```

This XML tells the workflow runtime tracking service a couple of things. First, it declares that there are two workflow-level events that should be tracked: the `Created` and `Completed` events.

Additionally, the nodes in the `ActivityTrackingLocation` element define which events of the base `Activity` class are noteworthy. Every time the `Executing` and `Faulting` events are fired, a call is made to record this information. Because the `Type` node points to the `System.Workflow` `.ComponentModel.Activity` class and all workflow activities derive from this class, these events are tracked for every type of activity.

Scheduling Services

Scheduling services enable you to define how workflows are executed related to threading. By default, Windows Workflow Foundation runs workflows in an asynchronous manner. This means that when a workflow is started from within a host application, the workflow spawns on a separate thread, and control is immediately returned to the host. This is a nice way to do things if you are developing in a Windows Forms application because the end user should be able to manipulate the user interface (UI) while workflows are running in the background. It wouldn't make much sense to lock the application's UI for a long period of time while the user is waiting for the workflow to finish.

However, in application scenarios such as in ASP.NET web forms or web services, which execute on the server, it might make sense to lock the thread until the workflow returns control. Both of the scenarios mentioned are provided natively with Windows Workflow Foundation.

Custom Services

The previous sections related to workflow runtime services discuss the out-of-the-box functionality included with Windows Workflow Foundation. Although these classes provide a rich set of services, often specific needs arise that call for the development of custom runtime services.

For example, a workflow development effort might require that workflow tracking data be sent to a web service upon failure of a workflow instance. This is relatively easy to implement given the base framework provided with Windows Workflow Foundation.

You can extend every type of runtime service and develop new types of runtime services. Chapter 7 discusses out-of-the-box runtime services in more detail and explains how to develop custom services.

Rules

Business processes and business rules go hand in hand. *Business rules* are the entities that define how software makes workflow decisions. One distinction between business rules and business processes is how often each of them changes.

Business processes are assumed to be well tested and defined; therefore, you do not need to modify their workflow on a regular basis. Conversely, business rules can change all the time. For example, a set of pricing rules for an e-commerce website might dictate how promotions are handled. The user might receive free shipping on his or her order if the order total is more than $50, and this threshold could change weekly or monthly. The important thing is that business rules should be flexible and easy to modify.

Windows Workflow Foundation provides a rich infrastructure for designing and executing rules. However, to define simple decision-making logic, you can use traditional code. For example, the IfElse activity, which is introduced in the Hello World example in Chapter 2, determines the branch to execute based on code written in C#.

However, for serious process implementation that depends on a great deal of business logic, you should consider the business-rules framework. In general, these rules are related *sets*. One rule set might contain rules related to human resources and recruiting, whereas another set might define rules for inventory management.

You can think of rules as `if-then-else` statements. The `if` portion of a rule generally inspects some property or properties of the current execution process, such as an order amount or a user's security roles. The `then` actions define what occurs when the Boolean output of the `if` condition evaluates to `true`. The `else` actions occur when the `if` statement evaluates to `false`. Although these concepts are fairly elementary and familiar to anyone who has developed software, Windows Workflow Foundation enables you to define these rules in an encapsulated and flexible manner.

Windows Workflow Foundation provides the Rule Set Editor (see Figure 3-4) for defining rules within Visual Studio. You can access this screen with the `RuleSetReference` property of a Policy activity in the workflow designer.

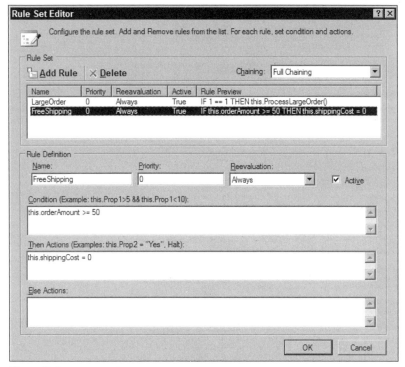

Figure 3-4

You can see here that the `FreeShipping` rule is inspecting a variable called `orderAmount` for a value greater than or equal to $50. If this turns out to be the case during runtime, the `shippingCost` variable is set to $0. In this example, an `else` action has not been provided.

Rule definitions are stored in a separate XML file that is external to the executable code. This allows for easy modification, even during workflow execution. The following is a snippet from the rules XML file for the `FreeShipping` rule:

```
...
<Rule Name="FreeShipping" ReevaluationBehavior="Always" Priority="0"
 Description="{p3:Null}" Active="True">
  <Rule.ThenActions>
    <RuleStatementAction>
      <RuleStatementAction.CodeDomStatement>
        <ns0:CodeAssignStatement LinePragma="{p3:Null}"
         xmlns:ns0="clr-namespace:System.CodeDom;Assembly=System, Version=2.0.0.0,
         Culture=neutral, PublicKeyToken=b77a5c561934e089">
          <ns0:CodeAssignStatement.Left>
            <ns0:CodeFieldReferenceExpression FieldName="shippingCost">
              <ns0:CodeFieldReferenceExpression.TargetObject>
                <ns0:CodeThisReferenceExpression />
              </ns0:CodeFieldReferenceExpression.TargetObject>
            </ns0:CodeFieldReferenceExpression>
          </ns0:CodeAssignStatement.Left>
```

```
            <ns0:CodeAssignStatement.Right>
              <ns0:CodePrimitiveExpression>
                <ns0:CodePrimitiveExpression.Value>
                  <ns1:Int32 xmlns:ns1="clr-namespace:System;Assembly=mscorlib,
                    Version=2.0.0.0, Culture=neutral,
                    PublicKeyToken=b77a5c561934e089">0</ns1:Int32>
                </ns0:CodePrimitiveExpression.Value>
              </ns0:CodePrimitiveExpression>
            </ns0:CodeAssignStatement.Right>
          </ns0:CodeAssignStatement>
        </RuleStatementAction.CodeDomStatement>
      </RuleStatementAction>
    </Rule.ThenActions>
    <Rule.Condition>
      <RuleExpressionCondition Name="{p3:Null}">
        <RuleExpressionCondition.Expression>
          <ns0:CodeBinaryOperatorExpression Operator="GreaterThanOrEqual"
            xmlns:ns0="clr-namespace:System.CodeDom;Assembly=System, Version=2.0.0.0,
            Culture=neutral, PublicKeyToken=b77a5c561934e089">
            <ns0:CodeBinaryOperatorExpression.Left>
              <ns0:CodeFieldReferenceExpression FieldName="orderAmount">
                <ns0:CodeFieldReferenceExpression.TargetObject>
                  <ns0:CodeThisReferenceExpression />
                </ns0:CodeFieldReferenceExpression.TargetObject>
              </ns0:CodeFieldReferenceExpression>
            </ns0:CodeBinaryOperatorExpression.Left>
            <ns0:CodeBinaryOperatorExpression.Right>
              <ns0:CodePrimitiveExpression>
                <ns0:CodePrimitiveExpression.Value>
                  <ns1:Int32 xmlns:ns1="clr-namespace:System;Assembly=mscorlib,
                    Version=2.0.0.0, Culture=neutral,
                    PublicKeyToken=b77a5c561934e089">50</ns1:Int32>
                </ns0:CodePrimitiveExpression.Value>
              </ns0:CodePrimitiveExpression>
            </ns0:CodeBinaryOperatorExpression.Right>
          </ns0:CodeBinaryOperatorExpression>
        </RuleExpressionCondition.Expression>
      </RuleExpressionCondition>
    </Rule.Condition>
  </Rule>
...
```

Although you don't have to understand completely what is going on in the preceding XML, you can see that the rule is defined in a declarative manner and that the markup should be consumable by anything that understands the rule-set schema.

There is a lot more to the rules infrastructure, such as rules-related activities and chaining. Chapter 9 covers the entire gamut of rules-related topics.

Visual Studio

Visual Studio is the key tool for developing workflows. Microsoft has made great strides to provide a consistent and familiar development environment across technologies, including ASP.NET, Windows

Forms, SQL Server, and BizTalk, to name a few. If you have used Visual Studio to develop software in the past, you should be able to find your bearings rather quickly when learning the Windows Workflow Foundation development paradigm.

Familiar components and concepts, such as project templates, the Toolbox, the Solution Explorer, debugging, and the like, are all part of the development experience in Visual Studio. Figure 3-5 shows a Visual Studio 2005 development screen with some of these items displayed.

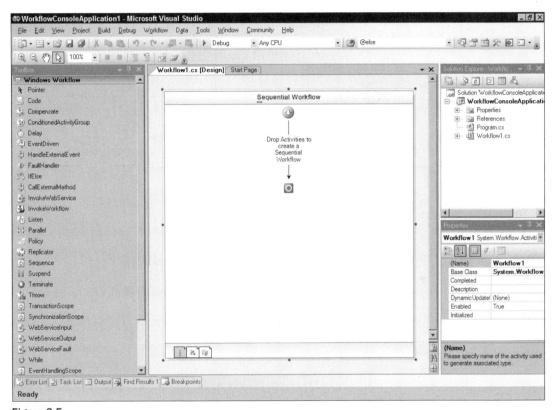

Figure 3-5

Visual Studio also supports the development of .NET code, which is important if you are going to use Windows Workflow Foundation to create custom components. In addition, the workflow components for Visual Studio provide several different authoring models, including the declarative XAML and the code-only style.

The Visual Studio environment for Windows Workflow Foundation is covered in detail in Chapter 4.

Windows Workflow Utilities

Just like the .NET software development kit (SDK), the Windows Workflow Foundation SDK ships with command-line utilities to assist with development.

wca.exe

Workflow-to-host communication has already been mentioned as a vital component of the Windows Workflow Foundation architecture. One of the ways a workflow can communicate with its host is through a data-exchange service. This is a class that implements a .NET interface with the `ExternalDataExchange` attribute.

The wca.exe command-line utility generates a set of strictly bound classes that are derived from already-written data exchange classes. Without these strictly bound classes, the Windows Workflow Foundation runtime engine uses reflection to manipulate the data exchange classes. Therefore, there is a slight performance advantage when you use the generated code. In addition, the generated classes provide designable components, which means that icons appear in the Toolbox for external methods and event handlers. This offers an improved development experience.

Because this utility is related to workflow communication, it is covered in greater detail in Chapter 5.

wfc.exe

The wfc.exe utility is the Windows Workflow Foundation command-line compiler. It enables you to compile workflows and activities outside the Visual Studio environment (as discussed in detail in Chapter 4). Table 3-2 lists the wcf.exe options.

Table 3-2: wcf.exe Options

Command-Line Option	Short Form	Description
`/out:<file>`		Outputs a file name.
`/target:assembly`	`/t:assembly`	Builds a Windows Workflow Foundation assembly (default).
`/target:exe`	`/t:exe`	Builds a Windows Workflow Foundation application.
`/target:codegen`	`/t:codegen`	Generates a partial class definition.
`/delaysign[+|-]`		Delays the signing of the assembly using only the public portion of the strong name key.
`/keyfile:<file>`		Specifies a strong name key file.
`/keycontainer:<string>`		Specifies a strong name key container.
`<XAML file list>`		Specifies XAML source file names.
`<vb/cs file list>`		Specifies code-beside file names.
`/reference:<file list>`	`/r:`	References metadata from the specified assembly files.
`/library:<path list>`	`/lib:`	Specifies a set of directories that contain references.
`/debug[+|-]`	`/d:`	Emits full debugging information. The default is +.

Command-Line Option	Short Form	Description
/nocode[+|-]	/nc:	Disallows code-beside and code-within models. The default is -.
/checktypes[+|-]	/ct:	Checks for permitted types in the wfc.exe.config file. The default is -.
/language:[cs|vb]	/l:	Specifies the language to use for the generated class. The default is cs (C#).
/rootnamespace:<string>	/rns:	Specifies the root namespace for all type declarations. Valid only for the VB (Visual Basic) language.
/help	/?	Displays this usage message.
/nologo	/n	Suppresses compiler copyright message.
/nowarn	/w	Ignores compiler warnings.

Windows Workflow Foundation Features and Principles

The previous sections described the tangible areas of the Windows Workflow Foundation platform. The following sections cover concepts and features at a higher level to help you gain a greater appreciation for what Windows Workflow Foundation has to offer. In turn, this should assist you in applying these concepts to workflow-related conversations and decisions in your organization.

Dynamic Update

Dynamic update describes the ability of Windows Workflow Foundation to modify a running workflow's execution path. This opens up a new world of scenarios related to capturing missed requirements during development or allowing for exception cases where a process might need to behave differently than it normally would.

For example, consider an approval process that requires an additional round of approvals from analysts. Because business processes are at the forefront of workflow, and processes are sometimes dynamic, this is a very important feature of Windows Workflow Foundation.

Chapter 11 discusses dynamic update in depth and explains how to apply this concept to your workflows.

Designer Hosting

Designer hosting is a unique feature of Windows Workflow Foundation. It enables you to display the workflow designer in your own applications.

The hosted designer enables ISVs to develop workflow-related products on top of Windows Workflow Foundation and allows end users to manipulate visual processes. You might be thinking something like, "Wow, allowing a business user to modify software sounds dangerous!" Well, there is a little more to the story. The designer is completely customizable so that the level of interactivity between the workflow engine and the end user is completely in control of the application developer. You, as the developer, can decide which activities the user has access to and provide limitations to what the user can do during design time.

Imagine that a set of custom activities has been developed that pertains to a specific business problem domain, such as call-center administration. The call-center manager could open his or her workflow designer, which was either built internally or purchased from a third party, and then drag and drop pre-built activities on to a visual design surface. This provides a great deal of flexibility to the business while ensuring that the user cannot get into too much trouble.

Chapter 11 covers designer hosting in greater detail, including technical implementation and example scenarios.

Extensibility

To ensure that Windows Workflow Foundation is able to meet the needs of various problem domains and specific technology requirements, the framework is extensible through and through. Essentially *everything* on the platform can be extended or enhanced, even down to customization of the look and feel of the workflow designer.

One of the more common scenarios for using Windows Workflow Foundation will probably be the development of new activities. Because activities are the building blocks of workflow solutions, they will likely be the most visible. In addition, because the out-of-the-box activities that ship with Windows Workflow Foundation are generic and do not relate to areas such as healthcare or law, custom activities will be developed to solve problems in these fields.

Runtime services are another great example of the extensibility of this platform. For example, if an organization requires workflows to persist themselves to XML rather than use the native SQL persistence service, you can develop this with the base classes provided.

Extensibility is not something that is applied to only one area of the framework. Therefore, this concept is reinforced throughout the book through examples and scenarios of how you can expand Windows Workflow Foundation.

Configuration

With the release of the .NET Framework in 2002, configuration became a first-class citizen. There are entire class libraries and runtime elements that support dynamic settings defined in XML files.

Windows Workflow Foundation configuration uses this same principle to allow developers greater flexibility in their workflow applications. A common configuration scenario is one where runtime services are defined and configured in an app.config or web.config file. The following is an example configuration file that adds the SQL tracking service to the workflow runtime. It is important to note that the ConnectionString key/value pair is used by the SqlTrackingService class that is referenced in the Services node:

```xml
<?xml version="1.0" encoding="utf-8" ?>
<configuration>
  <configSections>
    <section name="WorkflowConfig"
     type="System.Workflow.Runtime.Configuration.WorkflowRuntimeSection,
          System.Workflow.Runtime, Version=3.0.0.0, Culture=neutral,
          PublicKeyToken=31bf3856ad364e35" />
  </configSections>
  <WorkflowConfig Name="WorkflowConfig">
    <CommonParameters>
      <add name="ConnectionString"
           value="Initial Catalog=WorkflowTracking;
                 Data Source=localhost;Integrated Security=SSPI;" />
    </CommonParameters>
    <Services>
      <add type="System.Workflow.Runtime.Tracking.SqlTrackingService,
           System.Workflow.Runtime, Version=3.0.0.0, Culture=neutral,
           PublicKeyToken=31bf3856ad364e35"/>
    </Services>
  </WorkflowConfig>
</configuration>
```

Chapter 5 discusses configuration in more detail.

Workflow Monitoring

The Windows Workflow Foundation platform provides an extensive library of performance counters to assist in diagnosing performance issues in a production environment. *Performance counters* are pieces of code that expose key metrics related to processes execution. You can view the data that these pieces of code expose in the Windows Performance Monitor application. For example, Figure 3-6 shows the Performance Monitor displaying operating system metrics.

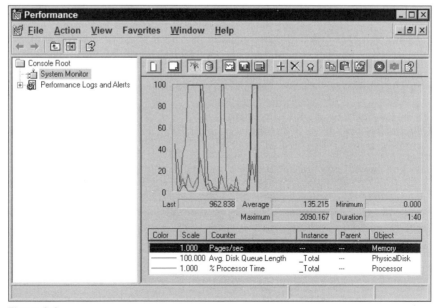

Figure 3-6

Performance counters are built on an extensible framework, which means that any application developer can create counters that generate meaningful data for custom applications. The Windows Workflow team has done just that. Table 3-3 lists a subset of the workflow performance counters.

Table 3-3: Workflow Performance Counters

Counter	Description
Workflows Created	The number of workflows created on a system
Workflows Completed	The number of completed workflows on a system
Workflows Executing	The number of workflows currently executing
Workflows Persisted	The number of workflows that have been persisted

Chapter 12 covers the rest of the performance monitors and workflow monitoring scenarios.

Namespaces

To immerse yourself in the Windows Workflow Foundation API, you need to know what namespaces are available and what kind of classes you can expect to find in each. The following namespaces are available in Windows Workflow Foundation:

- ❑ `System.Workflow.Activities` — Contains classes that represent the concrete activities included with Windows Workflow Foundation, such as the Code activity and the IfElse activity.

- ❑ `System.Workflow.Activities.Rules` — Contains classes related to rules in Windows Workflow Foundation, including classes for conditions and their associated actions.

- ❑ `System.Workflow.Activities.Rules.Design` — Contains classes that represent the Rule Set Editor and Rule Condition Editor user-interface dialog boxes in Visual Studio. These dialog boxes are discussed in greater detail in Chapter 9.

- ❑ `System.Workflow.ComponentModel` — Contains all of the classes and interfaces that are used as the basis for workflows and activities. This includes the base class for all activities, which is aptly called `Activity`. Other supporting elements such as delegates and enumerations are located here as well.

- ❑ `System.Workflow.ComponentModel.Compiler` — Contains classes that support the compilation process of activities and workflows. In addition, the classes that perform validation of activities during design time are located here.

- ❑ `System.Workflow.ComponentModel.Design` — Contains classes and constructs to create and extend design-time components. (Visual design is a core concept of Windows Workflow Foundation.) Classes of note include `WorkflowTheme`, which provides properties related the look and feel of a workflow during design time, and `ActivityToolboxItem`, which is the base class for all Toolbox activity items.

- ❑ `System.Workflow.ComponentModel.Serialization` — Contains classes that support the serialization of workflows and activities.

- ❑ `System.Workflow.Runtime`—Contains classes and interfaces related to the workflow runtime. The most notable class in this namespace is `WorkflowRuntime`, which is responsible for the execution and maintenance of running workflow instances. The `WorkflowInstance` class is also important because it represents an active workflow.

- ❑ `System.Workflow.Runtime.Configuration`—Contains classes that allow the runtime to access predefined configuration data. (Configuration is an important part of Windows Workflow Foundation.)

- ❑ `System.Workflow.Runtime.Hosting`—Contains classes related to the workflow runtime services introduced previously. All workflow runtime hosting classes are located here, from the base `WorkflowRuntimeService` class to the concrete default classes for treading and transactions.

- ❑ `System.Workflow.Runtime.Tracking`—Contains the actual runtime service classes as well as classes that define tracking profiles and channels. (Even though tracking falls under the umbrella of runtime services, this concept is sizeable enough to warrant its own namespace.)

Windows Workflow Foundation and Other Technologies

Windows Workflow Foundation by itself is a great tool, but when combined with other technologies, it can do even greater things. Over the past few years, Microsoft's strategy has included providing an encompassing set of complementary technologies. The following sections highlight these technologies and how they relate to developing workflow applications.

SQL Server

You can use SQL Server as the backbone to workflow application development. You can persist workflow instances and store tracking data in SQL Server's relational tables. Basically, you can write any data to the database and later recall it. As you continue to read this book, you'll see that SQL Server plays an important role in the Windows Workflow Foundation platform and architecture.

BizTalk Server

If you've had any exposure to Microsoft's BizTalk Server, you may have had had a knee-jerk reaction when you first heard about Windows Workflow Foundation. This is because on the surface, there might appear to be some traits of both technologies that seem to overlap. Some of the differences between BizTalk and Windows Workflow Foundation are described later, including pointers on when you should use one technology over the other. First, here's some background information on what BizTalk is and how it works.

Microsoft initially released BizTalk as BizTalk 2000. At a high level, BizTalk was built to tackle the problem domain of Enterprise Application Integration (EAI). EAI describes the concept of helping applications talk to one another. This becomes difficult because applications speak myriad dialects. For example, an enterprise's payroll system might communicate with the outside world by dumping a flat file on an FTP site. Conversely, the system that handles new hires is a little more progressive and exposes some XML web services. Without some kind of translation between the two systems, you're out of luck regarding communication.

A common way to describe a system such as BizTalk is as a *hub-and-spoke* model. That is, BizTalk sits in the middle (the hub) and branches out to a series of software systems (the spokes) while sending and receiving messages to and from each application (see Figure 3-7). This minimizes the amount of glue code that developers have to write and maintain to make each system talk to another one. Without a system like BizTalk, a developer would have to write custom code for the CRM system to talk to the ERP system, and vice versa. There would also have to be code for the custom application to talk to the external trading partner and SharePoint site. The list goes on and on. As you can see, the number of touch points increases greatly every time a new system is added to the mix.

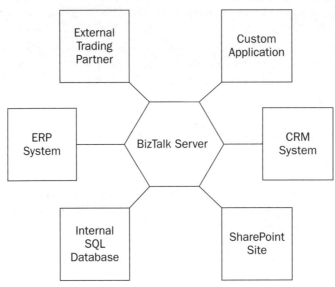

Figure 3-7

The concept of messages is key to the purpose of BizTalk in life. BizTalk receives messages from certain applications and delivers pertinent information to other applications interested in particular data. Because of this, BizTalk has to be able to understand each message type an application generates. If BizTalk understands how Application A and Application B talk, it is reasonable that BizTalk can act as a translator between the two.

Though integrating two applications isn't very interesting and probably not a worthy use of BizTalk, the value starts to go up when numerous systems are added to the picture. For example, say an HR system exposes data related to employee training efforts, and there are three pieces of software in an organization that are interested in this information. Furthermore, one of these applications might be interested in only the training related to information technology. All three systems could easily be informed when an employee takes a training class, but the application concerned with technology training can *subscribe* to messages exposing that specific data.

BizTalk Components

A typical BizTalk project contains several common entities that facilitate the concept of EAI. First, because BizTalk has to be able to understand the messages from all involved applications, there needs to be a definition of what these messages look like. This definition is called a *schema* and is a standard XSD file.

Mapping enables one application's messages to be sent to another system. Mapping is a visual, typically straightforward process. The *source* schema is displayed on the left side of the screen, and the *destination* is displayed on the right. In simple scenarios, a field-to-field translation is as easy as dragging one node of the schema from the source to another node on the destination. See Figure 3-8 for an example of the BizTalk mapping interface.

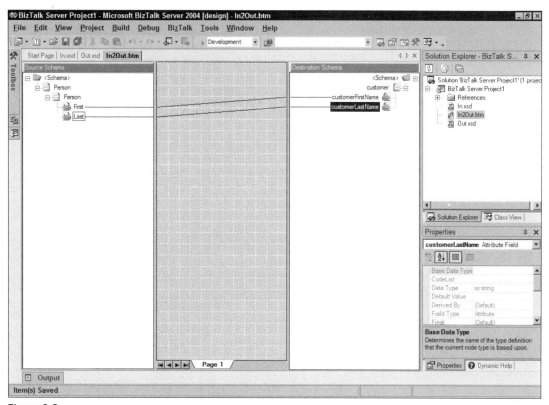

Figure 3-8

The schema map can take an XML file that looks like this:

```
<Person>
  <Person>
    <First>Bryan</First>
    <Last>Roberts</Last>
  </Person>
</Person>
```

and make it look like this:

```
<customer customerFirstName="Bryan" customerLastName="Roberts" />
```

Ports are another core concept within BizTalk. Ports in BizTalk are conceptual and do not correlate directly to ports in a networking sense (such as port 80 for a web server). A port defines a location where a message can be received or sent. During development, you can keep these ports completely conceptual and not tied to a physical location such as a file drop or web service URL. However, after the project moves to production, you must *bind* a port to a real location. There are many different types of transports for sending and receiving messages, such as FTP, e-mail, web services, and SharePoint document libraries. BizTalk provides an *adapter* infrastructure to handle different transport types. Each adapter has to be configured to allow BizTalk to use a specific port. For example, the FTP adapter needs a URL, user name, password, and a folder in which to look for messages.

Finally, the piece that might cause some confusion related to BizTalk and Windows Workflow Foundation is called *orchestration.* As you might imagine, the fact that BizTalk can act as an organization's central hub for message handling and delivery means that it should also be able to facilitate complex business processes related to all this data. For example, if BizTalk is used to handle messages related to customer orders, it should be able to make decisions and *route* messages based on predefined processes and rules. A simple scenario might be one where all orders over $500 are routed to a customer specialist for approval and special service. Furthermore, this process of orchestration, like many other things in BizTalk and Windows Workflow Foundation, is visual. You drag and drop *shapes* from the Toolbox on to the orchestration designer to define a process. This is where the knee-jerk reaction mentioned previously comes in — initially, you might be confused about how these two pieces of software relate to each other. The next section covers this topic.

Although other pieces of BizTalk are quite interesting and important, those topics are better left to the numerous comprehensive resources that are readily available. Other key components include the BizTalk Rules Engine, Business Activity Monitoring, and pipelines. For more about BizTalk Server, refer to *Professional BizTalk Server 2006, R2* (available at www.wrox.com).

Differences and When to Use What

Because both and Windows Workflow Foundation share the concept of process definition, you may wonder why they exist separately. There is a compelling answer for this dilemma, and key differences exist between the two entities.

This biggest differentiator between the two is that BizTalk is a server product that is installed, configured, and subsequently maintained in a production environment. As mentioned, Windows Workflow Foundation is a software development framework that is not meant to run on its own. Because BizTalk is a product, it also costs a lot more than Windows Workflow Foundation, which is free. The Enterprise edition of BizTalk 2006 currently costs $29,999, and for that price tag, you get the application integration features previously mentioned. In addition, Windows Workflow Foundation does not include technology out of the box that parallels the BizTalk adapter and schema mapping functionality.

After reading the previous paragraph, you might be wondering what is so great about Windows Workflow Foundation compared with BizTalk. BizTalk is not better than Windows Workflow Foundation; it is simply different. First, not all development efforts require the enterprise-level features BizTalk provides, such as guaranteed message delivery.

In addition, you can use Windows Workflow Foundation in scenarios where BizTalk would not make sense, and vice versa. For example, if you're tackling the problem of integrating internal applications and external business partners on a singular platform, BizTalk makes sense. However, when you're automating a process that does not contain an integration component, Windows Workflow Foundation might be a better solution.

Windows Workflow Foundation also provides functionality that BizTalk does not. For example, BizTalk does not provide dynamic update. After an orchestration is defined at design time in a BizTalk project, it cannot change without a developer performing alterations and a redeployment of the solution. Windows Workflow Foundation also contains functionality for state-driven processes, whereas BizTalk does not.

Another feature specific to workflows is the availability of extensible activities. The shapes that come with BizTalk are set in stone and cannot be changed, and new shapes cannot be developed. This point plays further into the extensibility aspects of Windows Workflow Foundation compared with BizTalk — the workflow framework essentially is fully extensible. Although BizTalk is very customizable, there is a limit to what you can develop on its platform; the sky is the limit for Windows Workflow Foundation.

To reiterate, BizTalk and Windows Workflow Foundation are separate although complementary technologies that are meant to solve different categories of problems. You need to evaluate a project's needs on a case-by-case basis in order to decide which software to use.

The Future

Because BizTalk's concept of visual orchestration is similar to what Windows Workflow Foundation provides, Microsoft has announced that the next version of BizTalk (likely around 2008) will use that framework as its core for the orchestration component. This makes sense because it is probably not a great idea for Microsoft to maintain two separate process design technologies going forward. This is also good news for developers because it signifies that Microsoft is serious about supporting Windows Workflow Foundation in the long term.

Office and SharePoint

The integration between Windows Workflow Foundation and SharePoint will likely be an extremely compelling area as the workflow platform becomes more widely adopted. SharePoint, Microsoft's answer to portals, is a server-side product for activities such as team collaboration, document management, and search.

End users of the SharePoint web front end are able to create sites and web pages related to different topics as well as customize these items to fit the different needs of individual organizations. For example, a project manager could set up a site to monitor the progress of a company's latest acquisition efforts. Other sites and pages might be set up so that developers can share technical articles found on the web. Figure 3-9 shows a sample SharePoint site.

Because document management is one of SharePoint's strong points, the adoption of workflow is an obvious progression. Typical scenarios will include document approval and expiration, and some of this technology is included out of the box. However, because workflows are able to run in the context of SharePoint, there will be many scenarios geared toward specific business domains. Insurance claim processing and HR-related tasks come to mind.

Figure 3-9

InfoPath is another increasingly popular front end for process-based software. InfoPath is used to easily model data entry forms. In the past, developers had to create ASP.NET web forms or Windows Forms applications for even the simplest of data entry scenarios. InfoPath provides a rich interface that can be used by developers and end users alike to create and deploy forms. InfoPath 2003 was a client-only tool, so the end user was required to have the InfoPath software installed on his or her machine to fill out developed forms. In Office 2007, the InfoPath Server does not have this requirement. Forms are designed and deployed to the server and then, when requested, are rendered in HTML and displayed in the ubiquitous web browser.

Because workflows should easily interact with people, InfoPath or another forms technology is often a natural fit. A form requesting assistance from the help desk might actually kick off a workflow, whereas another InfoPath form might enable the help-desk worker to update a user's case. Figure 3-10 shows a sample InfoPath form representing an expense report.

Chapter 15 goes into more detail about how Windows Workflow Foundation fits in with the Office and SharePoint technologies.

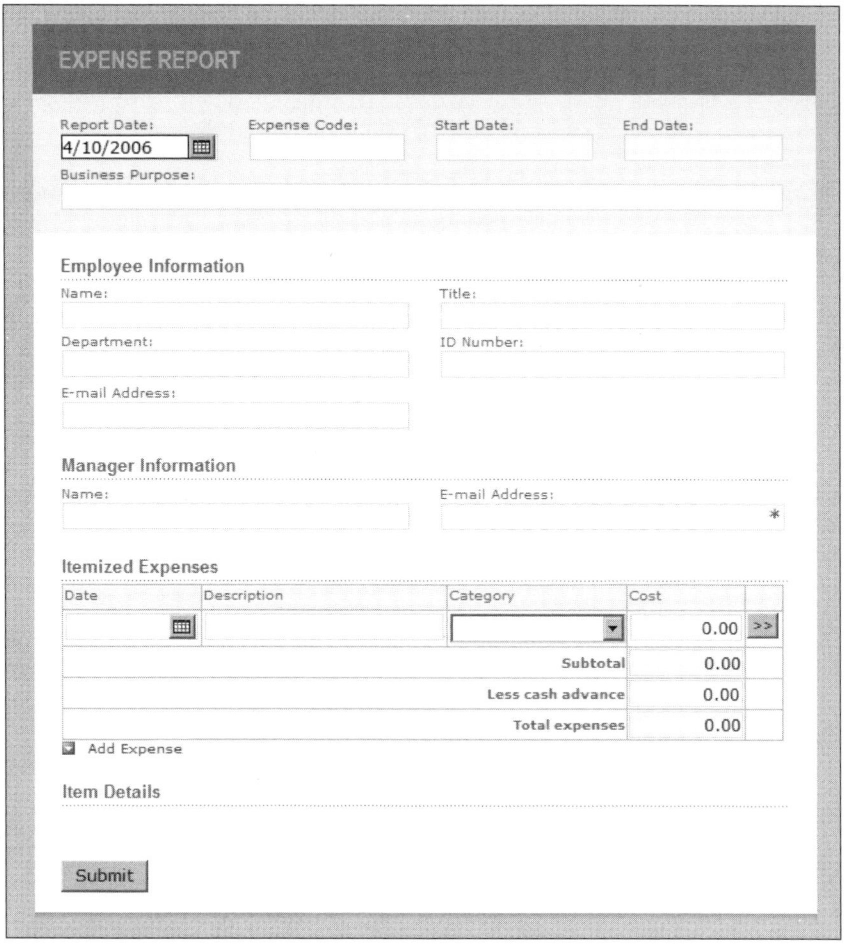

Figure 3-10

Windows Communication Foundation

Chapter 1 gave a short introduction to service-oriented architecture (SOA). Windows Communication Foundation (WCF) is Microsoft's next-generation platform for developing distributed, or services-oriented, applications. Although Windows Workflow Foundation and WCF are two mutually exclusive pieces of technology, they can also go hand in hand.

Just as activities are the building blocks of workflows, services are the building blocks for SOA. Furthermore, services are generally built to support business processes. They are meant to perform one discrete piece of functionality and nothing more. This means that typically services are meaningless by themselves. This is where workflow comes into the picture. Workflow can *orchestrate* these standalone services into a meaningful set of steps governed by rules and logic.

Chapter 14 provides more insight into WCF and how it relates to Windows Workflow Foundation.

ASP.NET

Because workflows can be hosted in any type of .NET application, in many respects ASP.NET is no more special than a Windows Forms or a console application. However, anyone who has done web development can attest to the fact that there many factors that set the web paradigm apart from other forms of client-side development.

The most glaring characteristic of web development is the fact that it is a stateless environment. This means that every request made by an end user is separate from any other request made by the same user. Web development platforms such as ASP.NET provide the infrastructure to deal with these issues using concepts such as Sessions and ViewState.

Another trait that sets web development apart from Windows development is the fact that the user has a different experience related to processing and UI interactivity. On the web, a page isn't returned until it is processed and ready for viewing. In Windows, the UI is always visible even if something is going on in the background. In this case, developers generally perform long-running tasks asynchronously so that the UI appears to be responsive and the user is able to interact with the form even if other work is being done behind the scenes.

By default, workflow instances are started asynchronously and control is immediately returned to the host. Although this behavior may be desirable in a Windows application, you may not want this to occur in your ASP.NET applications. The workflow platform enables you to modify this type of behavior.

Windows Workflow Foundation's relation to ASP.NET is discussed in Chapter 13.

Summary

This chapter introduced you to the core technology of Windows Workflow Foundation. Items such as activities, runtime services, and rules make up the core of the workflow platform. There is also a rich set of functionality provided to developers out of the box. However, to ensure that Windows Workflow Foundation is able to handle just about any scenario related to process management, many core pieces of the architecture are extensible.

Windows Workflow Foundation can also work with many other technologies that provide complementary functionality. You can combine workflows with systems such as SQL Server, Windows Communication Foundation, and ASP.NET to build process-oriented systems.

4

Workflow Development and Visual Studio

This chapter covers the core concepts of workflow development, including the workflow infrastructure, compilation, serialization, and development modes. It also discusses the Visual Studio development environment. As a key component of the workflow development process, Visual Studio provides a rich set of tools for developing and debugging workflow-based applications.

The Composition of a Workflow

Most developers use Visual Studio to create and modify workflow applications, but it is by no means required for workflow development. Just as with C# and the .NET SDK, all you need to develop managed software is notepad.exe and csc.exe (the command-line C# compiler). Granted, most people don't use Notepad to develop workflows, but you can use it to break down the components of the workflow infrastructure that are abstracted by Visual Studio.

Workflow Development Styles

In Windows Workflow Foundation, there are three modes of workflow development and composition, and there are pros and cons associated with each. These development modes are discussed in the following sections.

Markup Only

This style of workflow enables you to declaratively define a workflow entirely in one file. The layout of the workflow file is a flavor of XML called XAML (eXtensible Application Markup Language). To use this type of workflow you have two options. The first is to compile the file with the Windows Workflow Foundation command-line compiler. You can also use the `CreateWorkflow` overloads of the `WorkflowRuntime` class that take an `XmlReader` instance. (Chapter 5 covers creating workflow instances.)

Defining Workflows in XAML

XAML is a means for declaratively developing software. XAML is not specific to Windows Workflow Foundation—you can also use it to develop user interfaces in Microsoft Windows Presentation Foundation. Previously, Windows user interfaces were developed programmatically by declaring controls and manipulating properties such as size and location to control the look and feel. With XAML, you can define a user interface hierarchically with XML elements that correspond to controls. The same goes for Windows Workflow Foundation workflows.

Each XML element corresponds to an activity class, with the root element corresponding to one of the workflow activity types. So the root element can be either `SequentialWorkflowActivity` or `State MachineWorkflowActivity`. Just as elements map to classes, attributes map to properties on these classes. The following code is a short example of a workflow written entirely in XAML. The workflow basically loops five times and prints a short message on each iteration:

```
<SequentialWorkflowActivity
  xmlns="http://schemas.microsoft.com/winfx/2006/xaml/workflow"
  xmlns:x="http://schemas.microsoft.com/winfx/2006/xaml"
  Name="XomlWorkflow"
  x:Class="XomlWorkflow">

  <WhileActivity x:Name="myWhileLoop">
    <WhileActivity.Condition>
      <CodeCondition Condition="WhileCondition" />
    </WhileActivity.Condition>
    <CodeActivity x:Name="myCodeActivity"
      ExecuteCode="myCodeActivity_ExecuteCode" />
  </WhileActivity>

  <x:Code>
    <![CDATA[
      int count = 0;

      private void WhileCondition(object sender, ConditionalEventArgs e)
      {
        e.Result = count++ < 5;
      }

      private void myCodeActivity_ExecuteCode(object sender, EventArgs e)
      {
        Console.WriteLine("The count is " + count.ToString());
      }
    ]]>
  </x:Code>
</SequentialWorkflowActivity>
```

Figure 4-1 shows what this workflow looks like in the workflow designer.

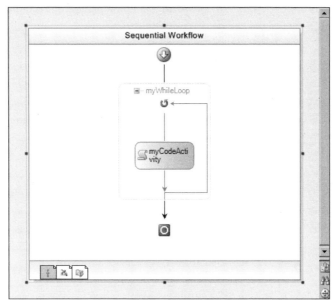

Figure 4-1

Because the workflow is implemented entirely in XAML, the supporting C# code is listed in a CDATA block inside an x:Code element (The CDATA block allows the representation of any kind of text.) To see how this XAML works, compile it with the command-line compiler, wfc.exe as follows (wfc.exe is discussed in more detail later in this chapter):

```
wfc.exe XomlWorkflow.xoml /target:assembly /out:XomlWorkflow.dll
```

This command compiles your .xoml file into XomlWorkflow.dll. By using a .NET developer's best friend, Lutz's Reflector (www.aisto.com/roeder/dotnet), you can take a look at what was done with your XAML markup. The following shows the workflow class metadata:

```
[WorkflowMarkupSource(@"C:\Documents and Settings\Administrator\My Documents\Visual
Studio 2005\Projects\Book\Chapter 4\XomlWorkflow\XomlWorkflow.xoml",
"7EB9EE5D6FFF9178C357DFC35593D31C")]
public class XomlWorkflow : SequentialWorkflowActivity
{
    // Methods
    public XomlWorkflow();
    private void InitializeComponent();
    private void myCodeActivity_ExecuteCode(object sender, EventArgs e);
    private void WhileCondition(object sender, ConditionalEventArgs e);

    // Fields
    private int count;
    private CodeActivity myCodeActivity;
    private WhileActivity myWhileLoop;
}
```

The following code is in the `InitializeComponent` method generated by the workflow compiler:

```
private void InitializeComponent()
{
    base.CanModifyActivities = true;
    CodeCondition condition1 = new CodeCondition();
    this.myWhileLoop = new WhileActivity();
    this.myCodeActivity = new CodeActivity();
    this.myWhileLoop.Activities.Add(this.myCodeActivity);
    condition1.Condition +=
        new EventHandler<ConditionalEventArgs>(this.WhileCondition);
    this.myWhileLoop.Condition = condition1;
    this.myWhileLoop.Name = "myWhileLoop";
    this.myCodeActivity.Name = "myCodeActivity";
    this.myCodeActivity.ExecuteCode +=
        new EventHandler(this.myCodeActivity_ExecuteCode);
    base.Activities.Add(this.myWhileLoop);
    base.Name = "XomlWorkflow";
    base.CanModifyActivities = false;
}
```

Pretty cool, huh? The compiler took the XAML code, parsed it, and generated common language runtime (CLR) code that was then compiled into a .NET assembly.

Because markup-only workflows are contained in a single file, end users can define and run their own workflows. Granted, a user would probably use a front-end application that has been custom developed with a specific problem domain in mind. In this type of situation, you, as the developer, can use the `WorkflowCompiler` class to compile the XAML workflow programmatically, just as the wfc.exe utility does. (The `WorkflowCompiler` class is discussed later in this chapter.)

Drawbacks

Despite the niceties of this model, it has its drawbacks. Most obvious, the inclusion of .NET code for logic is not implemented in the most natural way for developers. Even though the code included in the `x:Code` element is eventually compiled into a .NET class, you are forced to write code inside an XML element with none of the features available in Visual Studio or outside the object-oriented paradigm. If you decide to go this route, you should first develop the code inside a real code file and class and then copy the code contents into the XML file. This way, you can use features such as IntelliSense, code highlighting, and developing in a true object-oriented manner.

Code and Markup

Also called *code-beside,* the code-and-markup development model is very similar to what ASP.NET developers are familiar with. The workflow definition exists in a markup file, as discussed in the previous section, but a standard .NET code file exists for the implementation of other business logic. This is a very elegant development mode because it allows for complete separation of the declarative workflow definition and logic implemented in code.

The code-beside model uses the concept of partial classes. *Partial classes* allow the definition of one class to be in multiple files or locations. By splitting key parts of a class into different files, multiple developers can work on the class at the same time. However, the functionality of partial classes in this development model is a little different (more on why in a moment).

To use this workflow development method, you must declare the .NET code file as a partial class. This is extremely simple — you just use the `partial` keyword on the class definition. For example:

```
public partial class MyWorkflow : SequentialWorkflowActivity
{
    ...
}
```

Aside from the `partial` keyword, there is really nothing special about this file. In the following workflow markup, the `x:Class` attribute points to the class defined in the previous code. This tells the workflow compiler to create a class called `MyWorkflow` when parsing the markup and generating the CLR code:

```
<SequentialWorkflowActivity
    x:Class="MyNamespace.MyWorkflow"
    Name="MyWorkflow"
    xmlns="http://schemas.microsoft.com/winfx/2006/xaml/workflow"
    xmlns:x="http://schemas.microsoft.com/winfx/2006/xaml">
    ...
</SequentialWorkflowActivity>
```

The magic happens during the compilation process. The XAML workflow definition is parsed into a partial class of the same name as the .NET code file. At this point, the partial classes are merged and compiled as any standard .NET partial classes would be.

Code-Only

The code-only workflow development model will probably be one of the more commonly used methods because it is the default in the Visual Studio development environment. In this model, the workflow definition is defined entirely in a CLR language, such as C# or Visual Basic .NET. If you've done any development with Windows Forms in Visual Studio, this method will probably seem familiar (more on that in the Visual Studio section of this chapter).

The following is an example of a code-only workflow that prints a message using a Code activity. There are a couple things to notice here. First, `MyCodeOnlyWorkflow` inherits from `SequentialWorkflowActivity`, which means the class is a sequential workflow. Next, take a look at the class's private field, `myCode Activity`, and the lone constructor. The constructor initializes the Code activity, wires an event handler for the `ExecuteCode` event, and then adds the activity to the workflow's `Activities` collection. Finally, the `ExecuteCode` event handler is defined as `myCodeActivity_ExecuteCode`.

```
public class MyCodeOnlyWorkflow : SequentialWorkflowActivity
{
    private CodeActivity myCodeActivity;

    public MyCodeOnlyWorkflow()
    {
        this.CanModifyActivities = true;

        this.myCodeActivity = new System.Workflow.Activities.CodeActivity();
```

```
            this.myCodeActivity.Name = "myCodeActivity";
            this.myCodeActivity.ExecuteCode +=
                new System.EventHandler(this.myCodeActivity_ExecuteCode);

            this.Activities.Add(this.myCodeActivity);
            this.Name = "CodeOnlyWorkflow";
            this.CanModifyActivities = false;
        }

        private void myCodeActivity_ExecuteCode(object sender, EventArgs e)
        {
            Console.WriteLine("Hello world!");
        }
    }
}
```

Although this might not look like the workflows you're used to, it is just as much a workflow as anything in Windows Workflow Foundation. You can compile this code file into a .NET assembly and use it as you would a workflow developed with any other mode.

You will probably not use this development mode very often, if at all. Windows Workflow Foundation is all about declaratively and visually developing workflows, so piecing together a workflow definition with C# or Visual Basic .NET is not the best or easiest choice given the alternatives available. Visual Studio can write this initialization code for you while you focus on the visual definition of the workflow itself.

Workflow Serialization

Workflow serialization is the process of persisting a workflow definition to XAML. Workflow serialization is similar to standard XML serialization of .NET objects; however, workflow serialization takes a workflow definition, no matter how it was developed, and writes that to an XAML file. Standard XML serialization of .NET classes is generally used to persist the state of a class instance rather than its definition. After a workflow has been serialized, the workflow runtime can execute it. The workflow namespaces provide several classes to assist in the serialization process.

So what is serialization used for? Well, in this author's opinion, one of the most useful things that serialization provides is the ability to persist workflows created by end users. You can develop applications that allow end users to create workflows of their own and save them to a durable medium. This could be the filesystem or a database table. Because the output of the serialization process is plain XML, it is highly portable and flexible.

The following code example builds a workflow definition programmatically and then serializes to a .xoml file. First, an instance of the `SequentialWorkflowActivity` class that represents the workflow definition is created. Next, several child activities are created and added to the workflow or their respective parent activities. Finally, an instance of `WorkflowMarkupSerializer` is created and used to write the workflow definition that was just created to a file called myWorkflow.xoml.

```
SequentialWorkflowActivity myWorkflow = new SequentialWorkflowActivity();
myWorkflow.Name = "myWorkflow";

ParallelActivity parallelActivity1 = new ParallelActivity();
```

```
SequenceActivity sequenceActivity1 = new SequenceActivity();
SequenceActivity sequenceActivity2 = new SequenceActivity();

parallelActivity1.Activities.Add(sequenceActivity1);
parallelActivity1.Activities.Add(sequenceActivity2);

CodeActivity codeActivity1 = new CodeActivity();
CodeActivity codeActivity2 = new CodeActivity();

sequenceActivity1.Activities.Add(codeActivity1);
sequenceActivity2.Activities.Add(codeActivity2);

myWorkflow.Activities.Add(parallelActivity1);

WorkflowMarkupSerializer serializer = new WorkflowMarkupSerializer();
XmlWriter xmlWriter = XmlWriter.Create(@"C:\myWorkflow.xoml");
serializer.Serialize(xmlWriter, myWorkflow);
```

This results in the following XML:

```xml
<?xml version="1.0" encoding="utf-8"?>
<SequentialWorkflowActivity
  x:Name="myWorkflow"
  xmlns:x="http://schemas.microsoft.com/winfx/2006/xaml"
  xmlns="http://schemas.microsoft.com/winfx/2006/xaml/workflow">

    <ParallelActivity x:Name="parallelActivity1">
        <SequenceActivity x:Name="sequenceActivity1">
            <CodeActivity x:Name="codeActivity1" />
        </SequenceActivity>
        <SequenceActivity x:Name="sequenceActivity2">
            <CodeActivity x:Name="codeActivity2" />
        </SequenceActivity>
    </ParallelActivity>

</SequentialWorkflowActivity>
```

Serialization Classes

The major classes in the Windows Workflow Foundation serialization infrastructure are located in the `System.Workflow.ComponentModel.Serialization` namespace. They are as follows:

❑ `WorkflowMarkupSerializer` — This is the base class for all serialization classes in Windows Workflow Foundation. You can use it to serialize workflows and activities to workflow markup XAML. In addition, you can deserialize workflow markup into corresponding workflow and activity objects.

❑ `ActivityMarkupSerializer` — You use this class used to serialize the definition of non-composite workflow activities.

❑ `CompositeActivityMarkupSerializer` — This class allows you to serialize more complex, composite activities. Composite activities act as containers for other activities.

Custom Serialization

You can specify which serializer should be used on a particular custom-developed activity. To do so, decorate the activity class with the `DesignerSerializer` attribute that exists in the `System .ComponentModel.Design.Serialization` namespace, as shown in the following code:

```
[DesignerSerializer(typeof(MyCustomSerializer), typeof(WorkflowMarkupSerializer))]
public class MyActivity : Activity
{
    ...
}
```

The first parameter of the `DesignerSerializer` attribute is a type reference to the serializer for this activity. The second parameter represents the first parameters base type that defines the serialization schema.

Workflow Compilation

Workflow compilation is just as important as workflow development because it enables you to execute workflows. A couple of methods of workflow compilation that are discussed next. In addition to the two methods outlined here, when you're developing in Visual Studio, you can compile workflows from within the tool, as with any other type of .NET application built in Visual Studio.

wfc.exe

The Windows Workflow Foundation SDK includes a command-line utility, wfc.exe, for manually compiling workflow files into executable assemblies. As discussed earlier in this chapter, this utility takes a workflow definition and compiles it into a .NET assembly for distribution and execution. You can use any type of workflow development model with the wfc.exe compiler. The following examples use different development types.

The first example uses the markup-only mode and outputs the XAML to an assembly called MyAssembly.dll:

```
wfc.exe /out:MyAssembly.dll /target:assembly MyWorkflow.xoml
```

The command-line compiler also shows errors in compilation just as though you were compiling inside Visual Studio. The following example shows an attempt to compile a workflow developed in the code-only mode. However, because there are a couple Code activities inside the workflow, and their corresponding `ExecuteCode` event handlers are not wired, wfc.exe cannot compile, and a message is displayed. Also, note that the code and markup development mode are supported by providing both .xoml and .cs files as parameters.

```
wfc.exe /out:MyAssembly.dll /target:assembly MyWorkflow.cs MyWorkflow.designer.cs

Microsoft (R) Windows Workflow Compiler version 3.0.0.0
Copyright (C) Microsoft Corporation 2005. All rights reserved.
```

```
The compiler generated the following messages(s):

MyWorkflow.cs : error 278: Activity 'codeActivity1' validation failed: Property
'ExecuteCode' is not set.

MyWorkflow.cs : error 278: Activity 'codeActivity2' validation failed: Property
'ExecuteCode' is not set.

Compilation finished with 0 warning(s), 2 error(s).
```

There are also a few other options for the wfc.exe utility, such as whether to create the debugging information for the assembly and strong name information. If you type **wfc.exe /?** on the command line, you are presented with a full list of the utility's options, as follows:

```
                    Windows Workflow Compiler Options

wfc.exe <XAML file list> /target:assembly [<vb/cs file list>] [/language:...]
  [/out:...] [/reference:...] [/library:...] [/debug...] [/nocode...]
  [/checktypes...]

                          - OUTPUT FILE -
/out:<file>               Output file name
/target:assembly          Build a Windows Workflow assembly (default).
                          Short form: /t:assembly
/target:exe               Build a Windows Workflow application.
                          Short form: /t:exe
/delaysign[+|-]           Delay-sign the assembly using only the public portion
                          of the strong name key.
/keyfile:<file>           Specifies a strong name key file.
/keycontainer:<string>    Specifies a strong name key container.

                          - INPUT FILES -
<XAML file list>          XAML source file name(s).
<vb/cs file list>         Codebeside file name(s).
/reference:<file list>    Reference metadata from the specified assembly file(s).
                          Short form is '/r:'.
/library:<path list>      Set of directories where to lookup for the references.
                          Short form is '/lib:'.

                          - CODE GENERATION -
/debug[+|-]               Emit full debugging information. The default is '+'.
/nocode[+|-]              Disallow code-beside and code-within models.
                          The default is '-'. Short form is '/nc:'.
/checktypes[+|-]          Check for permitted types in wfc.exe.config file.
                          The default is '-'. Short form is '/ct:'.

                          - LANGUAGE -
/language:[cs|vb]         The language to use for the generated class.
                          The default is 'CS' (C#). Short form is '/l:'.
/rootnamespace:<string>   Specifies the root Namespace for all type declarations.
                          Valid only for 'VB' (Visual Basic) language.
                          Short form is '/rns:'.
```

```
                              - MISCELLANEOUS -
/help                    Display this usage message. Short form is '/?'.
/nologo                  Suppress compiler copyright message. Short form is '/n'.

/nowarn                  Ignore compiler warnings. Short form is '/w'.
```

The WorkflowCompiler Class

You can also compile workflows in .NET code with the WorkflowCompiler class. This comes in handy in scenarios where end users are developing and modifying workflows in custom applications. In the following example, a WorkflowCompiler instance compiles a file called XomlWorkflow.xoml. In addition, the WorkflowCompilerParameters class is used to tell the compiler to reference MyAssembly.dll, output the workflow to MyWorkflow.dll, and tell the compiler not to generate debugging information. After the workflow is compiled, there is a check to make sure that no errors occurred. If that is the case, the compiler output is printed to the console, and the types in the newly generated .NET assembly are printed as well. If errors did occur during compilation, they are shown to the user.

```csharp
WorkflowCompiler compiler = new WorkflowCompiler();
WorkflowCompilerParameters parms =
    new WorkflowCompilerParameters(new string[] { @"C:\MyAssembly.dll" },
    "MyWorkflow.dll", false);

WorkflowCompilerResults res = compiler.Compile(parms, @"C:\XomlWorkflow.xoml");

if (res.Errors.Count == 0)
{
    if (res.Output.Count > 0)
    {
        // print the compiler output
        Console.WriteLine("Compiler output:");
        foreach (string msg in res.Output)
        {
            Console.WriteLine(msg);
        }
    }

    // print the types in the assembly
    Console.WriteLine("Types in the assembly:");
    Type[] types = res.CompiledAssembly.GetTypes();
    foreach (Type type in types)
    {
        Console.WriteLine(type.FullName);
    }
}
else
{
    foreach (CompilerError err in res.Errors)
    {
        Console.WriteLine("Error: " + err.ErrorText);
    }
}
```

Because the `WorkflowCompilerResults` class exposes the `CompiledAssembly` property, the developer is instantly given access to run the newly compiled workflow. The following is an example of this scenario:

```
WorkflowRuntime runtime = new WorkflowRuntime();

WorkflowInstance instance =
    runtime.CreateWorkflow(typeof(res.CompiledAssembly.GetTypes()[0]));

instance.Start();
```

Compilation Steps

No matter which compilation method you use — the command-line compiler, the `WorkflowCompiler` class, or Visual Studio — the following steps occur to ensure a successful compilation:

1. Validation is performed on workflow activities. If errors occur here, compilation stops.

2. A partial class is generated, which is fed to the workflow compiler.

3. Code is generated to wire event handlers and set properties (as described earlier regarding the output from Lutz's Reflector).

4. The partial class generated in step 2 is fed with any partial code classes written by the developer to the workflow compiler, and a .NET assembly is generated.

The Visual Studio Development Environment

Visual Studio is the epicenter of workflow development. It provides virtually all the tools and functionality required to develop all kinds of workflow-related software. In the past, Visual Studio was generally used for traditional software development — namely, writing code. However, in the past few years, Microsoft has made Visual Studio the place for seemingly all types of development on its platform. The following products utilize Visual Studio for development purposes: BizTalk, SQL Server Analysis Services, Integration Services, and other SQL Server products, as well as the more traditional items, such as ASP.NET and Windows Forms.

The major advantage of utilizing Visual Studio across so many products is consistency. There are many concepts specific to the Visual Studio development environment that can be carried across technologies. Microsoft has applied this idea to other products as well — the Office system is a great example. Back in the day, many software applications, even from the same vendor, had dissimilar user interfaces. The Office suite of applications has long since standardized interfaces so that they are consistent across the board. The idea is that after the user becomes comfortable with Word or Access, learning Excel is much easier.

Solutions and Projects

To facilitate the logical grouping of items in your development effort, Visual Studio provides the concepts of solutions and projects. A *solution* is the overall container of all items; therefore, you can have only one solution open in an instance of Visual Studio. A solution can contain one or more projects and other ancillary solution items. These *solution items* can be items such as text documents, images, assemblies to reference in projects, or any other supporting items aside from code.

A *project* represents one .NET assembly and has one of the following project output types:

❑ Windows Application

❑ Console Application

❑ Class Library

The Windows and Console Application project output types generate an .exe file, whereas the Class Library project output type generates a .dll file.

Creating New Solutions and Projects

Creating new solutions and projects is easy, and you have a couple of options for starting a new workflow development effort. To create a new project within a solution by default, which is one of the more common methods, open Visual Studio and select File ➪ New ➪ Project from the main menu. The New Project dialog box is displayed (see Figure 4-2). To access the workflow project templates (discussed in the next section), select the Workflow option from the tree control under your desired language.

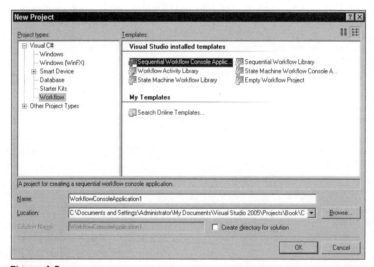

Figure 4-2

Give your new project a name and a location. If you want Visual Studio to create a separate directory for the solution, select the corresponding option. Click OK, and your new solution and project are created and loaded into the Visual Studio environment.

You also have the option of creating an empty solution first and then adding one or more projects to it. To do this, select the Other Project Types ➪ Visual Studio Solutions option from the New Project dialog box and then select Blank Solution from the right side of the screen. You can use this method to maintain complete control over where and how your solutions and projects are created.

You can add new projects to an existing solution from the Solution Explorer window in Visual Studio. Right-click the solution and select Add ⇨ New Project from the context menu. This displays the same New Project dialog box shown in Figure 4-2.

Workflow Project Types

By default, the Workflow Extensions for Visual Studio provide six project templates that contain default files related to each project type and automatic references to key workflow-related assemblies.

Sequential Workflow Console Application

A project created from this template has the Console Application output type and provides you with two files initially: Program.cs and Workflow1.cs.

Program.cs contains a class called `Program`, which contains a method with the signature `static void Main(string[] args)`. This is the standard entry point method signature for a classic console application.

Workflow1.cs is a sequential workflow generated with the code-only workflow development model. You would generally not use this development mode manually, because Visual Studio is responsible for the code that defines properties and adds activities to the workflow.

The Workflow1.cs code file does not contain the code that is generated automatically for adding activities, wiring event handlers, and the like; rather, Visual Studio creates another code file called Workflow1.designer.cs. Figure 4-3 shows these two files in the Visual Studio Solution Explorer window.

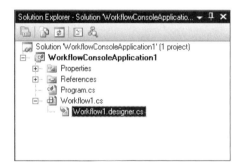

Figure 4-3

The Workflow1.designer.cs file contains a partial class that corresponds to the `Workflow1` class in Workflow1.cs. This keeps the generated code out of your way when you're working in the Workflow1.cs file. The following code shows the contents of a Workflow1.designer.cs file. The workflow corresponding to this code contains an IfElse activity with two branches.

```
partial class Workflow1
{
    #region Designer generated code

    /// <summary>
    /// Required method for Designer support - do not modify
    /// the contents of this method with the code editor.
```

```
/// </summary>
[System.Diagnostics.DebuggerNonUserCode]
private void InitializeComponent()
{
    this.CanModifyActivities = true;
    System.Workflow.Activities.CodeCondition codecondition1 =
        new System.Workflow.Activities.CodeCondition();
    this.ifElseBranchActivity2 =
        new System.Workflow.Activities.IfElseBranchActivity();
    this.ifElseBranchActivity1 =
        new System.Workflow.Activities.IfElseBranchActivity();
    this.ifElseActivity1 = new System.Workflow.Activities.IfElseActivity();
    //
    // ifElseBranchActivity2
    //
    this.ifElseBranchActivity2.Name = "ifElseBranchActivity2";
    //
    // ifElseBranchActivity1
    //
    codecondition1.Condition +=
        new System.EventHandler<System.Workflow.Activities.ConditionalEventArgs>(
            this.MyCondition);
    this.ifElseBranchActivity1.Condition = codecondition1;
    this.ifElseBranchActivity1.Name = "ifElseBranchActivity1";
    //
    // ifElseActivity1
    //
    this.ifElseActivity1.Activities.Add(this.ifElseBranchActivity1);
    this.ifElseActivity1.Activities.Add(this.ifElseBranchActivity2);
    this.ifElseActivity1.Name = "ifElseActivity1";
    //
    // Workflow1
    //
    this.Activities.Add(this.ifElseActivity1);
    this.Name = "Workflow1";
    this.CanModifyActivities = false;

}

#endregion

private IfElseBranchActivity ifElseBranchActivity2;
private IfElseBranchActivity ifElseBranchActivity1;
private IfElseActivity ifElseActivity1;
}
```

By letting Visual Studio manage this code, you can more easily perform the specified activities — setting properties in the Properties window and dragging and dropping them visually.

Sequential Workflow Library

This project template is similar to the Console Activity project output type except that it is not executable. The project's output type is Class Library, which enables you to start a collection of workflows without having to develop a host.

The only files added to this project by default are Workflow1.cs and Workflow1.designer.cs.

Workflow Activity Library

The Activity Library project template provides you with a starting point for a set of custom workflow activities. The project's output type is Class Library.

The only default files in the project are Activity1.cs and Activity1.designer.cs. Just as with the code-only workflows, all designer-related properties are contained in the Activity1.designer.cs file.

State-Machine Workflow Console Application

This project template is very similar to the Sequential Workflow Console Application project template. By default, the project contains Program.cs, the workflow host, and the workflow files Workflow1.cs and Workflow1.designer.cs.

The only difference in this project template is that Workflow1 is a state-machine workflow rather than a sequential workflow.

State Machine Workflow Library

The State Machine Workflow Library project template is similar to the Sequential Workflow Library project template, except this template contains a state-machine workflow by default rather than a sequential workflow.

Empty Workflow Project

This project template is what it sounds like — an empty project. The only advantage it has over creating a standard class library project is that the references to workflow assemblies are added by default.

Although this template doesn't give you much by default, it gives you complete flexibility out of the gate.

Menus

Several menu items in Visual Studio provide functionality related specifically to Windows Workflow Foundation development.

The Workflow Menu

This menu provides workflow-specific activities in Visual Studio (see Figure 4-4).

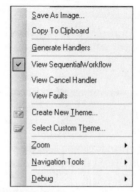

Figure 4-4

The Save As Image option enables you to take a snapshot of a workflow in its current state and save it as various different image types, such as a bitmap or JPEG. You can use this to validate workflow functionality with others in your organization through e-mail or some other medium, or for documentation purposes. The Copy to Clipboard option is similar, except that instead of saving the image, it copies it to your computer's clipboard.

The Generate Handlers option is another time-saving option. It automatically generates event handler methods for the currently selected item's events. This works for activities and the workflow itself.

You can select various workflow views when designing a workflow in Visual Studio. You then navigate these views in the Workflow menu. As you can see in Figure 4-4, the current workflow has three views: the SequentialWorkflow, Cancel Handler, and Fault Handler views. (The various views for each workflow type are discussed later in this chapter.)

The Create New Theme and Select Custom Theme options are related to workflow designer themes, which are discussed later in this chapter. You use the Zoom and Navigation Tools menu options to visually manipulate the workflow designer. The last option in this menu, Debug, enables you to set debugging options for your workflow. (Debugging is discussed later in this chapter.)

The Project Menu

Although the Project menu is not specific to Windows Workflow Foundation, it does have some context-specific items related to workflow development. As you can see in Figure 4-5, you can add several workflow-related items to your current project.

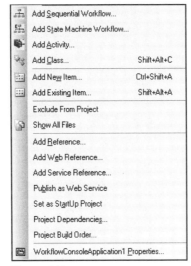

Figure 4-5

The Workflow Toolbar

The workflow toolbar provides zooming, workflow navigation, and themes options (see Figure 4-6).

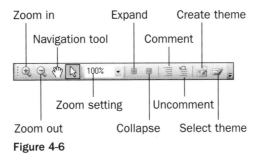

Figure 4-6

These workflow toolbar options are also available from the Workflow menu in the main menu.

The Toolbox

The Visual Studio Toolbox provides you with all the components necessary for developing workflows. The Toolbox drag-and-drop functionality enables you to visually build your application. Figure 4-7 shows the Toolbox with all out-of-the-box Windows Workflow Foundation activities.

Figure 4-7

Displaying Custom Components in the Toolbox

In addition to displaying the standard workflow activities, the Toolbox can display custom components that you or others have developed. Visual Studio Toolbox can detect all workflow activities in the current solution. For example, if a project in your current solution contains custom-developed workflow activities, you can set it up so that these activities are automatically displayed in the Toolbox (see Figure 4-8).

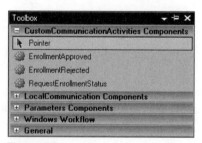

Figure 4-8

To enable this Toolbox functionality, all you need to do is to decorate your activity class with `ToolboxItemAttribute`. For example:

```
[ToolboxItemAttribute(typeof(ActivityToolboxItem))]
public class MyCustomActivity : Activity
```

Adding Items to the Toolbox

You can also add items that are located in external assemblies to the Toolbox. In addition, you can logically group Toolbox components in tabs. To add a new tab, right-click an empty area of the Toolbox and select Add Tab from the context menu. Then give the tab a name.

At this point, you can add external components to your newly created tab. Right-click an empty area in your new tab and select the Choose Items option. This displays the Choose Toolbox Items dialog box, where you can select the components you want to add to the Toolbox (see Figure 4-9).

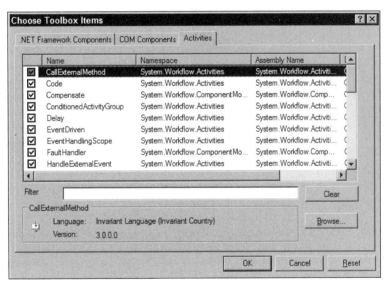

Figure 4-9

This dialog box contains the following tabs:

❑ **.NET Framework Components** — This tab shows .NET assemblies that are currently in the Global Assembly Cache and their status related to whether or not they have been added to the Toolbox.

❑ **COM Components** — This tab does not pertain to workflow development.

❑ **Activities** — This tab is specifically related to Windows Workflow Foundation and shows all activities that have been added to the Global Assembly Cache. The items on this tab are a subset of the .NET Framework Components tab.

You can either select an item from the .NET Framework Components or Activities tab or click the Browse button to locate a .NET assembly on the filesystem. After you select an assembly that contains custom activities, they appear in the list and are selected by default. You can modify your selection using the corresponding check boxes and click OK. The custom activities that you selected appear in your new Toolbox tab, and you can use them in workflows.

This dialog box also contains a filtering text box that allows you to type a few letters of the item you are looking for to display only matching items.

Project Item Types

There are several item types that are specific to a Windows Workflow Foundation project. To add these items to your project, you can use the Project menu (discussed earlier), or right-click your project and use the context menu. To provide easy access to common items, the context menu enables you to add the items by selecting the Add from the Project context menu. This displays the Add submenu (see Figure 4-10).

Figure 4-10

If you select the New Item option from the Add submenu, you are presented with a long list of available project items. The Add New Item dialog box is shown in Figure 4-11.

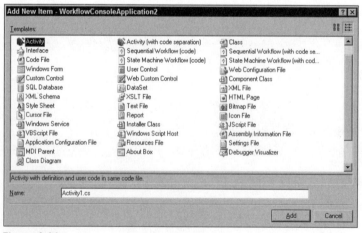

Figure 4-11

The items displayed on your machine may differ based on the installation options of Visual Studio. This dialog box allows you to add new items such as sequential and state workflows using the different development modes discussed earlier in this chapter as well as new activities.

The Properties Window

The Properties window enables you to manipulate values and settings on various items in Visual Studio. If you have used Visual Studio for development in the past, you are already very familiar with this window. However, because this window is so important to Windows Workflow Foundation, it is described briefly here.

The Properties window displays properties in a context-specific manner related to what is selected in the Visual Studio document region. For example, if you select the workflow designer by clicking a blank area of the workflow, the Properties window displays the corresponding property names and descriptions (see Figure 4-12).

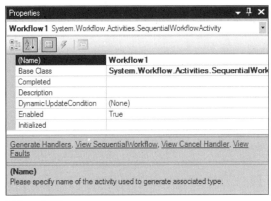

Figure 4-12

The Properties window also allows you to configure event handlers related to the item that is currently selected. To access the item's events, click the lightning-bolt icon. The events view of the Properties window is displayed, as shown in Figure 4-13.

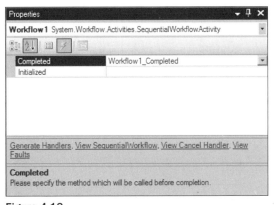

Figure 4-13

As you can see in Figures 4-12 and 4-13, there are some context-sensitive links that enable you to perform actions on the currently selected item. In these figures, the selected item is a sequential workflow, and the items are related to generating event handlers and navigating to the different workflow views.

The bottom of the Properties window shows the description of the currently selected property or event.

The Designers

You will probably spend the majority of your workflow development time using the workflow designers. The designers are located in the document region of Visual Studio, and you drag and drop activities to and from them to build your workflows. Each workflow type has its own designer and specific features. In addition, you can visually develop and modify activities with a designer.

The designers enable you to do things like comment individual activities by right-clicking and selecting the Disable option from the context menu. After you have disabled an activity, it appears with a green, slightly opaque overlay.

The designers also have various views that represent different areas of development for that workflow or activity. The following sections discuss each designer view with its respective parent.

Sequential Workflows

The sequential workflow designer enables you to visually design ordered workflows by dragging and dropping graphical activities and manipulating their properties.

The sequential workflow designer has three different views that separate distinct areas of functionality for the workflow. You can navigate to these views by using the icons in the lower-left corner of the workflow designer or by using the drop-down menu. To display the drop-down menu, hover over the Sequential Workflow title at the top of the designer and click the down arrow.

The Workflow View

The workflow view is what you are probably most used to and is the default view for the sequential workflow designer. If you are currently in another view, you can return to the default workflow view by using the icons at the bottom left of the workflow designer (see Figure 4-14). The leftmost icon moves you to the workflow view.

The Cancellation Handler View

The cancellation handler view enables you to define a set of activities that occur when a workflow instance is cancelled. This view automatically contains the CancellationHandler activity, which must to exist and cannot be removed. The default view of the CancellationHandler was shown in Figure 4-14.

This view executes and behaves no differently from the main workflow designer view. You drop activities into it that you want to occur if the workflow is canceled.

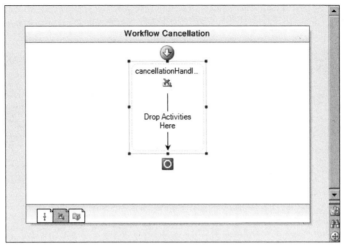

Figure 4-14

The Faults View

The faults view of the sequential workflow designer is analogous to a `try-catch` block in any CLR language. The following code represents a standard exception-handling block in C#. Here, code that may cause an exception is wrapped in a `try` block. Then several `catch` blocks are defined in order to monitor for specific exception types. The order in which `catch` blocks are defined is important, so you should place more specific exceptions types at the top of the chain and more generic exception types at the bottom.

```
try
{
    // below is some potentially dangerous code
    ...
}
catch(SqlException ex)
{
    // handle the SQL exception
}
catch(InvalidOperationException ex)
{
    // this is a more generic catch block
}
catch
{
    // this catch block will catch anything missed so far in the chain
}
```

The workflow fault handler view follows the same logic as `try-catch` blocks. You add FaultHandler activities to the FaultHandlers activity in order, from left to right, to monitor for specific fault types. You map each added FaultHandler activity to an exception type, along with its own flow of other activities in the area below the fault types list. (Chapter 12 discusses fault handling in more detail.)

Figure 4-15 shows the sequential workflow's faults view for a fault handler that catches a `SqlException`.

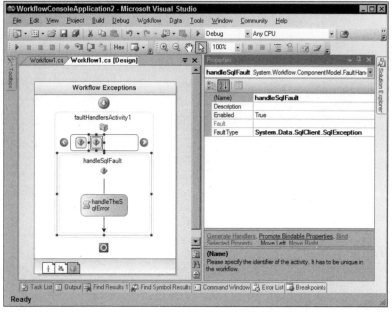

Figure 4-15

State-Machine Workflows

State-machine workflows have two views within the Visual Studio designer. You use the workflow development view (Figure 4-16) to define the states that exist in a state-machine workflow and the events that occur in each. You use the EventDriven activities view to define a flow of work whenever a configured event is raised (see Figure 4-17).

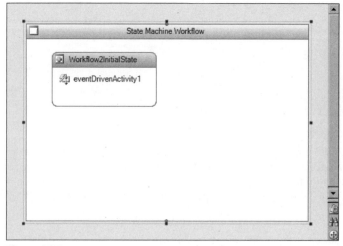

Figure 4-16

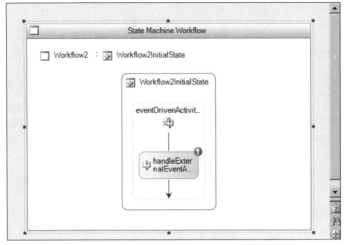

Figure 4-17

For more information about state-machine workflows, see Chapter 10.

Activities

In addition to developing the two workflow types visually, you can visually create standalone activities. A Sequence activity enables you to define a set of activities to form a reusable workflow. The activity designer has the following three views, which are the same as the sequential workflow designer views:

❑ Activity view (analogous to the sequential workflow view of a sequential workflow)

❑ Cancel handler view

❑ Faults view

Figure 4-18 shows the default view for the activity designer.

Figure 4-18

Chapter 6 covers activity development, including this type of visual sequence activity development.

Design-Time Validation

Activities can have built-in validation logic, which enables Visual Studio to check for configuration errors at design time. This means you do not have to wait until compilation or even runtime to find errors in your activities.

Each activity can determine if it is configured correctly. The workflow designer can also determine each activity's status. Workflow activities that do not pass validation are flagged with a red exclamation point, as shown in Figure 4-19. Clicking this exclamation point displays a drop-down menu with details about what is causing the problem. In the case of the Code activity shown in the figure, the `ExecuteCode` event needs to be wired.

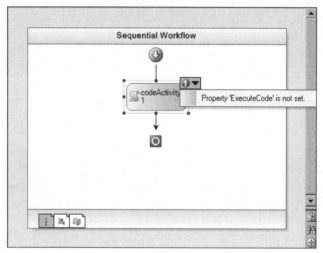

Figure 4-19

The steps required to implement this type of validation behavior in custom activities are covered in Chapter 6.

Themes

Because the visual aspect of workflow development is key to this platform, the Windows Workflow Foundation team has provided an extensible architecture that enables you to customize how workflows look and feel.

Visual Studio provides the Theme Customization dialog box, which allows you to view and modify a properties for different workflow activities. You can access this dialog box by clicking the Create New Theme button on the workflow toolbar or by selecting the Workflow ⇨ Create New Theme in Visual Studio. Figure 4-20 shows the Theme Customization dialog box displaying the properties for the IfElse activity. As you can see, there are properties such as `Background Start Color` and `Background End Color` that allow gradient color schemes for activities.

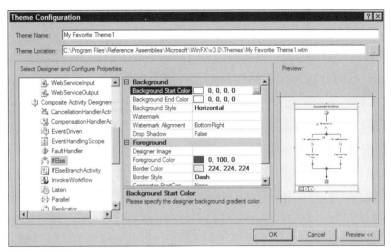

Figure 4-20

If you make modifications to the default workflow activity themes, you have the option of saving your changes to a .wtm file. Doing this generates an XML file that defines the colors, images, and other options that you specified for your theme. You can load existing themes into the Visual Studio environment by clicking the Select Custom Theme button on the workflow toolbar or from the Workflow main menu.

Debugging

Although debugging strategies are covered in Chapter 12, it is important to point out that Visual Studio plays a vital role in this process.

Debugging workflows in Visual Studio is very similar to debugging traditional code. You can place breakpoints on workflow activities by right-clicking and selecting Breakpoint ⇨ Insert Breakpoint from the activity's context menu. Standard commands such as Step Into, Step Over, and Start Debugging provide you with a consistent debugging experience. This includes the ability to configure workflow variables as watch variables so that their values can be monitored during execution.

The Type Browser

The Type Browser dialog box enables you to select .NET interfaces for the CallExternalMethod and HandleExternalEvent data-exchange activities. To access this dialog box, click the ellipsis button on the `InterfaceType` property of either of these activities.

The dialog box scans the current project for any interfaces decorated with the `ExternalDataExchange` attribute and displays them to the user. In addition, the user has the option of pointing to another assembly outside the project. All interfaces decorated with the same attribute are displayed from the assembly (see Figure 4-21).

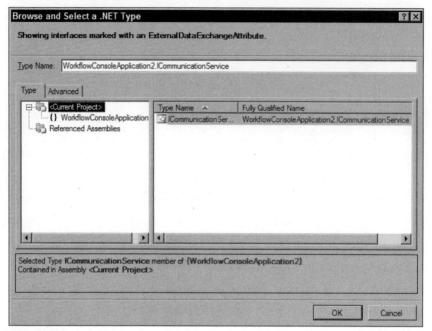

Figure 4-21

In addition, you can use the Type Browser to add FaultHandler activities to a FaultHandlers activity. Each FaultHandler activity corresponds to .NET exception class through its `FaultType` property. If you click the ellipsis button on this property in the Properties window, the Type Browser dialog box displays the classes that inherit from the base `System.Exception` class.

Summary

This chapter described how you can use Windows Workflow Foundation to develop workflows. Topics covered included workflow development modes, compilation, serialization, and the Visual Studio development environment.

As you learned in this chapter, the workflow development modes include markup only, markup with code, and code only. Workflow markup is defined by a standard called extensible application markup language, or XAML. Nodes in a XAML document correspond to classes, and attributes in nodes correspond to properties in those classes.

Compilation was also covered as it relates to workflow development. There are several ways to compile workflows, no matter what mode you use for development, including the wfc.exe command-line compiler, the `WorkflowCompiler` class, and Visual Studio.

Workflow serialization enables you to persist a workflow, perhaps defined in code, to a durable medium such as the filesystem. There are several classes provided in Windows Workflow Foundation that facilitate this functionality.

Finally, the Visual Studio development environment was discussed as it relates to Windows Workflow Foundation. Visual Studio provides a rich, familiar, and visual environment for developing workflow-based software. This chapter discussed Visual Studio basics, including project templates, the Toolbox, and the Properties window. The chapter also discussed workflow designers and their various views.

Workflow Hosting, Execution, and Communication

Workflows need a host application to run. The host is responsible for starting and maintaining workflows — the workflow itself doesn't need to know anything about the infrastructure in which it is running. However, this infrastructure is very important to the lifecycle of workflows.

Part of the concept of hosting is workflow communication. Workflows need to be able to communicate important information to the outside world, and vice versa. Windows Workflow Foundation provides the necessary components and architecture to facilitate this communication.

This chapter covers the following topics:

- ❑ Workflow hosting
- ❑ Workflow runtime
- ❑ Workflow and runtime management
- ❑ Workflow communication methods

Workflow Hosting

Workflows can be hosted in any type of .NET application, which opens up myriad possible scenarios for workflow-enabled software. The flexible workflow architecture allows individual workflows and their respective instances to be hosted in multiple types of applications across their execution lifecycle. Just as with classes in .NET, workflows have a definition and can have any number of instances of a definition.

A workflow instance might be started from within a Windows Forms application when a user enters data and clicks a button. Next, the workflow may require some interaction with an ASP.NET web form. The same workflow instance and its associated state and context are used in the Windows Forms and ASP.NET applications, which are known as the *hosts*. The workflow runtime enables hosting in applications.

The Workflow Runtime

The workflow runtime is the gateway between the host application and workflow instances. Even though workflow is the star of the show, the runtime plays a very important role in workflow lifecycle management.

The WorkflowRuntime Class

The `System.Workflow.Runtime.WorkflowRuntime` class represents the workflow runtime and exposes a great deal of functionality to manage the runtime environment. Using this class, you have complete control over the execution of workflow instances and the runtime itself.

The `WorkflowRuntime` class is responsible for the following important tasks:

- ❑ Managing the workflow runtime
- ❑ Starting and managing runtime instances
- ❑ Managing runtime services
- ❑ Handling runtime events

Managing the Workflow Runtime

Obtaining a reference to this important class is quite simple. You just create a new instance like any other .NET class, as shown in the following code:

```
// create a runtime instance
WorkflowRuntime theRuntimeInstance = new WorkflowRuntime();
```

As previously mentioned, the workflow runtime can be hosted in any .NET application or application domain (AppDomain). Because AppDomains and threads are recurring and important themes related to Windows Workflow Foundation, these concepts are covered in the following section.

AppDomains, the Common Language Runtime, and Threads

An AppDomain is a concept specific to the .NET Common Language Runtime (CLR). AppDomains provide an environment for the secure and safe execution of managed code. Just like a process is the smallest unit of isolation on the Windows operating system, an AppDomain is the smallest unit of isolation within the CLR. AppDomains are located within processes and have a one-to-many relationship with them.

AppDomains provide execution isolation and boundaries. This means that code running within one AppDomain cannot affect, adversely or otherwise, code or memory in another AppDomain or process. (You can take deliberate steps to enable an AppDomain to affect the execution of code outside its boundaries, but that is outside the scope of what is discussed here.)

Threads define a further level of code execution. There can be multiple threads in a process and within an AppDomain. A thread does not belong to one AppDomain — it can be executing in one AppDomain one minute and another the next minute, but it can be actively executing within only one application domain at a time. See Figure 5-1 for a representation of the .NET execution model.

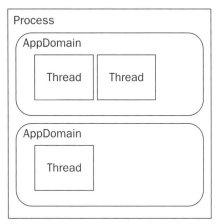

Figure 5-1

Generally, .NET developers are not concerned with the management of application domains. The CLR always creates a default application domain for a .NET application in which a developer's code runs. However, the .NET class libraries expose a class called AppDomain for application domain management and manipulation. This class also enables you to create new application domains. For example, you may want to create a new application domain for code that is long running, unstable, or both. This provides a level of stability to other code running on the system and in the same process.

Runtime Management

The WorkflowRuntime class exposes two public methods that relate the management of the workflow runtime itself: StartRuntime and StopRuntime.

StartRuntime causes a couple of important actions to take place. First, there are core runtime services that must always exist in a running workflow runtime: a workflow transaction service and a workflow scheduler service. When StartRuntime is called, a check is performed to see if either of these two services has been manually added to the runtime. If not, the runtime creates default instances of each service type. The default class for the transaction service is DefaultWorkflowTransactionService, and the default class for the scheduler service is DefaultWorkflowSchedulerService. After the services have been successfully instantiated and added to the runtime, each service is started with its Start method. In addition to the service configuration that occurs during the runtime startup process, the IsStarted property of the runtime is set to true, and the Started event is raised.

Calling the StopRuntime method has an opposite effect. All services are stopped, all workflow instances are unloaded, the IsStarted property is set to false, and the Stopped event is raised.

Starting and Managing Workflow Instances

One of the most important tasks the workflow runtime can perform is starting workflow instances. In addition to starting instances, the runtime exposes functionality for managing them.

To start a workflow instance, simply call the `CreateWorkflow` method of your `WorkflowRuntime` instance. There are several overloads to this method, but the one most commonly used takes a `Type` instance, which represents a workflow class type. For example:

```
// MyWorkflow is a workflow definition class
Type workflowType = typeof(MyWorkflow);

// use the workflow runtime to create an instance of MyWorkflow
WorkflowInstance workflowInstance =
    theRuntimeInstance.CreateWorkflow(workflowType);
```

Although the preceding code creates a workflow instance, it does not actually start the workflow. The `Start` method of the `WorkflowInstance` class does that, as shown here:

```
// start the workflow instance!
workflowInstance.Start();
```

In addition, if the `StartRuntime` method of the `WorkflowRuntime` class has not yet been called, it is called when a workflow instance start is attempted.

Managing Runtime Services

The `WorkflowRuntime` class plays an important role in managing runtime services. A runtime service is a class that inherits from the `System.Workflow.Runtime.Hosting.WorkflowRuntimeService` class and provides functionality related to runtime management. These services run in the background of the workflow runtime, remaining generally invisible to users.

Several runtime services are provided out of the box for transactions, workflow persistence, tracking, threading, workflow communication, and more. These runtime services are covered in detail in Chapter 7.

To enable runtime classes in a host application, you need to add them to the workflow runtime class. The following code is an example of how to do this:

```
// create an instance of the SqlWorkflowPersistenceService class
SqlWorkflowPersistenceService sqlPersistence =
    new SqlWorkflowPersistenceService();

// create a runtime instance reference
WorkflowRuntime theRuntime = new WorkflowRuntime();

// add the persistence service to the runtime
theRuntime.AddService(sqlPersistence);

// start the runtime
theRuntime.StartRuntime();
...
```

As you can see, the workflow runtime exposes a method called `AddService` that takes a workflow runtime service instance as its sole argument. Conversely, the runtime contains a method for removing services, called `RemoveService`, as shown here:

```
// start the runtime
theRuntime.StartRuntime();
...
// remove the SqlWorkflowPersistenceService from the runtime
theRuntime.RemoveService(sqlPersistence);
```

In addition, the workflow runtime exposes methods for obtaining references to services already added to the runtime. If you need to obtain a reference to one specific type of service, use the `GetService` method, as follows:

```
// obtain a reference to the SQL persistence service by specifying its type
SqlWorkflowPersistenceService sqlPersistence =
    theRuntime.GetService(typeof(SqlWorkflowPersistenceService));

// you can also use the generics overload to get the runtime service you want
sqlPersistence = theRuntime.GetService<SqlWorkflowPersistenceService>();
```

The `GetService` method works only if there is one instance of the service type. If you try to call `GetService` for a service type that has two or more instances added to the runtime, an `Invalid OperationException` is thrown, as follows:

```
WorkflowRuntime workflowRuntime = new WorkflowRuntime();

MyRuntimeService service1 = new MyRuntimeService();
MyRuntimeService service2 = new MyRuntimeService();

workflowRuntime.AddService(service1);
workflowRuntime.AddService(service2);

// the following line will throw an exception
MyRuntimeService serviceReference =
    workflowRuntime.GetService(typeof(MyRuntimeService));
```

If you need a list of all runtime services, or if there is more than one service of the same type currently in the runtime, use the `GetAllServices` method. For example, the following code returns only the runtime services that are added by default after starting the `WorkflowRuntime` instance:

```
WorkflowRuntime workflowRuntime = new WorkflowRuntime();
workflowRuntime.StartRuntime();

// the following line will retrieve all runtime services
// notice the Type we are passing is WorkflowRuntimeService
// which is the base class for all runtime services
System.Collections.ObjectModel.ReadOnlyCollection<object> services =
    workflowRuntime.GetAllServices(typeof(WorkflowRuntimeService));
```

Handling Runtime Events

The `WorkflowRuntime` class exposes events related to runtime and workflow activities. You can implement these events in the host to handle certain types of workflow and runtime actions.

Table 5-1 describes the workflow runtime events that relate to the runtime.

Table 5-1: Workflow Runtime-Related Events

Event	Description
Started	Fired when the workflow runtime is started by calling to `Start Runtime` method or when the first workflow instance is started.
	Passes a `WorkflowRuntimeEventArgs` instance to the event handler.
Stopped	Fired when the `StopRuntime` method is called.
	Passes a `WorkflowRuntimeEventArgs` instance to the event handler.
ServicesException NotHandled	Raised when a runtime service that has been added to the runtime does not handle an exception.
	Passes a `ServicesExceptionNotHandledEventArgs` instance to the event handler.

Table 5-2 lists the events related to workflow instances. These events pass useful information back to the host though a `WorkflowEventArgs` instance or class that inherits from it. The `WorkflowEventArgs` class exposes its `WorkflowInstance` property to provide a reference to the workflow instance from which the event was raised. (The `WorkflowInstance` is covered later in this chapter.)

Table 5-2: Workflow Instance-Related Events

Event	Description
WorkflowAborted	Raised when a workflow instance is aborted.
	Passes a `WorkflowEventArgs` instance to the event handler.
WorkflowCompleted	Raised when a workflow instance completes.
	Passes a `WorkflowCompletedEventArgs` instance to the event handler.
WorkflowCreated	Raised when a workflow instance is created.
	Passes a `WorkflowEventArgs` instance to the event handler.
WorkflowIdled	Raised when a workflow becomes idle.
	Passes a `WorkflowEventArgs` instance to the event handler.
WorkflowLoaded	Raised when a workflow instance is loaded into memory.
	Passes a `WorkflowEventArgs` instance to the event handler.

Event	Description
WorkflowPersisted	Raised when a workflow is persisted to a durable medium via a persistence service.
	Passes a `WorkflowEventArgs` instance to the event handler.
WorkflowResumed	Raised when a workflow instance is resumed.
	Passes a `WorkflowEventArgs` instance to the event handler.
WorkflowStarted	Raised when a workflow instance is started. Passes a `Workflow EventArgs` instance to the event handler.
WorkflowSuspended	Raised when a workflow instance becomes suspended. This can occur when the `Suspend` or `RequestSuspend` method of the `Workflow Instance` is called by a `SuspendActivity` inside a workflow instance or when the runtime needs to suspend the instance.
	Passes a `WorkflowSuspendedEventArgs` instance to the event handler.
WorkflowTerminated	Raised when a workflow instance is terminated.
	Passes a `WorkflowTerminatedEventArgs` instance to the event handler.
WorkflowUnloaded	Raised when a workflow instance is unloaded from memory.
	Passes a `WorkflowEventArgs` instance to the event handler.

The following code listing is a simple example of how the host handles runtime events. A `Workflow Runtime` instance is created, and there are several event handlers wired in the `Main` method. The event handlers use their respective event argument parameters to display relevant information about each event.

```
static void Main(string[] args)
{
    WorkflowRuntime workflowRuntime = new WorkflowRuntime();

    workflowRuntime.Started += new
      EventHandler<WorkflowRuntimeEventArgs>(workflowRuntime_Started);
    workflowRuntime.Stopped += new
      EventHandler<WorkflowRuntimeEventArgs>(workflowRuntime_Stopped);
    workflowRuntime.WorkflowCreated += new
      EventHandler<WorkflowEventArgs>(workflowRuntime_WorkflowCreated);
    workflowRuntime.WorkflowCompleted += new
      EventHandler<WorkflowCompletedEventArgs>(workflowRuntime_WorkflowCompleted);
    workflowRuntime.WorkflowTerminated += new
      EventHandler<WorkflowTerminatedEventArgs>(workflowRuntime_WorkflowTerminated);
    workflowRuntime.WorkflowIdled += new
      EventHandler<WorkflowEventArgs>(workflowRuntime_WorkflowIdled);

    workflowRuntime.StartRuntime();

    WorkflowInstance instance = workflowRuntime.CreateWorkflow(typeof(MyWorkflow));
```

```
        instance.Start();
    }

    // runtime related event handlers
    private void workflowRuntime_Started(object sender, WorkflowRuntimeEventArgs e)
    {
        Console.WriteLine("The workflow runtime has been started. It's status is: " +
            e.IsStarted ? "running" : "not running" + ".");
    }

    private void workflowRuntime_Stopped(object sender, WorkflowRuntimeEventArgs e)
    {
        Console.WriteLine("The workflow runtime has been stopped. It's status is: " +
            e.IsStarted ? "running" : "not running" + ".");
    }

    // workflow instance related event handlers
    private void workflowRuntime_WorkflowCreated(object sender, WorkflowEventArgs e)
    {
        Console.WriteLine("A workflow instance has been created with the identifier " +
            e.WorkflowInstance.InstanceId.ToString() + ".");
    }

    private void workflowRuntime_WorkflowCompleted(object sender,
        WorkflowCompletedEventArgs e)
    {
        Console.WriteLine("The workflow instance with the identifier " +
            e.WorkflowInstance.InstanceId.ToString() + " has completed.");
    }

    private void workflowRuntime_WorkflowIdled(object sender, WorkflowEventArgs e)
    {
        Console.WriteLine("The workflow instance with the identifier " +
            e.WorkflowInstance.InstanceId.ToString() +
            " has gone idle.");
    }

    private void workflowRuntime_WorkflowTerminated(object sender,
        WorkflowTerminatedEventArgs e)
    {
        Console.WriteLine("The workflow instance with the identifier " +
            e.WorkflowInstance.InstanceId.ToString() +
            " has been terminated.");

        Console.WriteLine("It threw an exception, here are the details: " +
            e.Exception.Message);
    }
```

Persistence Points

You can use Windows Workflow Foundation to persist running workflows and their respective states, such as when a workflow instance is long running, and you do not want to store the workflow state in memory.

Persistence is a topic deeply imbedded in the concept of the workflow runtime. The runtime dictates when a workflow should be persisted to a designated store and makes the necessary persistence services method calls to do so.

The milestones when the runtime tells an active persistence service to persist a workflow instance are known as *persistence points.* To effectively manage a long-running workflow environment, you need to understand where in the workflow lifecycle these points exist. Persistence points occur at the following times in the lifecycle:

❑ Directly before a workflow instance is completed or terminated

❑ After a workflow instance becomes idle

❑ When the workflow instance is explicitly unloaded, which occurs when the Unload or TryUnload method of the workflow instance is called

❑ When activities that are decorated with the PersistOnClose attribute are completed

The workflow runtime is generally smart enough to know when to save a workflow's state to a data store. This is generally seamless to developers and most definitely invisible to end users.

Workflow persistence services are covered in detail in Chapter 7, along with the other runtime services.

The WorkflowInstance Class

The WorkflowInstance class represents all workflows in their instantiated form. You use this class to monitor and manipulate an instance related to its execution. Think of it as a wrapper around an instance of a workflow definition class.

The standard technique for obtaining a reference to a new workflow instance is to call the CreateWorkflow method of the WorkflowRuntime class. Calling this method returns a reference to a workflow instance representing a workflow of the type passed as a parameter. Calling CreateWorkflow does not start the workflow. The Start method of WorkflowInstance must be explicitly called to begin the execution of the workflow itself.

Table 5-3 lists the methods of the WorkflowInstance class.

Table 5-3: WorkflowInstance Methods

Method	Description
Abort	Ends execution of the current workflow instance in a synchronous manner. Calling Abort causes all changes made since the most recent persistence point to be discarded. Therefore, this method is usually used when a workflow cannot recover from a serious error. Calling Resume starts the workflow instance from the most recent persistence point after an Abort call.
ApplyWorkflow Changes	Takes a WorkflowChanges instance as its sole parameter and is used for dynamic update (see Chapter 11).

Table continued on following page

Method	Description
EnqueueItem	Places a message to the specified workflow in the queue.
EnqueueItemOnIdle	Places a message to the specified workflow in the queue only after the workflow instance has gone idle.
GetWorkflow Definition	Returns the workflow definition class that the workflow instance represents.
GetWorkflow QueueData	Returns a collection that contains information related to workflow queues and their associated work.
Load	Loads an unloaded workflow instance from a persistence store. The workflow state is read from the store, and the workflow continues execution.
ReloadTracking Profiles	Causes each TrackingProfile related to a workflow instance to be reloaded.
Resume	Resumes execution of a workflow instance that was previously suspended or aborted.
Start	Begins execution of a workflow instance.
Suspend	Suspends a workflow instance's execution.
Terminate	Terminates an active workflow instance and attempts to persist the workflow's state. This method is also called when an unhandled exception is raised from within a workflow instance.
TryUnload	Makes a request to unload the workflow instance's state to a persistence store at the point when the instance is next suspended or idle.
Unload	Synchronously makes a request to unload the workflow instance's state to a persistence store.

Workflow Execution

When the Start method of a WorkflowInstance class is called, two things have to happen to begin the workflow. Because activities make up a workflow definition and define the process flow, the runtime must find the root activity of a workflow and call its protected Execute method. From here, the work-flow continues until an action causes a disruption in the flow.

Several events can halt or otherwise modify a workflow's execution. The host can call the Abort, Terminate, Unload, or TryUnload method of the WorkflowInstance class to manually stop or pause the execution of a workflow instance. Workflow execution can also come to a stop when there is no work that can be immediately performed. This happens when the workflow is waiting for input from an outside entity, such as a person or external software system. Finally, exceptions that are not properly handled in a workflow instance cause the workflow execution to come to an end.

Conventional wisdom tells developers to put code that initializes variables and otherwise readies a class for execution in the class constructor. However, in Windows Workflow Foundation, this is not the recommend way to do things, because the workflow class constructor is actually called twice: once to validate the workflow's activities and again when the class is instantiated for execution. Therefore, you should place code that usually goes in the constructor in the `ExecuteCode` event handler of a Code activity.

The WorkflowEnvironment Class

The `WorkflowEnvironment` class enables you to access the transactional context of the workflow instance executing on the current thread. This class exposes two properties of interest: the `WorkflowInstanceId`, which is the globally unique identifier (GUID) for a particular workflow instance, and `IWorkBatch`, which enables transactional functionality in the workflow. Work batching and transactional services are discussed in the following section.

Work Batching

Windows Workflow Foundation provides transactional functionality through *work batching*. This concept allows discrete chunks of work to be added to a set and completed at the same time. During the execution of a workflow, units of work can be added to the `WorkBatch` property of the `WorkflowEnvironment` class. When the workflow runtime reaches a commit point, all work items are performed within the context of a single transaction. That way, if any errors occur during this work, the workflow remains in a valid state after a rollback.

To enable this transactional process, you need to create a class that implements the `IPendingWork` interface. This interface describes a class with a couple of methods, including `Commit`, which is where the actual work happens. The `Commit` method receives an `ICollection` instance that contains a list of all objects added with the `WorkBatch` property of `WorkflowEnvironment`. The `Commit` method can iterate through each object in the `ICollection` instance and perform some kind of work.

Developing Batch Services

Services that inherit from `WorkflowCommitWorkBatchService` are responsible for taking the items in the work batch and performing their actions in a transactional manner. You are, of course, free to inherit from this class and develop your own batch service. However, if you do not specify that such a service be added to the workflow runtime, an instance of `DefaultWorkflowCommitWorkBatchService` is automatically added for you. (Chapter 7 has more on batching and transactions related to this type of runtime service.)

Workflow Communication

Workflow-to-host communication and host-to-workflow communication are vital components of Windows Workflow Foundation. Without the necessary hooks to send data back and forth, workflows would not be nearly as useful. Host applications are the most common locations where workflows receive information from the outside world.

For example, in a scenario where a user interacts with a Windows Forms application that is hosting a helpdesk ticket workflow, the Windows application needs to inform the workflow when the user starts a new ticket or updates an existing one. In addition, the workflow might need to tell the host application when an action of interest occurs, such as a request for further information from the user.

There are two main methods of workflow communication. The first, and the simpler of the two, uses parameters to pass data to a workflow when it is created. The second and richer form of communication is called *local communication services.* This technique uses method and events to facilitate communication. Both of these methods are covered in the following sections.

You might be thinking, "What about web services?" Although web services are becoming more vital for distributed application communication, they are outside the scope of this type of communication. That does not mean that web services and other distributed communication technologies are not important to Windows Workflow Foundation. Chapter 14 discusses Windows Workflow Foundation as it relates to web services, and Chapter 15 covers how Windows Communication Foundation relates to the workflow platform.

Parameters

Parameters provide a simple way to pass data to a workflow instance during its creation. A `Dictionary <string, object>` generics collection is used to pass parameters to the `CreateWorkflow` method of the `WorkflowRuntime` class. Because the collection is passed before the workflow is started, it is helpful only for initialization purposes and cannot be used to communicate with a workflow that is already running.

Each parameter key added to the dictionary collection *must* correspond to a public property in the workflow definition class that has a `set` accessor. These properties are used to hold the values added to the collection in the host.

Conversely, parameters can be passed from a workflow out to its host upon completion. Event handlers for the `WorkflowCompleted` event are passed an instance of the `WorkflowCompletedEventArgs` class. This class holds a property called `OutputParameters`, which is of type `Dictionary<string, object>`. Just as with the input parameters, the workflow class must expose its output parameters as public properties, but this time with the `get` accessor.

Using this method of communication is quite simple, as displayed in the following code. The input parameters are prepared in the host application and passed to the `CreateWorkflow` method. The `runtime_WorkflowCompleted` event handler method uses the `OutputParameters` collection to access the output parameters.

```
public static void Main(string[] args)
{
    WorkflowRuntime runtime = new WorkflowRuntime();

    runtime.WorkflowCompleted +=
        new EventHandler<WorkflowCompletedEventArgs>
            (runtime_WorkflowCompleted);

    runtime.StartRuntime();

    Dictionary<string, object> parameters = new Dictionary<string, object>();
    parameters.Add("SomeMessage",
        "This is a message which goes in to the workflow instance...");

    WorkflowInstance wi =
```

```
        runtime.CreateWorkflow(typeof(ParametersWorkflow), parameters);

    wi.Start();
}

private static void runtime_WorkflowCompleted(object sender,
    WorkflowCompletedEventArgs e)
{
    Console.WriteLine("The workflow instance with the ID '" +
        e.WorkflowInstance.InstanceId.ToString() + "' has completed.");
    Console.WriteLine("It told us: " +
        e.OutputParameters["SomeOtherMessage"]);
}
```

The following code shows the workflow definition class. As you can see, there is a property for
`SomeMessage`, which is the input parameter, and `SomeOtherMessage` acts as the output parameter.
These properties have a `set` and `get` accessor, respectively.

```
public sealed partial class ParametersWorkflow : SequentialWorkflowActivity
{
    private string someMessage;
    private string someOtherMessage;

    public string SomeMessage
    {
        set { someMessage = value; }
    }

    public string SomeOtherMessage
    {
        get { return someOtherMessage; }
    }

    public ParametersWorkflow()
    {
        InitializeComponent();
    }

    private void caEchoInputMessage_ExecuteCode(object sender, EventArgs e)
    {
        Console.WriteLine("The host told me: " + this.someMessage);
    }

    private void caSetOutputMessage_ExecuteCode(object sender, EventArgs e)
    {
        this.someOtherMessage = "This message will be accessed by the host...";
    }
}
```

103

Local Communication Services

You can use Windows Workflow Foundation to communicate back and forth between a host and an executing workflow instance. Essentially, you use standard .NET interfaces and classes to facilitate workflow communication through method calls and events.

When a workflow wants to tell something to the host, it calls a method predefined in a .NET interface and subsequently implemented in a concrete class. When the host is ready to notify the workflow of some event or data, it raises an event that is then handled by the workflow.

Relevant Classes

The following sections review several classes that enable local communication services.

Custom Communication Service Interfaces and Classes

To allow communications to occur between a workflow host and workflow instances, you must define communication contracts that dictate which messages can be sent back and forth. These contracts are implemented through .NET interfaces, and they can contain any public methods that can be called from the workflow. The interface methods represent concrete methods that will exist on the workflow host. You can pass any type of data as parameters to these methods for communication purposes, and you can specify return values to set variables in the workflow instance. However, any type passed to a workflow and its host must be decorated with the `Serializable` attribute (more on this requirement later in this chapter).

After you define the communication interfaces, you must create concrete classes to implement the behavior specified in the interfaces. The following sections cover classes and entities important to local communication services. An example is then shown and discussed to further explain these concepts.

ExternalDataExchangeService

This class is a runtime service that manages all the communication service classes. To use local communication services, you must add an instance of this class to the workflow runtime (as you do with any other runtime service that uses the `AddService` method of `WorkflowRuntime`). Then you can add communication service classes to the `ExternalDataExchangeService` instance using its own `AddService` method, as follows:

```
WorkflowRuntime workflowRuntime = new WorkflowRuntime();

// create an instance of the data exchange service
ExternalDataExchangeService dataService = new ExternalDataExchangeService();

// add the external data exchange service to the runtime
workflowRuntime.AddService(dataService);

// create an instance of my custom communication service
MyCommunicationService commService = new MyCommunicationService();

// add the communication service to the data exchange runtime service
dataService.AddService(commService);
```

The `ExternalDataExchange` service class exposes the following public methods for managing local communication services:

❏   `AddService` — Adds communication service instances to the data exchange service.

❏   `GetService` — Takes a `Type` reference as its sole parameter and returns any communication services of that type. Because `GetService` returns an `object`, you must first cast it to the appropriate type.

❏   `RemoveService` — Takes a communication service instance as a parameter and removes it from the data exchange service. `RemoveService` throws an `InvalidOperationException` if the class reference passed is not already registered with the data exchange service.

The data exchange service is also responsible for managing the communications between the host and workflow instances. When the communication is handled through interfaces as described previously, the runtime uses .NET reflection to make method calls and raise events.

ExternalDataExchangeAttribute

This attribute is used to decorate custom communication-service interfaces. It acts as a marker so that the Windows Workflow Foundation infrastructure knows which interfaces are to be treated as a communication contract.

The following is a simple example of this attribute on a communication interface:

```
[ExternalDataExchangeAttribute]
public interface ICommService
{
    void CallTheHost();
    event EventHandler<ExternalDataEventArgs> NotifyTheWorkflow;
}
```

When you decorate an interface with this attribute, Visual Studio perceives that interface as a communication contract. This is important when you want to designate an interface as the contract for communicating with the host in a workflow.

ExternalDataEventArgs

This class is passed to event handlers of local communication services and represents the context of the event. Like any other event in the .NET Framework, this class inherits from `System.EventArgs`. Any event that participates in the communication process between workflows and hosts must use this class or an inherited class to represent the event.

Just because you have to use this class for workflow communication events does not mean you are limited in what you information you can pass to the workflow. To create an event-arguments class that passes data specific to your problem domain, you can simply inherit from `ExternalDataEventArgs`. The following is an example of an inherited class that passes a person's first and last name:

```
[Serializable]
public class NewPersonEventArgs : ExternalDataEventArgs
{
```

```
    private string firstName;
    private string lastName;

    public string FirstName
    {
        get { return this.firstName; }
    }

    public string LastName
    {
        get { return this.lastName; }
    }

    public NewPersonEventArgs(Guid instanceId, string firstName, string lastName)
        : base(instanceId)
    {
        this.firstName = firstName;
        this.lastName = lastName;
    }
}
```

There are a couple of important things to notice in this example. First, the class is marked with the `Serializable` attribute. This is required because the `EventArgs` class is actually serialized when it is passed from the workflow's host to the workflow instance. If you do not decorate your custom class with this attribute, an `EventDeliveryFailedException` is thrown when an event passing your custom class is raised.

Also notice that the constructor receives not only the `firstName` and `lastName` variables, but also an `instanceId` that is subsequently passed to the base class constructor. This is also a requirement because the runtime must know the workflow instance on which to raise an event.

Table 5-4 lists the properties in the `ExternalDataEventArgs` class.

Table 5-4: ExternalDataEventArgs Properties

Property	Description
Identity	This property is the identity of the entity that is raising the event. This value is used for security purposes to ensure that the calling entity has access to pass data to the workflow.
InstanceId	This property is a `Guid` that maps to an existing workflow instance that is to handle the event.
WaitForIdle	This Boolean property indicates whether the event about to be raised should be raised immediately or when the workflow instance becomes idle.
WorkflowType	This property is a `Type` instance representing the type of the workflow instance.

Property	Description
WorkHandler	This property is of type `IPendingWork` and allows the workflow host to interact with the transactional work batch.
WorkItem	This property is a reference to the object that caused the current event to be raised.

Communication Activities

The classes discussed so far are related mostly to the workflow runtime host. However, several important entities facilitate communication on the workflow side, as described in the following sections.

The CallExternalMethod Activity

The CallExternalMethod activity is used to call methods in the workflow host that have been defined with the workflow communication contracts. To do this, you place this activity in a workflow and set a couple of key properties.

First, you set the `InterfaceType` property to specify that this interface should be used to define the workflow communication.. In Visual Studio, you set the `InterfaceType` property in the .NET type browser. The Browse and Select a .NET Type dialog box, shown in Figure 5-2, enables you to select interfaces that have been decorated with the `ExternalDataExchangeAttribute`. To access this dialog box, click the ellipsis button in the `InterfaceType` property box in the properties window.

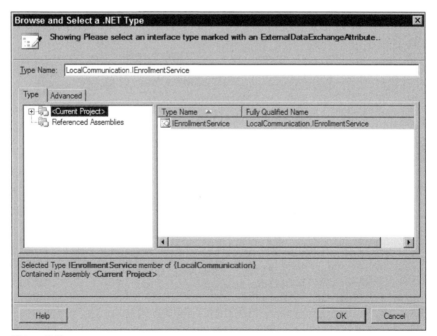

Figure 5-2

107

From here, you can select interfaces defined in the current project or in referenced assemblies, which is useful for separating key code entities. For example, you can place all interfaces in a single Visual Studio project for ease of versioning and reusability.

After setting the interface, you need to define which method on that interface is called when the CallExternalMethod activity is executed. You do this with the `MethodName` property. A drop-down list is provided so that you can choose among all methods defined in the communication interface.

When you select the method, the properties list changes based on parameters that are to be passed to that method and that method's return value. These new properties allow you to specify which properties or fields in your workflow are bound to the method parameters and return value. You have several options for binding values.

The first binding option is to select a field or property declared in the workflow's code-beside class or a property of the same type on another activity. For example, if the method chosen has a parameter of type `System.String`, you can choose a `string` field defined in the workflow. This `string` field is then passed to the method in the workflow host. The same holds true for the method's return value — the field selected is set after the method is finished and returns.

The other option is to have Visual Studio create a new property or field to which the method's return value or parameters can be bound. You can accomplish both binding options by using the dialog box that appears when you click the ellipsis in one of the parameter's or return value's properties dialog box. Figure 5-3 shows the first tab of this dialog box. Figure 5-4 shows the second tab, which allows you to create a new member to which the value will be bound.

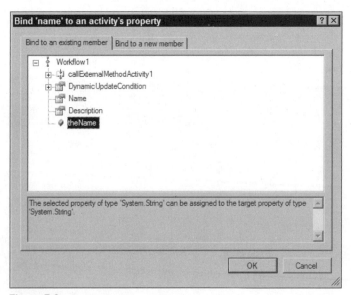

Figure 5-3

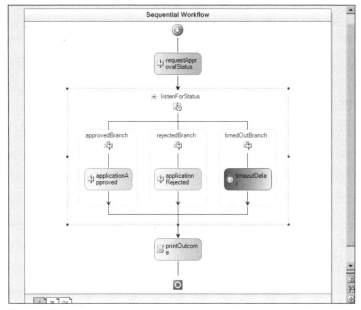

Figure 5-4

When you create a new property, a `DependencyProperty` instance is created in the workflow definition. Dependency properties represent the data storage and retrieval processes for workflow activities. The generated dependency property points at a newly generated class property of the same type as the method parameter that was promoted. This new property uses the dependency property instance to access and retrieve the data associated with the parameter. The following is an example of the code generated during property promotion:

```
public static DependencyProperty MyParameterProperty =
    DependencyProperty.Register("MyParameter",
        typeof(System.Boolean),
        typeof(LocalCommunication.EnrollmentWorkflow));

[DesignerSerializationVisibilityAttribute(DesignerSerializationVisibility.Visible)]
[BrowsableAttribute(true)]
[CategoryAttribute("Parameters")]
public Boolean MyParameter
{
    get
    {
        return ((bool)(base.GetValue(
            LocalCommunication.EnrollmentWorkflow.MyParameterProperty)));
    }
    set
    {
        base.SetValue(LocalCommunication.EnrollmentWorkflow.MyParameterProperty,
            value);
    }
}
```

Notice the attributes that are decorating the `MyParameter` property. These are used by the Visual Studio designer to provide important information during design time. `DesignerSerializationVisibility Attribute` defines how the property is serialized, `BrowsableAttribute` dictates whether the property will be visible in the properties window of Visual Studio, and `CategoryAttribute` is used by the properties window when properties are categorized (as opposed to being sorted alphabetically).

The HandleExternalEvent Activity

The HandleExternalEvent activity is used to handle events raised from the workflow host — specifically, events defined in communication interfaces. Just like the CallExternalMethod activity, this activity has an `InterfaceType` property that defines the interface with the event. After setting the `InterfaceType` property, you must set the `EventName` property from the drop-down menu.

This activity is very important because it acts as the listener in the workflow, waiting for a message from the outside host. You can use many different patterns to initiate and coordinate conversations between workflow instances and their hosts. For example, the HandleExternalEvent activity is commonly used directly after a CallExternalMethod activity. In this scenario, a workflow uses a method on a workflow data service to request information and then waits for a response through an event. More patterns are discussed in the next section.

The Listen and EventDriven Activities

These activities work together to allow a workflow to wait and listen for an event from the workflow host. The Listen activity can have two or more branches, but only one is actually executed. Each branch on this activity is an EventDriven activity.

EventDriven activity instances are parents to other activities that are executed by an event. To support this behavior, the first child activity of an EventDriven activity must be an event-handling activity. More specifically, the first child activity must implement the `IEventActivity` interface — `HandleExternal EventActivity`, for example. After execution in a particular branch is started through the event-handling activity, no other branch can be executed. This type of behavior is useful when the workflow does not know what type of action to anticipate next in its series of events.

A Communication Example

This section provides an example of local communication services using the classes and concepts introduced in this chapter. The code is for an application-for-enrollment process at an educational institution.

When the sample workflow instance starts, a college application is created and passed to the workflow. The first step in the sample workflow is to request an application status from the host. Because this is just a sample workflow application showcasing local communication services, the software simply asks the host for an approved or nonapproved status. In a more complex scenario, the external method call could present the user with a rich user interface requesting further data about the application's status.

Next, the workflow listens for an answer from the host. It does this using the Listen, EventDriven, and HandleExternalEvent activities. The Listen activity also has a branch containing a Delay activity. Because this activity implements `IEventActivity` interface, it can cause the Listen activity to execute a given branch if nothing happens within a configured amount of time. Remember that only one branch of a Listen activity executes, so as soon as one branch executes, the activity ends its execution. Figure 5-5 shows the completed workflow in Visual Studio.

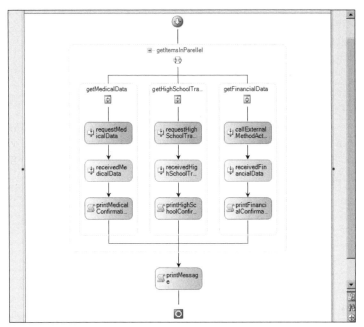

Figure 5-5

The following listing shows the code in the workflow host. In this example, the host is simply a console application that starts a new workflow instance and passes the applicant's name as a parameter. Also notice that an instance of the ExternalDataExchangeService is added to the workflow runtime. Subsequently, an instance of a custom local communication service, EnrollmentService, is added to the ExternalDataExchangeService instance.

```
public class Program
{
    static AutoResetEvent waitHandle = new AutoResetEvent(false);

    public static void Main(string[] args)
    {
        // create a workflow runtime instance
        WorkflowRuntime runtime = new WorkflowRuntime();
        runtime.WorkflowCompleted += new
            EventHandler<WorkflowCompletedEventArgs>(
                runtime_WorkflowCompleted);

        // create the data exchange runtime service
        // and add it to the runtime
        ExternalDataExchangeService dataService =
            new ExternalDataExchangeService();
        runtime.AddService(dataService);

        // add a new instance of the enrollment communication
        // service and add it to the data exchange service
```

```
        dataService.AddService(new EnrollmentService());

        // create a parameters object to pass the "application"
        Dictionary<string, object> parms = new Dictionary<string, object>();
        parms.Add("ApplicantName", "Todd Kitta");

        // create an instance of the enrollment workflow and pass
        WorkflowInstance wi =
            runtime.CreateWorkflow(typeof(EnrollmentWorkflow), parms);

        // start the workflow instance
        wi.Start();
        waitHandle.WaitOne();
    }

    static void runtime_WorkflowCompleted(object sender,
        WorkflowCompletedEventArgs e)
    {
        waitHandle.Set();
    }
}
```

The following code shows the communication contract that is implemented as a .NET interface deco-rated with the ExternalDataExchange attribute. The communication service allows the back-and-forth passing of data; the workflow can request a status from the workflow host, and the host can raise an event to the workflow signifying that an application has been approved or rejected.

```
[ExternalDataExchange]
public interface IEnrollmentService
{
    void RequestEnrollmentStatus(string name);

    event EventHandler<ExternalDataEventArgs> EnrollmentApproved;
    event EventHandler<ExternalDataEventArgs> EnrollmentRejected;
}
```

The data event arguments class that is passed to the workflow event handlers is shown in the following code. Notice that the EnrollmentEventArgs class inherits from ExternalDataEventArgs. Remember, this is a requirement for all event-arguments classes used in workflow communication. In this example, the inherited class simply adds a property for the applicant's name. Although the workflow should already have a copy of the applicant's name, this example illustrates the flexibility of the communication services.

```
[Serializable]
public class EnrollmentEventArgs : ExternalDataEventArgs
{
    private string applicantName;

    public string ApplicantName
    {
        get { return this.applicantName; }
    }

    public EnrollmentEventArgs(Guid instanceId, string applicantName)
```

```
            : base(instanceId)
    {
        this.applicantName = applicantName;
    }
}
```

The next block of code shows the communication service itself, which is called `EnrollmentService`. The class implements the `IEnrollmentService` interface (defined earlier). The `RequestEnrollment Status` method calls another private method, which then requests a response through the console interface. If the user enters **y**, the `EnrollmentApproved` event is raised with a new instance of the `EnrollmentEventArgs` class. Otherwise, the `EnrollmentRejected` event is raised. After one of the events is raised, the workflow continues from its idle state and executes the appropriate branch. (That is, of course, unless the workflow times out based on the Delay activity's configuration.)

```
public class EnrollmentService : IEnrollmentService
{
    public void RequestEnrollmentStatus(string name)
    {
        ThreadPool.QueueUserWorkItem(GetResponse,
            new EnrollmentEventArgs(
                WorkflowEnvironment.WorkflowInstanceId,
                name));
    }

    private void GetResponse(object o)
    {
        EnrollmentEventArgs args = o as EnrollmentEventArgs;

        Console.WriteLine("Will you approve the application for " +
            args.ApplicantName + "?");

        // read the user's response from the command line
        char response = Console.ReadKey().KeyChar;
        Console.WriteLine();

        // check the user's response
        // and raise the appropriate event
        if (response == 'y')
        {
            EnrollmentApproved(null, new EnrollmentEventArgs(
                args.InstanceId,
                args.ApplicantName));
        }
        else
        {
            EnrollmentRejected(null, new EnrollmentEventArgs(
                args.InstanceId,
                args.ApplicantName));
        }

    }

    public event EventHandler<ExternalDataEventArgs> EnrollmentApproved;
    public event EventHandler<ExternalDataEventArgs> EnrollmentRejected;
}
```

The workflow's code follows. There are a few important things to observe in this code. First, notice the `ApplicantName` property. This is set through the parameters collection passed from the host upon the workflow's creation. A couple of private class members act as flags. The first, `responseReceived`, is set to `true` when one of the two branches with HandleExternalEvent activities executes. The next, `isApplicationApproved`, is set to `true` if the `EnrollmentApproved` event is raised from the host. These flags are then used in the `ExecuteCode` event handler of the Code activity called `printOutcome`. This method simply prints a status message to the console window.

```
public sealed partial class EnrollmentWorkflow : SequentialWorkflowActivity
{
    private string applicantName;
    public string ApplicantName
    {
        set { this.applicantName = value; }
    }

    private EnrollmentEventArgs enrollmentEventArgs;
    private bool responseReceived = false;
    private bool isApplicationApproved = false;

    public EnrollmentWorkflow()
    {
        InitializeComponent();
    }

    private void printOutcome_ExecuteCode(object sender, EventArgs e)
    {
        string message;

        if (this.responseReceived)
        {
            message = "The workflow produced an outcome of ";

            if (this.isApplicationApproved)
            {
                message += "approved.";
            }
            else
            {
                message += "rejected.";
            }
        }
        else
        {
            message =
                "The workflow timed out before it received a response.";
        }

        Console.WriteLine(message);
    }

    private void applicationApproved_Invoked(object sender,
        ExternalDataEventArgs e)
    {
```

```
            this.responseReceived = true;
            this.isApplicationApproved = true;
        }

        private void applicationRejected_Invoked(object sender,
            ExternalDataEventArgs e)
        {
            this.responseReceived = true;
            this.isApplicationApproved = false;
        }
    }
```

Developing Custom Communication Activities

The previous section showed you how to develop custom communication services and then how to use these services in a workflow with the HandleExternalEvent and CallExternalMethod activities. In this section, you learn how to take those concepts a step further to build a library of custom activities that represent the communication interfaces built for a specific problem domain.

Doing this is a relatively simple process—it involves inheriting from the activities introduced in the preceding section. The following code listings expand on the college application communication service. Remember, the IEnrollmentService interface defined one method, RequestEnrollmentStatus, and two events, EnrollmentApproved and EnrollmentRejected. Custom communication activities need to be created for the method and each of the events.

In the following code, notice the ToolboxItemAttribute that decorates the class. This lets Visual Studio know that it should add the custom activity to the Toolbox so the developer can drag and drop it on to the workflow designer. Also, the name parameter of the RequestEnrollmentStatus method is represented as a DependencyProperty wrapped in a public property.

```
[ToolboxItemAttribute(typeof(ActivityToolboxItem))]
public class RequestEnrollmentStatus : CallExternalMethodActivity
{
    public static DependencyProperty nameProperty = DependencyProperty.Register(
        "name", typeof(string), typeof(RequestEnrollmentStatus));

    public RequestEnrollmentStatus()
    {
        this.InterfaceType = typeof(IEnrollmentService);
        this.MethodName = "RequestEnrollmentStatus";
    }

    [ValidationOptionAttribute(ValidationOption.Required)]
    public string name
    {
        get
        {
            return ((string)
                (this.GetValue(RequestEnrollmentStatus.nameProperty)));
        }
        set
        {
            this.SetValue(RequestEnrollmentStatus.nameProperty, value);
```

```
            }
        }

        protected override void OnMethodInvoking(EventArgs e)
        {
            this.ParameterBindings["name"].Value = this.name;
        }
    }
```

The following code is similar to the previous RequestEnrollmentStatus class. However, it represents one of the two events in the IEnrollmentService interface, EnrollmentApproved. Because the class represents one of the events on the interface, it inherits from HandleExternalEventActivity. It also represents the EnrollmentEventArgs and sender parameters of the event handler.

```
[ToolboxItemAttribute(typeof(ActivityToolboxItem))]
public class EnrollmentApproved : HandleExternalEventActivity
{
    public static DependencyProperty senderProperty =
        DependencyProperty.Register(
            "sender", typeof(object), typeof(EnrollmentApproved));

    public static DependencyProperty eventArgsProperty =
        DependencyProperty.Register(
            "eventArgs", typeof(EnrollmentEventArgs), typeof(EnrollmentApproved));

    public object sender
    {
        get
        {
            return (object)base.GetValue(EnrollmentApproved.senderProperty);
        }
        set
        {
            base.SetValue(EnrollmentApproved.senderProperty, value);
        }
    }

    public EnrollmentEventArgs eventArgs
    {
        get
        {
            return (EnrollmentEventArgs)base.GetValue(
                EnrollmentApproved.eventArgsProperty);
        }
        set
        {
            base.SetValue(EnrollmentApproved.eventArgsProperty, value);
        }
    }

    public EnrollmentApproved()
    {
```

```
        this.InterfaceType = typeof(IEnrollmentService);
        this.EventName = "EnrollmentApproved";
    }

    protected override void OnInvoked(EventArgs e)
    {
        this.eventArgs = (EnrollmentEventArgs)e;
    }
}
```

Generating Communication Activities

Although you can create strongly typed communication activities, as shown in the previous section, you can also generate these classes using wca.exe, a command-line utility included with the Windows Workflow Foundation SDK.

wca.exe is a very useful utility that basically does what you did manually in the previous section. Table 5-5 lists the command-line switches that you can use to modify the behavior of this utility.

Table 5-5: wca.exe Command-Line Switches

Command Option	Description
/collapseArgs, /c	Collapses all public properties in the event-arguments class into a single public property. By default, the generated classes contain a property for each property of the event-arguments class.
/includeSender, /I	Includes the sender parameter as a public property of the generated classes. This does not appear by default.
/language:, l:<language>	Allows you to specify in which language the generated classes are created. Possible values are CS for C# and VB for Visual Basic .NET. CS is the default if a value is not provided.
/out:, /o:<directoryName>	Allows you to indicate which directory should be used as the output for the generated files. If this option is not specified, the current folder is used.
/namespace:, /n:<namespace>	Allows you to specify the namespace to which the generated classes belongs. If the namespace option is not specified, the namespace in which the communication interface is defined is used.

The following is an example of how you can use the wca.exe utility. The utility checks LocalCommunication.exe for any interfaces decorated with the ExternalDataExchange attribute and then generates strongly typed communication classes in the GeneratedActivities folder:

```
wca.exe LocalCommunication.exe /o:GeneratedActivities
```

The following code is an example of what the wca.exe utility generates given the `EnrollmentRejected` event of the `IEnrollmentService` interface:

```
[ToolboxItemAttribute(typeof(ActivityToolboxItem))]
public partial class EnrollmentRejected : HandleExternalEventActivity {

    public static DependencyProperty ApplicantNameProperty =
        DependencyProperty.Register("ApplicantName", typeof(string),
            typeof(EnrollmentRejected));

    public EnrollmentRejected() {
        base.InterfaceType = typeof(LocalCommunication.IEnrollmentService);
        base.EventName = "EnrollmentRejected";
    }

    [BrowsableAttribute(false)]
    [DesignerSerializationVisibilityAttribute(
        DesignerSerializationVisibility.Hidden)]
    public override System.Type InterfaceType {
        get {
            return base.InterfaceType;
        }
        set {
            throw new InvalidOperationException(
                "Cannot set InterfaceType on a derived
                    HandleExternalEventActivity.");
        }
    }

    [BrowsableAttribute(false)]
    [DesignerSerializationVisibilityAttribute(
        DesignerSerializationVisibility.Hidden)]
    public override string EventName {
        get {
            return base.EventName;
        }
        set {
            throw new InvalidOperationException(
                "Cannot set EventName on a derived HandleExternalEventActivity.");
        }
    }

    [ValidationOptionAttribute(ValidationOption.Required)]
    public string ApplicantName {
        get {
            return ((string)
                (this.GetValue(EnrollmentRejected.ApplicantNameProperty)));
        }
        set {
            this.SetValue(EnrollmentRejected.ApplicantNameProperty, value);
        }
    }
}
```

```
protected override void OnInvoked(System.EventArgs e) {
    LocalCommunication.EnrollmentEventArgs castedE =
        ((LocalCommunication.EnrollmentEventArgs)(e));
    this.ApplicantName = ((string)(castedE.ApplicantName));
}
}
```

Notice that the generated class inherits from `HandleExternalEventActivity`, as you'd probably expect. The properties that you would otherwise have to set manually are set for you automatically. Take a look at the `InterfaceType` property for an example. Its value is set in the constructor, but its `set` accessor throws an exception if called. This is by design and prevents other code from inadvertently setting it to something that doesn't make sense. Also interesting is the overridden `OnInvoked` method. Here, the `ApplicantName` property is set to the relevant value whenever the event is raised.

Correlation

Correlation describes the concept of correctly delivering messages to a particular event handler in a workflow instance. As you have seen so far, you can easily get your message to its intended workflow by using the `InstanceId` GUID. However, there may be times when you want to deliver a message to a specific HandleExternalEvent activity that is waiting for its associated event to be raised.

Think about a workflow scenario that requires several inputs from outside sources in no particular order. To illustrate this point, take the college enrollment process a step further. After a student has been accepted to a school, there are several items the institution might need before the enrollment can be considered complete. For example, the student may be required to have his or her medical history, financial records, and high school transcript sent to the university before classes and living arrangements can be assigned.

To do this in Windows Workflow Foundation, you can use the Parallel activity. The activity should have at least three branches, one each for the items required by the school. You could also add a fourth branch with a Delay activity that sends a reminder to the appropriate parties if items are not received within an acceptable timeframe.

Figure 5-6 is a workflow that meets these requirements. The workflow contains a Parallel activity that contains three branches. Each branch represents the request and subsequent retrieval of required data for the college enrollment process. The first branch is for medical data, the second for the high school transcript, and the third for financial data.

The nice thing about how this workflow is designed is that any of the three activities can occur in any order. All three requests are sent out simultaneously, but the responses can occur at very staggered intervals, even if one response occurs weeks after another. The important thing to note is that after the requests are sent out and responses are subsequently received, the response data has to know which ExternalEventHandlerActivity activity to execute.

The following sections explain the Windows Workflow Foundation infrastructure that handles message correlation. After that, the code for this example scenario is provided.

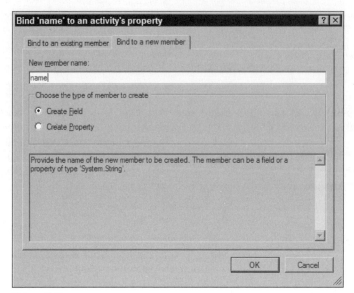

Figure 5-6

CorrelationParameterAttribute

The `CorrelationParameterAttribute` attribute is used to decorate the communication service definition interface. Its sole parameter is a string that represents the name of the variable acting as the correlation identifier. This variable name can exist on any method in the interface as well as any event. When
present, it is used to tie the incoming or outgoing message to a specific activity instance in the workflow.

For example, think about a scenario where multiple messages are sent out to external sources, all of which
eventually receive some kind of response. This could be applied in a document approval or voting workflow. After messages are sent out requesting a response, HandleExternalEvent activities are waiting for
the messages. The workflow must somehow know which activity to notify upon the arrival of a message.
The incoming message must have a copy of the unique correlation identifier that was mapped when the
message was originally sent out of the workflow. The CallExternalMethod and HandleExternalEvent
activities have a property called `CorrelationToken`, which is of type `CorrelationToken`. Because both
activities point to the same `CorrelationToken` instance, you can map them to each other during runtime. Don't forget — the CallExternalMethod activity you are using to send out a message must pass a
variable that acts as the correlation identifier defined by the `CorrelationParameterAttribute` on the
communication service interface.

CorrelationInitializerAttribute

The `CorrelationInitializerAttribute` is used to decorate the method on the communication service
interface that first introduces the correlation identifier to the message correlation process. The decorated
method must contain a parameter that matches the name supplied to the `CorrelationParameter`
`Attribute`. This attribute marks the method so that the workflow runtime knows when to start a new
message conversation.

CorrelationAliasAttribute

The `CorrelationAliasAttribute` enables you to provide the correlation identifier in a method or event but by using a different parameter name from what was defined using the `CorrelationParameter Attribute`. This comes in handy with events that provide the identifier in an event-arguments class. For example, the original correlation parameter could have been defined as `employeeId`, but the event-arguments class, e, might have a property called `EmployeeID`. In this case, you give the event an attribute definition similar to the following:

```
[CorrelationAlias("employeeId", "e.EmployeeID")]
event EventHandler<MyCustomEventArgs> MyEvent;
```

A Correlation Example

Now back to the example introduced earlier. The scenario involved a request for data required for a student to enroll at a college. The workflow sends out three simultaneous requests for a student's medical data, high school transcript, and financial information that are used for financial aid purposes.

The first logical step in developing such a solution is to define the communication interface, as follows:

```
[ExternalDataExchange]
[CorrelationParameter("itemType")]
public interface IObtainRequiredItemsService
{
    [CorrelationInitializer]
    void RequestItem(string ssn, string itemType);

    [CorrelationAlias("itemType", "e.ItemType")]
    event EventHandler<RequiredItemEventArgs> ItemReceived;
}
```

The interface looks a lot like a standard communication service interface, without a few extra attributes. The `CorrelationParameterAttribute` tells the workflow runtime to pay attention to any method or event that passes the `itemType` variable. The `ItemReceived` event that is decorated with the `CorrelationAliasAttribute`, which tells the workflow runtime to map the `itemType` identifier to the `e.ItemType` property on the `RequiredItemEventArgs` instance passed to the event handler.

The following code is the service implementation itself. Because the `RequestItem` method is called for any type of item request, it has a `switch` statement that checks the `itemType` variable. In a real-life solution, this method might send an e-mail or call an external web service requesting the desired information. The service also adds three public methods not included in the interface. These methods are called from the host when the requested data becomes available. Each method then raises the `ItemReceived` event, passing the appropriate `itemType` flag so the correct HandleExternalEvent activity is executed in the workflow. The item type passed is crucial for the correlation to work correctly.

```
public class ObtainRequiredItemsService : IObtainRequiredItemsService
{
    public void RequestItem(string ssn, string itemType)
    {
        switch (itemType)
        {
            case "medical":
                Console.WriteLine(
                    "Medical records were requested! Get on it!");
```

```
                            break;
                    case "highschool":
                        Console.WriteLine(
                            "High school transcript was requested! Get on it!");
                        break;
                    case "financial":
                        Console.WriteLine(
                            "Financial records were requested! Get on it!");
                        break;
                }
            }

            public event EventHandler<RequiredItemEventArgs> ItemReceived;

            public void SubmitMedicalRecords(Guid instanceId, object data)
            {
                if (ItemReceived != null)
                {
                    ItemReceived(null, new RequiredItemEventArgs(
                        instanceId, "medical", data));
                }
            }

            public void SubmitHighSchoolTranscript(Guid instanceId, object data)
            {
                if (ItemReceived != null)
                {
                    ItemReceived(null, new RequiredItemEventArgs(
                        instanceId, "highschool", data));
                }
            }

            public void SubmitFinancialRecords(Guid instanceId, object data)
            {
                if (ItemReceived != null)
                {
                    ItemReceived(null, new RequiredItemEventArgs(
                        instanceId, "financial", data));
                }
            }
        }
    }
```

The following code shows a portion of the workflow code-behind. Notice the three instances of `RequiredItemEventArgs`. These fields are set when a message is received into the workflow through the HandleExternalEvent activities.

```
public sealed partial class ObtainRequiredItemsWorkflow
    : SequentialWorkflowActivity
{
    private RequiredItemEventArgs medialArgs;
    private RequiredItemEventArgs highSchoolArgs;
    private RequiredItemEventArgs financialArgs;

    ...
}
```

The workflow host code follows. Of interest here is the `WorkflowIdled` event hander. This method is called after the request messages are sent from the workflow and the workflow enters a waiting state. At this point, the code simulates delays and then passes the requested data to the workflow through the communication service class.

```
public class Program
{
    private static ObtainRequiredItemsService itemService;
    private static WorkflowInstance instance;

    public static void Main(string[] args)
    {
        WorkflowRuntime workflowRuntime = new WorkflowRuntime();
        ExternalDataExchangeService dataService =
            new ExternalDataExchangeService();
        workflowRuntime.AddService(dataService);
        itemService = new ObtainRequiredItemsService();
        dataService.AddService(itemService);

        AutoResetEvent waitHandle = new AutoResetEvent(false);

        workflowRuntime.WorkflowCompleted +=
            delegate(object sender, WorkflowCompletedEventArgs e)
                { waitHandle.Set(); };
        workflowRuntime.WorkflowIdled +=
            new EventHandler<WorkflowEventArgs>(workflowRuntime_WorkflowIdled);

        Dictionary<string, object> parms = new Dictionary<string, object>();
        parms.Add("Ssn", "111223333");

        instance = workflowRuntime.CreateWorkflow(
            typeof(CorrelationWorkflow.ObtainRequiredItemsWorkflow), parms);

        instance.Start();
        waitHandle.WaitOne();
    }

    public static void workflowRuntime_WorkflowIdled(object sender,
        WorkflowEventArgs e)
    {
        // sleep for 2 seconds to simulate a delay in submission
        Thread.Sleep(2000);
        itemService.SubmitMedicalRecords(instance.InstanceId,
            "All shots up-to-date.");

        Thread.Sleep(2000);
        itemService.SubmitHighSchoolTranscript(instance.InstanceId,
            "Graduated top of the class.");

        Thread.Sleep(2000);
        itemService.SubmitFinancialRecords(instance.InstanceId,
            "Qualifies for aid.");
    }
}
```

To bring this example together, think about why correlation was needed in the first place. There were several activities waiting for the same event to be raised from the outside world. However, even though each activity was waiting for the same event, a distinction existed for each that could be used to allow the correct activity to receive the event. This distinction, known as the *correlation parameter,* is specified in the communication contract interface. Therefore, any communication between the workflow and host related to these activities needs to include this correlation parameter. If the facilities for correlation did not exist in Windows Workflow Foundation, the runtime would get confused when delivering messages to the workflow, which could be received by more than one activity.

Summary

This chapter covered quite a few topics related to workflow hosting and communication between a host and a workflow instance. The `WorkflowRuntime` class is responsible for creating new workflow instances and managing runtime services. Runtime services are classes that perform specialized work related to runtime management, such as workflow persistence and threading behavior. The workflow runtime also exposes several events that enable you to monitor for relevant activities related to the workflow runtime itself as well as workflow instances.

Communication is an important part of the workflow infrastructure. You can use parameters to pass data to workflows upon their creation and receive data upon workflow completion. This chapter also introduced local communication services. Local communication services enable a workflow host and a workflow instance to communicate with each other using a communication contact defined as a .NET interface and its subsequent implementation as a class.

6

Activities

This chapter covers the workflow building blocks—activities. First, the chapter provides an overview of the activity architecture and relevant components of Windows Workflow Foundation. After that, the chapter presents a detailed list and discussion of each out-of-the-box activity. The chapter names each activity, and discusses important relationships between it and other activities.

The second half of the chapter covers custom activity development. The chapter describes pertinent steps and pitfalls related to creating new activities and provides examples to illustrate the text.

An Introduction to Activities

As previously mentioned, activities are the basic building blocks of a workflow definition. An activity represents a discrete piece of functionality that generally does only one thing, but it does that one thing very well. Your goal is to make activities as reusable and generic as possible so that you can use them across many different workflows. Although the previous sentence is generally true, you can also use activities in very specific problem domains. For example, you could implement a library of custom activities related to a very narrow field, such as organic chemistry or a specific process at a healthcare institution.

Generally, activities come in two flavors: standard and composite. Standard activities are standalone components, such as the Code or CallExternalMethod activity. Composite activities contain child activities that are executed according to the logic implemented in the parent. For example, the IfElse activity can have many branches, each representing a particular path to be executed according to specified Boolean logic. A composite activity can also be something like a Sequence activity, which simply executes its children in the order in which they are defined.

Out-of-the-Box Activities

The following sections cover the out-of-the-box activities included in the Windows Workflow Foundation API. Each section begins by showing the class definition for an activity and then provides useful information, including whether you can inherit from the activity, which class the activity inherits from, and any interfaces the activity implements. There are different base classes an activity can inherit from and other miscellaneous interfaces that add functionality to an activity.

In addition, a few activities are specific to certain types of workflows. More specifically, activities such as State and SetState can be used only in state-machine workflows. Whenever an activity has a requirement such as this, it is pointed out in the text.

The CallExternalMethod Activity

The syntax of the CallExternalMethod activity is as follows:

```
public class CallExternalMethodActivity : Activity, IDynamicPropertyTypeProvider
```

This activity is a vital component of the local communication services (covered in Chapter 5). To use this activity, you must set the `InterfaceType` and `MethodName` properties so that the workflow knows which external method to call. You set these properties from the properties window in Visual Studio, as described in Chapter 5. The `InterfaceType` property uses the .NET type browser to display and select the appropriate communication interface.

If you have not already done so, first you need to add the `ExternalDataExchangeService` to the workflow runtime's services collection. You can then implement the interface set to the `InterfaceType` property on the `ExternalDataExchangeService` communication service class.

You use the CallExternalMethod activity's `ParameterBindings` property to map parameters defined by the method referenced in the `MethodName` property. This property is of type `WorkflowParameter BindingCollection` and maps parameter names to fields in the workflow code. `WorkflowParameter BindingCollection` inherits from `KeyedCollection<string, WorkflowParameterBinding>`, which in turn maps a string to a parameter binding class. Return values work the same way.

The Code Activity

The syntax of the Code activity is as follows:

```
public sealed class CodeActivity : Activity
```

This activity is the utility player of the workflow activities. It is extremely useful for one-off scenarios that can be accomplished with a couple of lines of code. The Code activity works by exposing a single event called `ExecuteCode`, which fires when the activity is ready to execute.

In the corresponding code file, you need to include an event handler for the `ExecuteCode` event as well as your implementation of the desired functionality for the activity. You can use a variety of code types for this activity, from modifying workflow variables to performing calculations.

The `ExecuteCode` event handler executes on the same thread as the workflow and in a synchronous manner, meaning that the workflow does not proceed until the handler code has completed. Because of this, you should use the Code activity for relativity simple and short-running pieces of code (similar to code that runs on the UI thread of a Windows Forms application).

You may open up a workflow and see a load of Code activities strewn about. This is the antithesis of the workflow development paradigm. Not that using the Code activity is a bad thing in the right situation, but if you find yourself continually writing code behind the workflow, developing a new activity might be a better solution. As in object-oriented development, this enables you to reuse a piece of logic multiple times in a workflow as well as across workflows.

The CompensatableSequence, Compensate, and CompensationHandler Activities

These activities have the following syntax:

```
public sealed class CompensatableSequenceActivity : SequenceActivity,
    ICompensatableActivity

public sealed class CompensateActivity : Activity, IPropertyValueProvider,
    IActivityEventListener<ActivityExecutionStatusChangedEventArgs>

public sealed class CompensationHandlerActivity : CompositeActivity,
    IActivityEventListener<ActivityExecutionStatusChangedEventArgs>
```

These activities are commonly used together to provide the functionality for *long-running transactions.* Long-running transactions are not ACID transactions, which are the archetypal transactions most developers correlate with relational databases. Rather, a long-running transaction is just a chunk of logic that has an associated chunk of undo or recover logic. The classic example is online travel reservations.

If you book a trip on a travel website that includes airfare, hotel, and a rental car, these bookings likely occur in separate back-end transactions—meaning that the website books the flight, the hotel, and then the car with separate companies. However, if one of these booking fails, none of them should go through. However, because each of the pieces of work occurs with a different company and a different system, a traditional transaction is not easy to implement, if not impossible.

Therefore, some compensation logic needs to be implemented to make sure everything comes out in a valid state at the end of the day. The program flow should go something like this:

❏ Book the flight.

❏ Book the hotel. If something goes wrong, cancel the flight and then stop.

❏ Book the car. If something goes wrong, cancel the flight and hotel and then stop.

It is this type of scenario where the CompensatableSequence and Compensate activities come into play. Because the `CompensatableSequenceActivity` class inherits from `SequenceActivity`, it can contain any number of child activities that execute in order. What makes this activity special is that it implements the `ICompensatableActivity` interface. Activities that implement this interface can be compensated.

That is, they have a designated sequence of activities that can implement the recovering logic if something goes wrong, even if the CompensatableSequence activity has finished executing and/or the workflow has been persisted and reloaded many times. The sequence of recovering logic is implemented by the CompensationHandler activity. You cannot directly add this activity to a workflow from the Visual Studio Toolbox; instead, it is automatically available in a separate activity view on each `ICompensatable Activity`.

You initiate the compensation logic by setting the `TargetActivityName` property of the Compensate activity. The `TargetActivityName` must point to an `ICompensatableActivity` that already exists in the workflow. Another requirement of this activity is that you must use it inside a CompensationHandler, CancellationHandler, or FaultHandler activity, because these three activities are generally where things might go wrong and require compensation of another sequence of logic.

The CompensatableTransactionScope and TransactionScope Activities

These activities have the following syntax:

```
public sealed class CompensatableTransactionScopeActivity : CompositeActivity,
    IActivityEventListener<ActivityExecutionStatusChangedEventArgs>,
    ICompensatableActivity

public sealed class TransactionScopeActivity : CompositeActivity,
    IActivityEventListener<ActivityExecutionStatusChangedEventArgs>
```

Both of these activities implement the same execution logic except for one notable difference, which is covered in a moment. First, you need to understand what these activities were built to do. In .NET 2.0, which was released in October 2005, the `System.Transactions` namespace was introduced in the Base Class Library. The classes in this namespace, namely `Transaction` and `TransactionScope` (not to be confused with the TransactionScope activity), support the ability to implement automatically rolled-back transactions if something goes wrong.

Although .NET transactions are not necessarily related to Windows Workflow Foundation, you should have at least a basic understanding of how these classes work when you're using the CompensatableTransactionScope and TransactionScope activities. Here's a simple code sample:

```
// start a new transaction scope
using (TransactionScope tScope = new TransactionScope())
{
    SqlConnection db1;
    SqlConnection db2;

    try
    {
        // open database 1 and do some stuff
        db1 = new SqlConnection("the connection string for DB1");
        SqlCommand com1 = new SqlCommand("some SQL", db1);

        db1.Open();
        com1.ExecuteNonQuery();
```

```
            // open database 2 and do some stuff
            db2 = new SqlConnection("the connection string for DB2");
            SqlCommand com2 = new SqlCommand("some other SQL", db2);

            db2.Open();
            com2.ExecuteNonQuery();
        }
        finally
        {
            // make sure both connections are closed

            if (db1 != null && db1.State != ConnectionState.Closed)
                db1.Close();

            if (db2 != null && db2.State != ConnectionState.Closed)
                db2.Close();
        }

        // Complete the transaction; this performs a commit.
        // Because the exception is not handled in the try block above,
        // this line will not be called if something goes wrong
        tScope.Complete();
    }
```

If you've ever done database programming in .NET, the code wrapped in the using statement should look very familiar. Basically, there is a bunch of database access code (code that could easily break) wrapped inside an active TransactionScope object. When you structure your code in this manner, both of the database commands participate in a single transaction that either commits or rolls back everything that happened in either database. You get this behavior essentially for free from a coding standpoint. This is because the database access classes check to see if there is an active transaction scope, and if there is, they both use it to maintain integrity.

Both the CompensatableTransactionScope and TransactionScope activities use this concept to implement their behavior. Therefore, any logic implemented in either of these activities is automatically rolled back if something goes wrong during initial execution. This behavior follows the properties of an ACID transaction. After this, the two activities differ.

The CompensatableTransactionScope activity has the added trait of enabling you to compensate for long-running transactions. Therefore, you can think of the CompensatableTransactionScope activity as a hybrid between the TransactionScope activity and the CompensatableSequence activity (introduced in the previous section). With the CompensatableTransactionScope activity, you have two opportunities to make things right in a bad situation: when the activity is initially executing and it rolls back the ACID transaction, and when something goes wrong down the road and the manual compensation logic that was implemented is called. The manual compensation logic does not provide the same outcome as the ACID rollback, but it does provide an opportunity to put things in a stable state.

You don't need to understand everything related to .NET transactions to use these activities, but you should have a broad understanding of what is going on behind the scenes. You can find many good resources dedicated to this topic by searching the web for *System.Transactions.*

The ConditionedActivityGroup Activity

The syntax of the ConditionedActivityGroup activity (or CAG) is as follows:

```
public sealed class ConditionedActivityGroup : CompositeActivity,
    IActivityEventListener<ActivityExecutionStatusChangedEventArgs>
```

This is a composite activity that executes its child activities based on their conditions and does so until an overall condition is true.

Consider, for example, a CAG activity that has two child activities. The first child activity has a WhenCondition that executes as long as a countervariable is less than 5. The second child activity does not have a WhenCondition set; therefore, it executes only once. In addition, the CAG activity itself has an UntilCondition that checks another variable for a specific value indicating that the CAG activity execution should end. You can set this indicator variable during the first child activity's execution when an abnormal situation arises. So the first child activity executes either five times or until the indicator variable is set to a specific value, and the second child activity still executes only once.

The Delay Activity

The syntax of the Delay activity is as follows:

```
public sealed class DelayActivity : Activity, IEventActivity,
    IActivityEventListener<QueueEventArgs>
```

You can use the Delay activity in long-running workflows when waiting for an outside entity to complete its work. A typical scenario is when an e-mail asking for an interaction with the business process is sent to a person involved in the workflow. When the e-mail is sent, the workflow is essentially idle until the outside entity performs his or her part. In this case, you could use the Delay activity in a Listen activity (discussed later) along with another activity that is waiting for the response from the outside entity. You can define the actions to be taken if the Delay activity times out before the person performs his or her part in the process. For example, you could define a loop that resends the e-mail three times and then escalates the issue to a manager.

The most important property on the Delay activity is TimeoutDuration, which is of type System .TimeSpan. You can set this property to a static value during design time or at runtime by using the InitializeTimeoutDuration event that is called right before TimeoutDuration needs to be set. The format that this property uses is the same as the TimeSpan.Parse method. For example, the string 1.12:00:00 represents one day, twelve hours, zero minutes, and zero seconds.

The Delay activity implements the IEventActivity interface, which is the same interface used by the HandleExternalEvent activity. This interface defines the functionality necessary for an activity to raise events to the workflow. Hence, the Delay activity enables you to raise an event to the workflow when it reaches its maximum wait time.

The EventDriven Activity

The syntax of the EventDriven activity is as follows:

```
public sealed class EventDrivenActivity : SequenceActivity
```

You can use this activity across the two workflow types: sequential and state machine. Like the Sequence activity, the EventDriven activity executes child activities in a certain order. Unlike the Sequence activity, however, the EventDriven activity's execution is kicked off by an event being raised. This event is defined by the first child of the EventDriven activity, which must be an activity that implements IEventActivity, such as HandleExternalEvent or Delay.

In a sequential workflow, you can use the EventDriven activity in combination with other activities. For example, you can use it in the Events view of the EventHandlingScope activity (which is discussed next). In this view, you can use any number of EventDriven activities to define multiple sets of activities for sequential execution.

You can also use the EventDriven activity in state-machine workflows. In fact, the EventDriven activity is at the heart of what makes state-machine workflows function. Instances of the EventDriven activity can sit in State activities and are executed when configured events are raised. However, you must consider several things before using the EventDriven activity within a state-machine workflow. First, only one activity that implements IEventActivity can be contained within an EventDriven activity. In addition, to prevent deadlocks in the workflow runtime, this IEventActivity activity must be the first child of the EventDriven activity.

Chapter 10 discusses state-machine workflows in more detail.

The EventHandlingScope and EventHandlers Activities

These activities have the following syntax:

```
public sealed class EventHandlingScopeActivity : CompositeActivity,
    IActivityEventListener<ActivityExecutionStatusChangedEventArgs>

public sealed class EventHandlersActivity : CompositeActivity,
    IActivityEventListener<ActivityExecutionStatusChangedEventArgs>
```

On its surface, the EventHandlingScope activity is a sequential activity, meaning that it executes a string of defined activities in a specific order. However, there is more to it than that. The EventHandlingScope activity also has a view that shows an EventHandlers activity.

The EventHandlers activity can have any number of EventDriven activities as children, and as you already know, the EventDriven activity generally has something like a HandleExternalEvent activity as its first child.

So here's the catch: Any or all of the EventDriven activities contained within the EventHandlers activity might execute if, and only if, the main sequence activity of the EventHandlingScope activity has not finished. Furthermore, any of the EventDriven activities might execute multiple times, but again, only if the main sequence activity has not completed.

The FaultHandler and FaultHandlers Activities

These activities have the following syntax:

```
public sealed class FaultHandlersActivity : CompositeActivity,
    IActivityEventListener<ActivityExecutionStatusChangedEventArgs>

public sealed class FaultHandlerActivity : Sequence, ITypeFilterProvider,
    IDynamicPropertyTypeProvider
```

The FaultHandler activity can be likened to a `catch` block in C#. It basically watches for a fault, or exception, of a specified type and executes its child activities if that fault type is caught. Faults correspond to standard .NET exceptions, which are classes that inherit directly or indirectly from `System .Exception`. Therefore, the FaultHandler activity has a property called `FaultType`, which you use to specify an exception class. In addition, you use the `Fault` property to set a member variable of the same type as the `FaultType` property. This enables you to inspect the exception class after the fault is handled.

The FaultHandlers (notice the *s*) activity can hold any number of FaultHandler activities and provides a place to set up activities to be executed if a particular fault is caught. Consider Figure 6-1, for example.

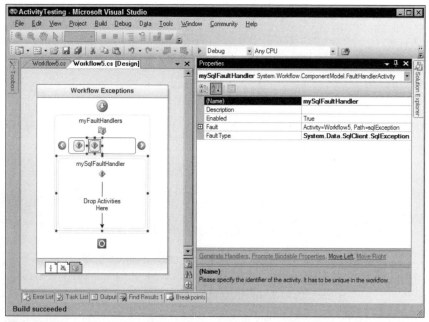

Figure 6-1

In the figure, the Faults view of the workflow shows an instance of a FaultHandlers activity ready for use. In addition, two FaultHandler activities have been added between the left- and right-facing arrowheads. The second FaultHandler activity is selected and configured to catch an exception of type

System.Data.SqlClient.SqlException. The Fault property is pointing to a class variable called sqlException in the workflow's code-beside class. The variable definition is shown in the following code:

```
private System.Data.SqlClient.SqlException sqlException;
```

The HandleExternalEvent Activity

The syntax of the HandleExternalEvent activity is as follows:

```
public class HandleExternalEventActivity : Activity, IEventActivity,
    IActivityEventListener<QueueEventArgs>, IDynamicPropertyTypeProvider
```

The HandleExternalEvent activity is generally used in concert with the CallExternalMethod activity to facilitate communications between a workflow instance and its host. Because this activity implements the IEventActivity interface, it is able to listen for a configured event and execute when that event fires. It uses its InterfaceType and EventName properties to identify the event to listen for on a corresponding communication service. The HandleExternalEvent activity also has a property called ParameterBindings that maps the parameters passed to the event's event handler to member variables in the workflow.

The HandleExternalEvent activity is also commonly used with the Listen activity. Each branch of a Listen activity takes an activity that implements IEventActivity as its first child. This enables a sequence of other activities to execute an event that is configured on a HandleExternalEvent activity.

The IfElse and IfElseBranch Activities

These activities have the following syntax:

```
public sealed class IfElseActivity : CompositeActivity,
    IActivityEventListener<ActivityExecutionStatusChangedEventArgs>

public sealed class IfElseBranchActivity : SequenceActivity
```

The IfElse and IfElseBranch activities enable you to define conditional logic flow, just as you can with logic flow constructs in traditional programming languages. Without the IfElseBranch activity, the IfElse activity is essentially useless.

The IfElse activity acts as a container for one to *n* IfElseBranch activities. Each branch can hold multiple child activities, which execute in a given order — the standard behavior for a Sequence activity, which the IfElseBranch activity inherits from.

Each IfElseBranch activity has a property called Condition of type ActivityCondition. This property defines a logical condition that must be true for that branch to execute. Every branch in an IfElse activity *must* have this property set without the last branch (which acts as the else branch). You can define the conditional logic using either of the following methods:

One method is to set the Condition property to an instance of the CodeCondition class. This class exposes an event, also called Condition, that is fired when the IfElseBranch activity's logic needs to be evaluated. The event is of type EventHandler<ConditionalEventArgs> and passes a ConditionalEventArgs instance to the event handler. The event handler implements the conditional logic and then sets the Result property of ConditionalEventArgs to true or false.

The other method of providing logic to the IfElse activity is to set the Condition property of an IfElseBranch activity to an instance of the RuleConditionReference class. This class acts as a pointer to a rule that exists in the workflow's rules set.

Chapter 9 discusses rules in detail.

The InvokeWebService Activity

The syntax of the InvokeWebService activity is as follows:

```
public sealed class InvokeWebServiceActivity : Activity,
    IDynamicPropertyTypeProvider
```

This activity enables a workflow to make calls to external web services. Adding this activity to your workflow is similar to adding a web reference in a .NET project. The Add Web Reference dialog box (shown in Figure 6-2) is displayed, where you enter a URL that points to the web service to be called. Then click the Add Reference button.

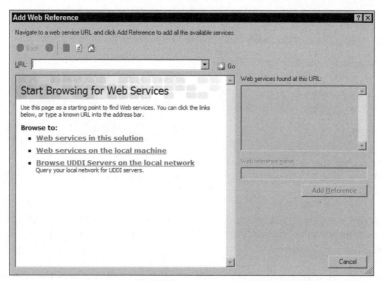

Figure 6-2

After you enter the URL and click the Add Reference button, a web service proxy class is generated, and the ProxyClass property of the InvokeWebService activity is set to point to this newly created class. For the activity to be fully configured, you must also set the MethodName property, which specifies the web service method to be called as well as any parameters and return values related to that method.

There is more to the InvokeWebService activity, such as dealing with the issue of ASP.NET sessions and cookies. Chapter 13 covers this issue and more details regarding web services and Windows Workflow Foundation.

The InvokeWorkflow Activity

The syntax of the InvokeWorkflow activity is as follows:

```
public sealed class InvokeWorkflowActivity : Activity, ITypeFilterProvider
```

You use this activity to asynchronously kick off the execution of another workflow. You point to the `Type` instance of the workflow to be executed using the `TargetWorkflow` property. The InvokeWorkflow activity also exposes an event called `Invoking`, which you can use to prepare parameter variables to be passed to the destination workflow.

Because the InvokeWorkflow activity calls another workflow asynchronously, the activity returns control to the calling workflow before the new workflow's execution.

The Listen Activity

The syntax of the Listen activity is as follows:

```
public sealed class ListenActivity : CompositeActivity,
    IActivityEventListener<ActivityExecutionStatusChangedEventArgs>
```

This activity allows a workflow to wait and listen for events without knowing which one will actually fire. The Listen activity can have any number of branches, each of which must have an activity that implements `IEventActivity` as its first child, the most obvious choices being the HandleExternalEvent and Delay activities.

This activity comes in most handy when you want to tell the workflow to wait for some response from the outside world, but that response could be any number of things. For example, a workflow might be waiting for a response to whether a loan should be approved. In this case, you could have one branch of the Listen activity containing a HandleExternalEvent activity to handle an `Approved` event, and another branch to handle an event called `Rejected`. You could even add a third branch with a Delay activity to handle the situation if a response is not provided in a timely fashion.

The Parallel Activity

The syntax of the Parallel activity is as follows:

```
public sealed class ParallelActivity : CompositeActivity,
    IActivityEventListener<ActivityExecutionStatusChangedEventArgs>
```

This activity enables you to have multiple activities executing independent of one another. You configure the Parallel activity with multiple branches, all of which have a Sequence activity as their first child.

Although the execution of each branch occurs independently of the other branches in a seemingly parallel fashion, this is actually not the case—so the name *Parallel* is a little deceiving. Because Windows Workflow

Foundation runs workflow instances on a single thread, multiple branches cannot run at the same time. Instead, the parallel execution is simulated. The Parallel activity runs the first activity of the first branch, and after that activity's execution has completed, the first activity of the second branch is run. This process continues until all activities in all branches have been executed.

See Figure 6-3 for an example of how the Parallel activity functions. In this workflow, the doStuffA activity of parallelBranchA is executed first, followed by doSomethingA, then doStuffB, and finally doSomethingB. After all four activities are run, the Parallel activity's execution is complete.

> **Although this example illustrates how the Parallel activity works, the order in which activities are executed is never guaranteed and should not be counted on during runtime.**

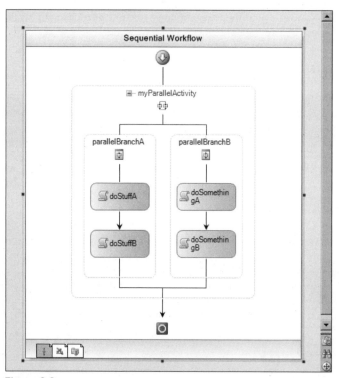

Figure 6-3

To illustrate the Parallel activity's execution model, Figure 6-4 shows a console window with messages printed from each Code activity.

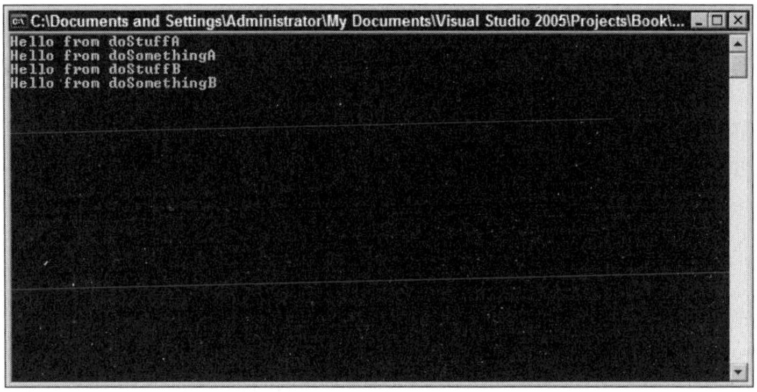

Figure 6-4

The Policy Activity

The syntax of the Policy activity is as follows:

```
public sealed class PolicyActivity : Activity
```

You use this activity to evaluate a set of predefined rules. It includes a `RuleSetReference` property, which is a pointer to the rules set.

Rules are a massive topic, and Chapter 9 is devoted to them. There is also more information about the Policy activity in that chapter.

The Replicator Activity

The syntax of the Replicator activity is as follows:

```
public sealed class ReplicatorActivity : CompositeActivity
```

This activity creates any number of instances of its single child activity. You can combine this activity with the Sequence activity or any other composite activity to allow multiple children.

The Replicator activity has a collection property called `CurrentChildData` that dictates how many times the child activity is replicated. You can populate this collection in an event handler for the `Initialized` event of the `Replicator` activity.

In addition, the Replicator activity has a property called `ExecutionType`, which you can set to one of two values in the `ExecutionType` enumeration. If you set this property to `ExecutionType.Sequential`, an instance of the child activity is created and executed before any other instances are created and subsequently executed. Conversely, if you set the `ExecutionType` property to `ExecutionType.Parallel`, all child activity instances are created first and then executed in a parallel fashion.

In some situations, you might want the execution of child activities to be canceled if a certain condition evaluates to `true`. In these cases, you can set the `UntilCondition` property to the desired code or rule condition.

The Sequence Activity

The syntax of the Sequence activity is as follows:

```
public class SequenceActivity : CompositeActivity,
    IActivityEventListener<ActivityExecutionStatusChangedEventArgs>
```

This is another utility activity. Its functionality is simple and allows the execution of child activities to occur in a defined order. The `SequentialWorkflowActivity` workflow class derives from `SequenceActivity` (discussed earlier).

This activity is most commonly used with other activities that allow only one child. For example, you can use the While activity with a Sequence activity to allow multiple children to execute in a loop iteration. In addition, the branches of the Parallel activity *require* that their sole child be a Sequence activity.

The SetState Activity

The syntax of the SetState activity is as follows:

```
public sealed class SetStateActivity : Activity
```

As you might imagine, the SetState activity is used with the state-machine workflow type and dictates which state the workflow should enter upon its execution. You can use this activity in the EventDriven, StateInitialization, and IfElse activities, but it must be the last child in each respective activity. The important property of this activity is `TargetStateName`, which is a string representing the desired subsequent state in the workflow.

Figure 6-5 shows an example of a SetState activity called `setTheState`. Here, the SetState activity is being used in an EventDriven activity within a workflow state called `StateMachineInitialState`. After the HandleExternalEvent activity called `eventFired` executes, the `setTheState` activity transfers the workflow from the `StateMachineInitialState` state to the `waitingState` state. Doing this also draws an arrow from the first to the second state in the main state-machine workflow view.

State-machine workflows are discussed in detail in Chapter 10.

The State Activity

The syntax of the State activity is as follows:

```
public class StateActivity : CompositeActivity
```

This activity is the heart of the state-machine workflow type. Each State activity represents a discrete status that a state-machine workflow can be in. The State activity doesn't really *do* anything—it is a container for all functionality that exists within that state. The EventDriven, StateInitialization, and StateFinalization activities can be children of a State activity, and all workflow logic is implemented in any of these three activities.

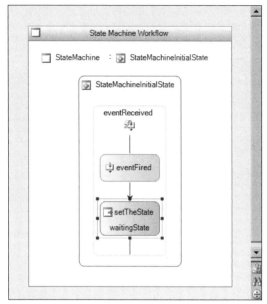

Figure 6-5

The StateFinalization and StateInitialization Activities

These activities have the following syntax:

```
public sealed class StateFinalizationActivity : SequenceActivity

public sealed class StateInitializationActivity : SequenceActivity
```

You can use the StateFinalization and StateInitialization activities to perform any kind of logic when a state-machine workflow's state is entered or exited. A State activity can contain zero or one of both of these activities. Because both of these activities inherit from `SequenceActivity`, child activities are executed in the order specified during workflow design.

All aspects of the state-machine workflow type are covered in Chapter 10.

The Suspend Activity

The syntax of the Suspend activity is as follows:

```
public sealed class SuspendActivity : Activity
```

You use this activity to pause a workflow instance's execution—generally, when an error occurs. The Suspend activity has a `System.String` property called `Error` that you can use to provide an error message describing what happened that caused the workflow to suspend itself.

When this activity is executed, the `WorkflowRuntime`'s `WorkflowSuspended` event is raised in the host, which then passes an instance of `WorkflowSuspendedEventArgs` to the event handler. This event arguments class has a property called `Reason` that contains a copy of the `SuspectActivity.Error` property.

You can write code to enable the workflow to restart after the issue that caused the suspension is resolved. To restart a suspended workflow instance, simply call the `WorkflowInstance.Resume` method from the host.

The SynchronizationScope Activity

The syntax of the SynchronizationScope activity is as follows:

```
public sealed class SynchronizationScopeActivity : Sequence
```

You can use this activity to synchronize the execution of a workflow when activities such as the Parallel activity execute children at the same time. Instead of simultaneously executing multiple activities, you can configure SynchronizationScope so that activities are executed separately, one after another.

As you learned previously, the Parallel activity enables you to have any number of branches, each containing Sequence activities, which execute pseudosimultaneously. However, there may be a workflow in which you want one branch to finish before the next starts execution. This is when you would use SynchronizationScope activities as children to the applicable Sequence activities. However, the simple act of adding a couple of SynchronizationScope activities to your workflow does not automatically create an isolated execution scope. You must set one or more of these activities' `SynchronizationHandles` properties to matching values. You can set these values in the Visual Studio's properties window.

To illustrate how this activity affects parallel execution, consider the example given in the Parallel activity section. If the activities in both parallel branches were wrapped in SynchronizationScope activities, and both SynchronizationScope activities had their `SynchronizationHandles` properties set to the same value, the execution order would change from this

- ❑ doStuffA
- ❑ doSomethingA
- ❑ doStuffB
- ❑ doSomethingB

to this:

- ❑ doStuffA
- ❑ doStuffB
- ❑ doSomethingA
- ❑ doSomethingB

The Terminate Activity

The syntax of the Terminate activity is as follows:

```
public sealed class TerminateActivity : Activity
```

As with the Suspend activity, when the Terminate activity is executed, the workflow instance's execution is interrupted. Unlike the Suspend activity, however, when you use the Terminate activity, the workflow is permanently terminated, and you cannot restart it at a later time.

When this activity is run, the `WorkflowTerminated` event of `WorkflowRuntime` is executed on the workflow host. This event passes an instance of `WorkflowTerminatedEventArgs` to the event handler that has a property called `Exception`. This property is of type `System.Exception` and allows the host to inspect the exception that caused the workflow to be terminated. Because the workflow instance is permanently terminated, all queued work items are deleted because they cannot be executed at a later time.

The Throw Activity

The syntax of the Throw activity is as follows:

```
public sealed class ThrowActivity : Activity, ITypeFilterProvider,
    IDynamicPropertyTypeProvider
```

This activity is similar to the `throw` keyword in C#. A .NET exception is tied to the Throw activity through its `Fault` property, which is of type `System.Exception`. When the Throw activity is executed, it calls a `throw` command on the exception instance specified in the `Fault` property. The exception is thrown outside the bounds of the workflow instance, to the workflow host. In addition, the workflow is terminated, and the `WorkflowTerminated` event of the `WorkflowRuntime` class is raised to the host.

The WebServiceFault Activity

The syntax of the WebServiceFault activity is as follows:

```
public sealed class WebServiceFaultActivity : Activity
```

The execution of this activity corresponds to sending a web service fault to a client during a request-response operation. You use this activity with the WebServiceInput activity, which is discussed next.

The WebServiceInput Activity

The syntax of the WebServiceInput activity is as follows:

```
public sealed class WebServiceInputActivity : Activity, IEventActivity,
    IActivityEventListener<QueueEventArgs>, IDynamicPropertyTypeProvider
```

You use this activity to expose a workflow as a web service. It represents the entry point of a web service method call. The WebServiceInput activity uses an interface to represent a method that exists on a web service. To configure the activity for this, you use the `InterfaceType` and `MethodName` properties.

In addition, the WebServiceInput activity has a Boolean property called `IsActivating`, which specifies whether the activity should create a new instance of the workflow and start it when the configured method is called. When this property is set to `true`, the WebServiceInput activity *must* be the first child of the workflow. Conversely, if the WebServiceInput activity is the first child, the `IsActivating` property *must* be set to `true`.

> *When using this activity, you must have a corresponding WebServiceOutput activity (discussed next). Chapter 14 discusses web services and how they affect Windows Workflow Foundation.*

The WebServiceOutput Activity

The syntax of the WebServiceOutput activity is as follows:

```
public sealed class WebServiceOutputActivity : Activity,
    IDynamicPropertyTypeProvider
```

You use the WebServiceOutput activity in conjunction with the WebServiceInput activity to expose workflows as web services. The WebServiceInput activity acts as a web service method's entry into a workflow, and the WebServiceOutput activity prepares values to be passed back to the calling application and acts as the logical exit point of the web service method.

A WebServiceOutput activity must follow a WebServiceInput activity. However, it does not have to directly follow the input activity—there can be other activities between the two. Also, just because the WebServiceOutput activity is the logical exit point for a web service method does not mean that it has to be the last child in a workflow. Other activities can follow the WebServiceOutput activity, but they do not have any affect on the return values of the web service method.

In addition, the WebServiceOutput activity must have its `InputActivityName` property set to the corresponding WebServiceInput activity.

The While Activity

The syntax of the While activity is as follows:

```
public sealed class WhileActivity : CompositeActivity,
    IActivityEventListener<ActivityExecutionStatusChangedEventArgs>
```

This is a logic flow activity with the same functionality as the `while` loop construct in C#. Like the IfElseBranch activity, which uses its `Condition` property to determine whether the branch executes, the While activity also has a `Condition` property. Also like the IfElseBranch activity, the While activity's Condition property is of type `ActivityCondition` and can take an instance of `CodeCondition` or `RuleConditionReference`.

The While activity can contain only one child activity. To overcome this limitation, just use the Sequence activity as the sole child activity. You can then drop as many activities in the Sequence activity as you wish. Figure 6-6 shows an example of this.

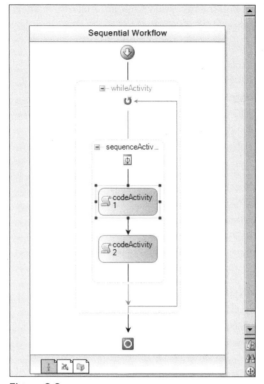

Figure 6-6

Developing Activities

Even though Windows Workflow Foundation provides a great deal of functionality and is extremely extensible, you may have situations where you want to develop custom workflow activities from scratch. For example, you there may be a need specific to your business that dictates the development of a new activity. This doesn't mean that you won't also need more generic activities that were not covered in the base API, but the online Windows Workflow Foundation community may have already solved a lot of these needs. For example, the Base Activity Library does not come with an activity that can execute commands against a SQL Server database. However, even before Windows Workflow Foundation was released, many community-contributed activities were available on the official website: wf.winfx.com.

With that said, there may be times when developing a new activity is the only answer. The following sections can help get you started in this area and make the most of your Windows Workflow Foundation platform.

To pique your interest before all the necessary foundational information is covered, here is a quick-and-dirty example of the simplest activity you could imagine. This `HelloWorldActivity` activity uses a property, `NameOfPerson`, which is set at design time to print a personalized message on the console.

```csharp
using System;
using System.ComponentModel;
using System.Workflow.ComponentModel;

namespace HelloWorldActivity
{
    public sealed class HelloWorldActivity : Activity
    {
        public static DependencyProperty NameOfPersonProperty =
            DependencyProperty.Register(
                "NameOfPerson",
                typeof(string),
                typeof(HelloWorldActivity));

        [Description("Someone's name who wants a personalized message.")]
        [Category("Display")]
        [Browsable(true)]
        public string NameOfPerson
        {
            get
            {
                return (string)base.GetValue(
                    HelloWorldActivity.NameOfPersonProperty);
            }
            set
            {
                base.SetValue(HelloWorldActivity.NameOfPersonProperty, value);
            }
        }

        public HelloWorldActivity()
        {
        }

        protected override ActivityExecutionStatus Execute(
            ActivityExecutionContext executionContext)
        {
            // present the personalized message if a name was provided
            if (!String.IsNullOrEmpty(this.NameOfPerson))
                Console.WriteLine(String.Format("Hello {0}!", this.NameOfPerson));
            else
                Console.WriteLine("I don't know who to say hello to :(");

            // we're done; return a "Closed" status
            return ActivityExecutionStatus.Closed;
        }
    }
}
```

The Activity Class

The `Activity` class is located in `System.Workflow.ComponentModel` and is the base class from which all other activities inherit. The `Activity` class itself inherits from `DependencyObject`, which is discussed later in this chapter (after a bit more context). This class provides all the basics you need to build your own activities.

To implement the logic necessary for a custom activity to function, you use three methods: `Initialize`, `Execute`, and `Cancel`. All three methods are called by the workflow runtime (not manually) and are passed context information related to the current execution environment. Both `Execute` and `Cancel` are passed an instance of the `ActivityExecutionContext` class, and the `Initialize` method is passed an `IServiceProvider` instance. You can use either of these parameter types to access valuable information about the runtime or to manipulate runtime behavior.

To implement a basic activity, you need only to inherit from the `Activity` class and override the `Execute` method. Of course, the interesting logic that the activity provides should be implemented in `Execute`. The `Execute` method returns a value from the `ActivityExecutionStatus` enumeration. In most normal circumstances in which the `Execute` method has done its business and is completely finished, it returns `ActivityExecutionStatus.Closed`. Other possible values are `Canceling`, `Compensating`, `Executing`, `Faulting`, and `Initialized`. The diagram shown in Figure 6-7 represents the states in which an activity can be and which states can transition to others.

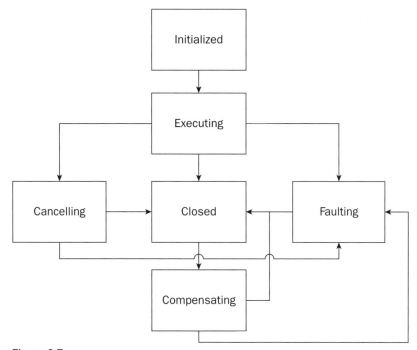

Figure 6-7

The CompositeActivity Class

The CompositeActivity class inherits from Activity and provides a base from which activities that provide a parent–child model can inherit. This level of the inheritance tree introduces the Activities property, which is a collection of all child activities that have been added to this, the parent. The CompositeActivity class also has a property called EnabledActivities, which retrieves all activities that would be returned from the Activities property, not including disabled and special activities such as CancellationHandler and CompensationHandler.

Activity Properties

As you have seen, activities generally expose properties that affect their runtime behavior. You may be familiar with exposing properties on standard .NET types, but Windows Workflow Foundation activity properties are different enough to cause a slight learning curve. The following sections cover activity properties and their associated traits.

DependencyObject and DependencyProperty

These classes provide the foundation for the activity data storage mechanism. Think back to the workflow tenets introduced in Chapter 1. The requirement that workflows remain stateful is very important, and these two classes play an important role in that constraint. In addition, dependency objects and their associated properties allow activities to project their properties onto their children.

For example, the ConditionedActivityGroup activity uses dependency properties to apply its WhenCondition property to its children. Figure 6-8 shows a Code activity added as a child to a ConditionedActivityGroup activity. In addition to the normal properties for a Code activity, there is a WhenCondition. Even though this appears to be part of the Code activity, it is actually inherited from its parent.

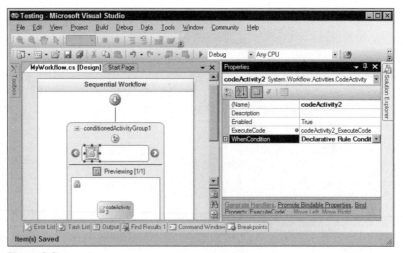

Figure 6-8

DependencyObject is basically a hash table that uses DependencyProperty instances as its key to retrieve values for a particular DependencyObject instance. To use dependency properties in activities, you generally follow a common pattern. You add a public static instance of a DependencyProperty to manage that property for all instances of the activity. Then you add a standard .NET property with get and set accessors. The get accessor uses the base GetValue method defined in the DependencyObject class (which the Activity class inherits from) to retrieve the stored value of the property for that activity instance by passing the static DependencyProperty instance mentioned earlier. Similarly, the set accessor uses the DependencyObject.SetValue method.

The previous paragraph describes a situation in which you use dependency properties to represent variable values such as strings or some other object type. You can also use dependency properties to manage other entities such as events. The following code shows an example of using dependency properties with events. Remember, the AddHandler and RemoveHandler methods are defined in the DependencyObject class, which is the base class for Activity.

```
public class MyActivity : Activity
{
    public static readonly DependencyProperty SomethingHappenedEvent;

    public event EventHandler SomethingHappened
    {
        add
        {
            base.AddHandler(MyActivity.SomethingHappenedEvent, value);
        }

        remove
        {
            base.RemoveHandler(MyActivity.SomethingHappenedEvent, value);
        }
    }
}
```

Property Types

In Windows Workflow Foundation, there are two types of activity properties: meta and instance. You must set meta properties to static values. You can set instance properties at runtime or bind them to another instance variable that provides the values during runtime.

Meta properties are like those introduced in the previous section. They use DependencyProperty instances and the DependencyObject infrastructure to manage their values. Conversely, if you added a standard .NET property to an activity, this is considered an instance property because its value is derived from an instance member during runtime. You can use traits from both of these property types through property binding.

Activity Property Binding

Property binding enables you to combine dependency properties with instance members that can be modified at runtime. To do this, you use the ActivityBind class to map a path from a dependency property to a dynamic instance member such as a variable, event, or method.

For example, the Throw activity has a dependency property called `Fault` that specifies an exception instance to throw when the activity is executed. In this case, you can use the `ActivityBind` class to map an `Exception` instance to the Fault property at runtime. This enables you to modify the exception instance during runtime, prior to the execution of the Throw activity. Here is the code you would use to configure this binding:

```
ActivityBind faultBinding = new ActivityBind();
faultBinding.Name = "MyWorkflow";
faultBinding.Path = "ex";
throwActivity.SetBinding(ThrowActivity.FaultProperty, faultBinding);
```

As you can see, two properties provide the path to the exception instance: `Name` and `Path`. `Name` specifies the name of the class where the member variable, `Path`, can be found. Then the `SetBinding` method of the Throw activity is called. The dependency property, `ThrowActivity.FaultProperty`, and the `ActivityBind` instance are passed to this method to complete the binding operation.

Visual Studio can automatically perform property binding. To set this up, you use the property binding dialog box (see Figure 6-9), which you can access by clicking the ellipsis button in the Fault property text box in the Properties Explorer. Figure 6-9 shows the property binding dialog box for the Throw activity example. From here, you can select an existing instance member, in this case `ex`, to bind to the `Fault` property. You can also have a new instance member or dependency property automatically generated using this dialog box's Bind to a new member tab.

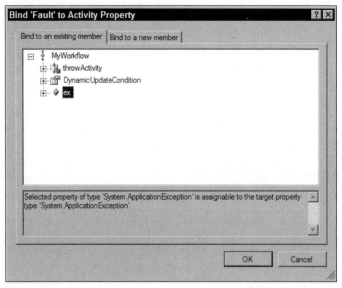

Figure 6-9

Property Attributes

You can apply attributes to activity properties to enhance their design-time and runtime behavior. Table 6-1 lists these attributes. Many of these attributes are used not only by Windows Workflow Foundation, but by many other components outside the workflow world as well.

Table 6-1: Activity-Related Attributes

Attribute	Description
BrowsableAttribute	Indicates whether or not the property will be displayed in the Properties Explorer of Visual Studio.
DefaultValueAttribute	Identifies a default value for the property.
DesignerSerialization VisibilityAttribute	Specifies the method of persistence to be used during design-time serialization of the property.
EditorAttribute	Specifies the class that should be used as the UI editor for the property. For example, the CallExternalMethod activity uses this attribute to specify that the TypeBrowser Editor class should be used to set the InterfaceType property.
ParenthesizeProperty NameAttribute	Indicates whether or not a property should be surrounded by parentheses. A property enclosed in parentheses appears at the top of an alphabetical list. This attribute is commonly applied to a component's Name property.
PersistOnCloseAttribute	This attribute is specific to Windows Workflow Foundation and denotes that a workflow should be persisted when the activity has been executed successfully.
MergablePropertyAttribute	When this attribute passes a value of true, it indicates that the property can be combined with properties belonging to other objects in Visual Studio's Properties Explorer.
RefreshPropertiesAttribute	Specifies which properties of the current object should be refreshed in the Properties Explorer when the current property is changed. This is useful when other properties' values are dependent on another property.
TypeConverterAttribute	Specifies the TypeConverter class type that should be applied to the property.

Activity Components

You can use component attributes to apply custom behaviors to an activity class. You implement these custom behaviors by inheriting from one of the following classes:

- ❑ System.Drawing.Design.ToolboxItem
- ❑ System.ComponentModel.Designer
- ❑ System.Workflow.ComponentModel.Compiler.ActivityValidator
- ❑ System.Workflow.ComponentModel.Serialization.WorkflowMarkupSerializer
- ❑ System.Workflow.ComponentModel.Compiler.ActivityCodeGenerator

The following sections discuss these classes.

149

ToolboxItem

You use the `ToolboxItem` class to specify how a designable component is represented in Visual Studio's Toolbox window. You can specify properties such as the component's display name and visual icon representation.

In addition, you use this class to define the component's default state. For example, think about the IfElse activity. When you drag and drop the IfElse component from the Toolbox to the workflow designer, it automatically contains two IfElseBranch activities. Although it may seem as though this happens by magic, it definitely does not.

The following code snippet is taken from an `IfElseToolboxItem` class that was reverse-engineered using Reflector. As you can see, the `CreateComponentsCore` method creates an instance of the `IfElseActivity` class and then adds two instances of the `IfElseBranchActivity` class to it. The `IfElseActivity` instance is then returned in an `IComponent` array and added to the workflow by Visual Studio.

```
protected override IComponent[] CreateComponentsCore(IDesignerHost designerHost)
{
    CompositeActivity activity1 = new IfElseActivity();
    activity1.Activities.Add(new IfElseBranchActivity());
    activity1.Activities.Add(new IfElseBranchActivity());
    return new IComponent[] { activity1 };
}
```

You apply a `ToolboxItem` class to an activity by decorating an activity class with the `System.ComponentModel.ToolboxItemAttribute` class and passing a `Type` reference to its constructor.

Designer

As you well know by now, activities have a visual component that is used during workflow design time. Traits such as text and image layout are defined in activity designer classes. Each activity designer ultimately inherits from the `ActivityDesigner` class that is defined in `System.Workflow.ComponentModel.Design`.

This class has important properties such as `ImageRectangle` and `TextRectangle` as well as important methods such as `Initialize` and `OnLayoutSize`. However, you can override these properties and methods to provide custom layout logic for new activities.

In addition, you can decorate custom activity designer classes with the `ActivityDesignerTheme` attribute to specify custom activity designer theme classes. These theme classes inherit from `ActivityDesignerTheme` and define various visual traits of a custom activity, such as the foreground and background colors as well as border styles. Here is a short example of a custom activity designer theme class:

```
public class MyActivityDesignerTheme : ActivityDesignerTheme
{
    public MyActivityDesignerTheme(WorkflowTheme theme) : base(theme)
    {
    }

    public override void Initialize()
```

```
    {
        this.BorderColor = Color.Black;
        this.BorderStyle = DashStyle.Solid;
        this.ForeColor = Color.Black;

        base.Initialize();
    }
}
```

ActivityValidator

You use `ActivityValidator` classes to specify the rules that govern whether an activity's given state is valid or not. Activity validation is the concept that provides the little red exclamation point icons on activities in the workflow designer. Validation can check for things as simple as whether or not a value is set or as complex as whether or not a given value is valid based on another property's value.

Most of the out-of-the-box activities have their own custom validation logic defined in `ActivityValidator` classes. For example, by looking at the `IfElseValidator` class in Reflector, you can see that the `Validate` method ensures that the child count is not less than 1 and that each child in its `EnabledActivities` collection is an `IfElseBranchActivity` instance. You can prove this logic by placing a new IfElse activity in a workflow and inspecting its errors.

WorkflowMarkupSerializer

You can serialize workflow activities according to logic you specify. You define the custom serialization logic in classes that inherit from `WorkflowMarkupSerializer`. Then you apply the serialization class to an activity using the `DesignerSerializer` attribute.

The following three markup serializers are provided out of the box for use in specific situations:

- ❑ `WorkflowMarkupSerializer`
- ❑ `ActivityMarkupSerializer`
- ❑ `CompositeActivityMarkupSerializer`

It is pretty easy to ascertain which entities these classes apply to based on their names.

ActivityCodeGenerator

Custom code generators can be written so that developers can participate in code generation during compile time. Generally, developers create new classes inheriting from `ActivityCodeGenerator` that pertain to a very specific need for code generation. Although you may rarely need to use code generation in your solutions, it is a very powerful tool when required.

A good example of how activity code generation is used in the Windows Workflow Foundation API is the WebServiceInput activity. When this activity is used to expose a workflow as an ASP.NET web service, code is generated when the workflow is compiled to create a new class inheriting from `Workflow WebService`. `WorkflowWebService` in turn inherits from `System.Web.Services.WebService`, which is the base class for all ASP.NET web services. Logic is then injected into the new class, which calls the workflow, and handles any input and output to and from the workflow.

The following code snippet represents a portion of the definition metadata of the `WebServiceInput Activity` class:

```
[SRCategory("Standard")]
[SRDescription("WebServiceReceiveActivityDescription")]
[ToolboxBitmap(typeof(WebServiceInputActivity), "Resources.WebServiceIn.png")]
[Designer(typeof(WebServiceReceiveDesigner), typeof(IDesigner))]
[ActivityValidator(typeof(WebServiceReceiveValidator))]
[ActivityCodeGenerator(typeof(WebServiceCodeGenerator))]
[DefaultEvent("InputReceived")]
public sealed class WebServiceInputActivity :
    Activity, IEventActivity, IPropertyValueProvider,
    IActivityEventListener<QueueEventArgs>, IDynamicPropertyTypeProvider
{
}
```

The important line to look at here is the second-to-last attribute of the class, `ActivityCodeGenerator`. This attribute references a class called `WebServiceCodeGenerator`, which, not surprisingly, inherits from `ActivityCodeGenerator`. This tells the compiler to call the code generator's `GenerateCode` method during compilation to create any necessary code and compile it as well. Code generation is a large topic in itself and not something specific to Windows Workflow Foundation; therefore, it is not discussed in detail here. However, having a basic understanding of what is going on in the `GenerateCode` method of `WebServiceCodeGenerator` may help you think of ways that you can use this infrastructure.

Basically, a new web service class definition is created using the `System.CodeDom.CodeType Declaration` class, and a method is created and added to the new class using the `CodeMemberMethod` class of the same namespace. To really get an idea of what is going here, use Lutz's Reflector to see what the code is trying to accomplish.

To summarize, if you need to create dynamically generate code at workflow compile time, you can inherit from the `ActivityCodeGenerator` class and apply the `ActivityCodeGenerator` attribute to your activity class.

An Example: Developing the WriteFile Activity

This activity development case study involves an activity that writes some text to a file. This goal of this case study is to cover the gamut of what you need to know for basic activity development. The WriteFile activity will have the following features:

❑ A custom Toolbox icon

❑ A custom Toolbox item type that will allow custom display text in the Toolbox

❑ A custom designer and a theme that includes an image

❑ Custom validation

❑ Its own execution logic

The first step in creating the new activity is to create a new class that inherits from `System.Workflow .ComponentModel.Activity`. The following code block shows the skeleton of the `WriteFileActivity` class, with numerous attributes decorating the new class:

```
[ToolboxItem(typeof(MyActivityToolboxItem))]
[ToolboxBitmap(typeof(WriteFileActivity), "Resources.write.ico")]
[Designer(typeof(WriteFileActivityDesigner), typeof(IDesigner))]
[ActivityValidator(typeof(WriteFileActivityValidator))]
public class WriteFileActivity : Activity
{
    ...
}
```

In this code, the `ToolboxItem` attribute is used to specify which class should be used to implement custom Toolbox behavior in Visual Studio. The code specifies a class called `MyActivityToolboxItem`, which was developed for this example and whose implementation is shown later. The `ToolboxBitmap` attribute specifies that the Toolbox should show an icon called `write.ico`, which has been included in the current assembly as a resource.

The `WriteFileActivity` class is also decorated with a `Designer` attribute instance that is used to specify a class that implements `IDesigner`. The `WriteFileActivityDesigner` class defines the behavior used when displaying the activity within the workflow designer. The implementation of this class is also shown later in the case study.

Finally, the activity class is decorated with the `ActivityValidator` attribute. This attribute simply specifies the type of a custom activity validator class — in this case, `WriteFileActivityValidator`. Like all of the other custom code developed for this example, this class is covered a little later.

Part of the actual implementation of `WriteFileActivity` is shown in the following code. There are a couple of important things to notice here. First, the required behavior of this activity dictates that you should be able to specify the name of the output file as well as the text to be written to that file. Therefore, there are two public properties defined: `FileName` and `FileText`. Notice that the `get` and `set` accessors of these two properties reference their corresponding static `DependencyProperty` instances.

```
public class WriteFileActivity : Activity
{
    public static DependencyProperty FileTextProperty =
        DependencyProperty.Register("FileText", typeof(string),
            typeof(WriteFileActivity));

    [Description("The text to write to the file")]
    [Category("File")]
    [Browsable(true)]
    [DesignerSerializationVisibility(DesignerSerializationVisibility.Visible)]
    public string FileText
    {
        get
        {
            return ((string)(base.GetValue(WriteFileActivity.FileTextProperty)));
        }
        set
        {
            base.SetValue(WriteFileActivity.FileTextProperty, value);
        }
    }

    public static DependencyProperty FileNameProperty =
```

153

```
        DependencyProperty.Register("FileName", typeof(string),
            typeof(WriteFileActivity));

    [Description("The file to write to")]
    [Category("File")]
    [Browsable(true)]
    [DesignerSerializationVisibility(DesignerSerializationVisibility.Visible)]
    public string FileName
    {
        get
        {
            return ((string)(base.GetValue(WriteFileActivity.FileNameProperty)));
        }
        set
        {
            base.SetValue(WriteFileActivity.FileNameProperty, value);
        }
    }
}
```

The next block of code is still in the `WriteFileActivity` class and is the meat of this entire exercise: the `Execute` method implementation. Here, the code simply creates a new instance of the `StreamWriter` class using the `System.IO.File.CreateText` method. Next, the text you specified in the `FileText` property is written to the stream; the stream is flushed and then closed. Finally, the `Closed` value from the `ActivityExecutionStatus` enumeration is returned to indicate a successful execution.

```
protected override ActivityExecutionStatus Execute(
    ActivityExecutionContext executionContext)
{
    StreamWriter writer = File.CreateText(this.FileName);
    writer.Write(this.FileText);
    writer.Flush();
    writer.Close();

    return ActivityExecutionStatus.Closed;
}
```

The next block of code shown is the implementation of the `MyActivityToolboxItem` class specified as the custom `ToolboxItem` class for the previous `WriteFileActivity`. Although this class doesn't have any behavior that is specific to this example, it shows how you can implement simple behavior that applies a custom description for any activity decorated with the `ToolboxItem` attribute and specifying this class.

```
[Serializable]
public class MyActivityToolboxItem : ActivityToolboxItem
{
    public MyActivityToolboxItem()
    {
    }

    public MyActivityToolboxItem(Type type)
        : base(type)
    {
        if (type != null)
```

```
            {
                if (type.Name.EndsWith("Activity") && !type.Name.Equals("Activity"))
                {
                    base.DisplayName =
                        type.Name.Substring(0, type.Name.Length - 8);
                }
            }
        }

        protected MyActivityToolboxItem(SerializationInfo info,
            StreamingContext context)
        {
            this.Deserialize(info, context);
        }
    }
```

Basically, this class changes the default display name of an activity in the Toolbox from its full name, in this case WriteFileActivity, to a shorter and friendlier name. In this example, the display name is WriteFile. This behavior is actually implemented in the ActivityToolboxItem class in the Windows Workflow Foundation APIs, but only for activities that have been included out of the box. So this custom class enables you to take advantage of the same behavior.

The following code is the WriteFileActivityDesigner class skeleton. Remember, this class was applied to WriteFileActivity earlier using the Designer attribute. Notice that there is an Activity DesignerTheme attribute decorating WriteFileActivityDesigner, which specifies a type of Write FileActivityDesignerTheme. As discussed earlier in this chapter, there are two classes that define how an activity is presented in the workflow designer. The designer class defines how an image and text are laid out, and the designer theme class defines other visual traits such as text and background color as well as the border's look and feel.

```
[ActivityDesignerTheme(typeof(WriteFileActivityDesignerTheme))]
public class WriteFileActivityDesigner : ActivityDesigner
{
    ...
}
```

The following code is the implementation of this WriteFileActivityDesigner class:

```
public class WriteFileActivityDesigner : ActivityDesigner
{
    private const int TEXT_WIDTH = 75;
    private const int PADDING = 4;

    protected override Rectangle ImageRectangle
    {
        get
        {
            Rectangle rect = new Rectangle();
            rect.X = this.Bounds.Left + PADDING;
            rect.Y = this.Bounds.Top + PADDING;
            rect.Size = Properties.Resources.Write.Size;
            return rect;
        }
    }
```

```
    }

    protected override Rectangle TextRectangle
    {
        get
        {
            Rectangle imgRect = this.ImageRectangle;

            Rectangle rect = new Rectangle(
                imgRect.Right + PADDING,
                imgRect.Top,
                TEXT_WIDTH,
                imgRect.Height);
            return rect;
        }
    }

    protected override void Initialize(Activity activity)
    {
        base.Initialize(activity);

        Bitmap image = Properties.Resources.Write;
        image.MakeTransparent();
        this.Image = image;
    }

    protected override Size OnLayoutSize(ActivityDesignerLayoutEventArgs e)
    {
        base.OnLayoutSize(e);

        Size imgSize = Properties.Resources.Write.Size;
        return new Size(imgSize.Width + TEXT_WIDTH + (PADDING * 3),
            imgSize.Height + (PADDING * 2));
    }
}
```

First, take a look at the two properties: ImageRectangle and TextRectangle. These two overridden properties define the logic that tells the designer where to place the activity image and text as well as the rectangle size of those two entities. There are two integer constants at the top of the class that are used during the visual layout process. TEXT_WIDTH simply says how wide the text's rectangle area will be, and PADDING says how large the margins will be in several areas of the activity's visual representation.

Next, the overridden Initialize method grabs the activity's image file from the assembly's resources store. The image is made transparent and then set to the Image property, which originally defined the base ActivityDesigner class.

Adding an image to an assembly's resources is simple. First, right-click the project icon in the Solution Explorer and select the Properties option from the context menu. This displays a multitude of properties and settings related to the project. On the Resources tab, click the down arrow on the Add Resource toolbar button and select Add Existing File (see Figure 6-10). This displays a dialog box where you can point to an image on your filesystem. After you select the image, it appears in the area below the toolbar. You

can now reference this image directly from code using the `Properties.Resources` class that is generated for you. This easy way of managing and accessing assembly resources was introduced in .NET 2.0
and Visual Studio 2005.

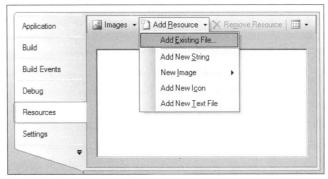

Figure 6-10

To get back to the example at hand, look at the overridden `OnLayoutSize` method in the `WriteFile`
`ActivityDesigner` class. Here, the code that specifies how the activity's size is calculated is implemented. Several variables are used to determine the activity's size, including the size of the activity
image, the desired padding, and the width of the text rectangle.

The following code shows the `WriteFileActivityDesignerTheme` class. This is the class that was
applied to the `WriteFileActivityDesigner` class using the `ActivityDesignerTheme` attribute. To
implement custom behavior here, the `Initialize` method was overridden, and numerous properties
defined in the base `ActivityDesignerTheme` class are set. As you can see, the foreground color, background color, border style, and a few other visual attributes are specified in this custom class.

```
public class WriteFileActivityDesignerTheme : ActivityDesignerTheme
{
    public WriteFileActivityDesignerTheme(WorkflowTheme theme)
        : base(theme)
    {
    }

    public override void Initialize()
    {
        this.ForeColor = Color.Black;
        this.BorderColor = Color.Black;
        this.BorderStyle = DashStyle.Solid;
        this.BackgroundStyle = LinearGradientMode.Vertical;
        this.BackColorStart = Color.White;
        this.BackColorEnd = Color.LightGray;

        base.Initialize();
    }
}
```

This next class covers a very interesting aspect of activity development. The `WriteFileActivity` `Validator` class, shown in the following code, defines the logic necessary to make sure the WriteFile activity is configured correctly during design time and runtime. The custom validator class inherits from `ActivityValidator` and is applied to the `WriteFileActivity` class using the `ActivityValidator` attribute. `WriteFileActivityValidator` defines its logic by overriding the `Validate` method of the `ActivityValidator` base class. In this example, an instance of the activity in question is acquired by casting the `obj` variable to a variable of type `WriteFileActivity`. From here, the code is able to analyze the activity to make sure that the necessary properties are set and that they are set correctly.

```
public class WriteFileActivityValidator : ActivityValidator
{
    public override ValidationErrorCollection Validate(
        ValidationManager manager, object obj)
    {
        if (manager == null)
            throw new ArgumentNullException("manager");

        if (obj == null)
            throw new ArgumentNullException("obj");

        WriteFileActivity activity = obj as WriteFileActivity;

        if (activity == null)
            throw new
                InvalidOperationException("obj should be a WriteFileActivity");

        if (activity.Parent != null)
        {
            ValidationErrorCollection errors = base.Validate(manager, obj);

            if (String.IsNullOrEmpty(activity.FileName))
                errors.Add(ValidationError.GetNotSetValidationError("FileName"));

            if (String.IsNullOrEmpty(activity.FileText))
                errors.Add(ValidationError.GetNotSetValidationError("FileText"));

            bool dirError = false;
            try
            {
                string fileDir = Path.GetDirectoryName(activity.FileName);
                dirError = !Directory.Exists(fileDir);
            }
            catch { dirError = true; }

            if (dirError)
            {
                errors.Add(new ValidationError(
                    "Directory for FileName is not valid or does not exist",
                    3,
                    false,
                    "FileName"));
            }
```

```
            if (Path.GetExtension(activity.FileName) != ".txt")
                errors.Add(new ValidationError(
                    "This activity only supports .txt files!",
                    4,
                    false,
                    "FileName"));

            return errors;

        }
        else
        {
            return new ValidationErrorCollection();
        }
    }
}
```

Notice the line that checks to see whether the `activity.Parent` property is null. Basically, the workflow compiler performs the validation logic even during the compilation of the activity class during design time. This means that if the activity does not pass validation given its default property values, it does not compile. Obviously, this isn't optimal because you are more concerned about whether the activity is configured correctly when it is actually being used. This is where the `Parent` property null check comes in. The activity has a parent only when it is being used in the workflow designer or during runtime. Therefore, none of the code within the `if` block is executed during the activity class' initial compilation. If there is no parent, an empty `ValidationErrorCollection` instance is returned, representing no errors.

Finally, take a look at the code that does the validation itself. This code checks for the following items:

❑   The `FileName` and `FileText` properties cannot be null or an empty string.

❑   A valid directory name must be specified in the `FileName` property, and it must already exist.

❑   The extension of the file specified in the `FileName` property must be .txt.

If any of these conditions is not met, a new instance of the `ValidationError` class is added to the `errors` collection, which is then returned at the end of the method. The logic defined in an `Activity Validator` class is what dictates when the red exclamation-point icon is added to activities in the workflow designer as well as whether or not the workflow can compile.

For general errors, a new instance of the `ValidationError` class is added to the errors collection. The `ValidationError` class has properties such as `ErrorText`, `IsWarning`, and `ErrorNumber`. In addition, the `ValidationError` class has a static utility method called `GetNotSetValidationError`, which allows you to easily create a validation error that is displayed when a property is not set.

The activity is complete. To test it, you can add the activity to Visual Studio's Toolbox by pointing to the compiled assembly on the filesystem. Doing this should result in something similar to Figure 6-11. Notice that the activity is using the custom naming defined in the `MyActivityToolboxItem` class — that is, the display name is WriteFile rather than WriteFileActivity. In addition, the activity's display image is using the icon that was defined using the `ToolboxBitmap` attribute in the activity's class definition.

Figure 6-11

Next, create a new workflow in a separate project, and add the new activity to the workflow by dragging and dropping it on the design surface. The size of the activity, the text, and the image adhere to the logic that was implemented in the `WriteFileActivityDesigner` class. In addition, the red validation icon appears on the activity, indicating that it is not correctly configured (see Figure 6-12).

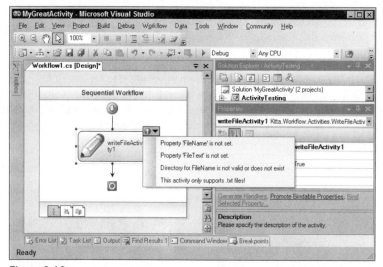

Figure 6-12

After you properly set each property, you should be able to execute the workflow, and a file will appear in the location specified with the `FileName` property.

Summary

This chapter introduced you to all the Windows Workflow Foundation activities. First, you were introduced to activities and their different types, including composite activities and how they are different from their standard counterparts. The Windows Workflow Foundation Base Activity Library was also covered from A to Z. There are no fewer than 30 activities provided out of the box for workflow development.

Custom activity development was also covered as a way for developers to implement functionality that was not included out of the box with Windows Workflow Foundation. Activity components provide the necessary framework to modify activity functionality and include toolbox items, activity designers, themes, activity validators, serializers, and code generators.

In addition, this chapter introduced activity properties and their surrounding infrastructure. Dependency objects and dependency properties provide the functionality necessary for activity data storage and property projection.

Finally, an activity development example gave some context to the subject matter of this chapter. The example covered the steps necessary to create a custom activity and briefly described the activity's execution, validation, and look and feel.

7

Runtime Services

This chapter covers the runtime services architecture within Windows Workflow Foundation. The Workflow API defines the base infrastructure for several runtime service types, including workflow persistence and tracking. In addition, several out-of-the-box services implement the base infrastructure. These services and examples of each can be found in this chapter.

The second half of the chapter covers custom runtime service development. The chapter covers alternatives to the out-of-the-box services and how to extend the base framework ,and provides examples that illustrate how to develop custom services.

Out-of-the-Box Services

The following sections discuss each runtime service type provided out of the box with Windows Workflow Foundation. These sections describe the concepts and instructions on how to use these runtime services as well as the drivers behind why each service type was developed.

Table 7-1 lists each out-of-the-box service type and corresponding implementations.

Table 7-1: Out-of-the-Box Services

Service Type	Description	Out-of-the-Box Implementations
Scheduling	Responsible for creating and scheduling new workflow instances for execution	`DefaultWorkflowScheduler Service`, `ManualWorkflow SchedulerService`
Work Batch	Enables behavior to maintain a stable and consistent execution environment	`DefaultWorkflowCommitWork BatchService`, `Shared ConnectionWorkflowCommit WorkBatchService`
Persistence	Provides an infrastructure for maintaining workflow instance state	`SqlWorkflowPersistence Service`
Tracking	Enables rich logging and tracking capabilities to monitor workflow execution	`SqlTrackingService`
Workflow Loader	Provides functionality to create workflow instances when the `CreateWorkflow` method is called	`DefaultWorkflow LoaderService`
Data Exchange	Manages custom communication services	`ExternalDataExchange Service`

Scheduling Services

Scheduling services are those that inherit from `WorkflowSchedulerService`. These services dictate the threading model that workflow instances use when started. The workflow runtime has to have one—and only one—scheduling service specified before starting. It is also important to have options related to threading because workflows can be hosted in any application type. Windows Forms applications, for example, might require a different threading model than an ASP.NET web application does.

Think about a Windows Forms application. Conventional wisdom tells developers to keep their Windows applications as fluid and responsive as possible. This commonly means running intense or long-running processes on background threads.

Conversely, consider an ASP.NET application. Spawning threads to perform work in the background doesn't add anything to the overall user experience. Any work that needs to be done should be completed by the time a response is returned to the client—not to mention the fact that IIS does not like it when you start to use a lot of its threads.

Considerations regarding ASP.NET and Windows Workflow Foundation are covered in Chapter 13.

Because requirements differ depending on the situation, Windows Workflow Foundation offers two distinct scheduling services out of the box. As its name implies, `DefaultWorkflowSchedulerService` is used by default when no scheduling service is specified explicitly. `ManualWorkflowScheduler Service` is also provided for use when required. The following sections describe each of these scheduling services.

DefaultWorkflowSchedulerService

As mentioned, `DefaultWorkflowSchedulerService` is automatically used by the workflow runtime when no other scheduling service is specified because the runtime *has* to have a scheduling service in order to start workflow instances.

This scheduling service uses threads from the thread pool to spawn workflow instances. Therefore, the host functions on its own thread, and workflow instances use their own thread to execute. One scenario where this is essential is in Windows Forms applications where the UI thread needs to remain available for user interaction and should not be bogged down with long-running or intensive processes.

Commonly in examples and in the host that is generated when you create a new console workflow project, you see code that forces the host to wait until after a workflow is completed. This is because the runtime is using `DefaultWorkflowSchedulerService`, and the console application completes and exits as soon as a workflow instance is started on another thread. Obviously, this is not optimal because any workflows started never get a chance to finish. The following code is an example of this pattern:

```
using(WorkflowRuntime workflowRuntime = new WorkflowRuntime())
{
    AutoResetEvent waitHandle = new AutoResetEvent(false);
    workflowRuntime.WorkflowCompleted += delegate(object sender,
        WorkflowCompletedEventArgs e)
    {
        // notify the host its OK to continue
        waitHandle.Set();
    };

    WorkflowInstance instance =
        workflowRuntime.CreateWorkflow(typeof(Temp.Workflow1));
    instance.Start();

    // wait until the workflow instance is done
    waitHandle.WaitOne();
}
```

This code waits to exit until the workflow instance completes by using the `AutoResetEvent` class. When the `WaitOne` method of this class is called, it blocks further execution on that thread until the `Set` method is subsequently called. That is why the `WorkflowCompleted` event is handled where the `Set` method is called. Therefore, when the workflow instance has finished executing, the final line is able to progress, and the application is able to finish.

ManualWorkflowSchedulerService

Unlike `DefaultWorkflowSchedulerService`, `ManualWorkflowSchedulerService` creates and executes workflow instances on a thread borrowed from the workflow runtime host. Therefore, you should consider using this alternative service when workflow instances should not be taking up too many threads or when the runtime host needs to wait for a response from the instance before doing anything else. An example of the former scenario is with ASP.NET. Because ASP.NET does not like all of its thread being used up by other processes, using `ManualWorkflowSchedulerService` here makes perfect sense.

Unlike with `DefaultWorkflowSchedulerService`, you need to explicitly add `ManualWorkflow SchedulerService` to the workflow runtime. When you do this, `ManualWorkflowSchedulerService` is used in place of the default service because the runtime can have one, and only one, scheduling service. The following code illustrates how to add and use `ManualWorkflowSchedulerService`:

```
WorkflowRuntime workflowRuntime = new WorkflowRuntime();

ManualWorkflowSchedulerService scheduler = new ManualWorkflowSchedulerService();
workflowRuntime.AddService(scheduler);

workflowRuntime.StartRuntime();

WorkflowInstance instance = workflowRuntime.CreateWorkflow(typeof(MyWorkflow));
instance.Start();

scheduler.RunWorkflow(instance.InstanceId);
```

First, a new instance of the manual scheduler class is created and added to the runtime's services using the `AddService` method as usual. In addition, a `WorkflowInstance` is created and started as it normally would be. The difference comes in when the `RunWorkflow` method of the `scheduler` object is called. This call is required to actually start your workflow's execution. Remember, this is a blocking call until your workflow is finished executing or idles.

Because you will most likely use `ManualWorkflowSchedulerService` in an ASP.NET environment, there is more on this topic in Chapter 13.

Work Batch Services

Workflow work batch services, also known as commit batch services, enable you to commit work batches at specified persistence points. Work batching, which was introduced in Chapter 5, is the process of building up a queue of work and then performing that work in the context of one transaction to make sure everything ends up in a consistent and stable state. Work batch services are responsible for making sure a transaction exists before the batching occurs and then starting the batch process.

All batch services inherit from the `System.Workflow.Runtime.Hosting.WorkflowCommitWork` `BatchService` class. This abstract class has a method called `CommitWorkBatch`, which performs the work described previously. Even though `WorkflowCommitWorkBatchService` is abstract, `Commit` `WorkBatch` is a concrete method — meaning that it can be called from any child classes by using the `base` keyword. You use this method when the base implementation contains only the logic you need in your new class. In addition, this method is passed a `CommitWorkBatchCallback` delegate that, when called, in turn calls the method that commits the work.

A work batching example is included later in this chapter, in the "Developing Persistence Services" section. First, however, here's a quick review of how this functionality is structured. If your solution requires that discrete chunks of code be queued up over time but executed at the same time, you need to create a custom class that implements the `IPendingWork` interface. The following example shows a skeleton class for implementing this interface:

```
public class MyWork : IPendingWork
{
    public void Commit(Transaction transaction, ICollection items)
    {
        foreach (object o in items)
```

```
        {
            // do some work on the object here
        }
    }

    public void Complete(bool succeeded, ICollection items)
    {
        // do some work when done here if you want
    }

    public bool MustCommit(ICollection items)
    {
        return true;
    }
}
```

The method that does all the work here is `Commit`. This method is called when the batch is being committed. Again, the commitment process is kicked off by the workflow runtime when a persistence point is reached. This method is passed a collection of objects that represent each chunk of work you added. You need to loop through this collection and do whatever work is required on each object. Note that in the code, the `foreach` loop is simply extracting a `System.Object` reference from the collection. However, the objects in this collection can be of any type.

The next step is to actually get objects into this collection so they can be iterated over. To do this, you use the static `WorkBatch` property of the `WorkflowEnvironment` class. You can add objects to this collection using its `Add` method from anywhere in your code, whether it's within the host or inside the workflow. This method takes an `IPendingWork` reference and an object reference. This object reference is added to the collection, which is then passed to the `Commit` method of your `IPendingWork` class. This is a pretty simple, but very elegant, architecture for transactional behavior in your workflow solutions.

DefaultWorkflowCommitWorkBatchService

Because a workflow batch service is always required, `DefaultWorkflowCommitBatchService` class is included out of the box. This class implements the basic functionality that can execute a work batch in the context of a transaction. Generally, this service provides all the batching functionality you need, and you don't even have to think about it because it is added to the runtime automatically. However, there may be situations, specifically dealing with database transactions, when this service cannot handle all your needs. That is where `SharedConnectionWorkflowCommitWorkBatchService` comes in.

SharedConnectionWorkflowCommitWorkBatchService

With what is probably the longest class name in the Windows Workflow Foundation API, `Shared ConnectionWorkflowCommitBatchService` enables you to use SQL Server transactions on a remote SQL Server database between various services that connect to that database. .NET transactions were introduced in Chapter 6, and this topic is beyond the scope of this book. However, this runtime service enables you to bypass the Distributed Transaction Coordinator (DTC), which would otherwise be necessary if the workflow host were running on a box other than the SQL Server.

Using this service is as simple as adding an instance of the class to the runtime as you do with any other service. The service class's constructor takes a string representing the connection string to the database. As a rule of thumb, if you are using both the SQL persistence and tracking services (discussed later), you should take advantage of the shared connection batch service to ensure that you are using SQL Server transactions and not adding extra overhead to your transactions by using the DTC.

Persistence Services

Persistence services exist to support the tenet that workflows must be long running and stateful. When a workflow instance is waiting for work to be performed or after important work has been completed, saving the workflow's state can help maintain a stable system.

The first way persistence services help is that they allow running workflow instances that are consuming valuable system resources to be taken out of memory and placed in a durable storage medium. The storage could be a database, an XML file, or any other method of a developer's choosing. The process of taking a workflow's data and execution state and persisting it is also known as *dehydration.* Conversely, when a workflow instance is ready to do work, the process of *rehydration* occurs to bring the workflow back to life.

Persistence services also help maintain the stability of a workflow instance by saving its state after important work has been performed. Think of a scenario that has a complex set of steps that make up a single transaction. After all the steps in the transaction have completed, why risk losing the work that has just been done? Saving state to a durable store can help you maintain important information about a process in progress.

Persistence services in Windows Workflow Foundation inherit from the `System.Workflow.Runtime` `.Hosting.WorkflowPersistenceService` class. This abstract class defines methods for writing and subsequently loading a workflow instance's state to and from a persistence store. These actions are supported by the `SaveWorkflowInstanceState` and `LoadWorkflowInstanceState` methods, respectively.

Two other important methods that persistence services are forced to implement are `SaveCompleted` `ContextActivity` and `LoadCompletedContextActivity`. These two methods deal with saving and loading activity scopes that are used for transactional compensation. When a transactional scope completes, its state is stored for later, when it may be needed for a rollback.

After workflow instances are persisted, they can be restored inside a host that is different from the original host. Although this is extremely useful for scenarios where multiple people or entities are involved in a process, it could also cause problems. If a workflow instance is saved to a persistence store and then loaded by two different hosts at the same time, the results could be pretty disastrous. Therefore, the `WorkflowPersistenceService` class supports the concept of instance locking. This safeguard basically flags a persisted workflow as unavailable, or in use, by another host and prevents multiple hosts from loading an instance simultaneously. As described in the upcoming "Locking Workflow Instances" section, workflow persistence services should implement custom locking if this behavior is required.

SqlWorkflowPersistenceService

This is the only persistence service provided out of the box, and it uses a Microsoft SQL Server database as its backing store. Like any persistence service, this class inherits from `WorkflowPersistence` `Service`. The database schema this service uses is defined by Microsoft and is discussed in more detail in the next section.

This service provides you with options regarding when to persist a workflow instance to the database, how long to maintain ownership of an instance, and how often to check the database for expired instances. Like some of the other runtime services (such as `DefaultWorkflowCommitWorkBatchService`, `Shared` `ConnectionWorkflowCommitWorkBatchService`, and `SqlTrackingService`, which are discussed later in this chapter), the SQL workflow persistence service enables you to retry operations if they do not succeed initially. You enable this behavior by setting each service's `EnableRetries` property. However, you cannot configure the number of retries allowable—this value is hard coded in the API.

Preparing SqlWorkflowPersistenceService

`SqlWorkflowPersistenceService` relies on the backing of a SQL Server database. Fortunately, the Workflow SDK provides scripts for creating the database schema and stored procedures.

> This book assumes that you have ready access to a graphical database management tool, such as SQL Server Management Studio, which ships with SQL Server 2005. If you do not have access to SQL Server 2005, Microsoft offers a free and very functional database engine called SQL Server Express (available for download at `http://msdn.microsoft.com/sql/express/`). Although SQL Server Express has some limitations, it is more than adequate for learning and testing purposes.
>
> The great thing about SQL Server 2005 Express Edition, as opposed to the previous free engine (MSDE), is that it has a free GUI tool called SQL Server Management Studio Express. As of this text's writing, this tool was available as a separate download from the Express database engine. It's a great alternative to SQL Management Studio for maintaining your SQL Server databases in a development environment.

The first step in preparing the workflow persistence data store is creating the database itself, which you can accomplish with Management Studio's user interface or by running the following T-SQL DDL:

```
CREATE DATABASE WorkflowPersistence
```

In this case, a database called `WorkflowPersistence` is created. (The database name is up to you, of course.) It is not even a requirement that a new database be created for the persistence store. You could create the supporting tables and stored procedures in an existing enterprise or application database. However, you should logically separate the persistence structure from other database entities to maintain a good division of business data and workflow support objects.

The next step in preparing the SQL persistence service is creating the database tables. A script called SqlPersistenceService_Schema.sql (located in C:\<WINDOWS DIR>\Microsoft.NET\Framework\ v3.0\Windows Workflow Foundation\SQL\<LANGUAGE DIR>) is used for this purpose. Open this file in SQL Management Studio, and select the appropriate database in which to run it—in this case, `WorkflowPersistence`. Click the Execute button on the toolbar or press F5 to execute the script. If everything goes well, two new tables should appear in the database: `InstanceState` and `CompletedScope`.

The `InstanceState` table is used to store workflow instances that have been dehydrated and that are in a waiting state. It includes the following columns:

❑   `uidInstanceID`—A unique identifier that corresponds to the `InstanceId` property of a workflow instance.

❑   `state`—The serialized and compressed version of the workflow instance's state as it stood before it was persisted.

❑ status — Indicates the current status of the workflow instance. Possible values are 0 for executing, 1 for completed, 2 for suspended, 3 for terminated, and 4 for invalid.

❑ unlocked — A status flag indicating the instance's locked state.

❑ blocked — A bit column indicating whether a workflow instance is waiting for some external stimulus or timeout. This essentially tells you whether a workflow instance is idle.

❑ info — An ntext column that contains extra information if the workflow instance was suspended or terminated. For example, SuspendActivity has an Error property that allows supporting information to be stored if the workflow was suspended for some reason.

❑ modified — A datetime column indicating when the workflow instance was last modified.

❑ ownerID — Represents the runtime host that has possession of this instance.

❑ ownedUntil — A datetime column that says how long the current owner will maintain ownership of the instance.

❑ nextTimer — A datetime column indicating the date and time at which the workflow instance's next timer will expire. (The "SqlWorkflowPersistenceService and Delays" section later in this chapter discusses timers in more detail.)

The CompletedScope table stores state information of activities that are participants in transactional behavior. When a transaction scope completes, its state is written to this table for later compensation if necessary.

To complete the initial SQL persistence setup, you need to add the stored procedures to the database, using a script called SqlPersistenceService_Logic.sql (again located in C:\<WINDOWS DIR>\ Microsoft.NET\Framework\v3.0\Windows Workflow Foundation\SQL\<LANGUAGE DIR>). Open the script in SQL Management Studio, and run it. Table 7-2 describes the stored procedures that appear in the database after you execute the script.

Table 7-2: SQL Persistence Stored Procedures

Stored Procedure	Description
DeleteCompletedScope	Deletes a record from the CompletedScope table
InsertCompletedScope	Inserts a record into the CompletedScope table
InsertInstanceState	Inserts a record into the InstanceState table
RetrieveAllInstance Descriptions	Gets a few key columns from the InstanceState table for all records
RetrieveANonblocking InstanceStateId	Gets the instance ID of one nonblocking record from InstanceState
RetrieveCompletedScope	Retrieves the state of a specific scope
RetrieveExpiredTimerIds	Gets all the InstanceState records that have expired timers
RetrieveInstanceState	Gets a specific InstanceState record

Stored Procedure	Description
RetrieveNonblocking InstanceStateIds	Gets the instance IDs of all nonblocking records from InstanceState
UnlockInstanceState	Sets an InstanceState record's owner to NULL, which unlocks it

Using SqlWorkflowPersistenceService

Now that you have prepared the SqlWorkflowPersistenceService infrastructure, you are ready to use it in workflow applications.

The first step in using this runtime service is creating an instance of the SqlWorkflowPersistence Service class. This class has a few overloaded constructors that enable you to set various options when creating an instance. The first overload takes a string as its only parameter, which represents the connection string to the persistence database.

The second overload takes four parameters, the first being the connection string. The next parameter is a Boolean value that indicates whether to unload workflow instances when they become idle. By default, this option is false, and it is important to set it to the desired value during object construction because it is not exposed as a public property to set later. The third parameter is a TimeSpan that indicates how long the runtime will maintain ownership of a persisted workflow instance — the default value is one year. The fourth and final parameter is another TimeSpan instance that indicates how often to check the database for expired timers — the default value is two minutes.

The final constructor overload takes an instance of a NameValueCollection object, which you can preload with applicable parameter values. The valid parameters are similar to the parameters in the previous overload — they are ConnectionString, OwnershipTimeoutSeconds, UnloadOnIdle, and LoadIntervalSeconds. This overload gives you the option of selectively setting these four values. The only required parameter is, of course, ConnectionString. If any of the four values is not explicitly specified, the default value is used.

After you have your SqlWorkflowPersistenceService instance, you need to add it to the Workflow Runtime's services using the AddService method. The following is an example of what this might look like. Notice that the code is using the NameValueCollection overload of the service's constructor to selectively set its properties.

```
WorkflowRuntime runtime = new WorkflowRuntime();

NameValueCollection parms = new NameValueCollection();
parms.Add("ConnectionString", "Initial Catalog=WorkflowPersistence;" +
    "Data Source=localhost;Integrated Security=SSPI;");
parms.Add("UnloadOnIdle", "true");

SqlWorkflowPersistenceService persistenceService =
    new SqlWorkflowPersistenceService(parms);

runtime.AddService(persistenceService);
```

After this code is called, everything is ready to go. Workflow instances running within this host are persisted at valid persistence points (covered next).

Persistence Points

The `SqlWorkflowPersistenceService` takes care of actually writing a workflow instance's state to the persistence database, but it is the workflow runtime that dictates when this occurs. The occasions when the runtime tells the persistence service to save a workflow's state are called *persistence points*. If a persistence service exists in the runtime, there are two occasions that always cause persistence to occur: just before a workflow instance completes and just before a workflow is terminated.

A few other events cause a workflow instance to be persisted. You can cause this to happen programmatically by calling the `Unload` or `TryUnload` method of the `WorkflowInstance` class. `Unload` is a blocking call that synchronously waits until the workflow can be persisted. `TryUnload` simply tries to unload the workflow instance, and if it cannot, it returns without doing so. Its Boolean return value indicates success or failure to persist.

These methods have a few things in common. First, if either method is called and a persistence service does not currently exist inside the runtime, an `InvalidOperationException` is thrown. Both methods also persist a workflow instance only when its status is idle or suspended. Finally, if a workflow is successfully persisted, the `WorkflowUnloaded` event of `WorkflowRuntime` is raised.

Another persistence point is when an activity that has been decorated with the `PersistOnClose` attribute has successfully completed. You can use this attribute to force workflows to persist themselves after crucial pieces of code have run. The following is a short example of using this attribute:

```
[PersistOnClose]
public class MyActivity : Activity
{
    ...
}
```

The final way you can cause persistence with a persistence point is to the set the `UnloadOnIdle` property of `SqlWorkflowPersistenceService` during that object's construction. The code at the beginning of the "Using SqlWorkflowPersistenceService" section shows the creation of a `SqlWorkflowPersistence` service that sets this value. If you set this value to `true`, the workflow instance is persisted when it has no immediate work to do. Obviously, this is a good time to persist and unload a workflow instance from system memory.

Aborting Workflow Instances

The `WorkflowInstance.Abort` method is specifically for workflows executed in a runtime that have a persistence service. If this method is called from the host, the workflow is aborted in a synchronous manner, meaning that the method does not return until the runtime has successfully aborted the instance.

What's interesting about this method and persistence is that all work performed since the last persistence point is thrown away. So calling `Abort` is kind of like an undo for workflows. After the workflow has been aborted, the runtime can retrieve the instance in its previous state by calling the `GetWorkflow` method of the `WorkflowRuntime` class.

SqlWorkflowPersistenceService and Delays

What about a scenario in which a workflow instance has been persisted to the persistence store but a Delay activity's execution is pending? SqlWorkflowPersistenceService handles this by keeping track of when its next persisted workflow will fire such an event.

Whenever a workflow instance's state is saved, the persistence service asks when its next timer will expire. The time at which this expiration will occur is stored in an internal object that is intelligent enough to determine, out of all the workflow instances it is managing, which workflow instance will expire next. At that time, the workflow instance is loaded from the persistence store, and the Delay activity is executed. All this happens automatically with no extra code needed from you.

Of course, if the host is not running when a timer expires, it cannot load the workflow and execute it. This is a common scenario if the host is a Windows Forms or web application, as opposed to a Windows service that is running continuously. In any event, SqlWorkflowPersistenceService covers this scenario as well.

The service uses its private loadingInterval field, which is of type TimeSpan, to determine how often to check the persistence store for expired timers. If expired timers are found, the workflow instances are loaded and executed as though the timers had just expired. This check is also performed when the persistence service is started.

Locking Workflow Instances

Workflow locking allows only one host to load a workflow instance at a time. This behavior is supported by SqlWorkflowPersistenceService out of the box. The service automatically sets the unlocked, ownerID, and ownedUntil columns in the persistence database.

When a workflow host pulls an instance's state from the data store because there is work to do, SqlWorkflowPersistenceService sets the aforementioned columns in the database, which in effect stakes a claim on the instance. After the work has completed and the instance is again unloaded from the runtime, ownerID and ownedUntil are set to null, and unlocked is set to 1. However, if a workflow host other then the locking owner tries to load the instance while these values are set, it gets an exception of type WorkflowOwnershipException.

Tracking Services

Tracking services enable you to identify the data related to workflow execution, capture and store that data in a durable medium, and then query that data for analysis at a later time. What kind of information can be tracked? Events and data related to workflows and activities.

The following sections cover some of the benefits of using workflow tracking, key concepts, and the out-of-the-box tracking functionality Windows Workflow Foundation provides. The base Workflow framework includes a SQL tracking service and a tracking service that monitors for terminated workflows and writes data to the Windows Event Log.

Monitoring Workflows

Tracking enables you to monitor currently running and completed workflows. This is a very powerful asset for workflow consumers. Imagine being able to know where all your workflows are in their progress at any given time. Further, imagine being able to say something like "Give me all 'create order' workflows that were created in the past 12 hours and are related to customer XYZ" or "Show me all workflows that are currently stuck in the 'waiting for confirmation' state."

Key Performance Indicators and Regulatory Compliance

The functionality provided by Windows Workflow Foundation to track important business data produced by executed workflow instances enables you to create and track Key Performance Indicators (KPIs). KPIs are metrics on which an organization's operations can be evaluated.

Generally, KPIs have two components: an actual value and a goal on which the value can be judged. For example, a company could have a KPI that represents its sales performance when compared with sales-plan data. Another example might be the percentage of help-desk tickets that are resolved within 24 hours, with a target of 75 percent.

Because you can extract business data from workflows using the tracking infrastructure, creating KPIs based on business processes becomes easier. In addition, workflow KPIs can be provided to end users in real time so that critical, time-sensitive decisions can be made.

In addition to producing KPIs, tracking workflows can assist public companies that are mandated to comply with such legislature as Sarbanes-Oxley. Having access to workflow- and processes-oriented software in such environments is extremely useful because the software itself documents its purpose by being declarative. This is an important part of regulatory compliance. Furthermore, tracking workflow execution can provide valuable information for auditors or for other compliance-related purposes.

Tracking Architecture

The following sections cover the architectural entities in Windows Workflow Foundation that support tracking. The major pillars of the tracking infrastructure are the following:

- ❑ The tracking runtime
- ❑ Tracking profiles
- ❑ Tracking channels
- ❑ Tracking services

The Tracking Runtime

The tracking runtime is actually built into the workflow runtime and is not an extensible part of the architecture. It is the liaison between workflow instances, which provide interesting events and data for tracking as well as the tracking services.

The runtime is responsible for delivering information from workflows to the appropriate services so that the correct information is captured. It does this by asking each tracking service (discussed later) what it is interested in. By doing this, the runtime can accurately and efficiently provide the correct data to the correct parties.

Tracking Profiles

Tracking profiles define what is interesting related to workflow execution. Items that can be tracked include workflow events, activity events and data, and user events and data. A tracking profile is completely customizable so that you can say that you are interested only in workflow events or in a specific subset of events.

There are a few classes relating to tracking profiles in the Windows Workflow Foundation API with which you should be familiar. The `System.Workflow.Runtime.Tracking.TrackingProfile` class is the container for all the rules that define the events and data that will be tracked during execution. The `TrackingProfile` class has a property called `ActivityTrackPoints`, which is a collection that holds `ActivityTrackPoint` classes.

In its `MatchingLocations` property, the `ActivityTrackPoint` class holds `ActivityTrackingLocation` classes, which define the types of activities that should be tracked.

You specify activities of interest in the `ActivityTrackingLocation` class constructor, which takes a `Type` instance. You can specify activities as low or high in the inheritance chain, as desired. For example, you might be interested in only the events that fire on custom-developed activities. Conversely, you could pass a `Type` instance representing the base `Activity` class so that every activity in a workflow is tracked. However, that happens only if the `MatchDerivedTypes` property is set to `true`. This property indicates whether classes that inherit from the `Type` specified in the constructor are tracked as well.

The `ActivityTrackingLocation` class has a property called `ExecutionStatusEvents`, which is a collection that holds values from the `ActivityExecutionStatus` enumeration. The values in this enumeration represent events that could occur on a given activity. Only the events added to the `ExecutionStatusEvents` collection are tracked. The following values are valid:

- ❑   Initialized
- ❑   Executing
- ❑   Canceling
- ❑   Closed
- ❑   Compensating
- ❑   Faulting

After you configure the `ActivityTrackingLocation` instance, you need to add it to the `ActivityTrackPoint` instance using its `MatchingLocation` property. At this point, you can add the `ActivityTrackPoint` instance to `TrackingProfile` in its `ActivityTrackPoints` property.

Similar to the `ActivityTrackPoint` and `ActivityTrackingLocation` classes, the `WorkflowTrackPoint` and `WorkflowTrackingLocation` classes support workflow-level tracking. The way these workflow tracking classes interact with one another and with the `TrackingProfile` class is virtually identical to their activity counterparts.

The `TrackingWorkflowEvent` enumeration provides the events that can be tracked for workflows. These values are added to a `WorkflowTrackingLocation` class in its `Events` property. The following event values are valid:

- Created
- Completed
- Idle
- Suspended
- Resumed
- Persisted
- Unloaded
- Loaded
- Exception
- Terminated
- Aborted
- Changed
- Started

Because of the way the tracking runtime handles profile caching, a versioning scheme is used so that newer profiles can be differentiated from their older counterparts. The `Version` property of `TrackingProfile` lets the runtime know that there have been changes to the profile and that it should be reloaded and used by the tracking service. This property is of type `System.Version`.

You have a couple of options for defining tracking profiles in your applications. The first method is to define profiles programmatically by using the `TrackingProfile` class. To do this, you use .NET code and the classes introduced previously, such as `WorkflowTrackPoint` and `ActivityTrackPoint`. The following is an example of creating a simplistic tracking profile using C#. This profile is interested in all activity events and all workflow events.

```
public static TrackingProfile GetTrackingProfile()
{
    // create a new profile and give it a version
    TrackingProfile profile = new TrackingProfile();
    profile.Version = new Version(1, 0, 0, 0);

    ActivityTrackPoint activityTrackPoint = new ActivityTrackPoint();
    ActivityTrackingLocation activityTrackingLocation =
        new ActivityTrackingLocation(typeof(Activity));

    // setting this value to true will match all classes that are in
    // the Activity class' inheritance tree
    activityTrackingLocation.MatchDerivedTypes = true;

    // add all of the activity execution status as something we are interested in
    foreach (ActivityExecutionStatus aes in
```

```
            Enum.GetValues(typeof(ActivityExecutionStatus)))
    {
        activityTrackingLocation.ExecutionStatusEvents.Add(aes);
    }

    activityTrackPoint.MatchingLocations.Add(activityTrackingLocation);
    profile.ActivityTrackPoints.Add(activityTrackPoint);

    WorkflowTrackPoint workflowTrackPoint = new WorkflowTrackPoint();
    WorkflowTrackingLocation workflowTrackingLocation =
        new WorkflowTrackingLocation();

    // add all of the tracking workflow events as something we are interested in
    foreach (TrackingWorkflowEvent twe in
        Enum.GetValues(typeof(TrackingWorkflowEvent)))
    {
        workflowTrackingLocation.Events.Add(twe);
    }

    workflowTrackPoint.MatchingLocation = workflowTrackingLocation;
    profile.WorkflowTrackPoints.Add(workflowTrackPoint);

    return profile;
}
```

This code creates a new `TrackingProfile` instance and immediately assigns a new version. The version number is hard-coded here, but this should obviously be more dynamic in a real-world application. Next, an `ActivityTrackPoint` instance is created that matches all activities. It does this because the `MatchDerivedTypes` property is set to `true`. In addition, every possible activity execution status is tracked due to the loop that iterates through the `ActivityExecutionStatus` enumeration. Finally, a workflow tracking point is created and added to the profile using a method that is similar to adding the activity tracking point. Again, each possible workflow event type is tracked in this example.

The following XML represents the same tracking profile as the one defined in the preceding code. Notice that the events the profile is interested in are the same events that were added using the enumeration loops in the code version. Defining tracking profiles in an XML format allows a more dynamic configuration scheme than does defining profiles in code. The XML can be swapped out very easily without your having to recompile or redistribute assemblies.

```xml
<TrackingProfile
    xmlns="http://schemas.microsoft.com/winfx/2006/workflow/trackingprofile"
    version="1.0.0.0">
    <TrackPoints>
        <WorkflowTrackPoint>
            <MatchingLocation>
                <WorkflowTrackingLocation>
                    <TrackingWorkflowEvents>
                        <TrackingWorkflowEvent>Created</TrackingWorkflowEvent>
                        <TrackingWorkflowEvent>Completed</TrackingWorkflowEvent>
                        <TrackingWorkflowEvent>Idle</TrackingWorkflowEvent>
                        <TrackingWorkflowEvent>Suspended</TrackingWorkflowEvent>
                        <TrackingWorkflowEvent>Resumed</TrackingWorkflowEvent>
                        <TrackingWorkflowEvent>Persisted</TrackingWorkflowEvent>
```

```
                    <TrackingWorkflowEvent>Unloaded</TrackingWorkflowEvent>
                    <TrackingWorkflowEvent>Loaded</TrackingWorkflowEvent>
                    <TrackingWorkflowEvent>Exception</TrackingWorkflowEvent>
                    <TrackingWorkflowEvent>Terminated</TrackingWorkflowEvent>
                    <TrackingWorkflowEvent>Aborted</TrackingWorkflowEvent>
                    <TrackingWorkflowEvent>Changed</TrackingWorkflowEvent>
                    <TrackingWorkflowEvent>Started</TrackingWorkflowEvent>
                </TrackingWorkflowEvents>
            </WorkflowTrackingLocation>
        </MatchingLocation>
    </WorkflowTrackPoint>
    <ActivityTrackPoint>
        <MatchingLocations>
            <ActivityTrackingLocation>
                <Activity>
                    <Type>
                    System.Workflow.ComponentModel.Activity,
                    System.Workflow.ComponentModel, Version=3.0.0.0,
                    Culture=neutral, PublicKeyToken=31bf3856ad364e35
                    </Type>
                    <MatchDerivedTypes>true</MatchDerivedTypes>
                </Activity>
                <ExecutionStatusEvents>
                    <ExecutionStatus>Initialized</ExecutionStatus>
                    <ExecutionStatus>Executing</ExecutionStatus>
                    <ExecutionStatus>Canceling</ExecutionStatus>
                    <ExecutionStatus>Closed</ExecutionStatus>
                    <ExecutionStatus>Compensating</ExecutionStatus>
                    <ExecutionStatus>Faulting</ExecutionStatus>
                </ExecutionStatusEvents>
            </ActivityTrackingLocation>
        </MatchingLocations>
    </ActivityTrackPoint>
    </TrackPoints>
</TrackingProfile>
```

In addition, you can serialize the tracking profiles created in code to XML by using the `TrackingProfile Serializer` class. The following is an example of how to do this by using a `StringWriter` instance:

```
// create an instance of the profile serializer
TrackingProfileSerializer serializer = new TrackingProfileSerializer();

// create the string writer
StringWriter sw = new StringWriter(new StringBuilder(),
   CultureInfo.InvariantCulture);

serializer.Serialize(sw, profile);
```

The code here simply creates a new instance of `TrackingProfileSerializer` and `StringWriter`, which work together to serialize the profile object to a string. After you serialize the profile to a string, you can save it to a file or use it in some other way. For example, you could call `sw.ToString()` and store the resulting value wherever you please.

Tracking Channels

Tracking channels inherit from the `System.Workflow.Runtime.Tracking.TrackingChannel` class. These entities do the actual persistence of tracking data when needed. Therefore, the tracking channels know how to communicate with a specified tracking store. For example, the `SqlTrackingService` (discussed in more detail in the next section) uses a class called `SqlTrackingChannel` that is responsible for storing tracking data in a SQL Server database. (Don't go looking for that class in the documentation — it is a private nested class inside `SqlTrackingService`.) There can be one channel per tracking service per workflow instance, and tracking channels are single threaded.

Tracking Services

Tracking services inherit from the `System.Workflow.Runtime.Tracking.TrackingService` class and provide the profiles and channels to the runtime. Tracking service instances are added to the workflow runtime in the host, just as with any other runtime service type.

Tracking services can optionally implement the `IProfileNotification` interface, which represents the ability to check tracking profiles for changes or removal. This interface exposes two public events: `ProfileRemoved` and `ProfileUpdated`. The tracking service that implements this interface should then provide behavior that checks the tracking profiles used for the service and raises one of these two events when appropriate. For an example, the `SqlTrackingService` implements this interface and uses a value passed to its constructor to determine how often to check for profile changes. Every time that interval passes, the SQL tracking service checks its profile table for changes and raises the relevant event.

Bringing It Together

All these entities come together to allow a cohesive tracking infrastructure. Figure 7-1 shows the interactions between tracking entities. The runtime sits between workflow instances and the tracking services. The runtime interacts with the services to get tracking profiles that are relevant for any given workflow instance. It says something like, "I am a workflow of type X; provide me with all profiles that I am interested in based on who I am." The runtime can contain any number of tracking services. So you could have one tracking service writing a specific type of information to one data store and another doing something completely different.

Workflow instances provide the tracking runtime with events and data, which is then filtered and sent to the appropriate tracking channels. The channels are responsible for writing that information to a medium. This medium can be *anything,* including a database, a file, XML, the console window, the Event Log, and so on.

After data is written to a durable store, you can review it with software that uses the workflow tracking query entities. You can perform searches for specific workflow types, instances, or workflows that meet specific criteria based on data values in activities. However, you need to implement this querying behavior specifically for each tracking store. There is no base infrastructure to support querying.

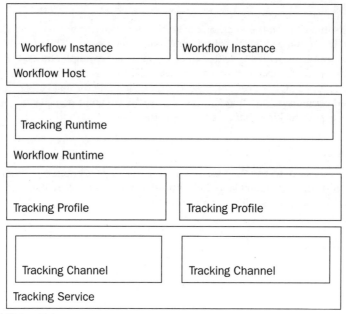

Figure 7-1

Tracking User Data

In addition to tracking activity and workflow events predefined in the workflow API, you can specify specific points in code at which data should be tracked—or, more accurately, *could* be tracked. This means that you can indicate that particular pieces of data at particular points of execution might be interesting enough to track. However, the relevant tracking profile must specify that the same data is interesting for it to get tracked. These points in code and the data are referred to as *user track points.*

The following is an example of modifying a tracking profile using C# to watch for a piece of data called FirstName with a value of Todd. This condition is specified by adding an ActivityTrackingCondition instance to the Conditions property of the UserTrackingLocation class. In addition, the ArgumentType property specifies the type of the data that will be tracked. Finally, the UserTrackingLocation instance is added to the UserTrackPoint class in its MatchingLocations collection.

```
UserTrackPoint userTrackPoint = new UserTrackPoint();

WorkflowDataTrackingExtract extract =
    new WorkflowDataTrackingExtract("MyWorkflow.myTestString");
extract.Annotations.Add("My annotation...");
userTrackPoint.Extracts.Add(extract);

UserTrackingLocation userTrackingLocation = new UserTrackingLocation();
userTrackingLocation.ActivityType = typeof(MyActivity);
userTrackingLocation.Conditions.Add(
    new ActivityTrackingCondition("FirstName", "Todd"));
```

```
        userTrackingLocation.ArgumentType = typeof(string);

        userTrackPoint.MatchingLocations.Add(userTrackingLocation);

        profile.UserTrackPoints.Add(userTrackPoint);
```

Notice that an instance of the `WorkflowDataTrackingExtract` class is added to the `UserTrackPoint`
`.Extracts` collection. This specifies the workflow members that are to be extracted and then tracked when
a user track point is matched. In the example, the code specifies that a member called `myTestString` on
the `MyWorkflow` class should be tracked.

In addition to extracting workflow members and storing their values, you can save annotations that
go along with these values by using the `WorkflowDataTrackingExtract.Annotations` property.
Annotations are strings that describe the extracted data and can be used to provide greater context when
viewing tracked data.

Now that you know what user track points are and how they are tracked, you need to define the user
track points. You do this by calling the `Activity.TrackData` or `ActivityExecutionContext`
`.TrackData` method. Both of these methods have two overloads: one that takes an object representing
user data and another that takes a user data object as well as a string representing the data's identifier key.

The following is a simple example of forcing the tracking infrastructure to track a piece of data that the
previous profile code would match. This code could be found in a workflow's code-beside class. Because
a workflow is an activity, it can access this method by using the `base` keyword.

```
        base.TrackData("FirstName", "Todd");
```

SqlTrackingService

The out-of-the-box service for tracking is `SqlTrackingService`, which uses SQL Server as its storage
medium. Like `SqlPersistenceService`, this service uses a defined database schema to perform its
functions. The SQL tracking service uses tables that store information related to events and data specified in tracking profiles. In addition, these tracking profiles are stored in the database and are associated
with a particular workflow type.

`SqlTrackingService` implements the `IProfileNotification` interface, which defines the functionality that informs the tracking runtime when a profile is removed or updated. `IProfileNotification`
exposes two events: `ProfileRemoved` and `ProfileUpdated`. The tracking runtime subscribes to these
events and takes the appropriate actions when either is raised.

The `ProfileRemoved` event passes a `ProfileRemovedEventArgs` object that contains a reference to the
type of workflow that had its profile removed. The `ProfileUpdated` event passes a `ProfileUpdated`
`EventArgs` object, which then passes a reference to the workflow type in question as well as a reference
to the tracking profile that it should now be using.

The `SqlTrackingService` uses an internal class, `SqlTrackingChannel`, as its channel for writing to
the backing SQL database. Because this class implements `IPendingWork`, workflow instances and the
tracking database can be kept in sync much better than if transactional behavior were not used.
However, the transactional behavior is not required. The `SqlTrackingService` has a property called
`IsTransactional`, which is in turn passed to the `SqlTrackingChannel` class. Then whenever some

data needs to be written to the database, the transactional flag is inspected, and if it is set to `true`, a work item is added to the batch for later execution. If the flag is set to `false`, the database write happens immediately.

Preparing SqlTrackingService

Before using `SqlTrackingService` in your workflow software, you have to set up and configure the database. As with `SqlWorkflowPersistenceService`, the first step is manually creating the tracking database by using the CREATE DATABASE T-SQL command, like this:

```
CREATE DATABASE WorkflowPersistence
```

Next, you must add the tables and stored procedures to the newly created database by running the Tracking_Schema.sql and Tracking_Logic.sql scripts, which are located in C:\<WINDOWS DIR>\ Microsoft.NET\Framework\v3.0\Windows Workflow Foundation\SQL\<LANGUAGE DIR>. These scripts create the database objects. Table 7-3 lists the tables that are created to support SQL tracking.

Table 7-3: SQL Tracking Tables

Table	Description
Activity	Records in this table represent activities that make up workflow definitions. So the table contains things like `myCodeActivity` rather than `CodeActivity`.
ActivityExecutionStatus	Holds possible values for an activity's execution status.
ActivityExecution StatusEvent	Stores data related to the execution of activities in workflow instances.
ActivityInstance	Represents a particular activity instance in a workflow instance.
AddedActivity	Stores information about activities added to a running workflow instance using dynamic update. (Dynamic update is covered in Chapter 11.)
DefaultTrackingProfile	Holds the default tracking profile for all workflow instances that have no profile specified.
EventAnnotation	Holds event annotations that were specified in code.
RemovedActivity	Stores information about activities removed from a running workflow instance using dynamic update. (Dynamic update is covered in Chapter 11.)
TrackingDataItem	Holds data values that are extracted from workflow activity instances.
TrackingDataItem Annotation	Holds annotations that were specified in code.
TrackingPartitionInterval	Holds a single row, which specifies the interval at which the workflow tracking data will be partitioned. The default is m, for *monthly.*
TrackingPartition SetName	Stores data surrounding the partitioned tables that are created and managed by the tracking runtime.

Table	Description
TrackingProfile	Stores tracking profiles related to workflow records stored in the Workflow table in their XML form.
TrackingProfileInstance	Data in this table represents an instance of a tracking profile in XML form.
TrackingWorkflowEvent	Holds possible values for workflow events, including `Completed`, `Idle`, and `Aborted`.
Type	Stores metadata about types that have been tracked, including types representing activities and workflows.
UserEvent	Represents user events captured during runtime about a workflow instance.
Workflow	The first time a particular version of a workflow is executed and tracked, its definition is stored here.
WorkflowInstance	When events and data related to workflow instances are tracked, they tie back to a record in this table. Records are identified by the same workflow instance IDs as in the code.
WorkflowInstanceEvent	Holds data related to workflow instance events.

After creating the database objects, using the SQL tracking service in your workflows is extremely simple. All you need to do is create an instance of the service class and add it to the runtime. The following is an example of what this might look like:

```
WorkflowRuntime workflowRuntime = new WorkflowRuntime();

SqlTrackingService trackingService = new SqlTrackingService(
    "Initial Catalog=WorkflowTracking;" +
    "Data Source=localhost;Integrated Security=SSPI;");
trackingService.IsTransactional = false;

workflowRuntime.AddService(trackingService);
```

A new instance of the `SqlTrackingService` class is created by using a constructor that takes a string representing the tracking database's connection string. In addition, the `IsTransactional` property of the service object is set to `false`, indicating that tracking data should be written to the database as events occur. Finally, the service instance is added to the `workflowRuntime` object using its `AddService` method.

Profiles and the SqlTrackingService

As noted in Table 7-3, tracking profiles used with `SqlTrackingService` are stored in the `Tracking Profile` table. The `SqlTrackingService` infrastructure provides a default profile, which is stored in the `DefaultTrackingProfile` table.

To create a new tracking profile and link it to a particular workflow type, you need to call the stored `UpdateTrackingProfile` procedure that was created during the initial setup of the tracking database. The following code is an example of how to do this:

```
private void CreateNewSqlTrackingProfile(TrackingProfile profile, Version version)
{
    // create the necessary objects to serialize the profile to a string
    TrackingProfileSerializer tpf = new TrackingProfileSerializer();
    StringBuilder sb = new StringBuilder();
    StringWriter stringWriter = new StringWriter(sb);
    tpf.Serialize(stringWriter, profile);

    Type workflowType = typeof(MyWorkflow);

    // create the database objects
    SqlConnection con = new SqlConnection(CONNECTION_STRING);
    SqlCommand com = new SqlCommand("UpdateTrackingProfile", con);
    com.CommandType = CommandType.StoredProcedure;

    // add required parameters to the SQL command
    com.Parameters.AddWithValue("@TypeFullName", workflowType.ToString());

    com.Parameters.AddWithValue("@AssemblyFullName",
        workflowType.Assembly.FullName);

    com.Parameters.AddWithValue("@Version", version.ToString());

    com.Parameters.AddWithValue("@TrackingProfileXml", stringWriter.ToString());

    try
    {
        // create the new profile in the database
        con.Open();
        com.ExecuteNonQuery();
    }
    finally
    {
        con.Close();
    }
}
```

The `CreateNewSqlTrackingProfile` method is passed not only a new `TrackingProfile` instance, but also a `Version` object. This allows tracking profiles in the `TrackingProfile` table to be versioned per workflow type. This code accesses the stored procedure by using the tracking SQL script included in Windows Workflow Foundation, `UpdateTrackingProfile`. This stored procedure takes parameters that identify the profile you are updating as well as the new profile definition in the `@TrackingProfileXml` parameter.

Querying SqlTrackingService

One of the really useful features of the SQL tracking infrastructure is its ability to query for workflows that have been tracked. There are several attributes you can use to specify which workflow instances you want to see, including the type of workflow, its status, and even specific values of activity properties.

Classes that participate in the querying process include SqlTrackingQuery, SqlTrackingQueryOptions, and TrackingDataItemValue.

SqlTrackingQueryOptions provides properties that enable you to filter the query results. You use the StatusMinDateTime and StatusMaxDateTime properties to specify the time window in which workflow instances were started. The WorkflowType property takes a reference to a Type instance representing a specific workflow. The WorkflowStatus property takes a value from the WorkflowStatus enumeration. Its values include Running, Completed, Suspended, Terminated, and Created. Both the WorkflowType and WorkflowStatus properties are nullable. If either of these properties is not set or set to null, that property is not used to filter the returned workflow instances.

The following code uses a SQL tracking query to search the workflow tracking database for helpdesk workflows that are considered *old* (a workflow that started more than two days ago and that is still running):

```csharp
private static void FindOldTickets(string user)
{
    SqlTrackingQuery query = new SqlTrackingQuery(CONNECTION_STRING);
    SqlTrackingQueryOptions queryOptions = new SqlTrackingQueryOptions();

    // filter workflow types to the HelpdeskWorkflow
    queryOptions.WorkflowType = typeof(MyWorkflow);

    // only get running workflows
    queryOptions.WorkflowStatus = WorkflowStatus.Running;

    // look for workflows which were started more than two days ago
    queryOptions.StatusMaxDateTime = DateTime.Now.AddDays(-2);

    // if a user was provided; use it as a filter
    if (user != null)
    {
        TrackingDataItemValue dataItemValue = new TrackingDataItemValue();
        dataItemValue.QualifiedName = "CreateTicket";
        dataItemValue.FieldName = "AssignedEmployee";
        dataItemValue.DataValue = user;
    }

    // add the criteria to the query options
    queryOptions.TrackingDataItems.Add(dataItemValue);

    // perform the query
    IList<SqlTrackingWorkflowInstance> matches = query.GetWorkflows(queryOptions);

    Console.WriteLine("Found " + matches.Count + " matching workflows.");
    foreach (SqlTrackingWorkflowInstance instance in matches)
    {
        Console.WriteLine("   Workflow Instance: " +
            instance.WorkflowInstanceId.ToString());
    }
}
```

There are two objects doing most of the work in this example. First, the `SqlTrackingQueryOptions` instance uses its `StatusMaxDateTime` property to specify that workflow instances older than two days should be retrieved. Next, the `TrackingDataItemValue` instance is configured to look for activities called `CreateTicket` that have their `AssignedEmployee` property set to the user string passed to this method. Finally, the `SqlTrackingQuery.GetWorkflows` method is called and returns a list of workflows that match the specified criteria.

Data Maintenance

Because workflow tracking can cause quite a bit of data to be written your SQL Server database, especially if you specify verbose tracking options, the SQL tracking service offers data maintenance capabilities. When you set the `PartitionOnCompletion` property of the tracking service instance, the tracking tables can be partitioned according to a specified time period.

The partition interval is dictated by a value in the `TrackingPartitionInterval` table in the tracking database. It has only one column, called `Interval`, and the value you set in this column specifies the partitioning behavior. For example, if you set the `Interval` column to `m`, the tracking service will create tables that are separated by month. Other valid values are `d` (for daily partitions) and `y` (for yearly partitions). You can set this value manually with a SQL script or through code, using the `SetPartitionInterval` stored procedure in the tracking database. This stored procedure takes one parameter, `@Interval`, which expects one of the interval codes (`m`, `d`, or `y`).

Tables are automatically created, along with new partition sets, when necessary. This happens when a new record is added to the `TrackingPartitionSetName` table. These records point to the separate partitioned tables and contain information such as when the partition was created and the last date that the partition should contain.

The previous paragraphs discuss the scenario in which partitioning occurs in real time as the application hosting the tracking service executes. This may not be optimal if you want more control over when the partitioning occurs. The SQL tracking database offers the `PartitionWorkflowInstance` stored procedure, which performs the same partitioning as previously mentioned, on demand. For example, you could set up a SQL Server job that runs the partitioning stored procedure nightly.

The Workflow Monitor

The Workflow Monitor sample application that ships with the Windows Workflow Foundation SDK connects to a SQL Server tracking database and enables you to query for and view executed workflow instances and, even better, workflows that are currently executing. Figure 7-2 shows this application in action.

The first thing that probably catches your eye is the workflow designer on the right side of the screen. It is obvious that this is a graphical representation of a workflow definition. However, it also represents the execution path of a workflow instance. The check marks on each activity represent a successful execution of the attached activity. In addition, they provide visual indicators as to which activities were executed and which were not. For instance, the figure shows a workflow instance of type `MyWorkflow` that has an IfElse activity. In this example, it was the left path, `isLargeValue`, that was executed.

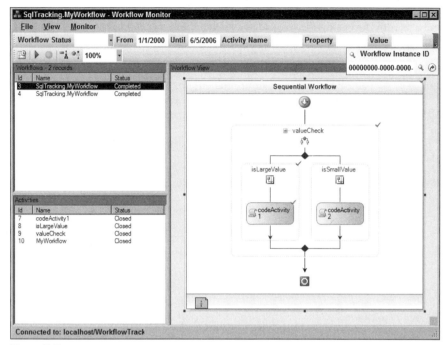

Figure 7-2

The top-right window in the Workflow Monitor shows workflow instances that have executed or are currently executing. The two workflows represent all of the instances that have been tracked in the database. However, take a look at the Workflow Status toolbar below the main menu. This gives you options for searching tracked workflow instances. Search criteria can include workflow status, a date range, and specific data values of activity properties. You can also use a workflow instance ID to search for a specific workflow instance. Any workflow instances matching the search criteria appear in the Workflows area on the left.

The bottom-left area of the application, the Activities window, shows the activities that were executed in the currently selected workflow instance. The activities that did not execute given the instance's path are not listed. In this example, isSmallValue and codeActivity2 were not executed and, therefore, are not shown in the Activities window.

This application is a simple but extremely compelling example of the power of Windows Workflow Foundation. Developed by using the platform's out-of-the-box capabilities, this application provides a great deal of insight into workflow execution. Imagine the possibilities when this idea is tailored to a specific organization and its business needs.

The TerminationTrackingService Application

TerminationTrackingService is another sample application that comes with the SDK. It enables the user to automatically log workflow instance terminations to the Windows Event Log. This gives the operations folks a simple method with which to quickly start troubleshooting workflow issues.

By default, `TerminationTrackingService` attempts to write to the event source `WinWF` unless another event source is provided using the constructor overload that takes a `NameValueCollection` instance. You can specify an alternative event source by adding a value with the key `EventSource`.

The following code shows an example of how to use `TerminationTrackingService`. By now, a lot of this code should look familiar. However, notice the `EnsureEventLog` method and its call from the `Main` method. This method uses the `System.Diagnostics.EventLog` class to make sure that a desired event log and event source exist. After that, an instance of `TerminationTrackingService` is created and added to the workflow runtime.

```
public static void Main(string[] args)
{
    EnsureEventLog("WinWF", "Workflow Log");

    WorkflowRuntime workflowRuntime = new WorkflowRuntime();

    TerminationTrackingService terminationService =
        new TerminationTrackingService();
    workflowRuntime.AddService(terminationService);

    WorkflowInstance instance =
        workflowRuntime.CreateWorkflow(typeof(MyWorkflow));
    instance.Start();
}

private static void EnsureEventLog(string eventSource, string eventLog)
{
    if (!EventLog.SourceExists(eventSource))
    {
        EventLog.CreateEventSource(eventSource, eventLog);
    }
}
```

If `MyWorkflow` is terminated either through the Terminate activity or through an unhandled exception, data describing this occurrence is written to the `Workflow Log` event log with the event source `WinWF`.

Figure 7-3 shows an example of an event written because of an exception that was manually thrown from inside a workflow.

This tracking service works by supplying the runtime with a tracking profile that is specifically interested in the event `TrackingWorkflowEvent.Terminated`. In addition, `TerminationTrackingService` gets a tracking channel that knows how to write the formatted data to the event log. This service is a simple but effective example of how workflow tracking can provide valuable information about workflow execution.

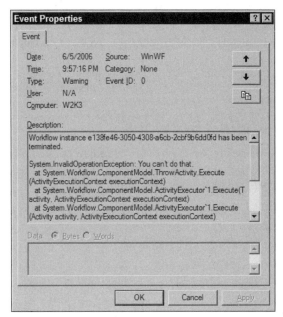

Figure 7-3

The Workflow Loader Service

The abstract `WorkflowLoaderService` class serves as the base class for services that load and create new instances of workflows. In most cases, the out-of-the-box behavior that is provided will suffice, but this extensibility point enables you to take essentially any input and create a workflow out of it. All that matters is that the custom class code can take the input and provide an activity tree.

Like the transaction and scheduler services, workflow loader services have a default type. `Default WorkflowLoaderService` is added automatically to the runtime if no other loader service is specified with the `AddService` method of `WorkflowRuntime`.

The Data Exchange Service

There isn't a lot more to cover related to the `ExternalDataExchangeService` that wasn't already covered in Chapter 5. Basically, this runtime service acts as a container for added local communication service instances. `ExternalDataExchangeService` itself is added to the workflow runtime through its `AddService` method, as with any other runtime service.

See Chapter 5 for an extensive discussion of the data exchange service and local communication services.

Developing Runtime Services

By now, the fact that Windows Workflow Foundation is extremely extensible should be prevalent in your mind. The runtime services architecture is no exception to this rule. Of course, there may be times when the functionality provided out of the box does not meet the needs of a given project or organization. In such situations, you are encouraged to extend the base infrastructure.

Developing Scheduling Services

You can develop custom scheduling services to allow workflows to start based on logic that is not provided in `DefaultWorkflowSchedulerService` or `ManualWorkflowSchedulerService`. The following is a skeleton class inheriting from `WorkflowSchedulerService`:

```
public class CustomWorkflowSchedulerService : WorkflowSchedulerService
{
    protected override void Cancel(Guid timerId)
    {
    }

    protected override void Schedule(WaitCallback callback,
        Guid workflowInstanceId, DateTime whenUtc, Guid timerId)
    {
    }

    protected override void Schedule(WaitCallback callback,
        Guid workflowInstanceId)
    {
    }
}
```

In this example, the `Cancel` method provides the logic to stop a workflow instance specified by a `Guid` value from running. The two `Schedule` overloads implement logic to queue the workflow instances for execution.

Developing Work Batch Services

Although the two work batch services included out of the box contain the functionality needed for most situations, the API allows you to develop your own custom batch service by inheriting from the `WorkflowCommitBatchService` class. The following code shows the skeleton of a custom batch service class. Basically, you just need to override the `CommitWorkBatch` service and implement your custom logic. You may want to do this if the transactional behaviors of the two other services do not meet your needs.

```
public class CustomWorkflowCommitWorkBatchService : WorkflowCommitWorkBatchService
{
    protected override void CommitWorkBatch(
        CommitWorkBatchCallback commitWorkBatchCallback)
    {
        // put your custom logic here     }
}
```

Developing Persistence Services

You can develop custom persistence services when the SQL Server persistence behavior is not adequate or appropriate for a particular project. For example, a disconnected application that is running on a user's laptop in the field may not have the option of running SQL Server. In such a scenario, persisting workflow state to the filesystem may be the next best thing. This section covers the necessary steps for building a custom persistence service. In addition, an example of what a file persistence service might look like is showcased.

The `WorkflowPersistenceService` abstract class defines several methods that must be implemented in a custom persistence service. The `SaveWorkflowInstanceState` and `LoadWorkflowInstance State` methods are responsible for keeping track of a workflow instance's state when it goes idle or is awakened from its sleep.

In addition, these two methods are responsible for implementing locking functionality. `LoadWorkflow InstanceState` needs to mark the persisted state as locked so that other workflow hosts are aware that the instance is spoken for at the moment. Furthermore, when this method attempts to load a workflow instance, it needs to check that same flag so that it doesn't step on anyone's toes.

`SaveWorkflowInstanceState` should respect the unlock parameter that is passed by the runtime. This variable is set to `true` after a workflow instance has already been persisted once before and subsequently loaded, and therefore locked.

`LoadCompletedContextActivity` and `SaveCompletedContextActivity` are responsible for managing the state of activity scopes related to compensation in transactions. The behavior implemented in these two methods is similar to the workflow instance methods that were just covered. The difference is the state that should be saved and subsequently restored represents a completed activity scope that needs to be restored if a transaction is rolled back.

The `UnloadOnIdle` method takes an `Activity` instance as its sole parameter and returns a Boolean value that indicates whether or not workflow instances should be unloaded and persisted when they run out of work and become idle. Depending on how you want your custom service to behave, you could either return a hard-coded `true` or `false`, or allow the host to set a variable indicating the unload functionality.

Finally, the `UnlockWorkflowInstanceState` method should implement behavior to unlock a currently locked workflow instance. To implement locking in a persistence service, you apply a flag or marker to a workflow instance's metadata. The unlock method simply removes or unsets this marker.

The following code is a sample implementation of what a file persistence service might look like. `FileWorkflowPersistenceService` writes workflow state data to a directory specified during the object's construction.

```
public class FileWorkflowPersistenceService
    : WorkflowPersistenceService, IPendingWork
{
    private bool unloadOnIdle;
    private string persistenceDirectory;

    public string PersistenceDirectory
```

```
    {
        get { return persistenceDirectory; }
    }

    public FileWorkflowPersistenceService(string persistenceDirectory,
        bool unloadOnIdle)
    {
        this.unloadOnIdle = unloadOnIdle;
        this.persistenceDirectory = persistenceDirectory;

        if (this.persistenceDirectory.EndsWith("\\"))
        {
            this.persistenceDirectory = this.persistenceDirectory.Substring(0,
                this.persistenceDirectory.Length - 1);
        }
    }

    protected override Activity LoadCompletedContextActivity(Guid scopeId,
        Activity outerActivity)
    {
        string fileName = this.GetScopeFilePath(scopeId);

        byte[] data = this.ReadData(fileName);

        this.EnsureDeleteInstanceFile(fileName);

        return WorkflowPersistenceService.RestoreFromDefaultSerializedForm(
            data, null);
    }

    protected override Activity LoadWorkflowInstanceState(Guid instanceId)
    {
        string fileName = GetInstanceFilePath(instanceId);

        if (Path.GetFileNameWithoutExtension(fileName).EndsWith("_lock"))
            throw new WorkflowOwnershipException(instanceId);

        byte[] data = this.ReadData(fileName);

        this.LockInstanceFile(fileName);

        return WorkflowPersistenceService.RestoreFromDefaultSerializedForm(
            data, null);
    }

    protected override void SaveCompletedContextActivity(Activity activity)
    {
        byte[] data =
            WorkflowPersistenceService.GetDefaultSerializedForm(activity);
        WorkflowStatus status =
            WorkflowPersistenceService.GetWorkflowStatus(activity);

        PendingWorkItem workItem = new PendingWorkItem(
            PendingWorkItem.WorkType.SaveCompletedContext,
            data,
```

```
            WorkflowEnvironment.WorkflowInstanceId,
            status);

        WorkflowEnvironment.WorkBatch.Add(this, workItem);
}

protected override void SaveWorkflowInstanceState(
    Activity rootActivity, bool unlock)
{
    byte[] data =
        WorkflowPersistenceService.GetDefaultSerializedForm(rootActivity);
    WorkflowStatus status =
        WorkflowPersistenceService.GetWorkflowStatus(rootActivity);

    PendingWorkItem workItem = new PendingWorkItem(
        PendingWorkItem.WorkType.SaveInstanceState,
        data,
        WorkflowEnvironment.WorkflowInstanceId,
        status);

    WorkflowEnvironment.WorkBatch.Add(this, workItem);
}

protected override bool UnloadOnIdle(Activity activity)
{
    return this.unloadOnIdle;
}

protected override void UnlockWorkflowInstanceState(Activity rootActivity)
{
    Guid id = WorkflowEnvironment.WorkflowInstanceId;
    this.EnsureUnlockInstanceFile(id);
}

// helper methods
private void WriteData(byte[] data, string filePath)
{
    try
    {
        FileStream stream = new FileStream(filePath, FileMode.OpenOrCreate);
        stream.Write(data, 0, data.Length);
        stream.Close();
    }
    catch(Exception ex)
    {
        throw new PersistenceException("Could not write the file.", ex);
    }
}

private byte[] ReadData(string filePath)
{
    try
    {
        FileInfo info = new FileInfo(filePath);
```

```
            byte[] data = new byte[info.Length];

            FileStream stream = new FileStream(filePath, FileMode.Open);
            stream.Read(data, 0, data.Length);
            stream.Close();

            return data;
        }
        catch(Exception ex)
        {
            throw new PersistenceException("Could not read the file.", ex);
        }
    }

    private string GetInstanceFilePath(Guid id)
    {
        string[] files = Directory.GetFiles(this.persistenceDirectory,
            id.ToString() + "*.wf");

        if (files.Length > 1)
            throw new PersistenceException("File confusion!");

        if (files.Length == 0)
            return null;

        return files[0];
    }

    private string GetScopeFilePath(Guid scopeId)
    {
        string fileName = this.persistenceDirectory +
            "\\scopes\\" + scopeId.ToString() + ".wf";

        if (!File.Exists(fileName))
            throw new PersistenceException("Could not file the scope file.");

        return fileName;
    }

    private void LockInstanceFile(string currentFileName)
    {
        try
        {
            string newFileName = Path.GetDirectoryName(currentFileName) +
                "\\" + Path.GetFileNameWithoutExtension(currentFileName) +
                "_lock.wf";

            File.Move(currentFileName, newFileName);
        }
        catch (Exception ex)
        {
            throw new PersistenceException("Could not rename file.", ex);
        }
    }
```

```
private void EnsureUnlockInstanceFile(Guid id)
{
    try
    {
        string oldFileName = this.persistenceDirectory +
            "\\" + id.ToString() + "_lock.wf";

        if(File.Exists(oldFileName))
        {
            string newFileName = id.ToString() + ".wf";
            File.Move(oldFileName, newFileName);
        }
    }
    catch (Exception ex)
    {
        throw new PersistenceException("Could not rename file.", ex);
    }
}

private void EnsureDeleteInstanceFile(string fileName)
{
    try
    {
        if (File.Exists(fileName))
        {
            File.Delete(fileName);
        }
    }
    catch(Exception ex)
    {
        throw new PersistenceException("Could not delete the file.", ex);
    }
}

// IPendingWork Members
public void Commit(Transaction transaction, ICollection items)
{
    foreach (PendingWorkItem item in items)
    {
        switch (item.WorkItemType)
        {
            case PendingWorkItem.WorkType.SaveInstanceState:
                string filePath = this.GetInstanceFilePath(item.Guid);

                if (item.InstanceStatus != WorkflowStatus.Completed &&
                    item.InstanceStatus != WorkflowStatus.Terminated)
                {
                    if (filePath == null)
                        filePath = this.persistenceDirectory + "\\" +
                            item.Guid.ToString() + ".wf";

                    this.WriteData(item.Data, filePath);
                }
                else
                {
```

```
                            this.EnsureDeleteInstanceFile(filePath);
                    }

                    break;

                case PendingWorkItem.WorkType.SaveCompletedContext:
                    this.WriteData(item.Data, this.persistenceDirectory +
                        "\\scopes\\" + item.Guid.ToString() + ".wf");
                    break;
            }

            this.EnsureUnlockInstanceFile(item.Guid);
        }
    }

    public void Complete(bool succeeded, System.Collections.ICollection items)
    {
        // do nothing...
    }

    public bool MustCommit(System.Collections.ICollection items)
    {
        return true;
    }
}
```

To ensure consistency in workflow instances, the persistence service implements the IPendingWork interface. This interface enables the code to queue chunks of work that will be performed at a time appropriate for maintaining a stable environment. The IPendingWork.Commit method is called when the queued work items are ready to be performed.

The service also supports instance locking. In this implementation, locking is indicated by renaming a workflow instance's file to include a lock suffix. This marker is checked whenever the service attempts to load an instance from the filesystem. If the service finds the lock flag, a WorkflowOwnership Exception is thrown. If the lock flag is not present and the workflow instance is successfully loaded, the service is responsible for adding the suffix so that other workflow hosts are not able to load the same instance. Finally, when the workflow instance is saved again and persisted, the lock flag should be removed.

The Commit method of the IPendingWork interface is passed a collection of objects that generally represent context related to the work to be done. For this example, a class was developed to hold the necessary information to perform the required persistence service tasks. The PendingWorkItem class is shown in the following code listing. The nested WorkType enumeration holds values that indicate what type of work should be performed in the IPendingWork.Commit method.

```
internal class PendingWorkItem
{
    private WorkType workItemType;
    private byte[] data;
    private Guid guid;
    private WorkflowStatus status;

    public WorkType WorkItemType
```

```
    {
        get { return this.workItemType; }
    }

    public byte[] Data
    {
        get { return this.data; }
    }

    public Guid Guid
    {
        get { return this.guid; }
    }

    public WorkflowStatus InstanceStatus
    {
        get { return status; }
        set { status = value; }
    }

    public PendingWorkItem(WorkType workItemType, byte[] data,
        Guid guid, WorkflowStatus status)
    {
        this.workItemType = workItemType;
        this.data = data;
        this.guid = guid;
        this.status = status;
    }

    public enum WorkType
    {
        SaveInstanceState,
        SaveCompletedContext
    }
}
```

Although this example shows a fairly interesting application of the persistence framework, several things could have been done to make it better. First, the current implementation does not clean up unused completed activity scopes after a workflow instance is completed or terminated. To add this functionality, a workflow instance ID needs to be tied to each activity scope so that these files can be deleted after they are no longer needed. You can accomplish this by prefixing each scope file name with the workflow instance ID to which it is associated.

Another potential enhancement for `FileWorkflowPersistenceService` would be to add code to load unloaded instances when child timers expire, just as the `SqlWorkflowPersistenceService` does. This code needs to check each workflow that is saved, get its next timer expiration, and then add the expiration to a list of other workflow instances' expirations. This list should be sorted so that the service fires an event to load the workflow instance with the next expiration.

There are probably other ways to make the `FileWorkflowPersistenceService` more functional and solid. However, this should be a good start to inspire a better rendition.

Developing Tracking Services

The ways in which organizations might want to capture information about the execution of their workflows are virtually limitless. So it's pretty exciting that the tracking infrastructure is so easily extensible. You could create tracking services to write XML to the filesystem or messages to an event log, or to call web services. Creating a new tracking service is relatively simple. The process involves creating two new classes that inherit from TrackingService and TrackingChannel.

The TrackingService class is what is actually added to the runtime with the AddService method and defines how profiles are used as well as how to access the TrackingChannel-associated class that knows how to track data. TrackingService has two overloads to the GetProfile method. The first receives a workflow instance ID and returns its corresponding profile. The second GetProfile overload receives a Type instance pointing to a workflow type as well as the version of the profile to get. A similar method, TryGetProfile, passes a profile back to the called method using an out parameter and returns a Boolean value to indicate whether the profile load was successful. Finally, inherited TrackingService classes must implement the GetTrackingChannel class, which returns the tracking channel to be used with the tracking service.

The TrackingChannel class is what does most of the work related to tracking itself. The Instance CompletedOrTerminated method is called when a workflow instance completes execution normally or is terminated. The implemented code is responsible for tracking this event. The meat of this class is the Send method, which receives a TrackingRecord object.

TrackingRecord is an abstract class; therefore, the instance passed to the Send method is actually one of three inherited classes: ActivityTrackingRecord, UserTrackingRecord, or WorkflowTracking Record. These classes contain useful information such as the date and time the event occurred, the type of object that caused the event to occur, and copies of the data captured by the tracking infrastructure.

The following is an example of a tracking service and corresponding channel that sends events by e-mail. Although tracking workflows using e-mail might not be entirely practical, situations where you want to watch for only workflow failures might be realistic.

```
public class EmailTrackingService : TrackingService
{
    // TrackingService methods
    protected override TrackingProfile GetProfile(Guid workflowInstanceId)
    {
        return this.GetDefaultProfile();
    }

    protected override TrackingProfile GetProfile(Type workflowType,
        Version profileVersionId)
    {
        return this.GetDefaultProfile();
    }

    protected override TrackingChannel GetTrackingChannel(
        TrackingParameters parameters)
    {
        return new EmailTrackingChannel("someone@here.com",
            "someoneelse@there.com",
            "smtp.here.com");
```

```
    }

    protected override bool TryGetProfile(Type workflowType,
        out TrackingProfile profile)
    {
        try
        {
            profile = this.GetDefaultProfile();
            return true;
        }
        catch
        {
            profile = null;
            return false;
        }
    }

    protected override bool TryReloadProfile(Type workflowType,
        Guid workflowInstanceId, out TrackingProfile profile)
    {
        // setting the output profile to null and returning false tells
        // the runtime that there is no new profile(s) to load
        profile = null;
        return false;
    }

    // Helper methods
    private TrackingProfile GetDefaultProfile()
    {
        // create a new profile and give it a version
        TrackingProfile profile = new TrackingProfile();
        profile.Version = new Version(1, 0, 0, 0);

        ActivityTrackPoint activityTrackPoint = new ActivityTrackPoint();
        ActivityTrackingLocation activityTrackingLocation =
            new ActivityTrackingLocation(typeof(Activity));

        // setting this value to true will match all classes that are in
        // the Activity class' inheritance tree
        activityTrackingLocation.MatchDerivedTypes = true;

        // add all of the activity execution status as
        // something we are interested in
        foreach (ActivityExecutionStatus aes in
            Enum.GetValues(typeof(ActivityExecutionStatus)))
        {
            activityTrackingLocation.ExecutionStatusEvents.Add(aes);
        }

        activityTrackPoint.MatchingLocations.Add(activityTrackingLocation);
        profile.ActivityTrackPoints.Add(activityTrackPoint);

        WorkflowTrackPoint workflowTrackPoint = new WorkflowTrackPoint();
        WorkflowTrackingLocation workflowTrackingLocation =
            new WorkflowTrackingLocation();
```

```
            // add all of the tracking workflow events
            // as something we are interested in
            foreach (TrackingWorkflowEvent twe in
                Enum.GetValues(typeof(TrackingWorkflowEvent)))
            {
                workflowTrackingLocation.Events.Add(twe);
            }

            workflowTrackPoint.MatchingLocation = workflowTrackingLocation;
            profile.WorkflowTrackPoints.Add(workflowTrackPoint);

            return profile;
        }
    }
```

The `EmailTrackingService` class inherits from `TrackingService` and contains logic to create a default profile that is interested in basically all activity and workflow events. The profile is defined in the `GetDefaultProfile` method, which says you are interested in everything related to activity and workflow events. Also notice that the `GetTrackingChannel` method creates and returns an instance of `EmailTrackingChannel`.

The following is the `EmailTrackingChannel` class, which inherits from `TrackingChannel`. As you can see in the `Send` method, there is logic to check for which type of record you are receiving. At that point, a specific private method is called to track the record in a custom manner. Each custom tracking method eventually calls the utility `SendEmail` method and passes along relevant data.

```
internal class EmailTrackingChannel : TrackingChannel
{
    private string from;
    private string to;
    private bool notifyOnCompletionOrTermination;

    private SmtpClient smtpClient;

    // TrackingChannel methods
    public EmailTrackingChannel(string from, string to, string smtpServer)
        : this(from, to, smtpServer, false)
    {
    }

    public EmailTrackingChannel(string from, string to, string smtpServer,
        bool notifyOnCompletionOrTermination)
    {
        this.from = from;
        this.to = to;
        this.notifyOnCompletionOrTermination = notifyOnCompletionOrTermination;

        smtpClient = new SmtpClient(smtpServer);
    }

    protected override void InstanceCompletedOrTerminated()
    {
        if (this.notifyOnCompletionOrTermination)
        {
```

```csharp
                this.SendEmail("Workflow Done",
                    "A workflow instance was completed or terminated.");
            }
        }

        protected override void Send(TrackingRecord record)
        {
            // check what kind of record we received
            if (record is WorkflowTrackingRecord)
            {
                SendWorkflowData((WorkflowTrackingRecord)record);
            }
            else if (record is ActivityTrackingRecord)
            {
                SendActivityData((ActivityTrackingRecord)record);
            }
            else if (record is UserTrackingRecord)
            {
                SendUserData((UserTrackingRecord)record);
            }
            else
            {
                // we don't know what it is...
            }
        }

        private void SendWorkflowData(WorkflowTrackingRecord workflowTrackingRecord)
        {
            SendEmail("Workflow event",
                workflowTrackingRecord.TrackingWorkflowEvent.ToString() +
                " happened at " + workflowTrackingRecord.EventDateTime.ToString());
        }

        private void SendActivityData(ActivityTrackingRecord activityTrackingRecord)
        {
            SendEmail("Activity event",
                activityTrackingRecord.ActivityType.FullName +
                " had execution status " +
                activityTrackingRecord.ExecutionStatus.ToString() +
                " at " + activityTrackingRecord.EventDateTime.ToString());
        }

        private void SendUserData(UserTrackingRecord userTrackingRecord)
        {
            SendEmail("User event",
                "The user data was: " + userTrackingRecord.UserData.ToString() +
                " at " + userTrackingRecord.EventDateTime.ToString());
        }

        // Helper methods
        private void SendEmail(string subject, string body)
        {
            this.smtpClient.Send(this.from, this.to, subject, body);
        }
    }
}
```

This overridden Send method of the class inspects the TrackingRecord parameter it receives and conditionally sends some information about the event by e-mail. The method that is called depends on whether the TrackingRecord instance is a WorkflowTrackingRecord, an ActivityTrackingRecord, or a UserTrackingRecord. Each utility method sends specific information about each record type.

Developing Workflow Loader Services

If the DefaultWorkflowLoaderService class functionality is not sufficient (perhaps because you are not using standard workflow definition markup or have your own workflow markup), you can create your own loader service. To do this, you inherit from the abstract WorkflowLoaderService class.

This class contains two overloaded methods that must be overridden in any inherited classes. The first overload of CreateInstance receives a Type reference of the class that represents a workflow definition. The second CreateInstance overload takes two XmlReader instances — the first representing the workflow definition and the second representing that workflow's rules.

To create a custom workflow loader class, you must effectively implement the behavior of both of these methods and return an Activity reference that represents the top level of the workflow activity tree — meaning the workflow itself. The following is a skeleton of what a custom workflow loader service looks like:

```
public class CustomWorkflowLoaderService : WorkflowLoaderService
{
    protected override Activity CreateInstance(XmlReader workflowDefinitionReader,
        XmlReader rulesReader)
    {
        Activity workflow = null;

        // parse the workflow definition
        ...

        // parse the workflow rules
        ...

        return workflow;
    }

    protected override Activity CreateInstance(Type workflowType)
    {
        Activity workflow = null;

        // use the type reference to create the activity tree
        ...

        return workflow;
    }
}
```

Developing Other Service Types

The runtime service types discussed so far are by no means the only types that can exist in the Windows Workflow Foundation runtime. You can develop and add any type of behavior that can interact with the runtime. This is why the `WorkflowRuntime.AddService` method takes an object. Services that fall outside the category of extended out-of-the-box services do not follow any particular architecture, so you can develop them to perform just about any task.

Although there are no required interfaces to implement or classes to inherit from, you can enhance runtime services by inheriting from the `System.Workflow.Runtime.Hosting.RuntimeService` class. This abstract class exposes the base behavior for services that can be started and stopped by the workflow runtime. You can implement initialization and cleanup code in the `OnStarted` and `OnStopped` methods. These methods are called when the `Started` and `Stopped` events are raised by the runtime, respectively. Finally, classes inheriting from `RuntimeService` can call the `RaiseServicesExceptionNotHandledEvent` method when there is an error that is not to be handled by the runtime service itself.

The following code is a skeleton of what a custom workflow runtime service class looks like:

```
public class CustomRuntimeService : WorkflowRuntimeService
{
    protected override void OnStarted()
    {
        // put some logic here for when the service starts

        base.OnStarted();
    }

    protected override void OnStopped()
    {
        // put some logic here for when the service stops

        base.OnStopped();
    }
}
```

Summary

Runtime services are distinct pieces of logic that run in the background of the workflow runtime and can provide behavior key to the workflow infrastructure or maintenance tasks.

Several service types included in the base API are provided as out-of-the-box services, including scheduling, work batch, persistence, tracking, workflow loader, and data exchange services. Several of these service types are so important to the functionality of the workflow runtime that there are default services that are used if no other services of that type are specified.

In addition, you can develop workflow runtime services to provide custom logic. This can occur by deriving from one of the base workflow service types in the API or by developing an entirely new service type from scratch.

8

Advanced Activity Development

The previous chapter introduces a lot of the core concepts related to Windows Workflow Foundation activities, such as key classes and the activity execution model. However, these topics just scratched the surface of the depth of activity concepts. This chapter introduces you to some of the more advanced activity themes, such as activity types, and takes a closer look at activity execution and communication.

This chapter covers the following topics:

❑   The activity execution model

❑   Activity execution contexts

❑   Iterative activities

❑   Event activities

The Activity Execution Model

The workflow runtime and the activity execution model are extremely interesting and deep topics in the world of Windows Workflow Foundation. Considerations had to be made when architecting this framework to ensure that each workflow tenet was appropriately implemented. For example, given the fact that workflow instances persisted to some durable medium at any given time, the state, including each activity's state, has to be persisted as well. Therefore, every time an activity executes, it does so within a special context that tracks information about the execution of that particular activity instance. This includes property data as well as status information related to the success of the activity's execution.

The advantage of this type of architecture is that it can act on an activity's previous execution, even if that activity executed months ago and the workflow instance has been persisted many times between then and now. This allows functionality such as compensation for an activity based on its state at one point in time if an error occurs and some logic needs to roll back previous actions. Imagine a scenario in which an activity initiates an order in a system. Perhaps an issue arises down the road, and the order needs to be canceled. The activity that created the order has access to its prior state, so it is potentially able to make a cancel order call while passing relevant information such as an order number.

The activity execution context comes into play for custom activity developers in two different instances. The first is related to custom composite activities where the parent needs to create new execution contexts for each child. In addition, if a custom activity is being developed that performs iteration, it needs to create a new execution context for the child activities each time they execute. The out-of-the-box While activity follows this rule by spawning a new context for each of its children during every loop iteration.

The goal of this chapter is to help you understand these concepts through further explanation and concrete examples.

The Activity Execution Context

The activity execution model is encapsulated in a class called `ActivityExecutionContext`. An instance of this class is passed to each method that needs access to an activity execution context, most notably the `Activity.Execute` method. The following code shows the metadata for this class:

```
namespace System.Workflow.ComponentModel
{
    public sealed class ActivityExecutionContext : IServiceProvider, IDisposable
    {
        public static readonly DependencyProperty CurrentExceptionProperty;

        public Activity Activity { get; }
        public Guid ContextGuid { get; }
        public ActivityExecutionContextManager ExecutionContextManager { get; }

        public void CancelActivity(Activity activity);
        public void CloseActivity();
        public void ExecuteActivity(Activity activity);
        public T GetService<T>();
        public object GetService(Type serviceType);
        public void TrackData(object userData);
        public void TrackData(string userDataKey, object userData);
    }
}
```

The `Activity` property provides access to the activity instance in the current execution context. Remember that every time an activity executes, a new instance is created. Therefore, an activity instance on a workflow definition is not the same as the `Activity` property of the `ActivityExecutionContext` class. The following code illustrates this concept:

```
if (MyWorkflow.Activities[0] == context.Activity)
{
    // this will never happen
}
```

The `ActivityExecutionContext` class also exposes a property that returns an instance of the `Activity ExecutionContextManager` class. Basically, this class enables you to create new execution contexts for an activity's children. You do this by calling the `CreateExecutionContext` method, which takes an activity instance from the workflow definition. In addition, the `ActivityExecutionContextManager` class allows you to flag an already-created execution context as completed. Because execution contexts can be persisted when a persistence service is present, you can use the `ActivityExecutionContextManager` class to obtain access to persisted, as well as nonpersisted, contexts. To obtain a reference to a persisted execution context, you must have access to its `ContextGuid`. (This class is covered again shortly in a development example.)

The `ActivityExecutionContext` class also exposes methods that control an activity's execution. `CloseActivity` causes the activity associated with the context to close. The `CancelActivity` and `ExecuteActivity` methods control child activities, which is why they take an `Activity` instance as a parameter.

Developing an Iterative Activity

To illustrate the concepts related to activity execution contexts, the following code shows a sample activity that behaves like the C# `foreach` construct. Activities that possess the properties of a loop are referred to as *iterative activities.* The `ForEachActivity` class has a property of type `IEnumerable`, which means that basically any .NET collection can be provided for iteration. This activity was modeled after the out-of-the-box While activity, and like the While activity, the sample implements the `IActivityEventListener <ActivityExecutionStatusChangedEventArgs>` interface. This provides the ability to listen for events raised on an activity. In this case, the activity is interested in listening for events on itself, specifically the `Closed` event.

```
public class ForEachActivity : CompositeActivity,
    IActivityEventListener<ActivityExecutionStatusChangedEventArgs>
{
    private IEnumerator enumerator = null;

    // *** Dependency properties removed for brevity ***

    protected override ActivityExecutionStatus Execute(
        ActivityExecutionContext context)
    {
        if (context == null)
            throw new ArgumentNullException("context");

        // perform the first "loop"
        if (this.Iterate(context))
        {
            // if there are no items in the collection, we're done
            return ActivityExecutionStatus.Executing;
        }
```

```
                // nothing to do, the activity is done
                return ActivityExecutionStatus.Closed;
        }

        private bool Iterate(ActivityExecutionContext context)
        {
            if (this.enumerator == null)
                this.enumerator = this.Collection.GetEnumerator();

            // make sure there is another item and there is a child activity
            if (!this.enumerator.MoveNext() || this.EnabledActivities.Count != 1)
                return false;

            // set the CurrentItem property
            this.CurrentItem = this.enumerator.Current;

            ActivityExecutionContextManager aecManager =
                context.ExecutionContextManager;

            // create a new context for the child activity
            ActivityExecutionContext newContext =
                aecManager.CreateExecutionContext(this.EnabledActivities[0]);

            // register for the child activity's Closed event
            newContext.Activity.RegisterForStatusChange(Activity.ClosedEvent, this);

            // execute the child activity
            newContext.ExecuteActivity(newContext.Activity);

            return true;
        }

        void IActivityEventListener<ActivityExecutionStatusChangedEventArgs>.OnEvent(
            object sender, ActivityExecutionStatusChangedEventArgs e)
        {
            if (e == null)
                throw new ArgumentNullException("e");

            if (sender == null)
                throw new ArgumentNullException("sender");

            // get the execution context of the child activity
            ActivityExecutionContext context = sender as ActivityExecutionContext;
            if (context == null)
            {
                throw new ArgumentException(
                    "sender should be an ActivityExecutionContext instance");
            }

            // unsubscribe from the Closed event
            e.Activity.UnregisterForStatusChange(Activity.ClosedEvent, this);
            ActivityExecutionContextManager aecManager =
                context.ExecutionContextManager;

            // complete the execution context
```

```
            aecManager.CompleteExecutionContext(
                aecManager.GetExecutionContext(e.Activity));

        // do the next "loop"
        if (!this.Iterate(context))
        {
            // no more loops, close the for each activity
            context.CloseActivity();
        }
    }
}
```

The overridden Execute method basically just calls an Iterate helper method that holds the looping logic. In reality, there isn't a loop to be found anywhere in this code. It is simulated by using the enumerator object, executing a lone child activity, and calling Iterate again after the child activity is closed. When the enumerator.MoveNext method no longer returns true, the ForEachActivity is closed.

In the Iterate method in this example, an ActivityExecutionContextManager instance is used to create a new execution context based on the ForEachActivity's child. The new context is then able to execute the child activity using its ExecuteActivity method. This pattern ensures that the child activity executes in its own separate context for every iteration. In the OnEvent method, which captures the Closed event, the execution context is completed with ActivityExecutionContextManager.

Figure 8-1 shows an example workflow that a ForEachActivity method called forEachDate. The first Code activity initializes a List<T> collection, which is bound to the ForEachActivity. The Code activity inside the loop then prints out information about the current item.

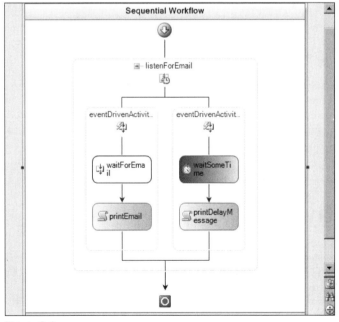

Figure 8-1

The following code represents the code-beside file for the workflow in Figure 8-1:

```
private void initCollection_ExecuteCode(object sender, EventArgs e)
{
    DateTime startDate = DateTime.Now;
    this.listOfDates.Add(startDate.AddHours(-5));
    this.listOfDates.Add(startDate.AddHours(-4));
    this.listOfDates.Add(startDate.AddHours(-3));
    this.listOfDates.Add(startDate.AddHours(-2));
    this.listOfDates.Add(startDate.AddHours(-1));
}

private void printInfo_ExecuteCode(object sender, EventArgs e)
{
    CodeActivity codeActivity = sender as CodeActivity;
    if (codeActivity != null)
    {
        ForEachActivity.ForEachActivity fea =
            codeActivity.Parent as ForEachActivity.ForEachActivity;

        if (fea != null)
        {
            Console.WriteLine("Current date: " +
                ((DateTime)fea.CurrentItem).Hour.ToString());
        }
    }
}
```

This workflow uses a collection of DateTime instances just to show that the activity can handle anything that implements IEnumerable. The printInfo event handler obtains a reference to the current item by first using the sender parameter to access the CodeActivity instance and then accessing its parent. The property of ForEachActivity's CurrentItem is of type object, so it needs to be cast as a DateTime before its Hour property can be accessed.

Although this is similar to how you develop other activity types, developing an iterative activity has its own set of considerations that must be addressed — the biggest of which is managing activity execution contexts. More specifically, the children of the iterative activity must be executed in their own execution contexts for each iteration so that each execution context can be persisted and treated separately for transactional purposes. The activity execution context is a great feature of Windows Workflow Foundation and really shows its benefits in iterative activities.

Event Activities

Previous chapters introduced the concept of event activities. Basically, event activities don't really do anything except hold the execution of a workflow until something happens. For example, the Delay activity doesn't do a bit of work aside from waiting a predetermined amount of time before allowing the next activity in the tree to execute. The same goes for the HandleExternalEvent activity, which blocks execution until the configured external event is raised. These event activities implement an interface called IEventActivity.

The IEventActivity Interface

`IEventActivity` is an interface that, when implemented by a custom activity, can be subscribed to by a listener. The metadata for the `IEventActivity` interface is shown in the following code:

```
namespace System.Workflow.Activities
{
    public interface IEventActivity
    {
        IComparable QueueName { get; }

        void Subscribe(ActivityExecutionContext parentContext,
            IActivityEventListener<QueueEventArgs> parentEventHandler);

        void Unsubscribe(ActivityExecutionContext parentContext,
            IActivityEventListener<QueueEventArgs> parentEventHandler);
    }
}

namespace System.Workflow.ComponentModel
{
    public interface IActivityEventListener<T> where T : System.EventArgs
    {
        void OnEvent(object sender, T e);
    }
}
```

The `Subscribe` and `Unsubscribe` events receive the same set of two parameters. The `parentContext` parameter is of type `ActivityExecutionContext` and holds a reference to the execution context of the activity that is subscribing an event of interest. The `parentEventHandler` parameter is of type `IActivityEventListener<QueueEventArgs>` and is shown the `IEventActivity` interface's metadata. This parameter holds a reference to the class that implements the `IActivityEventListener<QueueEventArgs>` interface and, therefore, has an `OnEvent` method.

The event handler is raised whenever the corresponding event is raised — more specifically, whenever data arrives in a workflow queue that has already been configured. Queues are discussed in the next section.

Workflow Queues

Workflow queues are at the heart of host-to-workflow communication. To ensure a consistent and robust communication mechanism, queues are used to facilitate the passing of data from the host to a workflow instance. However, data is never passed directly to a workflow instance, although it may appear that way in the code that performs such an operation. Rather, the workflow runtime acts as a mediator to make sure the communication takes place in an orderly fashion.

The `WorkflowQueue` class encapsulates the queue concept in Windows Workflow Foundation. The following code is a simple example of how to pass data from a workflow runtime host application to a workflow instance:

```
WorkflowInstance instance = workflowRuntime.GetWorkflow(instanceId);
string myData = "Hello from the outside";
instance.EnqueueItem("MyQueue", myData, null, null);
```

The EnqueueItem method of the WorkflowInstance class is responsible for passing data to a workflow. The first parameter is simply the name of the queue to which data is being passed. This queue must have been previously created; otherwise, an InvalidOperationException is thrown. Going back to workflow persistence for a moment, workflow queues created during runtime are persisted when unloading and are re-created during the hydration process.

The data passed in this example happens to be of type string. However, the second parameter is of type object, so anything can be passed as long as it is marked serializable. The final two parameters of the EnqueueItem method are related to work items for transactional execution and are an IPendingWork instance and object instance, respectively.

As shown in the following code, creating a queue and receiving data are almost as easy as sending data to an instance:

```
private void CreateQueue(Guid instanceId)
{
    WorkflowQueuingService queueingService =
        workflowRuntime.GetService<WorkflowQueuingService>();

    // create the queue
    WorkflowQueue queue = queueingService.CreateWorkflowQueue("MyQueue", true);

    // we want to be notified when a new piece of data becomes available
    queue.QueueItemAvailable += new EventHandler<QueueEventArgs>(itemAvailable)
}

private void itemAvailable(object sender, QueueEventArgs e)
{
    WorkflowQueuingService queueingService =
        workflowRuntime.GetService<WorkflowQueuingService>();

    // get the existing queue
    WorkflowQueue queue = queueingService.GetWorkflowQueue(e.QueueName);

    string message = (string)queue.Dequeue();
    Console.WriteLine("Message was: " + message);

    // unsubscribe from this event
    queue -= new EventHandler<QueueEventArgs>(itemAvailable);
    queueingService.DeleteWorkflowQueue(e.QueueName);
}
```

First, you can create a new queue by calling the WorkflowQueueingService.CreateWorkflowQueue method. The WorkflowQueueingService can be obtained from the workflow runtime and is added by default. Finally, by subscribing to the QueueItemAvailable event of the WorkflowQueue class, your code is notified whenever an item is added with the EnqueueItem method.

Finally, after the data from the queue is received and the queue is no longer needed, it should unsubscribe from the QueueItemAvailable event. You can then delete the queue by calling the Workflow QueueingService's DeleteWorkflowQueue method. Before deleting the workflow queue, make sure to retrieve any data by using the Dequeue method of WorkflowQueue.

Developing an Event Activity

To illustrate the development of an event activity, this section creates an example activity that monitors an inbox for new e-mail. This activity could then be used to block workflow execution while waiting for an e-mail and continuing when it is received. The interesting thing about developing activities that implement IEventActivity is that they need to be able to function as children of an EventDriven activity as well as when they are used by themselves. When an event activity is used in an EventDriven activity, which in turn is the child of another activity such as Listen or State, the EventDriven activity parent is responsible for subscribing to the event activity. Conversely, when an event activity is used in a standalone fashion, it needs to be able to subscribe to itself. The good news is that the code needed for both situations is not too complicated and enables you to reuse the methods implemented for the IEventActivity interface.

The Runtime Service

Before digging into the activity code itself, you need to develop a few other support classes for everything to work. For this example, a custom runtime service must be developed to manage e-mail subscriptions. Here is the WaitForEmailService code:

```
public class WaitForEmailService : WorkflowRuntimeService
{
    private List<EmailChecker> watchers = new List<EmailChecker>();

    protected override void OnStarted()
    {
        base.OnStarted();

        // start each of the email checkers
        foreach (EmailChecker checker in this.watchers)
        {
            if (!checker.IsStarted) checker.StartChecking();
        }
    }

    protected override void OnStopped()
    {
        base.OnStopped();

        // stop each of the email checkers
        foreach (EmailChecker checker in this.watchers)
        {
            if (checker.IsStarted) checker.PauseChecking();
        }
    }

    public void AddNewWatch(string server, string userName, string password,
        int checkFrequencyInSeconds, Guid workflowInstanceId,
        IComparable queueName)
    {
        // here we create a new email checker and subscribe to the
        // EmailReceived event
        // we also keep track of each subscription in a collection
```

```
            EmailChecker checker = new EmailChecker(server, userName, password,
                checkFrequencyInSeconds, workflowInstanceId, queueName);

            checker.EmailReceived +=
                new EventHandler<EmailReceivedEventArgs>(checker_EmailReceived);

            checker.StartChecking();

            this.watchers.Add(checker);
        }

        private void checker_EmailReceived(object sender, EmailReceivedEventArgs e)
        {
            // an email has been received! Tell the workflow instance!
            EmailChecker checker = sender as EmailChecker;
            if (checker != null)
            {
                WorkflowInstance instance =
                    Runtime.GetWorkflow(checker.WorkflowInstanceId);

                instance.EnqueueItem(checker.QueueName, e.Message, null, null);

                // the email checker is no longer needed
                checker.Dispose();
            }
        }
    }
}
```

The `WaitForEmailService` class inherits from `WorkflowRuntimeService`, which allows it to receive notifications when the workflow runtime is started and stopped. This enables it to respond accordingly — which in this example means starting and pausing e-mail checking.

`AddNewWatch` is a public method to be called from inside the activity (discussed in more detail later). The parameters include identifying items such as e-mail server information, the workflow instance ID of the workflow that is making the request, and the name of the queue to which messages should be delivered. With this information, a new instance of the `EmailChecker` class can be created, and the service can subscribe to its `EmailReceived` event. `EmailChecker` is a worker class that is responsible for notifying interested parties when new messages arrive. For the purposes of this example, the class does not check a real inbox; instead, it uses a `Timer` class to simulate an e-mail arriving. The e-mail checker instance is added to a class member collection for later reference.

The event handler for the `EmailReceived` event is pretty straightforward. It uses the `WorkflowRuntime` property to obtain a reference to the workflow instance that just received an e-mail and then calls its `EnqueueItem` method. Because the data passed to this method is accessible to the activity, the `Email Message` instance is passed as the second parameter. Finally, the `EmailChecker` is removed from the collection and disposed.

The E-Mail Activity

With the e-mail service developed, the `WaitForEmailActivity` is ready to be covered. The first part of the code is as follows:

```
public class WaitForEmailActivity : Activity, IEventActivity,
    IActivityEventListener<QueueEventArgs>
{
    public IComparable QueueName
    {
        get { return this.Name + "Queue"; }
    }

    public void Subscribe(ActivityExecutionContext parentContext,
        IActivityEventListener<QueueEventArgs> parentEventHandler)
    {
        if (parentContext == null)
            throw new ArgumentNullException("parentContext");

        if (parentEventHandler == null)
            throw new ArgumentNullException("parentEventHandler");

        // get the email service
        WaitForEmailService emailService =
            parentContext.GetService<WaitForEmailService>();

        if (emailService == null)
            throw new InvalidOperationException(
                "The WaitForEmailService is required");

        emailService.AddNewWatch(this.Server, this.UserName, this.Password,
            this.CheckFrequencyInSeconds, this.WorkflowInstanceId, this.QueueName);

        WorkflowQueuingService queuingService =
            parentContext.GetService<WorkflowQueuingService>();

        WorkflowQueue queue =
            queuingService.CreateWorkflowQueue(this.QueueName, false);
        queue.RegisterForQueueItemAvailable(parentEventHandler,
            base.QualifiedName);

        this.isSubscribed = true;
    }

    public void Unsubscribe(ActivityExecutionContext parentContext,
        IActivityEventListener<QueueEventArgs> parentEventHandler)
    {
        if (parentContext == null)
            throw new ArgumentNullException("parentContext");

        if (parentEventHandler == null)
            throw new ArgumentNullException("parentEventHandler");

        WorkflowQueuingService queuingService =
            parentContext.GetService<WorkflowQueuingService>();
        WorkflowQueue queue = queuingService.GetWorkflowQueue(this.QueueName);
        queue.UnregisterForQueueItemAvailable(parentEventHandler);
    }
}
```

The property members represent the required implementation according to the `IEventActivity` interface. The `QueueName` property simply provides a unique queue name for a particular workflow instance. Queue names need to be unique only across instances, so you can use the same names in separate instances — the workflow runtime knows which to use.

The `Subscribe` method is responsible for creating any required queues for communication as well as doing any internal subscription management. The activity uses `WaitForEmailService` to maintain subscription information for each workflow instance; therefore, the `Subscribe` method has to ensure that this service has been added to the workflow runtime's service collection. It is perfectly acceptable to have dependencies on specific runtime services.

Next, a new workflow queue is created, and the event handler passed to the `Subscribe` method is wired to receive notification whenever a new item is available in the queue. This is done using the `WorkflowQueue.RegisterForQueueItemAvailable` method. Next, a class field called `isSubscribed` is set to inform other methods in the class that the subscription is taken care of.

The `Unsubscribe` method simply obtains a reference to the previously created queue and unsubscribes from the item available event. The queue is not deleted in this step, as you might expect. If the queue is deleted at this point, the activity could not access the data that has been delivered. Rather, the queue is deleted by another method, which is discussed later.

The e-mail activity implements not only `IEventActivity`, but also the `IActivityEventListener<QueueEventArgs>` interface. This interface is implemented by a custom activity that needs to be informed when an event activity's event has occurred. In this case, the e-mail activity is interested when its own event is raised. However, it is important to understand when the implemented `OnEvent` method is called. When event activities are children of activities such as Listen, the parent is responsible for listening for the event. Therefore, it should be no surprise that these activities also implement `IActivityEventListener<QueueEventArgs>`. However, when the e-mail activity is used in a standalone manner, it is responsible for listening to itself and doing whatever is necessary to proceed. The following code shows the parts of the e-mail activity that illustrate these concepts:

```
public class WaitForEmailActivity : Activity, IEventActivity,
    IActivityEventListener<QueueEventArgs>
{
    void IActivityEventListener<QueueEventArgs>.OnEvent(object sender,
        QueueEventArgs e)
    {
        ActivityExecutionContext context = sender as ActivityExecutionContext;
        if (context != null &&
            this.ExecutionStatus == ActivityExecutionStatus.Executing)
        {
            if (this.CheckQueue(context) == ActivityExecutionStatus.Closed)
            {
                context.CloseActivity();
            }
        }
    }

    private ActivityExecutionStatus CheckQueue(ActivityExecutionContext context)
    {
        if (this.isSubscribed)
```

```
        {
            WorkflowQueuingService queuingService =
                context.GetService<WorkflowQueuingService>();
            WorkflowQueue queue = queuingService.GetWorkflowQueue(this.QueueName);

            if (queue.Count > 0)
            {
                object data = queue.Dequeue();
                if (!(data is EmailMessage))
                    throw new InvalidOperationException(
                        "This activity can only handle EmailMessage objects");

                base.SetValue(MessageProperty, data);

                // we're done with the queue, go ahead and delete it now
                queuingService.DeleteWorkflowQueue(this.QueueName);

                // we're done, so return a status of closed
                return ActivityExecutionStatus.Closed;
            }
        }

        // not done yet, return an Executing status
        return ActivityExecutionStatus.Executing;
    }
}
```

The OnEvent method performs a couple of checks up front to make sure everything is how it should be. It checks to make sure that the sender parameter is an ActivityExecutionContext instance, that the activity's execution status is Executing, and that the CheckQueue method returns a status of Closed. Because of the way the activity executes when not in a subscribing parent, all of these conditions should be true every time this method is called. The CloseActivity method of the context object is called to signal when the activity is done.

The CheckQueue method is next and is where most of the interesting work is performed in this activity. First, if the isSubscribed field is not set, no work is done, and a status of Executing is returned. However, the subscription has already been established, so an instance of the WorkflowQueueingService is acquired, which then allows access to the communication queue. Next, the queue is checked to make sure it has some data available—and the way the activity has been coded, this check should always evaluate to true. If the data dequeued is an EmailMessage instance, the activity's dependency property, MessageProperty, is set using the SetValue method. Finally, the message queue is deleted, and a status of Closed is returned.

The WaitForEmailActivity's Execute method is as follows:

```
public class WaitForEmailActivity : Activity, IEventActivity,
    IActivityEventListener<QueueEventArgs>
{
    protected override ActivityExecutionStatus Execute(
        ActivityExecutionContext context)
    {
        if (context == null)
```

```
            throw new ArgumentNullException("context");

        // subscribe will only be called here is we are not
        // in an activity like ListenActivity or StateActivity
        // i.e. if it is being used as a stand along activity
        if(!this.isSubscribed)
            this.Subscribe(context, this);

        return CheckQueue(context);
    }
}
```

The activity's Execute override is surprisingly simple. First, a check against the isSubscribed field is performed. Remember, you need to manually subscribe to the workflow queue only when the activity is not a child to a subscribing parent, such as the Listen activity. The CheckQueue method is then called to get the return status. If this is a standalone activity, Executing is returned; otherwise, a status of Closed is returned, and the activity is considered completed.

Testing the Activity's Execution

Now that WaitForEmailActivity is completed, it is interesting to see how it executes when used in different workflow scenarios. The execution path and order of method calls differ considerably, depending on whether the activity is in a subscribing parent. Figure 8-2 shows a workflow that has the e-mail activity as a child to a Listen activity. Because of this relationship, the Listen activity is responsible for listening for the event raised when a new item is added to the workflow queue.

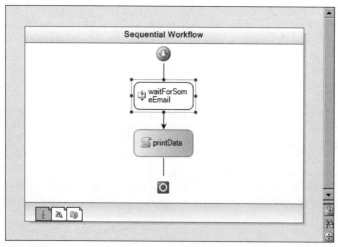

Figure 8-2

If you place strategic breakpoints in the code developed for this example, you can see an execution path like the following:

1. Subscribe is called (by the Listen activity), and a workflow queue is created and subscribed to.

2. The workflow goes idle while waiting for an e-mail.

3. An e-mail arrives, thereby notifying the e-mail runtime service, which adds an item to the queue.

4. Unsubscribe is called (by the Listen activity), and the subscription to the workflow queue is undone.

5. Execute is called, and the e-mail message is retrieved from the queue, which is then deleted.

6. A status of Closed is returned, and the workflow proceeds.

Figure 8-3 shows a workflow that uses the e-mail activity in a standalone fashion. As you know by now, this means that the activity is responsible for listening to itself when an item arrives in the queue rather than some other parent.

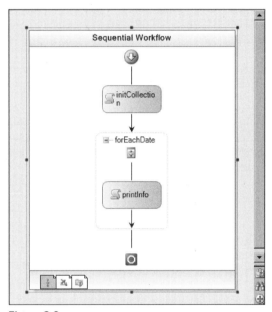

Figure 8-3

Again, if you use breakpoints and debug the workflow, you can see the following execution path:

1. Execute is called, which in turn calls the Subscribe method. A status of Executing is returned so that the activity does not close.

2. The workflow goes idle while waiting for an e-mail.

3. An e-mail arrives, thereby notifying the e-mail runtime service, which adds an item to the queue.

4. The activity's OnEvent method is called, which causes the e-mail to be retrieved from the queue. The queue is then deleted.

5. The ActivityExecutionContext.CloseActivity method is called, allowing the workflow to continue.

Other Considerations

Although `WaitForEmailActivity` is a fairly comprehensive example of how to implement an `IEventActivity` activity, a few other things could have been done to make it a little better and more robust. First, consider the workflow shown in Figure 8-2 earlier in this chapter. If the Delay activity in the second branch times out before the e-mail arrives, the workflow queue used in the e-mail activity is not deleted. Therefore, it would probably be a good idea to implement code in the activity's cancellation handler to clean up any resources.

In addition, a more interesting activity might look for very specific e-mails related only to the workflow instance in question. For example, perhaps all workflow instances are checking the same inbox. With the current implementation, only the instance that checks for e-mail first gets the notification. However, code could be implemented to correlate e-mails to a workflow instance. Perhaps each e-mail's subject is required to contain some GUID that ties back to a workflow instance. Regular expressions could be used to parse the text and raise the `EmailReceived` event only when appropriate.

Summary

The activity execution model is proof of a well-architected framework that can handle scenarios such as faults, persistence, and compensation. When an activity executes, it does so within the confines of an activity execution context. This context describes the activity's state during the time in which it executed. Each activity's execution context can be persisted so that compensation can occur weeks or months after it actually executed.

For activities that have multiple children or that have child activities executing multiple times, you must create separate execution contexts manually using the `ActivityExecutionContextManager` class, which is available from an `ActivityExecutionContext` instance. An example `ForEachActivity` was developed in this chapter to illustrate this concept. Even though this activity has only one child, each time that child executed, it was within a separate context.

The chapter also introduced workflow queues as the conduits for host-to-workflow communication. Instead of applications passing data directly to workflow instances, which may or may not even be in memory, the data is passed to a workflow queue. `WorkflowQueueingService` allows the creation and deletion of `WorkflowQueue` instances.

This chapter also introduced the concept of event activities. Event activities rely on input from the outside world to complete. The prime example of this type of activity is the out-of-the-box HandleExternalEvent activity. An example activity that blocks workflow execution until an e-mail arrives was developed to illustrate programming concepts related to event activities. This activity implements the `IEventActivity` interface, which allows it to be used in other event-specific activities, such as EventDriven and Listen. In addition, special considerations were made to ensure that it would execute correctly outside one of these activities.

9

Rules

Business rules are a crucial part of most software systems because they allow the translation of real business requirements to executable code. Many times business rules are treated as second-class citizens when they are simply lumped in with all the rest of the code that makes up an application. Because businesses can change over time, optimally you should be able to change business rules in a more eloquent way than just tweaking and redeploying the code it.

In addition, you may find that some implementations of business rules are looser or tighter than others. For example, there are well-known algorithms for evaluating rules in a set. A couple of these are the Rete algorithm and sequential algorithms. Plenty of resources on the Web discuss the semantics of business rules and various algorithms along with their pros and cons. The purpose of this chapter is to cover the rules implementation in Windows Workflow Foundation, so other extraneous information is kept to a minimum.

To some people, business rules are simply `if-else` statements in code that loosely tie to some business requirement. Luckily, in Windows Workflow Foundation, rules are much more than this.

The following topics are covered in this chapter:

- ❏ Code conditions
- ❏ Declarative rule conditions
- ❏ Rule sets
- ❏ Chaining
- ❏ Rules development

Business Rules and Windows Workflow Foundation

The business rules framework in Windows Workflow Foundation offers a great deal of functionality and flexibility. Everything from the simplest single rule to more complex sets of rules with involved execution logic is provided in the workflow API.

The classes that support rules in Windows Workflow Foundation exist in `System.Workflow.Activities.Rules` and `System.Workflow.Activities.Rules.Design`, and are discussed in this chapter. In addition, there are other rule-related entities throughout the API. For example, several activities are heavily tied to rules. This chapter also discusses these activities and how they are related to rules.

Before the chapter dives too deep into the world of rules, the next section covers code conditions — a simpler form of programmatic logic.

Code Conditions

When you think of rules, generally the most common trait that comes to mind is a Boolean condition. For example, comparing a number to a variable to see whether the number is larger than the variable produces a Boolean output. For simple Boolean checks, the *code condition* provides a programmatic way to define these expressions. Code conditions are represented by the `CodeCondition` class and are executed when its `Evaluate` method is called.

A few activities give you the option of using code conditions or rules when a condition is required. For example, the IfElseBranch activity has a property called `Condition` that requires you to choose the type of condition to use. The following code checks a variable to see whether it is greater than 200, and if so, it sets the `Result` property to `true` on the `ConditionalEventArgs` object that is passed to the method. All activities that allow the use of code conditions require the following method signature:

```
private void IsLargeOrder(object sender, ConditionalEventArgs e)
{
    e.Result = this.orderTotal > 200;
}
```

Although code conditions provide a simple way to specify Boolean values, there are some advantages to using rules over code conditions. First, rules allow dynamic updates, meaning that the conditions and subsequent actions can be updated during runtime if warranted. In addition, rules offer a rich authoring environment and a more customizable infrastructure, allowing them to be stored in a multitude of mediums. This includes XML out of the box, but the infrastructure could be extended to include stores such as SQL Server.

The Anatomy of Rules

In Windows Workflow Foundation, there are two different types of rules: declarative rules and rule sets.

Declarative Rule Conditions

Declarative rules are expressions that evaluate to `true` or `false`. This simpler form of rules is used in activities that require a Boolean expression to function, such as an IfElseBranch or While activity. Other activities that rely on rules are discussed a little later in the chapter.

There are no limitations on how rules are used in Windows Workflow Foundation because the platform is so extensible. You can develop custom activities to use rules, and, as you will see later, rules can be used programmatically and do not have to be used with activities at all.

Because declarative rule conditions are simply Boolean expressions, they are easy to read and create. The following is an example of a declarative rule condition that checks to see whether a customer is old enough to rent a car:

```
this.customer.Age >= 25
```

This rule could be referenced by an IfElseBranch activity to conditionally execute its child activities. If the condition is not met, the next branch is evaluated until a condition is eventually met or an `else` branch is reached.

Rule Sets

Rule sets are where the power of rules becomes evident. They are considerably more flexible than declarative rule conditions and provide quite a few more options for rule execution, also called *evaluation.* Rule sets are quite different from declarative rules; however, at the heart of things, they both provide a flexible architecture of maintainable rules.

The first and most obvious difference between declarative rules and rule sets is that as the name implies, rule sets can contain many rules. A set provides a container for rules that are presumably related to the same business problem domain. The rule set exposes an option applied to the set as a whole that specifies the behavior to be used during evaluation. This option, referred to as *chaining,* is discussed in detail later in this chapter. Briefly, chaining describes how rules are evaluated and reevaluated when properties on which the rules depend are changed.

The rules contained within rule sets are also different from individual declarative rule conditions. Instead of simply having a Boolean expression, rule set rules also have *actions* associated with them. Actions are analogous to the code within a C# `if` or `else` block. These actions are referred to as THEN and ELSE statements. However, you can develop custom actions.

Individual rules also have a few properties associated with them that are not applicable to declarative rule conditions. The first such property is a rule's *priority.* This value is coupled with the chaining option mentioned previously and states the order in which a rule should be evaluated related to other rules in the set. In the rule priority scheme, higher numbers are evaluated first.

Another rule property related to chaining is the *reevaluation* property. Possible values include `always` and `never`, which specify whether a rule is to be reevaluated if and when properties on which the rule is dependent are modified. Again, chaining with a reevaluation property is discussed in greater detail a little later.

The final rule-specific property is the *active* property. This value is represented by a check box in Visual Studio and specifies whether a rule should be evaluated at all. If the value is set to `false` or unchecked, the rule is ignored during runtime and has no impact on the outcome of the set's evaluation.

To give you an idea of how you can use rule sets, consider a set that specifies certain business rules related to an organization's new hire process. You could establish a rule that checks a candidate's years of experience against a job opening's requirements, as shown in the following example:

IF:

```
candidate.YearsOfExperience >= job.MinimumYearsOfExperience
```

THEN:

```
isValidCandidate = true
```

ELSE:

```
isValidCandidate = false
```

The rule set could also contain other rules that check for things such as whether the candidate has been convicted of a felony, all technical requirements are met, or the candidate is willing to relocate if the job's city is different from the candidate's current city of residence.

Windows Workflow Rules Language

You define rules in Windows Workflow Foundation using a syntax that isn't quite C# or Visual Basic .NET but is close to both. Because rules aren't much more than simplistic IF-THEN-ELSE statements, the syntax doesn't need to be that complex.

You can access fields, properties, and methods using the standard dotted notation, as with C# and Visual Basic .NET. The following is a simple IF statement that checks to see whether the customer placing an order is a Platinum customer:

```
this.customer.CustomerType == CustomerType.Platinum
```

Next is what could be a corresponding THEN statement:

```
this.order.Discounts.Add(new Discount(.15))
```

And the following is a possible ELSE statement:

```
this.order.Discounts.Add(new Discount(.05))
```

As you can easily ascertain, Platinum customers receive a 15 percent discount in this example, and other customer types receive only a 5 percent discount. In addition, the THEN and ELSE statements can access the `order` object's `Discounts` collection by calling `order.Discounts`. The rule could have just as easily referenced a method off the `order` object — perhaps one called `SetDiscount`.

A rule can reference any object that can be accessed in a workflow's code file. In the preceding example, there is a class field called `order`, which is why it is referenced with the `this` qualifier. The same goes for methods in the workflow code file. You can place more complex logic in an actual C# or Visual Basic .NET code file and then reference it as a method call from within a rule.

The following three tables list the expressions that you use in the rules language. Table 9-1 lists the relational expression operators that allow values, objects, and such to be compared with the output of `true` or `false`. The same types of expression operators exist in C# and Visual Basic .NET. If you use the Visual Basic .NET style of equality operators (= and <>), they are automatically changed to the C# style (== and !=).

Table 9-1: Rule Expressions

Expression	Expression Symbols
Equal	==, =
Not Equal	!=, <>
Greater Than	>
Greater Than or Equal	>=
Less Than	<
Less Than or Equal	<=

Table 9-2 lists the arithmetic-related operators available in rule expressions. You can use these operators in the `IF` portion of a rule or in the `THEN` or `ELSE` portion. For example, you could use them in the `IF` statement to compare a value with another value plus or minus a number you specify. Or you could use these operators in the `THEN` or `ELSE` statement to modify a value based on the outcome of the rule.

Table 9-2: Arithmetic Operators

Arithmetic Operation	Operator Symbols
Addition	+
Subtraction	–
Multiplication	*
Division	/
Modulus	MOD

Table 9-3 shows the operators that join Boolean expressions into larger, more complex Boolean expressions. As with the comparison expressions, workflow rules allow either C# or Visual Basic .NET flavors of expression joiners. However, when you use the Visual Basic .NET style operators, they are automatically translated to the C# style.

Table 9-3: Expression Joiners

Expression	Operator Symbols
And	`&&`, `AND`
Or	`||`, `OR`
Not	`!`, `NOT`
Bitwise And	`&`
Bitwise Or	`|`

Related Activities

Several activities rely on conditions and/or rules to function properly. This section discusses each out-of-the-box activity included in Windows Workflow Foundation.

The IfElse, While, Replicator, and ConditionedActivityGroup Activities

The IfElse, While, Replicator, and ConditionedActivityGroup activities can use code conditions or declarative rules to specify their conditional expressions. The IfElse and While activities have a property called `Condition`; the Replicator and ConditionedActivityGroup activities have a property called `UntilCondition`. Both of these properties are of the type `ActivityCondition`. Although this class is abstract, it has two derived classes that you can use to specify a condition: `CodeCondition` and `RuleConditionReference`.

As discussed earlier in this chapter, `CodeCondition` is a pointer to a method that sets a value in the `ConditionalEventArgs` instance passed to the method. `RuleConditionReference` is also a pointer, but to a declarative rule stored in the workflow's `.rules` file.

When you're setting the conditional properties in Visual Studio, you must first choose which condition class to use. Then, depending on your choice, you must specify the conditional expression.

If you choose `CodeCondition`, you must set its `Condition` property to an already-defined method with the signature `void Condition(object sender, ConditionalEventArgs e)`.

If you use `RuleConditionReference` to specify a conditional expression, Visual Studio provides a UI to select or create a new declarative rule in the workflow's rules store. To use this UI, select Declarative Rule Condition from the activity's conditional property. The `ConditionName` property becomes available and exposes an ellipsis button. Click this button to display the dialog box shown in Figure 9-1. From here, you can select an existing declarative rule or create a new one by clicking the New Condition button. As you can see, this dialog box displays all declarative rules that have already been defined in the workflow's .rules file.

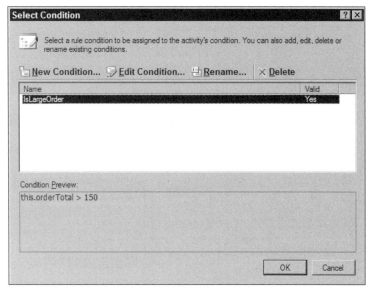

Figure 9-1

Creating a new declarative rule or editing an existing rule displays the dialog box shown in Figure 9-2. This dialog box enables you to define the IF portion of a rule using the same syntax described earlier in this chapter.

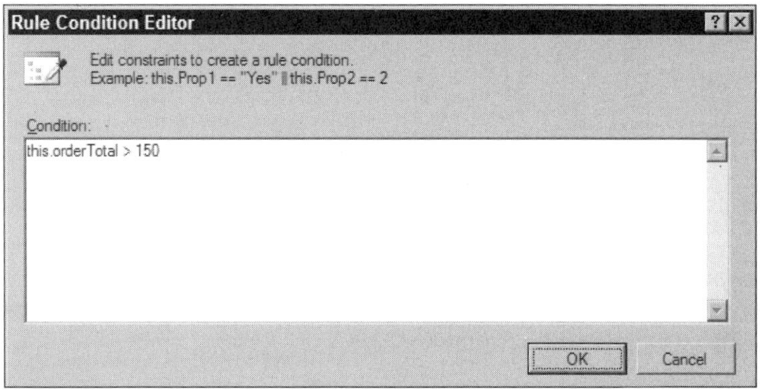

Figure 9-2

The advantage of using rules over code conditions is that you can modify declarative rules during runtime, which you cannot do with code conditions.

Policy

The Policy activity harnesses the power of rule sets. This activity pertains to conditions as well as the actions associated with each rule. You place a Policy activity within a workflow to point to a rule set reference (see Figure 9-3). When the activity is executed, it evaluates each rule in the set while executing the appropriate actions.

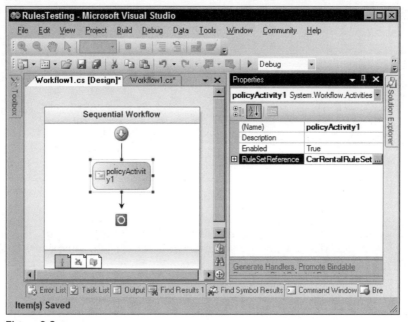

Figure 9-3

Evaluation of Rules

The evaluation of rules in a rule set is not a trivial process. There are many rules that dictate the execution path and reevaluation of rules based on changing properties. This evaluation process, also called *chaining,* is discussed in the following sections.

Chaining Options

Chaining describes the process of a rule's evaluation related to other rules' evaluations. The following options dictate how a rule set's rules are evaluated in relation to other rules in the set:

❏   Full chaining

❏   Explicit chaining

❏   Sequential (nonchained)

Full Chaining

Full chaining is a somewhat complex process of rule evaluation and reevaluation based on properties modified and rule priorities. Basically, the process goes something like this:

1. Highest-priority rules are evaluated first.

2. If a rule modifies the value of a property that a previously evaluated rule uses in its IF expression, the previous rule is reevaluated.

3. This process continues until all rules have been processed or the HALT command is called.

Perhaps an example is the best way to explain full chaining and the different techniques with which it is implemented. Consider the following rules and their associated actions related to a car rental scenario:

Require Insurance, Priority = 15

IF:

```
this.rental.CarType == CarType.Luxury && this.rental.Customer.Age <= 27
```

THEN:

```
this.rental.RequireInsurance = true
```

Is Premium Customer, Priority = 10

IF:

```
this.rental.Customer.Type == CustomerType.Premium
```

THEN:

```
this.rental.CarType = CarType.Luxury
```

Gas Option, Priority = 5

IF:

```
this.rental.GasOption == GasOption.RefillBeforeReturn
```

THEN:

```
this.rental.MinimumTankLevelUponReturn = this.rental.Car.CurrentTankLevel
```

ELSE:

```
this.rental.MinimumTankLevelUponReturn = 0
```

Given these rules, assume the following facts:

- ❑ The rental customer is 25 years old.

- ❑ The customer opted to rent a Yugo (in other words, not a luxury car).

- ❑ The customer is of Premium status.

- ❑ The customer opts to refill the tank prior to returning the car.

The first rule to be evaluated is the Require Insurance rule because its priority, 15, is the highest of the three rules. Because the customer chose to rent a Yugo, this rule's THEN expression is not executed even though the customer is under the age of 28. So far, nothing interesting has happened.

The next rule to be executed is the `Is Premium Customer` rule. This rule evaluates to true because the customer has achieved premium status. Because of this, the THEN expression is executed, thereby upgrading the rental to a luxury automobile.

Because the `rental.CarType` property was modified, and this property is read in the first rule, it must be reevaluated. Here's where the chaining comes into play. Rather than the next rule's being executed, the first rule is reevaluated. Now, because the rental car is considered luxury *and* the renter is only 25, the `RequireInsurance` flag is set to true.

After the `Require Insurance` rule has been evaluated the second time, and the insurance flag has been set, the final rule, `Gas Option`, is executed. The `Is Premium Customer` rule does not need to be evaluated a second time because the `rental.Customer.Type` property was not modified. At this point, because the customer has already opted to refill the tank himself prior to returning the vehicle, the `rental.MinimumTankLevelUponReturn` property is set to the current level of the car's gas tank, which may have been retrieved from a database.

Because no other rules in this set rely on the `MinimumTankLevelUponReturn` property, the rule set's execution is considered complete. As you can see, rule evaluation in the Windows Workflow Foundation rules engine is not as simple as 1-2-3. This is a good thing, of course, because it allows for powerful scenarios that otherwise would have to be implemented with custom code or a third-party package.

Implicit Chaining

The previous scenario used implicit chaining for rule evaluation and reevaluation. The workflow rules engine took it upon itself to investigate the properties each rule was inspecting and modifying. This is how the engine knew to reevaluate rules containing IF statements that might be affected by a value change in a subsequent rule.

Because there were no hints given to the rules engine related to what values might be looked at or modified, it had to make those assertions for itself. Hence, this method of chaining is called *implicit chaining*.

Attributed-Based Chaining

Quite often, the workflow engine cannot ascertain property dependencies across rules—such as when setting a property might modify the value of another property based on some logic in a class, or when a method call might do the same. For example, in the previous rental-car scenario, if calling a method named `PerformCarUpgrade` on a `rental` object modified the `CarType` property of the same object, the rules engine would have no way of knowing this. Therefore, you should provide hints to the rules engine so that the proper chaining behavior can take place. To do this, you use attributes defined in the workflow API, which are described in the following sections.

RuleRead

The `RuleRead` attribute tells the workflow engine that the property or method decorated with the attribute reads a specific property. For example, imagine if the `Require Insurance` rule's IF statement looked like this:

```
this.rental.GetCarType() == CarType.Luxury && this.rental.Customer.Age <= 27
```

Now the rule is comparing a value returned from a method rather than accessing the car type value from a known property. Therefore, the definition of the `GetCarType` method needs to look like the following code to enable proper chaining:

```
public class Rental
{
    private CarType _carType;

    ...

    [RuleRead("CarType")]
    public CarType GetCarType()
    {
        return this._carType;
    }

    ...
}
```

This enables the engine to act as though the `CarType` property itself were read in the `IF` expression.

RuleWrite

Just as the `RuleRead` attribute is necessary for nonimplicit property inspections, the `RuleWrite` attribute allows methods and other properties to be flagged as member modifiers. For example, imagine that the `Gas Option` rule used a method called `SetReturnGasLevel` instead of directly setting the `MinimumTankLevelUponReturn` property. This would allow member fields and properties to be modified in such a way that more complex logic can be applied in methods and properties, and still keep the rules engine in the loop. The following code shows how you could modify the `Rental` object so that a method can be used to set the `MinimumTankLevelUponReturn` property:

```
public class Rental
{
    // 1 would be a full tank
    private decimal _returnTankLevel = 1;

    public MinimumTankLevelUponReturn
    {
        get { return this._returnTankLevel; }
    }
```

```
   . . .

   [RuleWrite("MinimumTankLevelUponReturn")]
   public void SetReturnGasLevel(decimal level)
   {
       // custom logic here...
       this._returnTankLevel = level;
   }

   . . .
}
```

Alternatively, you could use the `set` accessor of the `MinimumTankLevelUponReturn` property to implement this custom logic, but the example gets the point across. There are plenty of occasions where you can modify the fields or properties of a class indirectly in a method or another property.

Notice that in the examples so far, the attributes to assist the rules engine in chaining have been applied in custom classes rather than in a workflow's code-beside code. This may not always be possible in the real world if classes were already defined during the original workflow development, or when you don't want to place workflow-specific dependencies in their enterprise business classes. To mitigate these situations, you could either create class wrappers or create methods in a workflow class to call the class methods directly. The following is an example of this pattern:

```
public class MyWorkflow : SequentialWorkflowActivity
{
    private Rental _rental;

    . . .

    [RuleWrite("rental.MinimumTankLevelUponReturn")]
    public void SetReturnGasLevel(decimal level)
    {
        this._rental.SetReturnGasLevel(level);
    }

    [RuleRead("rental.CarType")]
    public CarType GetCarType()
    {
        return this._rental.GetCarType();
    }
}
```

In this example, there is a class member variable of type `Rental` to contain business logic for a car rental. There are also methods in the workflow code-beside class that call `Rental` methods. Because these method calls read and write various values related to the rule, the `MyWorkflow.GetCarType` and `MyWorkflow.SetReturnGasLevel` methods are decorated with the appropriate rule attributes.

RuleInvoke

The `RuleInvoke` attribute tells the rules engine that the decorated method calls another method with the `RuleWrite` or `RuleRead` attribute applied. For example, the `Rental` object might have a method called `PerformPremiumUpgrade`, which among other things calls the `SetReturnGasLevel` method and passes a value of 0. This attribute brings together the other two chaining attributes to allow complete flexibility in code structure and workflow rules.

The following code listing is an example of what the PerformPremiumUpgrade method's implementation might look like:

```
public class Rental
{
    ...

    [RuleInvoke("SetReturnGasLevel")]
    public void PerformPremiumUpgrade()
    {
        ...
        this.SetReturnGasLevel(0);
        ...
    }

    ...
}
```

With this implementation, if you create a rule that looks like the following, the proper chaining path is followed when the rule set is evaluated:

IF:

```
this._manualPremiumUpgradeSelected == true
```

THEN:

```
this._rental.PerformPremiumUpgrade()
```

Explicit Chaining

The third and final method in which full chaining is implemented, *explicit chaining,* is the next natural progression after implicit and attribute-based chaining. Explicit chaining uses a rules-specific statement: Update.

The Update statement is called like a method and takes a path to a property that is said to be modified in the current rule. For example, if a method on a class modifies another value on that class, and you do not want to create method wrappers as shown previously, you can use explicit chaining to indicate that the value of interest is modified in a method call. The following example rule shows what this would look like in the car-rental scenario:

IF:

```
this._rental.GasOption == GasOption.RefillBeforeReturn
```

THEN:

```
this._rental.SetReturnGasLevel(this._rental.Car.CurrentTankLevel);
Update("_rental/MinimumTankLevelUponReturn")
```

ELSE:

```
this._rental.SetReturnGasLevel(0);
Update("_rental/MinimumTankLevelUponReturn")
```

As you can see, the Update statement passes a string representing a path to the member that was modified according to the actions taken in the THEN and ELSE statements. Note that just because the Update statement says that the MinimumTankLevelUponReturn property has been modified due to the code called in the THEN and ELSE statements does not necessarily mean that this is true. It is simply a flag that informs the rules engine to reevaluate any previous rules that rely upon that property in the IF statement. This is yet another way the rules engine provides complete control over rule evaluation.

You can also pass the Update statement a standard dotted path as opposed to the slash-delimited string. For example, you can express the Update call as follows (notice that the argument passed is not a string):

```
Update(this._rental.MinimumTankLevelUponReturn)
```

When you use the slash-delimited string method, the Update statement can also accept paths that include wildcards. For example, if a rules actions may cause every property of a given class to be updated, this can be represented in the following string:

```
Update("_rental/*")
```

If this statement is executed and full chaining is turned on, every rule that depends on a property of the _rental object is reevaluated. You can also use this slash-delimited property notation, including wildcards, with the RuleRead and RuleWrite attributes.

Explicit Chaining

The second option you can use to modify a rule set's evaluation scheme is *explicit chaining.* This option has the same name as one of the full chaining methods, and they are definitely related — but they are also slightly different.

The explicit chaining discussed previously refers to the pattern of using Update statements to control chaining behavior. The explicit chaining evaluation discussed in this section refers to one of the three options you can apply to a rule set to modify its evaluation method. The explicit-chaining rule set option has a dependency on the Update method of chaining.

When a rule set's chaining option is set to Full Chaining, explicit chaining is one of three ways in which chaining occurs. However, if a rule set's chaining option is set to Explicit Chaining, the Update pattern is used exclusively. The Explicit Chaining rule set option tells the rules engine to follow only the evaluation paths defined by the explicit chaining pattern.

Sequential (Nonchained)

When a rule set's chaining option is set to *sequential,* there is no chaining that occurs during evaluation. This means that rules are executed in order according to their priority (highest first), and no rules are reevaluated, regardless of any property dependencies.

The Rule Reevaluation Option

Each rule in a rule set has yet another option to control chaining behavior: the reevaluation option. The default value for a rule in the rules definition UI (covered later in this chapter) is `Always`, which means that a rule's chaining behavior is consistent with the behavior described so far in this chapter.

The other possible value for the reevaluation option is `Never`. If a rule is set to never reevaluate, the rules engine honors this setting regardless of the chaining behavior specified for a rule or rule set.

Creating Rules

There are a few ways to create rules: through the UI provided in Visual Studio (the most common method), by using XML, and programmatically by using standard .NET code.

The Rules UI

You can access the rules dialog boxes defined in the Windows Workflow Foundation API from a few predefined points in Visual Studio. The following sections describe these dialog boxes and how you can access and use them.

The Rule Set Editor

The Rule Set Editor dialog box (shown in Figure 9-4) provides all the functionality necessary to create new rule sets or modify existing ones. You access this dialog box from the Policy activity's `RuleSetReference` property.

> *Keep in mind that just because only one out-of-the-box activity uses the concept of rule sets does not mean that you can't develop custom activities to use them as well.*

You can accomplish quite a few things in this dialog box, including adding new rules to the current set, editing existing rules, and setting rule set chaining options. The list view toward the top of the screen lists all rules currently defined in the set. You can manipulate individual rules by selecting an item in the list and either deleting (by clicking the Delete button) or editing the rule's properties, which are populated in the area below the list.

The properties area provides essentially everything you need to modify a rule. The rule's IF, THEN, and ELSE statements are displayed here. In addition, the name, priority, and reevaluation properties can be modified. There is also an Active check box that specifies whether the currently selected rule should be evaluated during the rule set's evaluation.

One of the nice features of the rules UI in Windows Workflow Foundation is the inclusion of IntelliSense. When a rule's IF, THEN, or ELSE statements are being edited, contextual hints are given using the workflow's code-beside class as a baseline. This means that if you type **this.** in the IF box, you are presented with a list of variables from the workflow definition's class. For example, if a workflow's class had a member called `order`, it would appear in the IntelliSense list as shown in Figure 9-5.

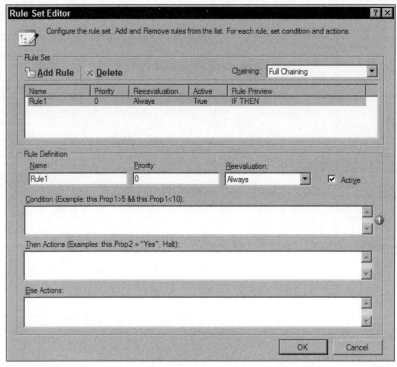

Figure 9-4

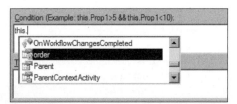

Figure 9-5

Even though there is only one custom field defined in this example, the list is quite long. This is because the list is showing all members of the workflow class and its parent classes.

The Rule Condition Editor

The declarative Rule Condition Editor, shown in Figure 9-6, allows you to specify simple rule conditions for use in conditional activities such as IfElse, While, and ConditionedActivityGroup. Not surprisingly, there is not a lot to this dialog box, because rule conditions are simply a Boolean expression. However, the UI provides nice features such as IntelliSense and rule validation. The red exclamation icon on the right side of the screen indicates a problem with the current condition. In this case, nothing has been entered in the required editor area.

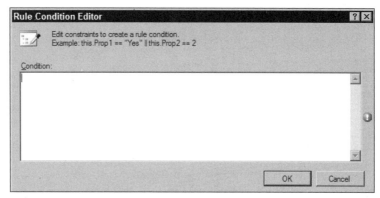

Figure 9-6

Embedding the Rules UI in Custom Applications

The workflow API exposes the rules UI dialog boxes for use in custom applications. These classes are located in the `System.Workflow.Activities.Rules.Design` namespace and include `RuleCondition Dialog` and `RuleSetDialog`.

The `RuleConditionDialog` is the UI that allows users to create declarative rule conditions based on the workflow that is passed to its constructor, as shown in the following code listing. Any members that have been defined in the `MyWorkflow` class are accessible in the rules UI, just as in Visual Studio. After the `ShowDialog` method is called and the user has created the desired condition, it is accessed with the `Expression` property. A `RuleDefinitions` instance is then created and the condition is added after being wrapped in a `RuleExpressionCondition` object. Finally, the `RuleSetDefinition` is serialized and written to an XML file.

```
private void CreateRuleCondition()
{
    MyWorkflow wf = new MyWorkflow();
    RuleConditionDialog rdc = new RuleConditionDialog(wf, null);
    rdc.ShowDialog();
    CodeExpression ce = rdc.Expression;

    RuleDefinitions ruleDefinitions = new RuleDefinitions();
    RuleExpressionCondition condition =
        new RuleExpressionCondition("MyCondition", ce);
    ruleDefinitions.Conditions.Add(condition);

    WorkflowMarkupSerializer serializer = new WorkflowMarkupSerializer();
    serializer.Serialize(new XmlTextWriter(@"C:\rules.xml", Encoding.Default),
        ruleDefinitions);
}
```

In addition to creating declarative rule conditions, the workflow API provides you with a dialog box where you can create more complex rule sets by using the `RuleSetDialog` class. The following code listing shows you how to use this class to create a rule set in a custom application:

```
private void CreateRuleSet()
{
    RuleSet ruleSet = new RuleSet("MyRuleSet");
    MyWorkflow wf = new MyWorkflow();
    RuleSetDialog rsd = new RuleSetDialog(wf, ruleSet);
    rsd.ShowDialog();
    ruleSet = rsd.RuleSet;

    RuleDefinitions ruleDefinitions = new RuleDefinitions();
    ruleDefinitions.RuleSets.Add(ruleSet);

    WorkflowMarkupSerializer serializer = new WorkflowMarkupSerializer();
    serializer.Serialize(new XmlTextWriter(@"C:\rules.xml", Encoding.Default),
        ruleDefinitions);
}
```

This code first creates an empty `RuleSet` instance simply to give it a name. The `RuleSetDialog` is then initialized by passing an instance of the `MyWorkflow` workflow class. As with the `RuleConditionDialog`, passing this workflow reference allows the user to access, with IntelliSense, any members defined in the workflow class.

After the rule set has been defined by the user, it is accessible through the `RuleSet` property. A `Rule SetDefinitions` class is created to hold the `RuleSet` object, and then it is serialized to XML on the filesystem.

Creating Rules Programmatically

Even with the rich UI experience provided out of the box with Windows Workflow Foundation, there might be situations when rules need to be created programmatically. Think about a project that requires end users to create rules without the assistance of IT. In many cases, you can just embed the provided dialog boxes in custom applications, but this is not always feasible. If there are very specific guidelines about how business rules can be defined, you may need to write custom code to fulfill the requirements.

The following sections describe how you can define rules in code and how these rules are subsequently evaluated.

Rules and the CodeDom

Internally, rules are created using classes defined in the .NET CodeDom namespaces (`System.CodeDom`). The CodeDom is not specific to Windows Workflow Foundation and is used for many different applications within and using .NET.

Essentially, the CodeDom enables you to create code by using code. Think about how you would describe a C# `if-else` statement using code. First, you need an object representing the `if` statement that has a construct for producing a value of `true` or `false` based on an expression. Next, you need an object representing the actions to be taken if the condition is `true` and another object representing the `else` portion of the code. Each discrete code construct and action should be able to be represented by objects that can then be compiled into actual executable code. This is what the CodeDom is for.

Table 9-4 lists the .NET CodeDom expression class types that are used to support the programmatic creation of workflow rules. Keep in mind that the classes listed here represent only a subset of what exists in the CodeDom namespaces. There are plenty of great resources available on the Web that discuss this topic in depth and in a more generic context.

Table 9-4: Relevant CodeDom Expression Classes

CodeDom Type	Description
CodeAssignStatement	Supports the assignment of a value to a variable. Example: `myName = "Todd"`
CodeBinaryOperatorExpression	Allows two code expressions to be operated on with a binary expression such as a comparison or mathematic operation. Example: `myAge == 25`
CodeDirectionExpression	Specifies the direction of a parameter being passed to a method. Example: `MyMethod(out int val)`
CodeExpressionStatement	Represents a single expression or line of code. Example: `myObject.ToString()`
CodeFieldReferenceExpression	Evaluates to a field reference. Example: `this.myVariable`
CodeMethodInvokeExpression	Represents a method call. Example: `Console.WriteLine("Hi")`
CodeMethodReferenceExpression	Represents a reference to a method. This object could then be passed to `CodeMethodInvokeExpression`.
CodePrimitiveExpression	Represents a single primitive value. Examples: `1`, `"Hello"`, `false`, `10.5`
CodePropertyReferenceExpression	Evaluates to a property reference. Example: `this.MyName`
CodeThisReferenceExpression	Represents a reference to the current class. For example, if you wanted to reference a method on the current, local class, it would look like this: `this.PerformValidation()`.
CodeTypeReference	Represents a reference to a .NET type. Example: `typeof(System.String)`
CodeTypeReferenceExpression	Represents a reference to a .NET data type. Example: `System.String`

Table 9-5 lists the CodeDom classes that allow operations to be performed between two expressions. These operators range from mathematical operations to Boolean comparison operations. All of these operators are values found in the `CodeBinaryOperatorType` enumeration.

Table 9-5: CodeDom Comparison Classes

Operators	Description
Add	Used to add expressions. Example: `2 + 2`
BitwiseAnd	Performs a bitwise and operation. Example: `val1 & val2`
BitwiseOr	Performs a bitwise or operation. Example `val1	val2`
BooleanAnd	Represents a Boolean and expression, as used with `if` statements. Example: `val1 == val2 && val3 == val4`
BooleanOr	Represents a Boolean or expression. Example: `val1 == val2 || val3 == val4`
Divide	Provides the division operator. Example: `10 / 2`
GreaterThan	Represents the greater than operator. Example: `x > 10`
GreaterThanOrEqual	Represents the greater than or equal to operator. Example: `val >= 24`
IdentityEquality	The identity equality operator. Example: `val == anotherVal`
IdentityInequality	The identity inequality operator. Example: `val != anotherVal`
LessThan	Represents the less than operator. Example: `5 < count`
LessThanOrEqual	Represents the less than or equal to operator. Example: `val <= 40`
Modulus	Allows the use of the modulus operator. Example: `(x % 2) == 0`

Operators	Description
Multiply	The multiplication operator.
	Example: 2 x 2
Subtract	The subtraction operator.
	Example: 40 - x
ValueEquality	The value equality operator.
	Example: val == 2

The Rules API

In addition to the functionality provided by the CodeDom to create rule expressions, the Windows Workflow Foundation API exposes classes that represent the rule entities. This includes items such as rules themselves, rule sets, and rule definitions that represent the container for all rule-related items in a workflow.

The rule-related objects in the API are located in the `System.Workflow.Activities.Rules` namespace and enable you to programmatically create rules just as they are created with the Visual Studio APIs. Building from the bottom up, the `Rule` class exposes properties such as `Condition`, `ThenActions`, and `ElseActions`. The `ThenActions` and `ElseActions` properties are collections that can have any number of actions associated with them.

Although the conditions and actions associated with a rule all come from the CodeDom classes, they are wrapped in rulecentric classes when associated with the `Rule` class. The `Condition` property is of type `RuleExpressionCondition`, which takes a `CodeExpression` as a parameter in one of its constructor's overloads. The `ThenActions` and `ElseActions` collections also wrap `CodeExpression` classes in a class called `RuleStatementAction`.

Next in the chain comes the `RuleSet` class. This class has properties such as `ChainingBehavior`, `Name`, `Description`, and `Rules`. The `ChainingBehavior` property takes a value from the `RuleChaining Behavior` enumeration. The `Rules` property is a collection of `Rule` objects that make up the rule set. You programmatically add `Rule` instances just as you would do visually in the rules UI.

The `RuleDefinitions` class essentially represents what you would find in the .rules file of a workflow. It is a container for all declarative rule conditions as well as all rule sets associated with a particular workflow. It has two properties: `Conditions` and `RuleSets`. As described in the following section, which provides an example of programmatic rule creation, the `RuleDefinitions` class can be serialized to an XML file, which gives you the equivalent of a .rules file created in Visual Studio.

A Programmatic Rules Example

This section studies some code that programmatically builds a rule set using the rules API and the CodeDom classes. To maintain consistency and so that you can see how the same rules can be modeled in different ways, the code builds the same three rules introduced earlier in the chaining section:

- ❑ One rule to check whether the renter requires insurance based on the car type and customer age
- ❑ One rule to provide a premium car upgrade if the customer is classified as Premium
- ❑ One rule to set the required gas level based on the option chosen by the renter

In addition to building the rules and rule set, the following code serializes the RuleDefinitions object to an XML file. The output XML is just as good as the XML created by the rules UI and can be used in the same way.

```
public static class RulesHelper
{
    // the following group of static members is simply obtaining references to
    // fields, properties, and types which will be used throughout the code
    private static CodeThisReferenceExpression thisReference =
        new CodeThisReferenceExpression();

    private static CodeFieldReferenceExpression rentalFieldReference =
        new CodeFieldReferenceExpression(thisReference, "rental");

    private static CodePropertyReferenceExpression customerFieldReference =
        new CodePropertyReferenceExpression(rentalFieldReference, "Customer");

    private static CodePropertyReferenceExpression carFieldReference =
        new CodePropertyReferenceExpression(rentalFieldReference, "Car");

    private static CodeTypeReferenceExpression carTypeReference =
        new CodeTypeReferenceExpression(typeof(CarType));

    private static CodeTypeReferenceExpression customerTypeReference =
        new CodeTypeReferenceExpression(typeof(CustomerType));

    private static CodeTypeReferenceExpression gasOptionReference =
        new CodeTypeReferenceExpression(typeof(GasOption));

    private static Rule BuildRequireInsuranceRule()
    {
        Rule rule = new Rule("RequireInsurance");
        rule.Priority = 15;

        // car type == luxury
        CodeBinaryOperatorExpression carTypeExp =
            new CodeBinaryOperatorExpression();
        carTypeExp.Left = new CodePropertyReferenceExpression(rentalFieldReference,
            "CarType");
        carTypeExp.Operator = CodeBinaryOperatorType.ValueEquality;
        carTypeExp.Right = new CodeFieldReferenceExpression(carTypeReference,
            "Luxury");

        // age <= 27
```

```
        CodeBinaryOperatorExpression ageExp = new CodeBinaryOperatorExpression();
        ageExp.Left = new CodePropertyReferenceExpression(customerFieldReference,
            "Age");
        ageExp.Operator = CodeBinaryOperatorType.LessThanOrEqual;
        ageExp.Right = new CodePrimitiveExpression(27);
        CodeBinaryOperatorExpression condition =
            new CodeBinaryOperatorExpression();
        condition.Left = carTypeExp;
        condition.Operator = CodeBinaryOperatorType.BooleanAnd;
        condition.Right = ageExp;

        rule.Condition = new RuleExpressionCondition(condition);

        // create the THEN action
        // require insurance = true
        CodeAssignStatement thenAction = new CodeAssignStatement(
            new CodePropertyReferenceExpression(rentalFieldReference,
                "RequireInsurance"),
            new CodePrimitiveExpression(true));

        rule.ThenActions.Add(new RuleStatementAction(thenAction));

        return rule;
    }

    private static Rule BuildIsPremiumCustomerRule()
    {
        Rule rule = new Rule("IsPremiumCustomer");
        rule.Priority = 10;

        // customer type ==premium
        CodeBinaryOperatorExpression customerTypeExp =
            new CodeBinaryOperatorExpression();
        customerTypeExp.Left =
            new CodePropertyReferenceExpression(customerFieldReference, "Type");
        customerTypeExp.Operator = CodeBinaryOperatorType.ValueEquality;
        customerTypeExp.Right =
            new CodeFieldReferenceExpression(customerTypeReference, "Premium");

        rule.Condition = new RuleExpressionCondition(customerTypeExp);

        // create the THEN action
        // car type = luxury
        CodeAssignStatement thenAction = new CodeAssignStatement(
            new CodePropertyReferenceExpression(rentalFieldReference, "CarType"),
            new CodeFieldReferenceExpression(carTypeReference, "Luxury"));

        rule.ThenActions.Add(new RuleStatementAction(thenAction));

        return rule;
    }

    private static Rule BuildGasOptionRule()
    {
        Rule rule = new Rule("GasOption");
```

```
            rule.Priority = 5;

            // gas option == refill before return
            CodeBinaryOperatorExpression customerTypeExp =
                new CodeBinaryOperatorExpression();
            customerTypeExp.Left =
                new CodePropertyReferenceExpression(rentalFieldReference, "GasOption");
            customerTypeExp.Operator = CodeBinaryOperatorType.ValueEquality;
            customerTypeExp.Right =
                new CodeFieldReferenceExpression(gasOptionReference,
                    "RefillBeforeReturn");

            rule.Condition = new RuleExpressionCondition(customerTypeExp);

            // create the THEN action
            // required return tank level = current tank level
            CodeAssignStatement thenAction = new CodeAssignStatement(
                new CodePropertyReferenceExpression(rentalFieldReference,
                    "MinimumTankLevelUponReturn"),
                new CodePropertyReferenceExpression(carFieldReference,
                    "CurrentTankLevel"));

            // create the ELSE action
            // required return tank level = 0
            CodeAssignStatement elseAction = new CodeAssignStatement(
                new CodePropertyReferenceExpression(rentalFieldReference,
                    "MinimumTankLevelUponReturn"),
                new CodePrimitiveExpression(0));

            rule.ThenActions.Add(new RuleStatementAction(thenAction));
            rule.ElseActions.Add(new RuleStatementAction(elseAction));

            return rule;
        }

        public static RuleDefinitions BuildRuleDefinitions()
        {
            Rule rule1 = BuildRequireInsuranceRule();
            Rule rule2 = BuildIsPremiumCustomerRule();
            Rule rule3 = BuildGasOptionRule();

            RuleSet ruleSet = new RuleSet("CarRentalRuleSet");
            ruleSet.ChainingBehavior = RuleChainingBehavior.Full;

            ruleSet.Rules.Add(rule1);
            ruleSet.Rules.Add(rule2);
            ruleSet.Rules.Add(rule3);

            RuleDefinitions ruleDefinitions = new RuleDefinitions();
            ruleDefinitions.RuleSets.Add(ruleSet);

            WorkflowMarkupSerializer serializer = new WorkflowMarkupSerializer();
            serializer.Serialize(new XmlTextWriter(@"C:\rules.xml", Encoding.Default),
```

```
                ruleDefinitions);

        return ruleDefinitions;
    }
}
```

There are a couple of things going on here. First, there is logic that builds the rules using the CodeDom classes — this code isn't specific to Windows Workflow Foundation. Here, the classes that were introduced in Table 9-4 and Table 9-5 are used to build the same rules that were built earlier using the UI. Second, there is code that takes the CodeDom expressions and creates `Rule` instances, and then adds these `Rule` instances to a `RuleSet` object in the `BuildRuleDefinitions` method. Finally, a `RuleDefinitions` instance is created and serialized to an XML file using `WorkflowMarkupSerializer`.

Creating Your Own Rules Editor

Given the knowledge conveyed in the last few sections, you could conceivably develop a completely customized rules editor. If end users need to be able to develop and maintain rules, the UI provided with the workflow API may or may not meet all requirements.

In reality, any interface given to users who are not developers would need to have tight controls and guidance during the rule development process. Although you may take for granted how easy it is to type **this.rental.CarType**, the average user's head might explode if you expect him or her to know how to do just that, and rightfully so. Users aren't developers, and it is not their job to be technical. It is up to you to provide an interface based on your users' level of expertise.

A user-friendly rules editor would probably be able to determine which properties users need to make comparisons on and provide these properties in something like a drop-down box so that there is no guessing involved. Comparison operators would probably also be displayed in a list for ease of use. Whatever your rules editor ends up looking like, the flexibility of the .NET Framework and Windows Workflow Foundation allow virtually endless possibilities to meet your needs.

Rules in XML

By default in Windows Workflow Foundation, rule definitions are associated with workflows in XML files. If you define rule conditions or rule sets in Visual Studio, the Solution Explorer window displays a *<Workflow Name>*.rules file associated with your workflow file (see Figure 9-7).

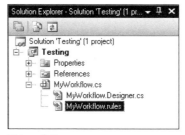

Figure 9-7

The following XML represents the three rental rules introduced earlier in this chapter. The nodes in the file correspond to types in the `System.CodeDom` namespace and are laid out in a similar fashion as the code implementation in the previous section. Some of the text has been abbreviated for spacing considerations.

```
<RuleDefinitions xmlns="http://schemas.microsoft.com/winfx/2006/xaml/workflow">
  <RuleDefinitions.RuleSets>
    <RuleSet Name="RentalRules" ChainingBehavior="Full" Description="{p3:Null}"
        xmlns:p3="http://schemas.microsoft.com/winfx/2006/xaml">
      <RuleSet.Rules>

        <Rule Name="Require Insurance" ReevaluationBehavior="Always" Priority="15"
            Description="{p3:Null}" Active="True">
          ...
        </Rule>

        <Rule Name="Is Premium Customer" ReevaluationBehavior="Always"
            Priority="10" Description="{p3:Null}" Active="True">
          <Rule.ThenActions>
            <RuleStatementAction>
              <RuleStatementAction.CodeDomStatement>
                <ns0:CodeAssignStatement LinePragma="{p3:Null}"
                    xmlns:ns0="clr-namespace:System.CodeDom;Assembly=System,
                    Version=2.0.0.0, Culture=neutral,
                    PublicKeyToken=b77a5c561934e089">
                  <ns0:CodeAssignStatement.Left>
                    <ns0:CodePropertyReferenceExpression PropertyName="CarType">
                      <ns0:CodePropertyReferenceExpression.TargetObject>
                        <ns0:CodeFieldReferenceExpression FieldName="rental">
                          <ns0:CodeFieldReferenceExpression.TargetObject>
                            <ns0:CodeThisReferenceExpression />
                          </ns0:CodeFieldReferenceExpression.TargetObject>
                        </ns0:CodeFieldReferenceExpression>
                      </ns0:CodePropertyReferenceExpression.TargetObject>
                    </ns0:CodePropertyReferenceExpression>
                  </ns0:CodeAssignStatement.Left>
                  <ns0:CodeAssignStatement.Right>
                    <ns0:CodeFieldReferenceExpression FieldName="Luxury">
                      <ns0:CodeFieldReferenceExpression.TargetObject>
                        <ns0:CodeTypeReferenceExpression>
                          <ns0:CodeTypeReferenceExpression.Type>
                            <ns0:CodeTypeReference ArrayElementType="{p3:Null}"
                                BaseType="RulesTesting.CarType" Options="0"
                                ArrayRank="0" />
                          </ns0:CodeTypeReferenceExpression.Type>
                        </ns0:CodeTypeReferenceExpression>
                      </ns0:CodeFieldReferenceExpression.TargetObject>
                    </ns0:CodeFieldReferenceExpression>
                  </ns0:CodeAssignStatement.Right>
                </ns0:CodeAssignStatement>
              </RuleStatementAction.CodeDomStatement>
            </RuleStatementAction>
          </Rule.ThenActions>
          <Rule.Condition>
            <RuleExpressionCondition Name="{p3:Null}">
              <RuleExpressionCondition.Expression>
                <ns0:CodeBinaryOperatorExpression Operator="ValueEquality"
                    xmlns:ns0="...">
                  <ns0:CodeBinaryOperatorExpression.Left>
```

```
                <ns0:CodePropertyReferenceExpression PropertyName="Type">
                  <ns0:CodePropertyReferenceExpression.TargetObject>
                    <ns0:CodePropertyReferenceExpression
                      PropertyName="Customer">
                      <ns0:CodePropertyReferenceExpression.TargetObject>
                        <ns0:CodeFieldReferenceExpression FieldName="rental">
                          <ns0:CodeFieldReferenceExpression.TargetObject>
                            <ns0:CodeThisReferenceExpression />
                          </ns0:CodeFieldReferenceExpression.TargetObject>
                        </ns0:CodeFieldReferenceExpression>
                      </ns0:CodePropertyReferenceExpression.TargetObject>
                    </ns0:CodePropertyReferenceExpression>
                  </ns0:CodePropertyReferenceExpression.TargetObject>
                </ns0:CodePropertyReferenceExpression>
              </ns0:CodeBinaryOperatorExpression.Left>
              <ns0:CodeBinaryOperatorExpression.Right>
                <ns0:CodeFieldReferenceExpression FieldName="Premium">
                  <ns0:CodeFieldReferenceExpression.TargetObject>
                    <ns0:CodeTypeReferenceExpression>
                      <ns0:CodeTypeReferenceExpression.Type>
                        <ns0:CodeTypeReference ArrayElementType="{p3:Null}"
                          BaseType="RulesTesting.CustomerType" Options="0"
                          ArrayRank="0" />
                      </ns0:CodeTypeReferenceExpression.Type>
                    </ns0:CodeTypeReferenceExpression>
                  </ns0:CodeFieldReferenceExpression.TargetObject>
                </ns0:CodeFieldReferenceExpression>
              </ns0:CodeBinaryOperatorExpression.Right>
            </ns0:CodeBinaryOperatorExpression>
          </RuleExpressionCondition.Expression>
        </RuleExpressionCondition>
      </Rule.Condition>
    </Rule>

    <Rule Name="Gas Option" ReevaluationBehavior="Always" Priority="5"
        Description="{p3:Null}" Active="True">
        ...
    </Rule>
  </RuleSet.Rules>
  </RuleSet>
 </RuleDefinitions.RuleSets>
</RuleDefinitions>
```

Using Workflow Rules

If you define your rules in Visual Studio, thereby creating a .rules file associated with your workflow, the runtime finds this file and uses it when your workflow is executed — that is, if your workflow is started by pointing to a .NET class type in the `WorkflowRuntime.CreateWorkflow` method.

With the XAML workflow style, on the other hand, you can specify the rules XML to be used when you call the `CreateWorkflow` method. The following code is an example of how this is done:

```
WorkflowRuntime workflowRuntime = new WorkflowRuntime();

XmlReader workflowReader = XmlReader.Create("MyWorkflow.xoml");
XmlReader rulesReader = XmlReader.Create("MyWorkflowRules.xoml");

WorkflowInstance instance = workflowRuntime.CreateWorkflow(
    workflowReader, rulesReader, null);

instance.Start();
```

There is an overload of the `CreateWorkflow` method that takes two `XmlReader` instances: one for the workflow definition itself and one for the workflow rules. The preceding code uses this method to create a workflow instance from the MyWorkflow.xoml definition file, with the rules that are in the MyWorkflowRules.xoml file.

Updating Rules Dynamically

One of the things that make rules so flexible is that they can be updated, even during runtime. Imagine a scenario where a workflow instance is running and reaches a point where it cannot continue because a rule has evaluated a certain way. This could happen when new customer gets rejected because of a credit check's results. However, a credit specialist might have the authority to lower the credit-score threshold. Because of situations like this, workflow rules can be changed fairly easily.

Generally, changes occur based on some code being called in the workflow host. A reference to the workflow instance in question must be acquired, because dynamic changes to rules occur at an instance level, not at the definition level. After a workflow instance reference is obtained, there are a few steps you must take to obtain a reference to a `RulesDefinition` object. After you have this object, you can make changes to rules programmatically, as shown earlier.

The following code is called from the workflow host when a request is made from the workflow to approve a decrease in the minimum credit score. This would likely happen in a CallExternalMethod activity. The workflow then determines which actions were taken by the user, if any, and proceeds appropriately.

```
static void ModifyMinimumCreditScore(WorkflowInstance instance)
{
    // this value is hardcoded for the example
    int creditScoreFloor = 600;

    WorkflowChanges workflowChanges =
        new WorkflowChanges(instance.GetWorkflowDefinition());

    CompositeActivity rootActivity = workflowChanges.TransientWorkflow;
    RuleDefinitions ruleDefinitions = (RuleDefinitions)rootActivity.GetValue(
        RuleDefinitions.RuleDefinitionsProperty);

    // loop through the rules collection and find the right one
    IEnumerator<Rule> rulesEnumerator =
        ruleDefinitions.RuleSets[0].Rules.GetEnumerator();
```

```
        Rule currentRule = null;
        while (rulesEnumerator.MoveNext())
        {
            currentRule = rulesEnumerator.Current;
            if (currentRule.Name == "CheckMinCreditScore")
            {
                break;
            }
        }

        // make sure we found our rule
        if (currentRule != null)
        {
            RuleExpressionCondition ruleCondition =
                (RuleExpressionCondition)currentRule.Condition;
            CodeBinaryOperatorExpression condition =
                (CodeBinaryOperatorExpression)ruleCondition.Expression;

            // update the condition with the new credit score floor
            condition.Right = new CodePrimitiveExpression(creditScoreFloor);

            // apply the changes
            instance.ApplyWorkflowChanges(workflowChanges);
        }
    }
```

This code example uses the concept of dynamic update to change a minimum credit score from whatever it was to 600. `WorkflowChanges` and its `TransientWorkflow` property facilitate this process by allowing access to the activities and rules inside a running workflow instance. After using some of the CodeDom classes to create the new rule expression, the `ApplyWorkflowChanges` method of the `WorkflowInstance` class is what finally cements the change in the workflow. The concepts illustrated in this code example are new and are part of the broader dynamic update topic that is discussed in detail in Chapter 11.

Summary

This chapter covered a great deal related to rules in Windows Workflow Foundation. The business rules framework provides a rich, flexible, and extensible platform on which rules can be developed, stored, and evaluated. Three types of rules were covered in this chapter: code conditions, declarative rule conditions, and rules as they exist in rule sets. Code conditions are static, code-based expressions that provide condition-dependent activities with their necessary Boolean values. Declarative rule conditions take code conditions to the next level by providing a more flexible, dynamic method of configuring certain activities, such as IfElseBranch and While.

Rule sets are where rules get interesting. This grouping of individual rules, which have their own associated actions such as THEN and ELSE, provides a great deal of functionality for business rules management and execution. Rule sets have several options related to how they are executed as a whole. This execution style is referred to as chaining. Rule sets are generally evaluated in a workflow with the Policy activity, which points to a specific rule set reference.

There are also several ways in which rules can be defined. Most of the time, rules will probably be authored and managed inside Visual Studio, which provides dialog boxes for rule conditions and rule sets. However, you can provide rule authoring capabilities in custom applications. In addition, you can programmatically create rules by using the Windows Workflow Foundation rules API and the classes in `System.CodeDom`.

10

State-Machine Workflows

This chapter covers a distinct type of workflow: the state machine. Although this workflow type has already been introduced to you, the sequential workflow tends to steal the spotlight. There is not really a reason for this except for the fact that most people tend to think of a sequential process when thinking of workflow. With that said, the state machine is no less important or useful when modeling processes.

Topics covered in this chapter include the following:

❑   Traits of a state-machine workflow

❑   When to use the state machine

❑   State-machine activities

❑   Developing state-machine workflows

❑   Advanced topics

Anatomy of a State Machine

State-machine workflows involve a few concepts that you should understand before trying to work with them, probably the most important of which is a state itself. A *state* in a state machine represents a mode or status a process can be in at a point in time. For example, consider a microwave. There are several states in which a microwave can be, including waiting for activity, cooking, and defrosting. Generally, a microwave — or any other state machine, for that matter — can be in only one state at a time.

Transitions are another vital concept of state machines. Whereas states represent what a workflow is doing at a given point in time, *transitions* define how a state machine moves from one state to another. It is extremely important to understand that a state machine does not necessarily have one defined path that dictates movement from State A to State B to State C. State machines can move from A to B, B to A, and finally from A to C, if appropriate. The execution path can vary every single time a state-machine workflow is executed. Transitions define the actions or events that may occur to cause the movement from one state to another.

State-machine workflows also have the concept of an initial and completed state. A state-machine workflow is in its *initial state* before anything happens and while it is waiting to transition to another state based on some event. As you may imagine, the *completed state* is what is transitioned to when the workflow has completed its final steps.

When to Use State Machines

Windows Workflow Foundation includes two very distinct types of workflows (state machine and sequential, which were introduced earlier in this book), and there are situations in which one type may work better than the other. However, sometimes this is not obvious, so it may come down to which type *seems* right given the problem at hand. However, there are several criteria that can give you a good idea of the workflow type that is right for your project.

One thing that can tip you off that you should use a state-machine workflow rather than the sequential variety is when the workflow has a large amount of human interaction. That is not to say that sequential workflows should not be used when humans are involved in the process, but workflows laden with human interaction are generally easier to model as a state machine. This is because whenever a person performs an action, a process progresses to another step; and in reality the word *progresses* is not completely accurate—it implies a forward movement. State machines are able to jump all over the place, depending on what the developer defines. Consider a state-machine workflow representing an order processing system. An active workflow instance could not jump from an Order On Hold state to a Waiting For Order state—that just wouldn't make sense. However, there are no restrictions on how many states another state can progress to.

State-machine workflows are also a natural fit when events that fire outside the bounds of the workflow are plentiful. This generally implies that the workflow is made up of a discrete set of steps, or states. State machines do well in these instances because each discrete step in a state machine is progressed to because of an event that is fired. Consider the order processing workflow again. There might be states called Pending Approval, Approved, and Completed. Each of these three example states is entered because the corresponding event occurred. Perhaps the workflow enters the Pending Approval state when the customer has finished entering an order for a large amount. The Approved state might be entered when an order specialist investigates the pending order and decides everything is good enough to ship. Finally, the Completed state might be entered when the customer's credit is verified.

If a process seems to have several instances when certain actions can occur at any point in the workflow, a state machine might be a good candidate. This is because as previously mentioned, states in a state machine can be entered in any order as long as you have defined the workflow this way. An order should probably be able to enter the On Hold or Canceled state at any time. If something goes wrong with a customer's order at any point in the process, a customer service representative can place the order on hold until the issue is resolved. The same applies if the order needs to be canceled.

Again, although there is no magical formula that tells you when to use a state-machine workflow instead of a sequential workflow, a lot of the time it comes down to what feels right. Because the sequential style is the most common workflow because it is the archetypal process modeling mode, developers will probably tend to choose a sequential workflow when a state machine could get the job done in a more efficient manner. If you are developing a sequential workflow and it starts to become difficult to allot for every execution path, or the process you are modeling just does not feel natural, it's time to consider a state machine.

State-Machine Activities

A handful of out-of-the-box activities are vital to modeling the state-machine workflow type. With the exception of the EventDriven activity, all activities discussed in this section can be used *only* in a state machine.

The StateMachineWorkflowActivity Class

As with the sequential workflow type, the state-machine workflow is represented as an activity. The StateMachineWorkflowActivity class inherits directly from CompositeActivity and implements the behavior that defines the concept of a state machine.

In contrast to the sequential workflow type, which can contain just about any activity as a direct child, the state-machine workflow can contain only State and EventDriven activities as direct children. These activity types and how they interact with the state machine are discussed in detail in the following sections.

The activity representing state machines has two properties that you use to configure vital behavior: InitialStateName and CompletedStateName. Both properties point to activities that are current children of the workflow. The InitialStateName property should point to the State activity, which is the first state that the workflow can be in (something like the Waiting For Order state in the previous example). Because a workflow logically has to have a first state, this property is required; otherwise, the workflow is in an invalid state.

The CompletedStateName property is equally useful and as important as the InitialStateName property. However, this property is not required, because it is conceivable to have a workflow that does not end. However, if you choose to have a completed state, the workflow knows it is finished whenever the referenced state is transitioned to. Most of the time, you specify a State activity in the CompletedStateName property, but there may be instances where it makes sense to have a never-ending workflow. For example, certain business processes might need to remain open for a long time, even if all work appears to have been completed. Keep in mind that just because the workflow has not completed, it does not need to be kept in memory. It can remain in a persisted state until more work needs to be performed.

The State Activity

The State activity is crucial to modeling a state machine because it represents the individual, discrete steps in a workflow. The State activity doesn't do anything per se — it is a container for other activities that perform the work. The State activity is simply representative of a position or status in a workflow.

State activities have names such as WaitingForOrder, OnHold, and PendingApproval. In these examples, and most of the time, a State activity represents one status in which a workflow can be. However, a State activity can also contain other State activities. In these special cases, the parent activity can act as an event handler for all child activities. This is called *recursive state composition* and is discussed a little later in this chapter.

State activities can contain only four activity types. You already know that a State activity can contain other State activities, but the EventDriven, StateInitialization, and StateFinalization activities can also be children of the State activity. These activities are discussed next.

The EventDriven Activity

You use the EventDriven activity to define the events that can occur in the workflow states or in the state-machine workflow itself. Like the State activity, the EventDriven activity doesn't really do anything by itself. Rather, because it inherits from `CompositeActivity`, it acts as a container for other activities that execute when the configured event is raised.

The EventDriven activity itself does not contain the facilities to point to a specific event to watch for. Events are listened for by using activities that implement the `IEventActivity` interface, such as the HandleExternalEvent and Delay activities. Therefore, one of these activities must be the first child of an EventDriven activity. Using an `IEventActivity` activity as the first child essentially blocks the execution of subsequent activities, which can be of any type, until the configured event fires — or, in the case of the Delay activity, when the timeout occurs. Furthermore, the EventDriven activity can contain only one activity that implements `IEventActivity`.

Each EventDriven activity can dictate which state the workflow transitions to upon the firing of the event and the subsequent execution of child activities. However, events can cause transitions only to State activities that are not parents to other State activities. These nonparent states are called *leaf states.* The nonleaf parent states act as a context container that accepts events for all child activities.

The StateInitialization Activity

The StateInitialization activity is an optional component of the State activity, and there can be only one of this type of activity, if any. This activity inherits from `SequenceActivity`, so it can have multiple child activities, which are executed in order. If this activity is present in a state, it is automatically executed when its parent state is entered.

Because the StateInitialization activity is unconditionally executed at the point a State activity is transitioned to, it cannot contain any `IEventActivity` activities.

The StateFinalization Activity

The StateFinalization activity has many of the traits of the StateInitialization activity. The most notable difference between the two activities is that the StateFinalization activity executes its child activities when the parent State activity is leaving by transitioning to another state.

Like the StateInitialization activity, the StateFinalization activity is optional. It cannot contain `IEventActivity` activities, and it inherits from `SequenceActivity`.

The SetState Activity

The SetState activity enables you to unconditionally transition to another state in the workflow without relying upon the firing of a specific event. However, there are restrictions on where this activity can be used. The SetState activity can be located only in an EventDriven or StateInitialization activity. Furthermore, in most cases, the SetState activity has to be the last child in the parent, because any other activities placed after it would never get executed. The exception to this rule is when the last child is an IfElse activity. In this case, the SetState activity has to be the last child in one of the branches.

Just like the EventDriven activity, the SetState activity can transition only to leaf states. You configure this activity by setting the `TargetStateName` property. Because of the way the state-machine workflow is meant to function, you should probably use the SetState activity sparingly, and state transitions should be dictated by events that are fired. However, this activity is available in the situations that warrant manual state transitions.

Recursive State Composition

There may be times in a state-machine workflow when multiple states need to respond to the same event or events. When modeling this type of functionality, developers commonly place the same event in multiple states, which causes replicated behavior. Obviously, this is not an optimal method.

The state-machine workflow type in Windows Workflow Foundation provides a way to implement this behavior in a more elegant manner. Essentially, states that want to listen for a common set of events are added to a parent state. This pattern is referred to as *recursive state composition.*

Refer back to the order workflow scenario. There might be states called Order Processing and Order Approved, with both states transitioning to an Order Completed state when an external event dictates this move. Figure 10-1 shows an example of what this workflow might look like, with each state taking care of its own transition.

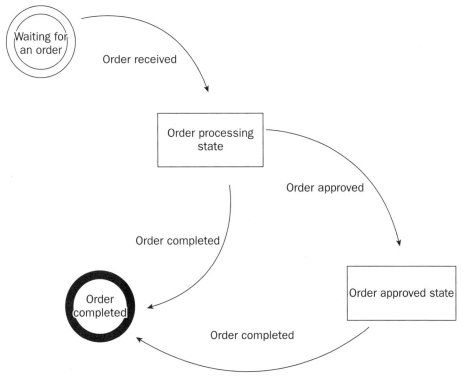

Figure 10-1

Again, this is not optimal because each state has the same logic as the other for transitioning to the Order Completed state. If both the processing and approved states are wrapped in a parent state that knows how to transition to a completed order, this duplicate logic can be eliminated. Figure 10-2 shows an example of what this might look like.

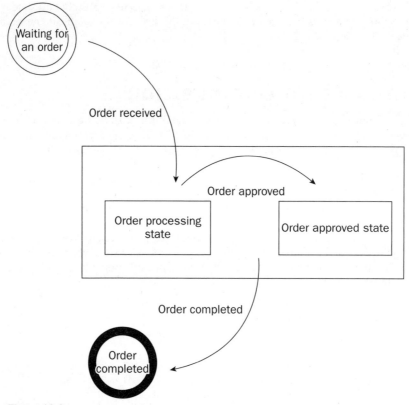

Figure 10-2

In recursive state composition, both the parent and child states are standard State activities by definition. A parent is a parent because the workflow developer added other State activities to it. Conversely, a child state is a child state because the developer added it to a parent State activity. However, when a State activity becomes a parent, its default behavior changes. The most glaring difference is the fact that a parent state cannot be directly transitioned to. Rather, transitions are made to child states, thereby activating the parent state. However, the parent state can have EventDriven activities just as a standard State would. Subsequently, while the workflow is in any of the child states, the parent's events will be raised and executed just as though the child state owned the event.

The concept of recursive state composition is commonly used to model a workflow's exception-handling scenarios. In this case, the word *exception* is referring not to a .NET exception but to a process exception. For example, if at any time during a workflow something goes wrong, it can enter a state called On Hold and notify a support agent of the issue. After the issue is resolved, the workflow can resume.

The State-Machine Designer

Now that the essentials of the state-machine workflow type have been introduced, it's time to cover the development of state-machine workflows in the Windows Workflow Foundation designer. Because state-machine workflows are different from sequential workflows, this workflow type has its own distinct designer.

Figure 10-3 shows an example of the state-machine workflow designer with a completed workflow. This example showcases a workflow modeling the process of a party. There is an initial state called `Party WorkflowInitialState` that transitions to `EntertainingState` when the `OnFirstGuestArrival` EventDriven activity is executed. If the food runs out during the `EntertainingState`, the workflow transitions to the `PreparingRefreshmentsState`. When the refreshments are ready, the workflow returns to the `EntertainingState`. When the party is active, guest arrivals are captured by the `OnGuestArrives` EventDriven activity. Finally, if at any time during the `EntertainingState` or `PreparingRefreshmentsState` the last guest leaves, the workflow transitions to the `PartyOver` state, signifying the end of the party workflow.

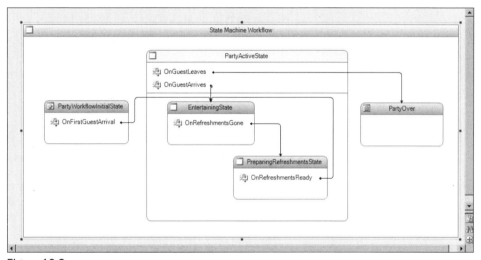

Figure 10-3

There are a few interesting things about the designer in this example. First, take a look at the `Party WorkflowInitialState` State activity. This state is the workflow's initial state, and as such, it has a special green icon on the top left. In addition, the `PartyOver` state is the workflow's completed state. This state has a special icon as well, denoted by the red image at its upper left. Remember, these two special states are configured by setting the `InitialStateName` and `CompletedStateName` properties of the workflow itself.

The state-machine workflow designer also provides a context menu where you can set these properties. Figure 10-4 shows the context menu that is displayed when you right-click a State activity in the designer. The Set As Initial State and Set As Completed State menu options provide an easy way to manipulate certain workflow properties.

Figure 10-4

This context menu also provides other options for manipulating the definition of a state-machine work-flow. In this example, there are four options to add context-appropriate activities to the selected State activity (the activity that was previously selected by right-clicking it in the designer). In this case, the activities that can be added are State, EventDriven, StateInitialization, and StateFinalization. If you right-click an empty area of the workflow itself, you are presented with a set of options to add State and EventDriven activities. Using the context menu to add activities yields the same results as dragging and dropping an activity from the Visual Studio Toolbox.

Drilling down, the designer view in Figure 10-5 shows the detail behind an EventDriven activity. In this case, the EventDriven activity shown is OnFirstGuestArrival, which is located in PartyWorkflow InitialState. This view was accessed by double-clicking the OnFirstGuestArrival EventDriven activity in the main workflow designer, as signified by the breadcrumb trail at the top of the designer. This shows that the current view is inside PartyWorkflowInitialState, which is inside Party Workflow. If you click an item in a breadcrumb trail, you are taken to whatever view is appropriate. This is a convenient way to navigate the workflow.

Remember that the first activity in an EventDriven activity has to implement IEventActivity, which the HandleExternalEvent activity does. The first activity in the example EventDriven activity is handleGuestArrivesEvent, which waits until a guest arrives to execute the next activities. There is also a Code activity that simply increments a workflow variable (in this case, keeping track of the number of guests). Last in the execution chain is a SetState activity. The setEntertainingState State activity specifies that the workflow should transition to EntertainingState at this point. Because this activity is configured to make the appropriate transition, the workflow designer automatically displays an arrow going from the EventDriven activity to the appropriate state, as shown in Figure 10-6.

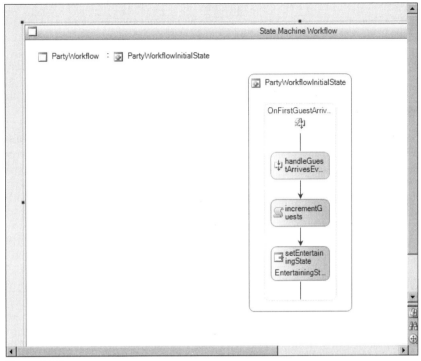

Figure 10-5

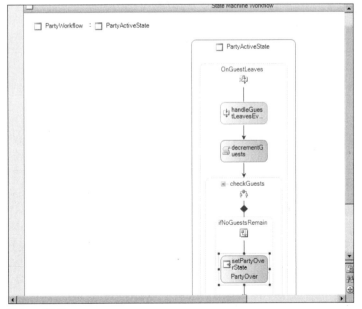

Figure 10-6

The EventDriven activity view displayed in Figure 10-5 shows the OnGuestLeaves EventDriven activity, which is defined in PartyActiveState. This activity is a little more interesting because there is logic that checks the guest count variable to whether if there are any guests left when one leaves. If, and only if, the last guest just left, the workflow transitions to the PartyOver state. Because the PartyOver state is designated at the completed state of the workflow, the execution of the instance ends when a transition moves to that state. Notice in Figure 10-6 that an arrow is drawn from the OnGuestLeaves EventDriven activity to the PartyOver state even though the transition is conditional and does not always occur.

As previously mentioned, if you have correctly configured the SetState activities, the state-machine workflow designer uses arrows to help you visualize these transitions. However, you can automate adding and configuring these SetState activities by simply clicking an anchor on an EventDriven activity and dragging it to an anchor on a State activity. After you perform this action in the designer, you can inspect the EventDriven activity view of the activity from which you dragged the anchor and see that a SetState activity has been added for you. In addition, the TargetStateName property is set to point to the chosen State activity.

Manipulating and Querying State-Machine Workflows

Windows Workflow Foundation provides the basic infrastructure to monitor and manipulate state-machine workflows. Monitoring is useful when you'd like to see where a running workflow is in its execution lifecycle. Manipulation comes in handy when outside input dictates that a state machine should take an alternative path. The following sections cover these topics.

The StateMachineWorkflowInstance Class

Because the state-machine workflow type is fundamentally unique, it has its own instance wrapper class that provides a wealth of data describing a running workflow instance as well as functionality to interact with the running workflow. This class is called StateMachineWorkflowInstance and can be found in the System.Workflow.Activities namespace.

To acquire an instance of this class for use in your workflow host, you need an instance of the WorkflowRuntime class and an InstanceId of the workflow instance of interest. The following code shows how to create an instance of StateMachineWorkflowInstance:

```
WorkflowRuntime runtime = new WorkflowRuntime();
WorkflowInstance instance = runtime.CreateWorkflow(typeof(MyWorkflow));
instance.Start();

stateMachineInstance
    = new StateMachineWorkflowInstance(runtime, instance.InstanceId);
```

Obviously, the workflow definition represented by the WorkflowInstance class needs to be a state-machine workflow; otherwise, the constructor throws an ArgumentException.

This class has properties that enable you to get information about the workflow instance and the workflow definition. The `WorkflowInstance` property returns an instance of the class of the same name. The `StateMachineWorkflow` property returns an instance of `StateMachineWorkflowActivity`, which is the definition of the workflow.

The `StateMachineWorkflowInstance` class also contains quite a few properties that enable you to query the workflow's current status. These properties and their uses are discussed in the next section.

Querying a State-Machine Instance

The `StateMachineWorkflowInstance` class gives you a great deal of information regarding the current state of a state-machine workflow instance. For example, you might have the following questions about the state machine:

- ❏ What are the states that make up the workflow?
- ❏ What state is the workflow currently in?
- ❏ Given the current state, what states can be next?
- ❏ What has the workflow done in the past?

To answer these questions, the `StateMachineWorkflowInstance` class provides you with several public properties. First, the `States` property returns a list of State activities through a `ReadOnly Collection<StateActivity>` instance, which represents all the states that make up the workflow.

To determine the state that the workflow is currently in, you can use the `CurrentStateName` or `CurrentState` property. The `CurrentState` property returns a string that represents the current state's name. The `CurrentState` property returns the State activity instance that represents the current state.

The third question regarding the available state changes can be answered by the `PossibleState Transitions` property. This property is of type `ReadOnlyCollection<string>`, thereby providing the list of possible states in string form.

The ability to access all this information is very useful, especially when you want to create a UI to monitor and interact with state-machine workflows. Imagine an application that has certain user interface components available when the workflow is in a given list of states. If information about the current workflow state were not available, you would have to implement duplicate logic in the client application to know when certain UI components should be available or enabled. However, the ability to query enables you to keep all the process logic in the workflow, where it should be. All the client application has to do is ask the workflow what state it is in and what states can come next. Logic can then be implemented to make the appropriate UI components available to the user.

Skipping Steps

Another way in which the `StateMachineWorkflowInstance` class provides flexibility in managing workflows is by allowing the client to programmatically set the current state of a workflow instance. This functionally is achieved by calling the `SetState` method and passing either a string representation of a state or an instance of a `StateActivity` class.

You should employ great restraint when using this method, because it basically sets a workflow's state using brute force. This means that no matter where the workflow is in its execution, and no matter what state the workflow is currently in, the SetState method obeys the command given by the code. It is important to let the workflow manage its own state; otherwise, the integrity of logic the workflow can degrade.

With that said, there are instances when using the SetState method is appropriate. Think of this method as an override option for certain steps in a workflow.

Imagine a workflow that manages certain processing states of data cleansing. Messages that come in to the workflow from outside sources might need to be processed into a common format. In this case, the workflow could have several states that represent different buckets of processing progress as well as exception states for when data cannot be easily transformed. For example, when an exception state is reached, the workflow application could notify the appropriate employee and ask him or her to manually fix the problem. However, there might be cases where the employee, who should be an expert in the data, decides that the message looks good enough to progress and decides to skip the manual step. In such a case, the SetState method provides a great alternative to modeling every manual override in the workflow itself. The client application used by the data analyst employees could have a button that enables them to override the manual intervention state, which then lets the data processing proceed as normal.

Although the SetState method can provide a great way to manage manual overrides and other workflow exceptions, it should be used only when necessary. As a rule of thumb, you should model override scenarios on the workflow itself rather than use this method. However, if accounting for the situations that might occur becomes daunting or starts to feel unnatural, perhaps the SetState method is a good candidate.

A Shopping Cart Example

The remainder of this chapter describes an example workflow application that models the familiar concept of a shopping cart. Although this workflow is nowhere near what a real-world shopping cart application needs to be, it is a great example for illustrating the concepts conveyed in this chapter regarding state machines.

The workflow starts out in a state that is simply waiting for something to happen. After a new shopping session is created, the workflow moves to the Shopping state. It is in this state that the user can add new items to the workflow, as well as check out. When the user says that he or she wants to check out, the appropriate EventDriven activity makes sure the cart is valid. In this workflow, the number of items a user can purchase cannot exceed three. (This may sound like a strange rule, but it works for this example.)

If the user's order is valid, the workflow proceeds to the WaitingToShip state. However, if more than three items were added to the order, the workflow enters the InvalidOrder state. When the workflow is in the InvalidOrder state, one of two things can happen. The first is a timeout. If nothing happens to correct the invalid state of the order within ten seconds, the order times out, and a transition is made to the workflow's completed state. However, if an administrator decides to override the order and allow it to ship, a manual state transition can occur through the ordering application (discussed later).

In addition, if the workflow is in either the `Shopping` or `InvalidOrder` state, a cancel event can be passed to the workflow, which immediately moves the state machine to its completed state. Finally, if a command to ship the order is passed while the workflow is in the `WaitingToShip` state, the completed state is transitioned to.

To illustrate the use of this workflow inside an application, a Windows Forms application has been developed to control the process (see Figure 10-7). As you can see, there is a button to start a new shopping session. When this button is clicked, a new workflow instance is started, and a description of the order is added to the list below.

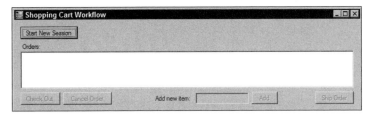

Figure 10-7

When at least one shopping session is started and selected in the list, the controls at the bottom of the screen that are appropriate for the current workflow state are enabled. For example, the Ship Order button is not enabled until a checkout command has been issued. Also, items can be added only while the workflow is in the `Shopping` state.

Now that the general application has been explained, it's time to get down to business. The first thing to be discussed is the shopping cart workflow itself. Figure 10-8 shows the state machine as it is displayed in the Visual Studio designer.

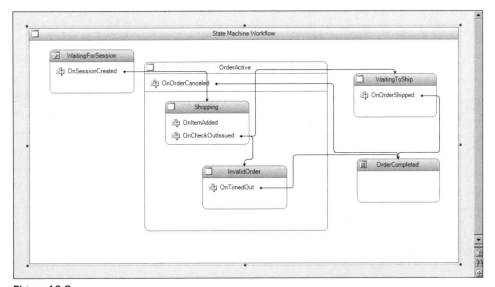

Figure 10-8

All the workflow states can be found here. You can see that the `WaitingForSession` state is designated as the workflow's initial state. This is the state that is immediately entered when the host application calls the `WorkflowInstance.Start` method. It does not exit that state and enter the `Shopping` state until the event configured in the `OnSessionCreated` EventDriven activity is raised.

The `Shopping` and `InvalidOrder` states are children, or leaf states, of the `OrderActive` state. As mentioned, this parent state handles the event configured in the `OnOrderCanceled` EventDriven activity. This employs the concept of recursive event composition introduced earlier in the chapter.

Also notice that the only connector line going from the `InvalidOrder` state is to the `OrderCompleted` state. This state transition occurs if there is a timeout while in the `InvalidOrder` state (as shown in Figure 10-9). As mentioned earlier, an administrator can override this invalid order and allow it to ship, if desired. Because there is no event wired to perform this transition, there is code in the client application that uses the `SetState` method to perform this transition. (The complete application code is shown later.)

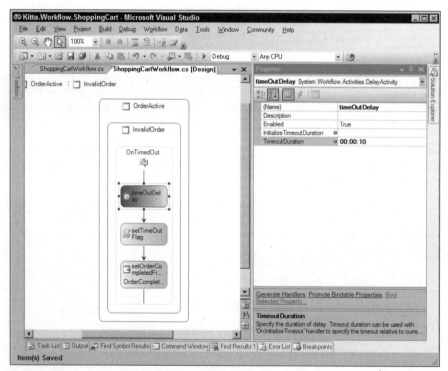

Figure 10-9

The final piece of the workflow is the code that sits behind the visual representation:

```
public sealed partial class ShoppingCartWorkflow: StateMachineWorkflowActivity
{
    public ItemAddedEventArgs itemAddedEventArgs = default(ItemAddedEventArgs);
    private Order order = new Order();
```

```
        private bool orderTimedOut = false;
        private bool canceled = false;

        public bool Canceled
        {
            get { return canceled; }
        }

        public Order Order
        {
            get { return this.order; }
        }

        public bool OrderTimedOut
        {
            get { return orderTimedOut; }
        }

        public ShoppingCartWorkflow()
        {
            InitializeComponent();
        }

        private void addItemToOrder_ExecuteCode(object sender, EventArgs e)
        {
            this.order.Items.Add(itemAddedEventArgs.Item);
        }

        private void CheckItemCount(object sender, ConditionalEventArgs e)
        {
            e.Result = this.order.Items.Count > 3;
        }

        private void setTimeOutFlag_ExecuteCode(object sender, EventArgs e)
        {
            this.orderTimedOut = true;
        }

        private void handleOrderCanceled_Invoked(object sender,
            ExternalDataEventArgs e)
        {
            this.canceled = true;
        }
    }
```

The public properties in this code allow communication back to the host after the workflow is completed. In addition, there are event handler methods that set flags for processing. One of these methods is the code condition that is called when the user issues a checkout command, which verifies that this is a valid order.

The following code is the Windows Forms application that controls the workflow and provides a front end for its functionality. (This application was previously shown in Figure 10-7.) Because this is a book about Windows Workflow Foundation, the focus of this discussion is the part of the code that interacts with the Windows Workflow Foundation API classes. The `EnableControls` method uses the `StateMachineWorkflowInstance` class to determine the state that the workflow is currently in and appropriately enable the form's controls.

```csharp
public partial class MainForm : Form
{
    private WorkflowRuntime runtime;
    private ShoppingCartService shoppingCartService;
    private List<StateMachineWorkflowInstance> orderWorkflows;

    private delegate void DefaultDelegate();
    private delegate void ShowOrderConfirmationDelegate(Order order,
        bool orderTimedOut);

    private StateMachineWorkflowInstance SelectedOrderWorkflow
    {
        get
        {
            if (lstOrders.SelectedItem != null)
                return orderWorkflows[lstOrders.SelectedIndex];
            else
                return null;
        }
    }

    public MainForm()
    {
        InitializeComponent();
    }

    private void MainForm_Load(object sender, EventArgs e)
    {
        this.orderWorkflows = new List<StateMachineWorkflowInstance>();
        this.DisableControls();
        this.ConfigureRuntime();
    }

    private void ConfigureRuntime()
    {
        runtime = new WorkflowRuntime();

        runtime.WorkflowIdled +=
            new EventHandler<WorkflowEventArgs>(runtime_WorkflowIdled);
        runtime.WorkflowCompleted += new
            EventHandler<WorkflowCompletedEventArgs>(runtime_WorkflowCompleted);
        runtime.WorkflowTerminated += new
            EventHandler<WorkflowTerminatedEventArgs>(runtime_WorkflowTerminated);

        ExternalDataExchangeService dataService =
            new ExternalDataExchangeService();
        runtime.AddService(dataService);

        shoppingCartService = new ShoppingCartService();
        dataService.AddService(shoppingCartService);
```

```
        }

        private void runtime_WorkflowIdled(object sender, WorkflowEventArgs e)
        {
            this.UpdateOrders();
        }

        private void runtime_WorkflowTerminated(object sender,
            WorkflowTerminatedEventArgs e)
        {
            this.UpdateOrders();
        }

        private void runtime_WorkflowCompleted(object sender,
            WorkflowCompletedEventArgs e)
        {
            this.UpdateOrders();

            if(!(bool)e.OutputParameters["Canceled"])
                this.ShowOrderConfirmation((Order)e.OutputParameters["Order"],
                    (bool)e.OutputParameters["OrderTimedOut"]);
        }

        private void ShowOrderConfirmation(Order order, bool orderTimedOut)
        {
            if (this.InvokeRequired)
            {
                this.Invoke(new ShowOrderConfirmationDelegate(ShowOrderConfirmation),
                    new object[] { order, orderTimedOut });
            }
            else
            {
                StringBuilder sb = new StringBuilder();

                if (!orderTimedOut)
                {
                    sb.Append("Your order was completed. " +
                        "The following items were ordered:");
                    sb.Append(Environment.NewLine);

                    foreach (Item item in order.Items)
                    {
                        sb.Append(Environment.NewLine);
                        sb.Append(item.ItemId);
                    }
                }
                else
                {
                    sb.Append("Your order was invalid and timed-out " +
                        "before someone approved it.");
                }

                MessageBox.Show(sb.ToString(), "Your Order",
                    MessageBoxButtons.OK, MessageBoxIcon.Information);
```

```
        }
    }

    private void btnNewSession_Click(object sender, EventArgs e)
    {
        WorkflowInstance instance = runtime.CreateWorkflow(
            typeof(ShoppingCartWorkflow));

        instance.Start();

        StateMachineWorkflowInstance stateMachineInstance =
            new StateMachineWorkflowInstance(this.runtime,
                instance.InstanceId);

        this.orderWorkflows.Add(stateMachineInstance);

        this.shoppingCartService.CreateSession(instance.InstanceId);
    }

    private void UpdateOrders()
    {
        if (this.InvokeRequired)
        {
            this.Invoke(new DefaultDelegate(UpdateOrders));
        }
        else
        {
            Guid tempGuid = default(Guid);

            if (this.SelectedOrderWorkflow != null)
                tempGuid = this.SelectedOrderWorkflow.InstanceId;

            this.DisableControls();
            lstOrders.Items.Clear();

            foreach (StateMachineWorkflowInstance i in this.orderWorkflows)
            {
                string description = i.InstanceId.ToString() + " (" +
                    (i.PossibleStateTransitions.Count > 0 ? i.CurrentStateName :
                        "Completed") + ")";

                int index = lstOrders.Items.Add(description);

                if (tempGuid != default(Guid) && tempGuid == i.InstanceId)
                    lstOrders.SelectedIndex = index;
            }
        }
    }

    private void DisableControls()
    {
        btnCheckOut.Enabled = false;
        btnCancelOrder.Enabled = false;
        btnShipOrder.Enabled = false;
```

```
            btnAddItem.Enabled = false;
            txtItem.Clear();
            txtItem.Enabled = false;
    }

    private void EnableControls()
    {
        switch (this.SelectedOrderWorkflow.CurrentStateName)
        {
            case "Shopping":

                txtItem.Enabled = true;
                btnAddItem.Enabled = true;
                btnCheckOut.Enabled = true;
                btnCancelOrder.Enabled = true;

                break;

            case "InvalidOrder":

                btnCancelOrder.Enabled = true;
                btnShipOrder.Enabled = true;

                break;

            case "WaitingToShip":

                btnShipOrder.Enabled = true;

                break;
        }
    }

    private void lstOrders_SelectedIndexChanged(object sender,
        EventArgs e)
    {
        this.DisableControls();

        if (lstOrders.SelectedItem != null)
            this.EnableControls();
    }

    private void btnCheckOut_Click(object sender, EventArgs e)
    {
        if (this.SelectedOrderWorkflow != null)
        {
            this.shoppingCartService.CheckOut(
                this.SelectedOrderWorkflow.InstanceId);
        }
    }

    private void btnCancelOrder_Click(object sender, EventArgs e)
    {
        if (this.SelectedOrderWorkflow != null)
```

```
        {
            this.shoppingCartService.CancelOrder(
                this.SelectedOrderWorkflow.InstanceId);

            this.UpdateOrders();
        }
    }

    private void btnShipOrder_Click(object sender, EventArgs e)
    {
        if (this.SelectedOrderWorkflow != null)
        {
            bool orderShipped = false;

            if (this.SelectedOrderWorkflow.CurrentStateName
                == "InvalidOrder")
            {
                DialogResult res = MessageBox.Show("Ship Order?",
                    "The order is currently in an invalid state, " +
                    "do you want to send it anyway?",
                    MessageBoxButtons.YesNo, MessageBoxIcon.Question);

                if (res == DialogResult.Yes)
                {
                    this.SelectedOrderWorkflow.SetState(
                        "OrderCompleted");
                    orderShipped = true;
                }
            }
            else
            {
                this.shoppingCartService.ShipOrder(
                    this.SelectedOrderWorkflow.InstanceId);
                orderShipped = true;
            }

            if (orderShipped)
            {
                this.UpdateOrders();
            }
        }
    }

    private void btnAddItem_Click(object sender, EventArgs e)
    {
        if (this.SelectedOrderWorkflow != null)
        {
            this.shoppingCartService.AddItem(
                this.SelectedOrderWorkflow.InstanceId,
                new Item(txtItem.Text.Trim()));
        }

        this.txtItem.Clear();
    }
}
```

The event handlers for the form's buttons use an instance of the `ShoppingCartService` class that was developed for this example. Although this class is not shown in this chapter, you can find it in the book's example code.

The event handler for the Ship Order button, `btnShipOrder_Click`, uses the `StateMachineWorkflow Instance` class as well as the call to the `SetState` method. A check is made in this method to see whether the workflow is currently in the `InvalidOrder` state. If it is, a confirmation message is displayed to make sure that the user really wants to ship an invalid order. If the order is not in this invalid state, it is shipped by calling the `ShipOrder` method of the `ShoppingCartService` class.

Summary

This chapter covered the concepts and patterns related to the Windows Workflow Foundation state-machine workflow style. The state machine provides a great deal of functionality to effectively model business processes inside the workflow infrastructure.

State machines include concepts such as states and transitions. Each state represents a discrete position a workflow can be in at a given point in time. Unlike sequential workflows, state machines do not have to have a predefined execution path. States can transition back and forth and all around the workflow if the current process dictates this behavior.

Because there are two distinct types of workflows, you need to have a feel for the best scenarios for each type. Some things that may necessitate a state-machine workflow include a lot of human interaction and a lot of external events that can fire at any point in the process. Or you may find it difficult to model all of a process's possible execution branches in a sequential workflow. Many times, it boils down to what feels right or natural for the current project.

Other topics relevant to state-machine workflows covered in this chapter include recursive state composition, querying a running workflow as to what state it is in or what transitions are possible, and moving states using a brute-force method. These concepts were illustrated in an extensive shopping cart example.

11

Dynamic Update and Designer Re-Hosting

This chapter discusses a few advanced topics that are in some ways related. First, the chapter covers the concept of dynamic update. Dynamic update enables you to modify the behavior of a workflow instance after it has started. The other topic is designer re-hosting, which enables you to include the rich Visual Studio workflow views in your own custom applications.

Although each topic has its own distinct functionality in Windows Workflow Foundation, you can use them together to provide a great deal of functionality in end-user applications.

This chapter covers the following topics:

- ❑ Dynamic update concepts and drivers
- ❑ Dynamic update infrastructure
- ❑ The workflow designer
- ❑ Hosting the designer in custom applications
- ❑ Applying dynamic update and designer re-hosting

Dynamic Update

Dynamic update is an extremely power feature of Windows Workflow Foundation that directly ties to one of the workflow tenets described in Chapter 1: Workflows are transparent and dynamic throughout their lifecycle, which means that running workflow instances should be flexible enough to have modifiable behavior.

Basically, dynamic update is provided for process scenarios that were not modeled in the workflow during development. Scenarios that might need such functionality are virtually endless. However, situations that might benefit from dynamic update include the following:

❑ Skipping specific steps in a workflow by deleting activities

❑ Adding additional approval steps in a workflow

❑ Modifying numeric thresholds that would allow processes to proceed in special instances

❑ Modifying business rules in extraordinary cases

❑ Adding an on-hold state to a workflow that requires out-of-band work

Dynamic update is applicable to sequential as well as state-machine workflows. However, when any dynamic changes are made to workflows, they are made to specific *instances* only, not to the workflow definition itself. It cannot be emphasized enough that dynamic update is to be used in circumstances calling for extraneous behavior that was not modeled by the original workflow developer. If a scenario is likely enough to occur a large percentage of the time, it should probably be added to the workflow definition.

There are many ways you can allow dynamic changes to be made to workflow instances. However, the same classes and patterns are used no matter where these changes are applied in the code. The workflow API provided for dynamic update is described in the following section.

The Dynamic Update API

Most of the classes that assist in the dynamic update process have already been introduced in this book and should be familiar to you. However, there is one class whose sole purpose is to allow dynamic update to occur: WorkflowChanges. This class is in the System.Workflow.ComponentModel namespace. To create an instance of this class, you need to pass a reference to the workflow's definition class to the constructor. You can easily obtain this reference by calling the GetWorkflowDefinition method of the WorkflowInstance class, as follows:

```
WorkflowInstance instance = workflowRuntime.GetWorkflow(instanceId);
WorkflowChanges changes = new WorkflowChanges(instance.GetWorkflowDefinition());
```

Now that you have an instance of the WorkflowChanges class, you can start making changes to the workflow definition. To do this, you need to use the workflow definition instance that is exposed in the WorkflowChanges.TransientWorkflow property. TransientWorkflow is of type CompositeActivity, which includes either SequentialWorkflowActivity or StateMachineWorkflowActivity.

To make changes to the workflow's activity tree, use the Activities property of the reference returned from TransientWorkflow. You can add activities directly to the workflow or as children of other composite activities. For example, you may want to add a new activity to a specific IfElseBranch activity. In addition, you can remove activities by calling the Remove method of the Activities property.

The following code shows an example of how to add an InvokeWorkflowActivity instance that calls another business process to an IfElseBranch activity:

```
WorkflowInstance instance = workflowRuntime.GetWorkflow(instanceId);
WorkflowChanges changes = new WorkflowChanges(instance.GetWorkflowDefinition());
```

```
// create a new InvokeWorkflowActivity instance and set its properties
InvokeWorkflowActivity invokeWorkflow = new InvokeWorkflowActivity();
invokeWorkflow.Name = "invokeMyWorkflow";
invokeWorkflow.TargetWorkflow = typeof(MyWorkflow);

// get the transient workflow definition and the IfElseBranch activity of interest
CompositeActivity wf = changes.TransientWorkflow;
IfElseBranchActivity elseBranch =
    wf.Activities["elseBranch"] as IfElseBranchActivity;

// add the InvokeWorkflowActivity instance to the IfElseBranchActivity
if (elseBranch != null)
    elseBranch.Activities.Add(invokeWorkflow);

// see if there are any errors in the changes we've made
ValidationErrorCollection errors = changes.Validate();
if (errors.Count == 0)
{
    // apply the changes to the workflow instance; we're done!
    instance.ApplyWorkflowChanges(changes);
}
else
{
    // there were some validation errors, throw an exception
    throw new ApplicationException(
        "There were errors when updating the workflow!");
}
```

The preceding code uses the `WorkflowChanges` class along with the workflow instance's `Transient Activity` property to add the `InvokeWorkflowActivity` instance to the running workflow. First, the `IfElseBranchActivity` instance is obtained using its name. Then the new activity is added as a change to the IfElseBranch activity. A call to the `Validate` method is made to make sure what was just done is legal. Finally, the changes are applied by calling `ApplyWorkflowChanges`.

Dynamic Update from within the Workflow

So far, the dynamic update examples in this chapter pertained to dynamically changing a running workflow from the context of the workflow runtime's host. However, there are times when a workflow can anticipate that it may need to change in the future during runtime. In these cases, you can inform a workflow that it is modifying itself.

Changing a workflow from the inside is not that different from doing the same thing from the outside. The biggest difference is that you need to create an instance of the `WorkflowChanges` class and then apply the changes. When updating workflows from the host, you have to first obtain a reference to a workflow instance you are interested in changing, and then use this reference to create the `Workflow Changes` instance and call the instance's `ApplyWorkflowChanges` method.

Conversely, you do not have access to a `WorkflowInstance` class internal to a workflow's definition class. Therefore, the way you create the `WorkflowChanges` class and apply the changes is slightly different. Consider the following code:

```
private void modifyMyself_ExecuteCode(object sender, EventArgs e)
{
    Console.WriteLine("About to modify myself; look out!");

    WorkflowChanges changes = new WorkflowChanges(this);
    CompositeActivity workflowCopy = changes.TransientWorkflow;

    WhileActivity whileActivity = new WhileActivity("loopStuff");

    CodeCondition codeCondition = new CodeCondition();
    codeCondition.Condition +=
        new EventHandler<ConditionalEventArgs>(codeCondition_Condition);

    whileActivity.Condition = codeCondition;

    CodeActivity writeStuff = new CodeActivity("writeStuff");
    writeStuff.ExecuteCode += new EventHandler(writeStuff_ExecuteCode);

    whileActivity.Activities.Add(writeStuff);
    workflowCopy.Activities.Add(whileActivity);

    this.ApplyWorkflowChanges(changes);
}

private void codeCondition_Condition(object sender, ConditionalEventArgs e)
{
    e.Result = i < 5;
}

private void writeStuff_ExecuteCode(object sender, EventArgs e)
{
    Console.WriteLine("Index is " + this.i.ToString());
    i++;
}
```

The first difference is that the `WorkflowChanges` constructor is passed a reference to the workflow definition class itself. Also, the last line of the example calls the `ApplyWorkflowChanges` method that is originally defined in the `CompositeActivity` class. In the example covering dynamic update from the host, there is a method of the same name defined on the `WorkflowInstance` class.

To Update or Not to Update?

Because workflows are all about defining business process and rules, a workflow should be able to accept or reject a set of changes. Just because the client application tells the workflow that it wants to add a new activity to its tree doesn't mean that performing the change would result in a valid business process. Therefore, the `SequentialWorkflowActivity` and `StateMachineWorkflowActivity` classes expose a property called `DynamicUpdateCondition` that is of type `ActivityCondition`. (This is in addition to the two other classes that inherit from `ActivityCondition`, which you learned about previously: `CodeCondition` and `RuleConditionReference`.)

Although the `DynamicUpdateCondition` property is not required to be set for dynamic update to work, its Boolean result dictates whether changes can be applied to a running workflow instance. This is an important property because at certain points during a workflow, changes might disrupt the business process, possibly corrupting data or resulting in an invalid end state. Examples of when you might not want to make changes to the workflow include after an order has already been shipped or before a specific logic branch has been reached in a sequential workflow.

For example, a workflow might want to apply dynamic updates only on odd days of the week (with Sunday being 0, Monday being 1, and so on). To implement this rule, you could set the `DynamicUpdate Condition` on the workflow with a declarative rule condition. The conditional code would look something like the following:

```
(int)System.DateTime.Today.DayOfWeek % 2 == 1
```

Figure 11-1 shows the Properties window with this property set.

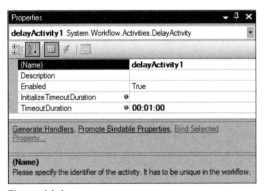

Figure 11-1

Now the code in the workflow host needs to attempt an update. The following code tries to create a new `CodeActivity` instance that writes a message to the console window:

```
WorkflowInstance instance = workflowRuntime.GetWorkflow(instanceId);
WorkflowChanges changes = new WorkflowChanges(instance.GetWorkflowDefinition());

CodeActivity newCode = new CodeActivity("newCode");
newCode.ExecuteCode += new EventHandler(newCode_ExecuteCode);

CompositeActivity wf = changes.TransientWorkflow;

// this will add the CodeActivity to the end of the workflow
wf.Activities.Insert(wf.Activities.Count, newCode);

// apply the changes
// if it is an even day of the week, this will throw an exception!
instance.ApplyWorkflowChanges(changes);
```

The event handler for the new `CodeActivity` looks like the following:

```
static void newCode_ExecuteCode(object sender, EventArgs e)
{
    Console.WriteLine("From newCode");
}
```

If you run this code on a Wednesday, everything works fine, and a `From newCode` message is displayed. However, if you run it on a Tuesday, you get an `InvalidOperationException` with a message similar to this: "Workflow changes cannot be applied to instance <your GUID> at this time. The `WorkflowChanges` condition property on the root activity has evaluated to `false`."

Dynamic Update of Rules

In addition to enabling you to make structural changes to workflows instances, the concepts of dynamic update apply to rules. This topic is covered in Chapter 9, so refer to that chapter for more information.

Designer Re-Hosting

This section covers the topic of re-hosting the Windows Workflow Foundation designer. Re-hosting enables you to display the workflow designer outside the bounds of Visual Studio. This can be extremely useful in many scenarios. For example, a custom Windows Forms application that enables end users to monitor the execution of running workflows in a visual manner can be a very powerful tool. Although this type of designer re-hosting does not necessarily provide interactive features such as modifying the workflow, that type of behavior is also possible.

There may be scenarios in which end users are responsible for developing and/or maintaining workflows. Although most developers are comfortable inside the Visual Studio environment, most end users are not. Therefore, an application that is a pared-down version of Visual Studio may be appropriate, depending on the comfort level of your users.

With that in mind, you may choose to include some of the features that make designing workflows in Visual Studio efficient and straightforward. The workflow designer itself is based on the same code that exists in Visual Studio, so its behavior is consistent outside that environment. However, you can provide elements such as an activity toolbox that contains only activities appropriate for what end users might need. You can also embed the properties grid in custom applications. Examples that illustrate how to do these things are shown a little later in this chapter.

The Designer API

The following sections describe the important designer API classes that make hosting the workflow designer in custom applications possible.

WorkflowDesignerLoader

This abstract class is in the `System.Workflow.ComponentModel.Design` namespace, and is responsible for obtaining a reference to a workflow definition and subsequently building the activity tree that is loaded in the workflow designer. Because this class is marked as `abstract`, you must implement a concrete inherited version. You can write code to load workflow definitions from a multitude of data sources, such as a filesystem or database.

In the following example, a custom `WorkflowDesignerLoader` class called `MyWorkflowLoader` reads a XOML workflow definition file from the filesystem. The points of interest in this class are the `PerformLoad` and `PerformFlush` methods.

```
public class MyWorkflowLoader : WorkflowDesignerLoader
{
    private string xomlPath = default(string);

    public override string FileName
    {
        get { return this.xomlPath; }
    }

    public MyWorkflowLoader(string xomlPath)
    {
        this.xomlPath = xomlPath;
    }

    protected override void PerformLoad(
        IDesignerSerializationManager serializationManager)
    {
        WorkflowMarkupSerializer workflowSerializer =
            new WorkflowMarkupSerializer();
        XmlReader xmlReader = XmlReader.Create(xomlPath);

        // obtain a reference to the workflow's root activity
        // via the markup serializer
        Activity rootActivity =
            workflowSerializer.Deserialize(xmlReader) as Activity;

        if (rootActivity != null)
        {
            // set the class name on the designer of our workflow
            this.SetBaseComponentClassName(rootActivity.GetType().FullName);

            // add the root activity to the designer
            // this call will recursively add all activities in the workflow
            this.AddActivityToDesigner(rootActivity);
        }
    }

    protected override void PerformFlush(
        IDesignerSerializationManager serializationManager)
    {
        // obtain a reference to the designer host
        IDesignerHost designerHost =
            (IDesignerHost)this.GetService(typeof(IDesignerHost));

        // obtain a reference to the root activity via the designer host
        Activity rootActivity = (Activity)designerHost.RootComponent;

        WorkflowMarkupSerializer workflowSerializer =
            new WorkflowMarkupSerializer();

        // this writes the XOML to the file system
        XmlWriter xmlWriter = XmlWriter.Create(xomlPath);
```

```
        workflowSerializer.Serialize(
            serializationManager, xmlWriter, rootActivity);
        // make sure to call the base flush method
        // this will ensure the layout information gets saved if necessary
        // i.e. for state machine workflows
        base.PerformFlush(serializationManager);
    }

    public override TextReader GetFileReader(string filePath)
    {
        return File.OpenText(filePath);
    }

    public override TextWriter GetFileWriter(string filePath)
    {
        return File.CreateText(filePath);
    }
}
```

PerformLoad uses the `FileName` property to read the XOML file and deserializes it using the `Workflow MarkupSerializer` class. The `Deserialize` method of `WorkflowMarkupSerializer` returns the root activity of the workflow, which is the workflow itself. This activity instance is then passed to the `AddActivityToDesigner` method, which is defined in the base `WorkflowDesignerLoader` class. When `PerformLoad` executes, the workflow definition is loaded and is ready to be displayed to the user. However, the custom workflow loader class must be instantiated and used in your application before this can happen. You learn how to do this shortly.

The `PerformFlush` method essentially does the opposite of `PerformLoad`—it takes the workflow definition as it exists in the designer and persists it to disk. It obtains an instance of the workflow by calling `IDesignerHost.RootComponent`. After all the work in `PerformFlush` has been completed, it calls the base implementation of the same method. There is code in the base class that persists layout information in a state-machine workflow.

DesignSurface

This class is the designer surface in the user interface. However, it is important to note that this class is not specific to Windows Workflow Foundation. The .NET Framework has quite a few classes that support the concept of *designability*—this being one of them. You can find this class in the `System .ComponentModel.Design` namespace of the Base Class Library.

Because this class implements the `IServiceProvider` interface, it acts as a source of services for the containing application. Designer services (discussed in more detail later) provide a pluggable architecture to implement designer-oriented behavior. By default, `DesignSurface` instances contain references to several services. Table 11-1 describes a few of these services.

Table 11-1: Designer-Related Services

Service	Description
ISelectionService	Provides hooks into the design to allow the containing application to select individual components in the designer. In the case of workflows, these components are activities.

Service	Description
IDesignerHost	Allows the calling application to, among other things, access already-added services as well as add new services to the designer.
IComponentChangeService	Exposes events to inform subscribers when something happens within the designable components. For example, this can be used to notify users when the designer is in an unsaved state or includes an undo function.

WorkflowView

The WorkflowView class is located in System.Workflow.ComponentModel.Design and is the UI control that does the drawing of the visual workflow representation. This class is workflow specific, unlike the other design types discussed so far.

To do the simplest of tasks with the workflow designer, you don't have to interact much with the WorkflowView class aside from adding it to your Windows Form. However, it does expose useful functionality, such as saving a snapshot of the workflow designer as an image, fitting the designer's view to the current screen size, and manipulating the selection of designer components.

Designer Services

Designer services provide distinct pieces of functionality during design time. Examples of designer services include context menu services, services for generating code-beside code, and services to enable toolbox functionality similar to the Visual Studio Toolbox. You can inherit many of these services from base API classes or implement them from base API interfaces and then custom-develop them for specific solutions.

Some of the interfaces that you can implement to create custom designer services are in the base .NET API in the System.ComponentModel.Design namespace. Others are workflow specific and can be found in various namespaces under the System.Workflow.ComponentModel namespace.

The non-workflow-specific designer service interfaces include IEventBindingService and IProperty ValueUIService. The IEventBindingService service defines the public members that provide the functionality to create event handler methods in a workflow's code-beside class. (This is similar to double-clicking an event name in the Properties Explorer window in Visual Studio.) The IPropertyValue UIService service defines the functionality that allows custom icons and tool tips to be displayed on the property grid. Figure 11-2 shows an example of what this service can do. In this screenshot, the InitializeTimeoutDuration and TimeoutDuration properties indicate that they are bindable workflow properties. You can also use the IMenuCommandService and IToolboxService designer services in workflow-related applications.

Other service interfaces are included in the Windows Workflow Foundation API itself. Two examples of these workflow designer services are IMemberCreationService and IDesignerGlyphProvider Service.

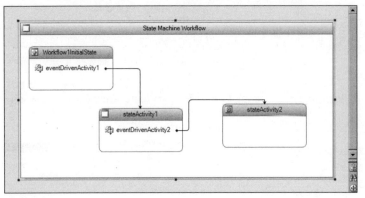

Figure 11-2

When implemented in a concrete class, IMemberCreationService is responsible for creating new members (properties, fields, and events) in classes. This is very useful in workflows because of the common need to create new fields and properties in a workflow's code-beside class for binding. This interface has methods like CreateEvent, CreateField, and CreateProperty.

The IDesignerGlyphProviderService interface defines a contract for a service that provides glyphs to workflow activities. *Glyphs,* represented by the DesignerGlyph class, are graphical indicators that can be displayed on activities to indicate the activity's status or anything else related to that activity. For example, the Workflow Monitor in the Windows Workflow Foundation SDK uses glyphs to indicate whether an activity was executed in a given workflow instance.

Bringing It Together

To better illustrate hosting the workflow designer, this section describes a sample application developed for this book. If you have not worked with designers and associated concepts such as designer services and providing toolbox functionality, this topic can be a bit tricky to understand at first; however, the concrete code example provided here should help speed your comprehension process.

The goals for this sample application are as follows:

❑   Allow opening and saving from the filesystem of workflows defined as XAML

❑   Provide a simple toolbox to show the out-of-the-box workflow activities

❑   Allow properties of the workflow and activities to be edited using a standard properties UI

For this example, the first piece of the application to be developed is the nonvisual section. A good place to start is to develop the WorkflowDesignerLoader class. The code shown in the "WorkflowDesignerLoader" section earlier in this chapter accurately represents the implementation for this sample, so it does not need to be displayed again.

Next, the development of the front-end code can commence. Start by fleshing out the user interface. Create a new Windows Forms project in Visual Studio, and rename the default form WorkflowDesigner.cs. To provide an environment similar to that of Visual Studio, the SplitterPanel control is used to segregate the various pieces of the UI.

In this example, the left side of the screen is reserved for the toolbox, the center for the actual workflow designer, and the right side for the properties grid. You can easily achieve this by using two SplitterPanel controls. One SplitterPanel will contain another SplitterPanel in its Panel1 property. When you do this, there are three panels available for the toolbox, designer, and properties grid, respectively.

You implement the toolbox simply by using a ListView control, and the properties on the right side use the PropertyGrid control. After these controls are added, along with a ToolStrip for easy access to opening and saving functions, the form looks like Figure 11-3.

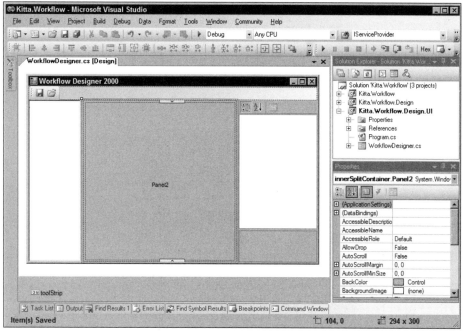

Figure 11-3

The following code creates the Windows Forms fields and the constructor, which prepares the designer for use:

```
private DesignSurface designSurface = new DesignSurface();
private WorkflowView workflowView = null;
private IDesignerHost designerHost = null;
private ISelectionService selectionService = null;
private IComponentChangeService componentChangeService = null;
private TypeProvider typeProvider = null;
private bool isDirty = false;

public WorkflowDesigner()
{
    InitializeComponent();

    // get a reference to the designer host service
```

```
    this.designerHost =
        (IDesignerHost)designSurface.GetService(typeof(IDesignerHost));

    // get the selection service instance
    this.selectionService =
        (ISelectionService)this.designerHost.GetService(typeof(ISelectionService));

    // subscribing to this event will allow us to
    // display the correct properties in the grid
    this.selectionService.SelectionChanged +=
        new EventHandler(selectionService_SelectionChanged);

    // get the component change service
    this.componentChangeService =
        (IComponentChangeService)this.designerHost.GetService(
            typeof(IComponentChangeService));

    // subscribing to this event will allow us to
    // monitor for changes in the workflow
    this.componentChangeService.ComponentChanged +=
        new ComponentChangedEventHandler(componentChangeService_ComponentChanged);

    this.typeProvider = new TypeProvider(this.designerHost);
    this.designerHost.AddService(typeof(ITypeProvider), typeProvider);

    this.LoadToolbox();
}
```

In this code, the constructor obtains references to various designer surfaces that can help the application function as desired. `ISelectionService` notifies the form when the selection of components in the designer is changed. This allows the property grid to be updated whenever a different component is selected.

Next, `IComponentChangeService` notifies the form through the `ComponentChanged` event that something in the workflow has changed. This allows the form to keep track of a workflow's status by using the `isDirty` field. If you subscribe to the form's `Closing` event, a warning can be displayed to the user asking whether the workflow should be saved first.

The constructor also takes care of creating an `ITypeProvider` service and adding it to the designer host's services. A type provider does what its name implies. If the designer needs access to a type in an assembly, it has to get it from somewhere. Therefore, if a type provider is added to the designer host's services, and all necessary assemblies are added to that provider, everything should work fine. (The code that adds an assembly reference to the type provider is shown next.) Finally, the constructor makes a call to the `LoadToolbox` method.

The next block of code is the method that loads the `ListView` control with activities from the `System.Workflow.Activities` assembly:

```
private void LoadToolbox()
{
    Assembly assembly = Assembly.Load("System.Workflow.Activities, " +
        "Version=3.0.0.0, Culture=neutral, PublicKeyToken=31bf3856ad364e35");
```

```
        this.typeProvider.AddAssembly(assembly);
        Type toolboxItemType = typeof(ToolboxItemAttribute);

        foreach (Type t in assembly.GetExportedTypes())
        {
            if (t.IsSubclassOf(typeof(Activity)))
            {
                object[] attributes =
                    t.GetCustomAttributes(toolboxItemType, false);

                if (attributes.Length == 0 || (attributes.Length == 1 &&
                    !ToolboxItemAttribute.None.Equals(attributes[0])))
                {
                    ListViewItem lvi = new ListViewItem(t.Name);
                    lvi.Tag = t;
                    lvwToolbox.Items.Add(lvi);
                }
            }
        }
    }
}
```

In this code block, the assembly is loaded using the `Assembly.Load` method and then it is added to the type provider that was introduced previously. Next, the code loops through each of the public classes in the assembly and checks to see whether it inherits from `Activity`. If there is a match, the type's attributes are checked for a `ToolboxItemAttribute`. This is logic that determines whether the activity is added to the toolbox, which is important because it may not make any sense to add certain activities. For example, an IfElseBranch activity should not be able to be directly added to a workflow; rather, it is always a branch of an IfElse activity.

Back in the form's constructor, the code subscribes to the events of a couple of the designer services. The event handlers are shown in the following code:

```
private void componentChangeService_ComponentChanged(object sender,
    ComponentChangedEventArgs e)
{
    // only call this code if the workflow has not yet been changed
    if (!this.isDirty)
    {
        // TODO: implement something here to indicate the workflow was changed
        this.isDirty = true;
    }
}

private void selectionService_SelectionChanged(object sender, EventArgs e)
{
    propertyGrid.SelectedObjects =
        (object[])this.selectionService.GetSelectedComponents();
}
```

In this code, the `ComponentChanged` event handler monitors for changes in the workflow designer and sets the `isDirty` flag to `true`. You could also add code that visually indicates to the user that the workflow is dirty. Visual Studio does this by placing an asterisk in the document's title tab.

The `SelectionChanged` event handler for the selection service simply notifies the `PropertyGrid` control that the selections in the designer have changed. This then changes the properties that are displayed in the grid. This is a simple but necessary step.

The next few methods are related to opening and saving XOML files from and to the filesystem.

The first method, shown in the following code, is `EnsureSaved`. This is simply logic that uses the `isDirty` flag to see whether the user needs to be prompted to save before doing something else. This method is used when the user tries to open a new workflow before saving the current workflow and when the user is exiting the application.

```
private bool EnsureSaved()
{
    if (this.isDirty)
    {
        DialogResult res = MessageBox.Show(
            "The current workflow is not saved. Save before continuing?",
            "Save?", MessageBoxButtons.YesNoCancel, MessageBoxIcon.Stop);

        if (res == DialogResult.Cancel)
            return false;

        if (res == DialogResult.Yes)
            this.SaveCurrent();
    }

    return true;
}
```

The next method is the event handler for the tool strip's Open button:

```
private void btnOpen_Click(object sender, EventArgs e)
{
    if (this.EnsureSaved())
    {
        OpenFileDialog ofd = new OpenFileDialog();
        ofd.Filter = "*.xoml|*.xoml";
        DialogResult res = ofd.ShowDialog();

        if (res == DialogResult.OK)
        {
            this.designSurface.BeginLoad(
                new KittaWorkflowDesignerLoader(ofd.FileName));

            propertyGrid.Site = this.designerHost.RootComponent.Site;

            IRootDesigner rootDesigner =
                (IRootDesigner)this.designerHost.GetDesigner(
                    this.designerHost.RootComponent);

            this.workflowView =
                (WorkflowView)rootDesigner.GetView(ViewTechnology.Default);

            this.workflowView.Dock = DockStyle.Fill;
```

```
            innerSplitContainer.Panel2.Controls.Add(workflowView);

            object[] selectedComponent =
                new object[] { this.designerHost.RootComponent };

            this.selectionService.SetSelectedComponents(selectedComponent);
            this.isDirty = false;
        }
    }
}
```

The first thing this method does is to call the `EnsureSaved` method to make sure that the user saved the workflow before opening a new one. The user is then presented with a dialog box to choose the XOML file to edit. This is where the workflow-specific code begins.

The `DesignerSurface` class has a method called `BeginLoad` that takes an instance of a `Workflow DesignerLoader` class. Of course, the loader developed for this example is what is passed. The remainder of the method configures the `WorkflowView` and the `PropertyGrid` controls.

The selection service configured in the form's constructor comes in handy here because it enables you to dictate which activity is selected by default. This is the opposite of what was discussed previously when the selection service was used to notify the host when something new was selected, not to actually programmatically select activities.

The remaining save and close methods are shown in the following code:

```
private void WorkflowDesigner_FormClosing(object sender, FormClosingEventArgs e)
{
    e.Cancel = !this.EnsureSaved();
}

private void btnSave_Click(object sender, EventArgs e)
{
    this.SaveCurrent();
}

private void SaveCurrent()
{
    KittaWorkflowDesignerLoader workflowLoader =
        (KittaWorkflowDesignerLoader)this.designSurface.GetService(
            typeof(WorkflowDesignerLoader));

    workflowLoader.Flush();

    this.isDirty = false;
}
```

In the `SaveCurrent` method, the custom `WorkflowDesignerLoader` class is obtained by calling the design surface's `GetService` method. Then the `Flush` method is called, which in turn saves the current workflow to the file it was opened from. Finally, the `isDirty` flag is set to `false` because the workflow is now saved.

Figure 11-4 shows what the example application looks like when running and with a loaded workflow definition.

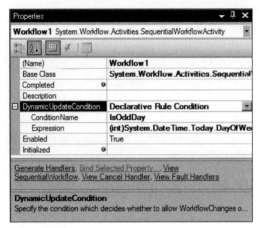

Figure 11-4

The last piece of code pertaining to the designer re-hosting example enables the user to drag and drop items from the toolbox to the designer. The most common way to achieve drag-and-drop functionality is to subscribe to the ListView's MouseMove event, as shown here:

```
private void lvwToolbox_MouseMove(object sender, MouseEventArgs e)
{
    if (e.Button == MouseButtons.Left && lvwToolbox.SelectedItems.Count == 1)
    {
        Type t = lvwToolbox.SelectedItems[0].Tag as Type;
        ToolboxItem toolboxItem = null;

        if (t != null && (toolboxItem = ToolboxService.GetToolboxItem(t)) != null)
        {
            IDataObject theData = null;
            IComponent[] components = toolboxItem.CreateComponents();
            if (components != null && components.Length > 0)
            {
                Activity newActivity = (Activity)components[0];

                IServiceProvider serviceProvider =
                    (IServiceProvider)this.workflowView;

                ComponentSerializationService service = serviceProvider.GetService(
                    typeof(ComponentSerializationService))
                        as ComponentSerializationService;

                if (service != null)
                {
                    theData =
                        CompositeActivityDesigner.SerializeActivitiesToDataObject(
```

```
                              this.workflowView, new Activity[] { newActivity });

                    lvwToolbox.DoDragDrop(theData,
                        DragDropEffects.Copy | DragDropEffects.Move);
                }
            }
        }
    }
}
```

The event handler in this code includes a lot of checks to make sure things are good enough to start the drag-and-drop process. First, the code ensures that the user has actually clicked something by inspecting the event argument's `Button` property against the `MouseButtons.Left` enumeration value. After this, the code extracts a `Type` instance from the selected `ListViewItem` and goes through steps to create an instance of that type.

The `ToolboxItem` class is used here to create a new instance of whatever the activity type is. For example, the way in which an `IfElseActivity` instance is created is interesting because two `IfElseBranch Activity` instances are created and added to the `IfElseActivity` instance. That is why you see two default branches when dragging that activity from the Visual Studio Toolbox.

After the code has an instance of the activity being dragged from the toolbox, it needs to be serialized so that it can be passed to the designer using the drag-and-drop framework. This serialization functionality is provided by the `ComponentSerializationService` designer service. Finally, the serialized data is passed to the `DoDragDrop` method of the toolbox `ListView`. After the user drags the mouse to a valid spot on the designer, the `WorkflowView`'s code takes care of the rest.

Although this example covers quite a bit in the way of loading a workflow and providing visual editing, it could do a lot more. The following list represents features that could be useful in a workflow designer hosting scenario:

❑ Improve the file management and error handling. This example was built with the bare minimum code to show workflow-specific functionality.

❑ Allow the workflow to have a code-beside class and implement the `IMemberCreationService` to allow new events, fields, and properties to be added.

❑ Implement `IEventBindingService` to allow various activities to perform logic when their events fire.

❑ Provide a more robust toolbox with images, and filter out activities in a context-specific manner. For example, don't show the State activity for sequential workflows.

❑ Allow the configuration of assemblies to check for activities for the toolbox.

❑ Implement code to allow the red validation glyphs to show error messages and transport the user to the affected property in the `PropertyGrid`.

❑ Implement the `IPropertyValueUIService` interface to allow the properties window to show custom icons for dependency properties.

The State-Machine Designer

As you've probably noticed in your workflow adventures so far, the state-machine designer has an added piece of functionality that does not apply to the sequential workflow designer. The designer for sequential workflows recreates the onscreen view every time a workflow definition is loaded — meaning that one activity is at the top followed by subsequent activities, and the spacing between activities is dynamic, based on the definition. Conversely, the state-machine workflow designer permits the workflow developer to place objects in user-defined positions on the canvas. This allows you to appropriately place State activity representations in clean arrangements on the screen.

However, this layout data must obviously be saved and subsequently reloaded when a state machine is loaded into the designer. Visual Studio handles this by saving a .layout file along with the workflow definition file.

Figure 11-5 shows a sample state-machine workflow.

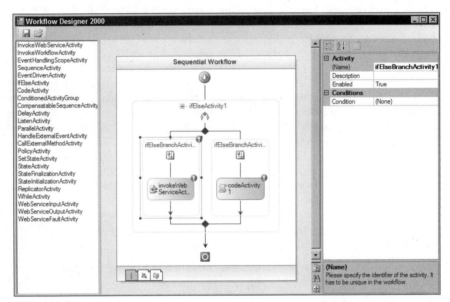

Figure 11-5

The following code listing is the layout file for the workflow shown in Figure 11-5:

```
<StateMachineWorkflowDesigner
    xmlns:ns0="clr-namespace:System.Drawing;Assembly=System.Drawing, Version=2.0.0.0,
    Culture=neutral, PublicKeyToken=b03f5f7f11d50a3a" Name="Workflow1"
    Location="30,30" Size="600, 287" AutoSizeMargin="16, 24"
    xmlns="http://schemas.microsoft.com/winfx/2006/xaml/workflow">
    <StateMachineWorkflowDesigner.DesignerConnectors>
        <StateDesignerConnector TargetConnectionIndex="0"
            TargetStateName="stateActivity1" SourceConnectionIndex="0"
            TargetConnectionEdge="Top" SetStateName="setStateActivity1"
```

```
        SourceStateName="Workflow1InitialState" SourceConnectionEdge="Right"
        TargetActivity="stateActivity1" SourceActivity="Workflow1InitialState"
        EventHandlerName="eventDrivenActivity1">
        <StateDesignerConnector.Segments>
          <ns0:Point X="194" Y="115" />
          <ns0:Point X="263" Y="115" />
          <ns0:Point X="263" Y="189" />
        </StateDesignerConnector.Segments>
      </StateDesignerConnector>
      <StateDesignerConnector TargetConnectionIndex="0"
        TargetStateName="stateActivity2" SourceConnectionIndex="0"
        TargetConnectionEdge="Top" SetStateName="setStateActivity2"
        SourceStateName="stateActivity1" SourceConnectionEdge="Right"
        TargetActivity="stateActivity2" SourceActivity="stateActivity1"
        EventHandlerName="eventDrivenActivity2">
        <StateDesignerConnector.Segments>
          <ns0:Point X="330" Y="230" />
          <ns0:Point X="355" Y="230" />
          <ns0:Point X="355" Y="173" />
          <ns0:Point X="499" Y="173" />
          <ns0:Point X="499" Y="181" />
        </StateDesignerConnector.Segments>
      </StateDesignerConnector>
    </StateMachineWorkflowDesigner.DesignerConnectors>
    <StateMachineWorkflowDesigner.Designers>
      <StateDesigner Name="Workflow1InitialState" Location="47, 74" Size="163, 80"
        AutoSizeMargin="16, 24">
        <StateDesigner.Designers>
          <EventDrivenDesigner Size="110, 152" Name="eventDrivenActivity1"
            Location="55, 105">
            <EventDrivenDesigner.Designers>
              <SetStateDesigner Size="90, 50" Name="setStateActivity1"
                Location="65,177" />
            </EventDrivenDesigner.Designers>
          </EventDrivenDesigner>
        </StateDesigner.Designers>
      </StateDesigner>
      <StateDesigner Name="stateActivity1" Location="183, 189" Size="160, 80"
        AutoSizeMargin="16, 24">
        <StateDesigner.Designers>
          <EventDrivenDesigner Size="110, 152" Name="eventDrivenActivity2"
            Location="191, 220">
            <EventDrivenDesigner.Designers>
              <SetStateDesigner Size="90, 50" Name="setStateActivity2"
                Location="201,292" />
            </EventDrivenDesigner.Designers>
          </EventDrivenDesigner>
        </StateDesigner.Designers>
      </StateDesigner>
      <StateDesigner Name="stateActivity2" Location="419, 181" Size="160, 80"
        AutoSizeMargin="16, 24" />
    </StateMachineWorkflowDesigner.Designers>
  </StateMachineWorkflowDesigner>
```

When you're working with workflow definitions in the filesystem, saving this layout information is easy. Code in the base `WorkflowDesignerLoader` class takes care of it for you. All you have to do is call `base.PerformFlush` from within an overridden `PerformFlush` method, as follows:

```
protected override void PerformFlush(
    IDesignerSerializationManager serializationManager)
{
    IDesignerHost designerHost =
        (IDesignerHost)this.GetService(typeof(IDesignerHost));
    Activity rootActivity = (Activity)designerHost.RootComponent;
    WorkflowMarkupSerializer workflowSerializer
        = new WorkflowMarkupSerializer();

    XmlWriter xmlWriter = XmlWriter.Create(xomlPath);
    workflowSerializer.Serialize(
        serializationManager, xmlWriter, rootActivity);

    // make sure to call the base flush method
    // this will ensure the layout information gets saved if necessary
    // i.e. for state machine workflows
    base.PerformFlush(serializationManager);
}
```

However, you may not be storing workflow definitions in the filesystem — you may be using a database. In this case, you should not make the `base.PerformFlush` method call. Instead, write code to call the `WorkflowDesignerLoader`'s `SaveDesignerLayout` method. This method has a signature that looks like the following code. Based on the arguments this method accepts, you simply need to write an `XmlWriter` instance to create something you can put in a database, like a string.

```
protected void SaveDesignerLayout(XmlWriter layoutWriter,
    ActivityDesigner rootDesigner, out IList layoutSaveErrors);
```

On the flip side, the following code shows how to load layout data from the filesystem and apply it to a state-machine workflow in a custom `WorkflowDesignerLoader` class. Just as you can when saving the layout information, you can easily modify this code to obtain a string representation of the layout XML from a database and pass it to the `LoadDesignerLayout` method.

```
private IList LoadStateMachineLayout(string fileName)
{
    if (!File.Exists(fileName))
    {
        throw new ArgumentException("The file " + fileName + " does not exist.");
    }
    else
    {
        IList layoutLoadErrors;
        XmlReader xmlReader = XmlReader.Create(fileName);
        this.LoadDesignerLayout(xmlReader, out layoutLoadErrors);
        return layoutLoadErrors;
    }
}
```

The `LoadStateMachineLayout` method shown here simply checks to make sure that the layout file exists. If it does, a new `XmlReader` instance is created and used to read the file by using the `LoadDesignerLayoutMethod`. If there are errors loading the file, an `IList` collection is returned.

Using Dynamic Update and Designer Re-Hosting

You can develop a lot of interesting things by combining the dynamic update capabilities of Windows Workflow Foundation with designer re-hosting. Although dynamic update is extremely powerful on its own, imagine the rich user experience you could provide by allowing users to modify running workflow instances with the designer.

You can accomplish this by using the concepts previously discussed. By loading a workflow definition in the designer and providing the ability to make modifications, you have already done a lot of the work.

Next, your code needs to keep track of changes made by users. To do this, you simply use the `IComponent ChangeService` discussed previously. After you have a trail of modifications that were made to the workflow, you use the dynamic update API introduced in this chapter to apply the changes to a transient workflow. As shown in the earlier code samples, the `IComponentChangeService` exposes an event called `ComponentChanged`. When this event is subscribed to and subsequently raised during execution, you can track what changed and use that information to update the workflow as described.

Summary

This chapter covered two powerful features of Windows Workflow Foundation: dynamic update and designer re-hosting. Dynamic update enables you to make modifications to running workflows using the APIs provided. It is important to note that changes made using dynamic update apply only to specific workflow instances and not to the workflow definition itself.

Designer re-hosting is another great feature that expands the possibilities for incorporating workflow into applications. By using the designer, you can provide features such as editing and creating workflow definitions, viewing the status of in-process and completed workflows, and even modifying running workflows.

12

Exceptions, Faults, and Debugging

This chapter is basically about what to do when things go wrong in your workflows. The major topics are exceptions and exception handling, workflow faults, and the debugging of workflows. This chapter explains the following areas in detail:

❑   Exceptions and the workflow runtime

❑   Common exception-handling techniques

❑   Debugging, troubleshooting, and diagnostics

❑   The Visual Studio debugging infrastructure

Exceptions

If you are reading this book, you probably have some experience with .NET development or development in general. You are probably also familiar with the concept of exceptions and exception handling. In .NET, exceptions are objects that derive directly or indirectly from System.Exception. Whenever something happens in the code that the developer deems bad, he or she can chose to *throw* an exception. The following is an example of this in C#:

```
// something bad happened, throw a new exception...

ApplicationException myException =
    new ApplicationException("Bad stuff happened, game over man!");

throw myException;
```

After an exception is thrown, the current method ceases to execute and the exception goes all the way up the call stack until it finds an appropriate exception handler or until the top of the stack is reached. If the latter scenario occurs, the application terminates abruptly with an error message from the .NET runtime.

Good developers not only account for exceptions in situations where something might go wrong, such as talking to a database, but they also are specific in their exception handling. This means you should be looking for very specific exception types when monitoring for exceptions. For example, if your code is performing an elaborate database insert operation, it should be no surprise that if something bad happens, it is probably a database-related error.

In .NET and other modern development platforms, you can specify multiple exceptions handlers for a block of code. Each handler should be looking for a different exception type, and each handler should be more generic than its previous handler. This tells you that the first handlers should be looking for very specific errors that might occur, whereas the latter handlers should be catch-alls. The following is an example of what this looks like in C#:

```
try
{
    // perform some database operation
}
catch (SqlException ex)
{
    // this handles an exception specific to MS SQL Server
}
catch (DataException ex)
{
    // this handles an exception related to ADO.NET
}
catch (ApplicationException ex)
{
    // this handles a custom application exception
}
catch
{
    // this is the catch all; most generic
}
```

Workflow Faults

Faults in Windows Workflow Foundation are a lot like exceptions in .NET. They differ in one major respect, however. In .NET, when an exception is thrown, it immediately starts looking for the closest relevant catch block up the stack. When a fault (exception) occurs in Windows Workflow Foundation, it is thrown to the workflow runtime, but the workflow is not immediately aborted. Instead, the exception is added to a special queue, which is handled at the appropriate time.

Workflow faults can occur for any number of reasons, such as issues in activity execution or with one of the runtime services. If any exceptions get raised from standard .NET code, they also get raised as workflow faults. Workflows can fail in just the same way that .NET code can, and you need to account for these failures with the techniques described in this section.

To illustrate how faults work in Windows Workflow Foundation, this section uses a simple example workflow. This workflow has a Parallel activity that contains two branches. The first branch prints a message, waits a specified time, and then prints another message. The second parallel branch prints a message, throws an exception, and then prints another message. The second message in the second branch never actually prints because the exception is being thrown. Figure 12-1 shows this workflow.

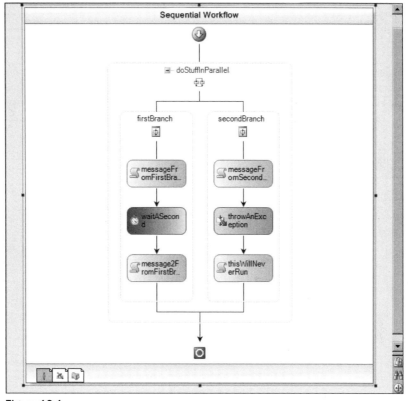

Figure 12-1

The following is some of the code from the workflow's host (not including the standard plumbing code, which was removed for brevity):

```
public class Program
{
    ...

    public static void Main(string[] args)
    {
        ...
        runtime.WorkflowTerminated +=
            new EventHandler<WorkflowTerminatedEventArgs>(
                runtime_WorkflowTerminated);
        ...
```

```
    }

    public static void runtime_WorkflowTerminated(object sender,
        WorkflowTerminatedEventArgs e)
    {
        Console.WriteLine("The workflow (" +
            e.WorkflowInstance.InstanceId.ToString() + ") was terminated!");
        waitHandle.Set();
    }
}
```

You can see that the `WorkflowRuntime`'s `WorkflowTerminated` event has been subscribed to. This is the event that is raised when an unhandled exception, or fault, is raised all the way up to the workflow runtime. Subscribing to this event and printing a message in the runtime host can help you figure out what's going on related to fault handling in the workflow instance and workflow runtime.

If you were to run the program in its current state, you would receive a series of messages similar to the console window in Figure 12-2.

Figure 12-2

By reviewing the messages that are printed from the workflow and the workflow host, you can start to decipher what happened:

1. The left branch executed its first `CodeActivity`.

2. The right branch executed its first `CodeActivity`.

3. The left branch executed its `DelayActivity`.

4. The right branch executed the `ThrowActivity`.

At this point, the fault gets thrown all the way up to the workflow runtime, and the workflow is terminated. Because a fault was raised in the middle of the Parallel activity's execution, the remainder of its work was canceled. The same goes for the workflow itself. If there were more work to do after the

Parallel activity, that work would never be started or completed. This seems pretty sloppy, right? In its current state, the workflow doesn't even have a chance to gracefully handle the fault or any of its consequences. However, Windows Workflow Foundation provides the infrastructure to do just this.

Handling Faults

To better manage the exception thrown in the example workflow, you could do one of a few different things. In all methods, the FaultHandlers and FaultHandler activities are part of the solution. The FaultHandlers activity is a container for zero or more FaultHandler activity instances.

You cannot directly add a FaultHandlers activity to your workflow, mainly because this activity is used only in certain instances, and the workflow designer takes care of doing this for you. Each composite activity in a workflow, including the workflow itself, has an associated FaultHandlers activity to manage faults raised while that activity and its children are executing. To access an activity's FaultHandlers activity, you need to access the activity's context menu and select the View Fault Handlers option. The workflow designer has a set of icons in the bottom-left corner that provide easy access to the workflow's fault handlers. To access a sequential workflow's fault handlers, click the View Fault Handlers button in the bottom-left corner of the workflow designer (see Figure 12-3). To access the IfElseBranch activity's fault handlers, click the View Fault Handlers button on the activity's view menu (see Figure 12-4).

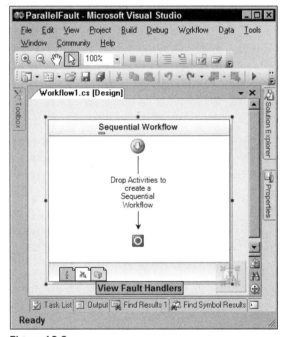

Figure 12-3

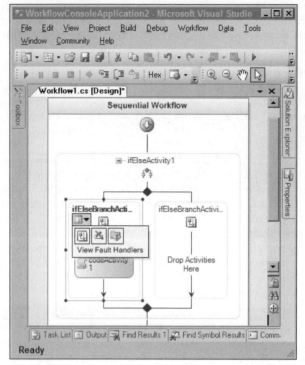

Figure 12-4

Remember the sample C# exception handlers shown earlier in this chapter? The FaultHandlers activity works like an entire group of `catch` blocks, whereas the FaultHandler activity is like an individual `catch` block. Given this comparison, it's not hard to understand why each FaultHandler activity instance has a particular exception type associated with it, which is done through the `FaultType` property. In addition, if a particular fault handler is executed because a certain exception type was raised, the exception instance can be captured and bound to a member of the workflow class. You do this by right-clicking a specific FaultHandler activity and selecting the Promote Bindable Properties option from the context menu. This creates a new dependency property in the workflow code-beside class and binds it to the fault handler's `Fault` property. Again, the FaultHandlers activity is like the set of `catch` blocks in C# because its child handler activities go from most to least specific.

Figure 12-5 shows what the FaultHandlers and FaultHandler activity instances look like in the workflow designer. You can see that a fault handler can contain child activities that are executed whenever the FaultHandler activity is executed. Also, some of a FaultHandler activity's properties are displayed on the right side of the screen. The selected activity is responsible for handling errors related to a SQL database.

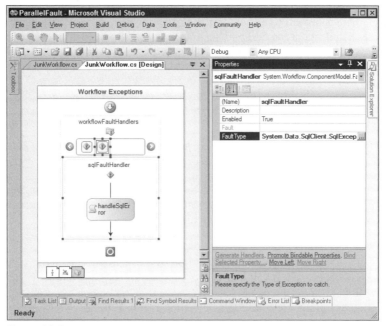

Figure 12-5

Now back to the example workflow with the parallel tasks. An appropriate fault handler needs to be placed somewhere in the workflow. Where you should place this fault handler depends on the application and what kind of error has occurred. In this example, a fault handler could be placed in the second parallel branch, in the Parallel activity itself, or on the workflow. In any event, the fault is raised up starting at the immediate parent until it finds a suitable handler. For example, if you place a FaultHandler activity on the example workflow and then rerun the program, the output would look like Figure 12-6.

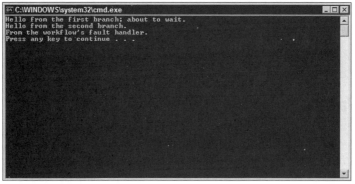

Figure 12-6

Now the workflow doesn't get terminated because the fault never had a chance to the leave the workflow. However, there is probably still some work to be done before the workflow really handles any issues gracefully. Think about the first parallel branch in this scenario. If the second branch is careless and causes an issue, the first branch is punished by prematurely being canceled. Although this is a fact of life, the first branch should at least be given a chance to perform some work before it is abruptly stopped. That is where cancellation handlers come in.

Cancellation Handlers

Just like fault handlers, cancellation handlers are located in composite activities, including the workflow itself. You can also access cancellation handlers in the same manner as fault handlers in the workflow designer. Cancellation handlers allow sibling activities in a composite parent to gracefully stop execution when another sibling has caused a fault. This is common when dealing with the Parallel activity, as in the example discussed in this chapter. However, any composite activity with multiple branches can take advantage of the cancellation handler infrastructure.

You implement cancellation handlers using the `CancellationHandlerActivity` class, which inherits from `CompositeActivity`. In the example with the Parallel activity, you could use the cancellation handler of the first parallel branch so that it has a chance to do something before it is killed off prematurely. If a Code activity that printed a message were added to the first branch's cancellation handler, the program would finally produce some output, as shown in Figure 12-7.

Figure 12-7

Throwing Faults

Just as it is important to be able to catch and handle exceptions that occur during workflow execution, it is equally important to be able to raise exceptions if something goes wrong. There are a couple of different ways to do this.

The traditional method is to throw .NET exception instances from .NET code. To do this, you could place the following code within the Code activity's `ExecuteCode` event handler:

```
private void myCodeActivity_ExecuteCode(object sender, EventArgs e)
{
   if (someInteger < 0)
      throw new ApplicationException("The value cannot be negative.");

   // perform some other operations...
}
```

This code simply throws a new `ApplicationException` instance when an `int` variable is not greater than zero. This causes the workflow runtime to handle the exception and create a new workflow fault.

Another method is to use the Throw activity to raise faults declaratively. This is not much different from throwing an exception from a block of code. It does, however, contribute to the declarative nature of workflows.

The Throw activity exposes the `Fault` and `FaultType` properties, which are both dependency properties. You can set these properties independently of each other, but you must set at least one of them to correctly configure the activity.

If you set `FaultType` to a .NET exception type, when the Throw activity executes, it throws a new instance of that exception type given its default constructor. Conversely, if you set the Fault property to point to an exception instance somewhere in the workflow, that instance is thrown when the Throw activity is executed. If you set these two properties at the same time, the `FaultType` property makes sure that the exception instance set using the `Fault` property is of the same type. If you try to set the `Fault` property to an exception instance that is not the same type as the one specified in the `FaultType` property, the activity does not pass validation.

The following is code from a workflow host application that subscribes to the `WorkflowRuntime`'s `Terminated` event:

```
workflowRuntime.WorkflowTerminated +=
    delegate(object sender, WorkflowTerminatedEventArgs e)
    {
        Console.WriteLine("Exception of type \"" +
            e.Exception.GetType().FullName + "\" was thrown: " +
            e.Exception.Message);
        waitHandle.Set();
    };
```

Because any exceptions that are unhandled in the workflow get thrown to the runtime, which then terminates the workflow, this event-handler code is called when any unhandled exceptions are raised.

Figure 12-8 shows the message that is printed when a Throw activity's `FaultType` and `Fault` properties are set. The `FaultType` property is set to `System.ApplicationException`, and the `Fault` property is bound to an `ApplicationException` instance in the workflow's code-beside class.

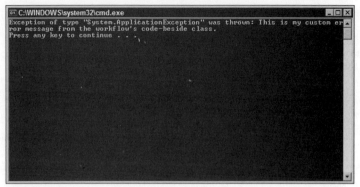

Figure 12-8

Debugging Workflows

Because bugs and code issues are real, finding and fixing problems in code is a common exercise. There are many different techniques used in software development to debug and track down issues. The following sections describe these techniques in relation to workflows.

Debugging in Visual Studio

If your background is in .NET software development, you are probably intimately familiar with the Visual Studio development environment, including vital components such as the Toolbox for visual designing, IntelliSense for quick access to object members, and helpful features such as code highlighting. In addition, Visual Studio provides a great debugging infrastructure that allows for detailed inspection of code, variables, and threads (among other things) during runtime.

The debugging functionality in Visual Studio involves several components. First, breakpoints are vital components that serve as placeholders in the code. A breakpoint basically says, "When this line of code is reached, pause execution and turn control over to the user." Then you, the developer, can do things such as check the values of variables using the Watch windows, change the execution path by dragging the execution indicator to a different line of code, or selectively step into or over blocks of code. You can access the step functionality by using keyboard shortcuts, by selecting buttons on the Debug toolbar (see Figure 12-9), or by selecting items in the Debug main menu.

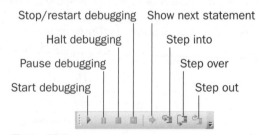

Stop/restart debugging   Show next statement

Halt debugging   Step into

Pause debugging   Step over

Start debugging   Step out

Figure 12-9

The first button, which looks like an A/V appliance's play button, issues the command to either start debugging a currently nonrunning piece of software, or to run until a breakpoint is reached if the software is running. The pause button tells the code to stop debugging and wait for further input from the user. The stop button halts the code debugging process. The left-pointing arrow button stops and restarts the debugging process.

The next group of buttons control stepping logic. The right-pointing arrow takes you to the current line of code that is ready to be executed. The step into, step over, and step out buttons control how you progress to the next statement in the code. Step over is useful if you don't want to debug the code in the method or property that is about to be executed.

Windows Workflow Foundation has been developed so that the Visual Studio debugging features are available to workflow developers, even in the visual designer. You can set breakpoints on activities in the workflow designer so that when they are about be executed, Visual Studio pauses on the activity and allows you to perform whatever actions you deem necessary. To do this, right-click an activity in the designer, expand the Breakpoint menu, and select Insert Breakpoint. At this point, you can use the standard debugging commands (start debugging, step over, and so on) to watch the workflow execute visually. Figure 12-10 shows the context menu that allows you to add the visual breakpoints.

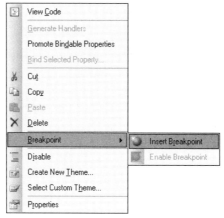

Figure 12-10

Figure 12-11 shows a screen shot of a workflow with an active breakpoint during execution. The Locals window toward the bottom of the screen gives you a view of the current variables that are local in scope. This enables you to inspect various values of activities and the workflow itself. In addition to debugging visually, you can set breakpoints and step through code, just as you can in standard .NET code.

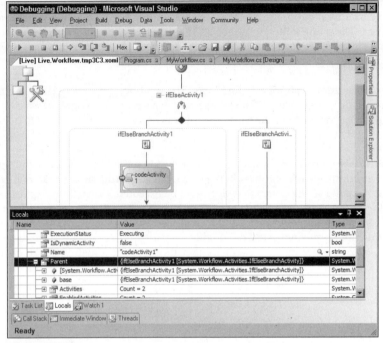

Figure 12-11

Using the WorkflowRuntime Events

A somewhat rudimentary but extremely useful method of debugging workflow instances is to simply subscribe to the various events exposed by the WorkflowRuntime class. Many times, if a particularly frustrating issue is causing problems, such as stalled execution or an elusive exception, attaching to a few of the runtime events and using some diagnostic code can clear things up.

Here is a list of each of the events in the WorkflowRuntime class, which you can use for reference:

- ❏ ServicesExceptionNotHandled
- ❏ Started
- ❏ Stopped
- ❏ WorkflowAborted
- ❏ WorkflowCompleted
- ❏ WorkflowCreated
- ❏ WorkflowIdled
- ❏ WorkflowLoaded
- ❏ WorkflowPersisted

- ❑   `WorkflowResumed`

- ❑   `WorkflowStarted`

- ❑   `WorkflowSuspended`

- ❑   `WorkflowTerminated`

- ❑   `WorkflowUnloaded`

Many of these events pass various types of `EventArgs` classes that contain useful information for that event. For example, the `WorkflowTerminated` event passes an instance of the `WorkflowTerminatedEventArgs` class, which has a property for exposing an exception thrown from within the workflow.

You can use the methods in the following code for debugging workflow issues. You can place breakpoints in each event handler or place debugging or tracing messages (discussed next) in the methods.

```
public static void Main(string[] args)
{
    WorkflowRuntime runtime = new WorkflowRuntime();
    AutoResetEvent waitHandle = new AutoResetEvent(false);

    runtime.WorkflowAborted +=
        new EventHandler<WorkflowEventArgs>(runtime_WorkflowAborted);
    runtime.WorkflowCompleted +=
        new EventHandler<WorkflowCompletedEventArgs>(runtime_WorkflowCompleted);
    runtime.WorkflowTerminated +=
        new EventHandler<WorkflowTerminatedEventArgs>(runtime_WorkflowTerminated);
    runtime.WorkflowIdled +=
        new EventHandler<WorkflowEventArgs>(runtime_WorkflowIdled);
    runtime.WorkflowPersisted +=
        new EventHandler<WorkflowEventArgs>(runtime_WorkflowPersisted);

    WorkflowInstance instance = runtime.CreateWorkflow(typeof(MyWorkflow));
    instance.Start();

    waitHandle.WaitOne();
}

static void runtime_WorkflowPersisted(object sender, WorkflowEventArgs e)
{
    Console.WriteLine("The workflow " + e.WorkflowInstance.InstanceId.ToString() +
        " was persisted.");
}

static void runtime_WorkflowIdled(object sender, WorkflowEventArgs e)
{
    Console.WriteLine("The workflow " + e.WorkflowInstance.InstanceId.ToString() +
        " has gone idle.");
}

static void runtime_WorkflowTerminated(object sender,
    WorkflowTerminatedEventArgs e)
{
    Console.WriteLine("The workflow " + e.WorkflowInstance.InstanceId.ToString() +
```

```
                " has been terminated.");
        Console.WriteLine("   ERROR MESSAGE: " + e.Exception.Message);
    }

    static void runtime_WorkflowCompleted(object sender, WorkflowCompletedEventArgs e)
    {
        Console.WriteLine("The workflow " + e.WorkflowInstance.InstanceId.ToString() +
            " has completed.");
    }

    static void runtime_WorkflowAborted(object sender, WorkflowEventArgs e)
    {
        Console.WriteLine("The workflow " + e.WorkflowInstance.InstanceId.ToString() +
            " has been aborted.");
    }
```

This code can be found in the workflow host and is simply subscribing to some of the events exposed by the `WorkflowRuntime` class. Many of the event handlers receive event arguments specific to the type of event that occurred. These arguments can provide useful information about what happened. For example, the `WorkflowTerminated` event handler can access an `Exception` instance that may provide more insight into why the workflow was terminated prematurely.

Tracing

Tracing is a concept not specific to workflows but built into the .NET Framework. The types in the `System.Diagnostics` namespace provide the necessary infrastructure for the tracing functionality. Tracing enables you to capture pieces of information that are important to the execution of a piece of software. This is a flexible architecture and is able to send messages to a variety of sources, such as the console window, text files, the event log, and any other logging medium you want to use.

Basic Tracing Concepts

To implement tracing, you must first configure the code to write messages at certain points in the application's execution. You do this by making calls to static methods on the `Trace` class, as follows:

```
string[] myArray = new string[] { "hi", "hello", "goodbye" };

Trace.WriteLine("About to loop through an array with " +
    myArray.Length + " items.");

Trace.Indent();
for (int i = 0; i < myArray.Length; i++)
{
    Trace.WriteLine("Performing operation on item: " + myArray[i]);

    // do something useful here...
}
Trace.Unindent();

Trace.WriteLine("Done looping...");
```

This code uses `Trace.WriteLine` calls and a method called `Trace.Indent` that allows for some additional formatting of the traced messages.

Now that you know how to add simple trace messages to your application, you need to know how to consume these messages. This occurs by using entities called trace listeners. A *trace listener* is a class that inherits from the `System.Diagnostics.TraceListener`. These classes receive messages that are broadcast using the various static `Trace` methods and then store or display these messages in whatever fashion you specify.

For example, the .NET Framework provides a `TextWriterTraceListener` class out of the box. This class takes the messages that were sent using the `Trace` class and writes them to a text file. In addition, there is a class that writes messages to the Windows Event Log called `EventLogTraceListener`.

You can easily develop new trace listeners by creating a new class; inheriting from `TraceListener`; and overriding, at a minimum, the `Write` and `WriteLine` methods of the base class. For example, you could develop a trace listener to write messages to a database table or an HTTP listener.

Whether you want to use an out-of-the-box trace listener or one that you custom-developed, you need to add an instance of the class to the `Trace.Listeners` collection. This collection can contain any number of listener instances, each of which is written to during runtime.

By default, the collection contains an instance of the `DefaultTraceListener` class, which simply writes messages to the Output window in Visual Studio. For example, if you run the preceding code with the default settings, the following text is displayed in the Output window of Visual Studio:

```
About to loop through an array with 3 items.
    Performing operation on item: hi
    Performing operation on item: hello
    Performing operation on item: goodbye
Done looping...
```

As you can see by this simple example, tracing can be an extremely powerful method of diagnosing issues and monitoring the execution of an application without using traditional Visual Studio debugging, which comes with its own overhead. However, it is important to note that tracing is meant to be used sparingly to diagnose issues. It should not be turned on and forgotten in a production application.

Luckily, the tracing infrastructure provides a way to turn messages on and off using configuration. The following code could be from an App.config or Web.config file and dynamically adds the `TextWriter TraceListener` to the `Trace.Listeners` collection without modifying the code. After you've completed your diagnostics, you can remove or comment out the text that adds the trace listener.

```
<configuration>
    <system.diagnostics>
        <trace autoflush="true">
            <listeners>
                <add name="TextFileListener"
                    type="System.Diagnostics.TextWriterTraceListener, System,
                        Version=2.0.0.0, Culture=neutral, PublicKeyToken=b77a5c561934e089"
                    initializeData="c:\logs\listener.txt" />
            </listeners>
        </trace>
    </system.diagnostics>
</configuration>
```

To further configure tracing in .NET, you can use the `TraceSwitch` class to categorize messages. These categories are defined in the `TraceLevel` enumeration and include the following options, in order from highest priority to lowest (aside from `Off`, which turns tracing off altogether):

❑   `TraceLevel.Off`

❑   `TraceLevel.Error`

❑   `TraceLevel.Warning`

❑   `TraceLevel.Info`

❑   `TraceLevel.Verbose` (includes all trace messages)

You can define multiple trace switches for a single application, each of which gets its own `TraceLevel` value. For example, the following configuration snippet says that the trace switch called `FileInfo` should show all messages at or above warnings, and the trace switch called `NetworkInfo` should show all messages:

```
<configuration>
  <system.diagnostics>
    ...
    <switches>
      <add name="FileInfo" value="Warning" />
      <add name="NetworkInfo" value="Verbose" />
    </switches>
  </system.diagnostics>
</configuration>
```

To use this switch information, you need to create instances of the `TraceSwitch` class given the names in the configuration file and use its properties with the `Trace.WriteIf` and `Trace.WriteLineIf` methods, as follows:

```
TraceSwitch fileInfoSwitch =
    new TraceSwitch("FileInfo", "Show information about reading files.");
TraceSwitch networkInfoSwitch =
    new TraceSwitch("NetworkInfo", "Show information about network activity.");

// file activity below
Trace.WriteLineIf(fileInfoSwitch.TraceInfo, "About to read a file.");
// read a file...
Trace.WriteLineIf(fileInfoSwitch.TraceError, "An error occurred reading a file.");

// network activity below
Trace.WriteLineIf(networkInfoSwitch.TraceInfo, "About to access the network.");
// try to access the network
Trace.WriteLineIf(networkInfoSwitch.TraceWarning,
    "The network might be down, will try again later.");
```

Given the settings in the preceding configuration file, the code's output would look like this:

```
An error occurred reading a file.
About to access the network.
The network might be down, will try again later.
```

The only message from the code not shown is the one that says it's about to read a file, because this message is classified as informational. The `FileInfo` switch shows only messages in the warnings category and higher.

Tracing the Windows Workflow Foundation Platform

Windows Workflow Foundation has quite a few built-in hooks for tracing. The developers of the workflow platform placed a great deal of tracing message throughout the code. Therefore, if the right switches are turned on, you can receive a great deal of useful information.

You can specify the following built-in switches for tracing:

❑   System.Workflow.Runtime

❑   System.Workflow.Runtime.Hosting

❑   System.Workflow.Runtime.Tracking

❑   System.Workflow.Activities

❑   System.Workflow.Activities.Rules

You must set these switches to a value from the `SourceLevels` enumeration, which includes `All`, `Critical`, `Error`, `Information`, and more.

In addition to these switches, the workflow tracing infrastructure has configurable options for tracing custom applications. The `System.Workflow LogToFile` switch specifies whether a file called WorkflowTrace.log should be written to the working directory. This option is off by default. If this switch is turned on, the file contains all the trace information specified with the source switches listed previously. Figure 12-12 shows an example of this file.

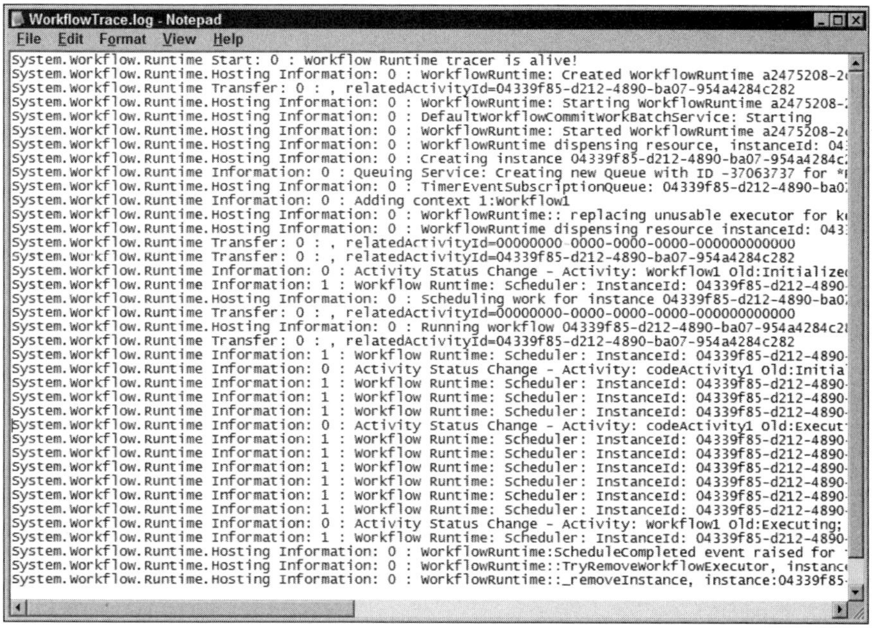

Figure 12-12

Another switch, `System.Workflow LogToTraceListeners`, specifies whether to send the workflow tracing information to any other configured trace listeners. By default, the workflow trace messages are sent to the file only if that switch is turned on. This is useful when you want to be able to view the built-in workflow tracing messages on the console window or another listener.

You can easily configure workflow tracing options in an App.config or Web.config file. The following XML shows a .NET configuration file that references all five workflow trace sources as well as the `System .Workflow LogToTraceListeners` and the `System.Workflow LogToFile` options. This file specifies various `SourceLevel` values for each of the five trace sources. In addition, the workflow tracing information is sent to a `ConsoleTraceListener` because the `System.Workflow LogToTraceListeners` option is on and the `System.Workflow LogToFile` option is off.

```xml
<?xml version="1.0" encoding="utf-8" ?>
<configuration>
  <system.diagnostics>
    <trace autoflush="true">
      <listeners>
        <add name="myConsoleListener"
          type="System.Diagnostics.ConsoleTraceListener" />
      </listeners>
    </trace>
    <switches>
      <add name="System.Workflow.Runtime" value="All" />
      <add name="System.Workflow.Runtime.Hosting" value="All" />
      <add name="System.Workflow.Runtime.Tracking" value="Critical" />
      <add name="System.Workflow.Activities" value="Warning" />
      <add name="System.Workflow.Activities.Rules" value="Off" />

      <add name="System.Workflow LogToFile" value="0" />
      <add name="System.Workflow LogToTraceListeners" value="1" />
    </switches>
  </system.diagnostics>
</configuration>
```

You can also implement you own tracing messages in workflow code, including custom activities, runtime services, and the workflow code-beside class. For example, if the code in the following listing is implemented using a Code activity's `ExecuteCode` event handler, the "My custom trace" message will be intermixed with the built-in trace messages:

```csharp
private void codeActivity1_ExecuteCode(object sender, EventArgs e)
{
    Trace.WriteLine("My custom trace.");
}
```

Performance Counters

You can also trace workflow activities on a systemwide level by using performance counters. *Performance counters* are measurable indicators exposed by various applications. An application that ships with Windows called Performance Monitor (perfmon.exe) enables you to use these metrics. Because performance counters are registered with Windows, the Performance Monitor application can see and display these counters. Figure 12-13 shows a view of Performance Monitor with some basic Windows-level counters displayed.

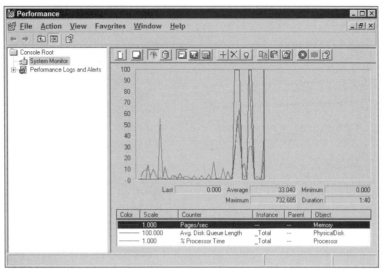

Figure 12-13

Workflow Counters

Windows Workflow Foundation provides several useful metrics, as described in Table 12-1.

Table 12-1: Workflow Performance Counters

Counter	Description
Workflows Aborted (count, per second)	The number of workflows aborted using `WorkflowInstance.Abort()`.
Workflows Blocked (count, per second)	The number of workflows that are blocked, currently waiting for an external event.
Workflows Completed (count, per second)	The number of completed workflows.
Workflows Created (count, per second)	The number of created workflows.
Workflows Executing (count)	The number of workflows currently executing.
Workflows Idle (count)	The number of workflows that have work to do but are not currently processing.
Workflows In Memory (count)	The number of workflows in memory. These are workflows that have been created; loaded from persistence; and not completed, terminated, or unloaded.
Workflows Loaded (count, per second)	The number of workflows loaded into memory.
Workflows Persisted (count, per second)	The number of workflows that have been persisted using a persistence service.

Table continued on following page

Counter	Description
Workflows Runnable (count)	The number of workflows that have received an external event to process but have not started processing.
Workflows Suspended (count, per second)	The number of suspended workflows.
Workflows Terminated (count, per second)	The number of terminated workflows.
Workflows Unloaded (count, per second)	The number of unloaded workflows.

You can view these performance counters at a system level, meaning across all `WorkflowRuntime` instances, or from the perspective of a single runtime instance. To view the workflow performance counters, first launch Performance Monitor by choosing Start ⇨ Run and typing **perfmon.exe**. By default, standard system counters are displayed, such as % Processor Time and Avg. Disk Queue Length. You can remove any counter you don't want to use by selecting the unwanted counter and pressing Delete.

Next, right-click the Performance Monitor background and select Add Counters. In the Add Counters dialog box, select Windows Workflow Foundation from the Performance object drop-down menu to display a list of the workflow performance counters (see Figure 12-14).

Figure 12-14

When you select one of the counters, the user interface allows you to apply that counter to all workflow instances on the machine, global instances, or individual `WorkflowRuntime` instances. Figure 12-14 indicates that the machine currently has two runtime instances: `workflowruntimea` and `workflowruntimeb`. These correspond to the names given to each workflow runtime section in the application's configuration file. You specify this name using the `Name` attribute of the main workflow runtime node.

Select the performance counters you want to use and the instances where you want to use them, and then add them to the graph with the Add button. Click the Close button to return to the main screen, where you can easily monitor the selected measures.

Creating Logs and Alerts

You can use the Performance Monitor to tell Windows to capture counter data based on the parameters you specify. For example, you may want to record the number of active and created workflows for a certain two-hour period every day. The recorded data is written to a log file in a directory of your choosing to be later inspected, just as though you were looking at a snapshot in time.

To configure a log, open Performance Monitor and expand the Performance Logs and Alerts tree item in the left pane. Next, select the Counter logs item; a listing of currently configured logs appears on the right. To add a new log configuration, right-click an empty area in the right pane and select New Log Settings from the context menu. Enter an appropriate name for the new log; the dialog box shown in Figure 12-15 is displayed.

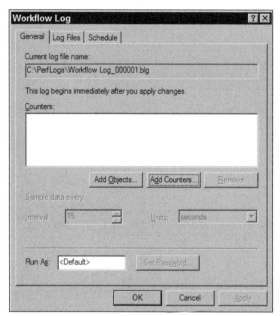

Figure 12-15

From this dialog box, you can configure the counters to be included, the counting interval, log file name and location, and the log scheduling. All of these options are pretty straightforward and allow a great deal of flexibility, depending on what data you want and when you want it.

The data of interest will now be captured by Windows, but it needs to be consumable. Again, you do this using the Performance Monitor. From the main System Monitor screen (the one with the graph), click the View Log Data button on the toolbar (or press Ctrl+L). From the subsequent dialog box, specify that the data source should be a log file and then point to where the log files of interest can be found.

Next, click the Add button on the Data tab. This displays a list of the counters available for viewing. The list consists of the same counters that were specified when you first configured the log. Click the OK button; the graph is loaded with the data captured during logging.

This is a great way to proactively keep tabs on system metrics. If performance issues start to crop up, you can review the counter logs for the past week to see what happened. Although this is just one of a multitude of system monitoring tools, it is a powerful and fairly simply way of troubleshooting potential issues.

Along with logging data for later use, you can configure alerts to perform an action based on a predetermined counter threshold being crossed. For example, if the Workflows Terminated counter reaches an unacceptable level, the operations team may want to be notified, because this could be a sign that something is seriously wrong. Configuring alerts is as simple as configuring new counter logs.

From within Performance Monitor, expand the Performance Logs and Alerts tree item in the left pane and then select Alerts. To create a new alert, right-click the right pane and select New Alert Settings. You are asked to enter a name for this set of alerts. After this, a dialog box is displayed, where you configure the counters of interest and the desired threshold for each.

After you configure the counter thresholds, you need to configure the corresponding actions. You do this on the Action tab, which is shown in Figure 12-16. As you can see, there are different actions that can be triggered when a counter threshold is breached.

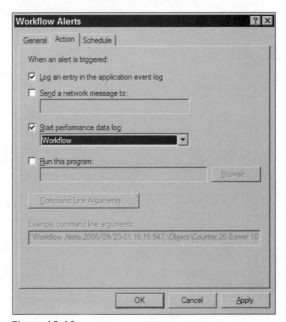

Figure 12-16

Summary

This chapter covered quite a bit related to exceptions in workflow execution, how to handle these exceptions, and how to track down and diagnose issues with workflows and code. Exceptions are situational events that are not the norm. When these types of events come up, they must be gracefully handled, or things can go seriously wrong.

In Windows Workflow Foundation, exceptions are presented as faults. Workflow faults correspond directly to .NET types that inherit from the `System.Exception` class. There are several activities that directly support the concept of faults. The `FaultHandlersActivity` and `FaultHandlerActivity` classes are responsible for monitoring and gracefully handling faults that are raised during workflow execution. `ThrowActivity` enables you to initiate the throwing of a workflow fault. The CancellationHandler activity enables you to gracefully handle the situation if an activity's execution is interrupted by the raising of a fault elsewhere in the workflow.

Because problems with workflows and code can occur due to bugs or other extraneous factors, there are several techniques available for tracking and logging these issues. This chapter discussed debugging in Visual Studio, .NET tracing, and performance counters. These techniques all have workflow-specific components that can assist you in the troubleshooting process.

13

Windows Workflow Foundation and ASP.NET

With the release of ASP.NET in 2002, Microsoft took web development to the next level by providing an object-oriented way to develop web applications in an extremely rapid manner. And as you know by now, Windows Workflow Foundation also provides a new method of architecting applications. You can use these two technologies together to enable new types of systems.

This chapter covers the following topics regarding the use of ASP.NET with Windows Workflow Foundation:

❑   Various application scenarios

❑   Pitfalls of using ASP.NET with workflows

❑   Hosting Windows Workflow Foundation in an ASP.NET environment

❑   Using a workflow as a page flow engine

Application Scenarios with ASP.NET

As mentioned several times throughout this book, one of the greatest things about Windows Workflow Foundation is the fact that it can be hosted in any .NET application type, including ASP.NET. One way that you could use a workflow and ASP.NET is to provide wizard- or step-based functionality — such as for an online store. Users start by visiting the site and adding various items to a basket. When they are ready to purchase items, the web application must check to see whether they are already members. If not, they must go through some kind of enrollment process. A workflow is a great way to model the various steps users might go through during a shopping experience online.

Consider also a lengthy application process that must maintain state across user visits. For example, a college admissions application could use Windows Workflow Foundation to provide a stateful page-flow back end. Applicants could start the process during their first visit, save their changes, and continue the process during subsequent visits. You could easily implement this by using the persistence functionality provided out of the box. This concept of using Windows Workflow Foundation as a page flow engine is discussed later in this chapter.

Technology Considerations

One of the most important technical considerations when you're determining whether to use Windows Workflow Foundation with ASP.NET is the hosting of the workflow runtime. By default, the workflow runtime is hosted so that new workflow instances are executed asynchronously, on a separate thread from the runtime. This generally works great, especially in applications that have a user interface because the work goes on in the background and the user interface thread is freed up to respond to user interaction. However, this is a different story in ASP.NET, for a couple of reasons.

First, workflows might need to behave differently in web applications because of the way users interact with web forms. When a button is clicked, a round trip is performed, and a response page is generated and returned to the user after the work on the server is complete. Because of this, and if the workflow steps are short in duration, the work should probably take place on the same thread as the web response so that control is not returned to the user until the workflow has completed a unit of work.

In addition, there are threading considerations because of the fact that ASP.NET is hosted in the IIS web server. IIS is particular about having many of its threads consumed. Because of this, the Windows Workflow Foundation API provides a scheduler service as an alternative to `DefaultWorkflowSchedulerService`. You can add `ManualWorkflowSchedulerService` to the workflow runtime's services just as you would any other runtime service. Instead of launching workflow instances on their own thread, `ManualWorkflowSchedulerService` executes instances on the calling thread in a synchronous manner.

The following is an example of using the `ManualWorkflowSchedulerService`:

```
WorkflowRuntime runtime = new WorkflowRuntime();

ManualWorkflowSchedulerService schedulerService =
    new ManualWorkflowSchedulerService();
runtime.AddService(schedulerService);

WorkflowInstance instance = runtime.CreateWorkflow(typeof(MyWorkflow));
instance.Start();

// the workflow instance is still not running!
// start it using the scheduler service
schedulerService.RunWorkflow(instance.InstanceId);
```

As you can see in the code, this is different from the `DefaultWorkflowSchedulerService` in that the `ManualWorkflowSchedulerService` requires an additional method call to start instance execution — even after the `WorkflowInstance.Start` method is called. The `RunWorkflow` method takes an instance GUID and causes a blocking call until the workflow returns control to the host application. Remember that if the `RunWorkflow` method is not called by the host, the workflow instance never executes.

This type of scenario makes perfect sense in an ASP.NET application that hosts a workflow with bite-size chunks of execution — meaning that a page request calls a workflow that performs work that does not take more than a few seconds. However, even for scenarios in which the workflow takes extended periods of time to execute and return control to the caller, using the `DefaultWorkflowSchedulerService` might not be the answer. Execution in web applications is generally reserved for performing work that has some impact on a page's outcome. Instead of using background threads for long-running work that will not be later utilized by a page, you can offload this work to an outside application. This type of scenario is discussed in Chapter 14, using a Windows Service as a workflow runtime host that runs outside the context of ASP.NET and IIS.

Managing the Workflow Runtime

Generally, you want to keep one instance of the workflow runtime for your entire application. Doing this in ASP.NET is a bit different from a Windows Forms application. A common way to manage the workflow runtime is to use the Global.asax file and the `Application_Start` and `Application_End` event handlers, as follows:

```
<%@ Application Language="C#" %>
<%@ Import Namespace="System.Workflow.Runtime" %>

<script runat="server">

    void Application_Start(object sender, EventArgs e)
    {
        WorkflowRuntime runtime = new WorkflowRuntime("WorkflowRuntime");
        runtime.StartRuntime();

        Application["WorkflowRuntime"] = runtime;
    }

    void Application_End(object sender, EventArgs e)
    {
        WorkflowRuntime runtime = Application["WorkflowRuntime"]
            as WorkflowRuntime;
        runtime.StopRuntime();
        runtime.Dispose();
    }

</script>
```

In this example, the constructor for the `WorkflowRuntime` class passes a string that is a reference to a section in the Web.config file. The following code shows a sample Web.config file:

```xml
<?xml version="1.0"?>
<configuration>
  <configSections>
    <section name="WorkflowRuntime"
        type="System.Workflow.Runtime.Configuration.WorkflowRuntimeSection,
        System.Workflow.Runtime, Version=3.0.0.0, Culture=neutral,
        PublicKeyToken=31bf3856ad364e35"/>
  </configSections>
  <appSettings/>
  <connectionStrings/>
  <WorkflowRuntime>
    <Services>
      <add
        type="System.Workflow.Runtime.Hosting.ManualWorkflowSchedulerService,
        System.Workflow.Runtime, Version=3.0.0.0, Culture=neutral,
        PublicKeyToken=31bf3856ad364e35"/>
    </Services>
  </WorkflowRuntime>
  <system.web>
    <compilation debug="true">
      <assemblies>
        <add assembly="System.Workflow.Activities, Version=3.0.0.0,
          Culture=neutral, PublicKeyToken=31BF3856AD364E35"/>
        <add assembly="System.Workflow.ComponentModel, Version=3.0.0.0,
          Culture=neutral, PublicKeyToken=31BF3856AD364E35"/>
        <add assembly="System.Workflow.Runtime, Version=3.0.0.0,
          Culture=neutral, PublicKeyToken=31BF3856AD364E35"/>
      </assemblies>
    </compilation>
    <authentication mode="Windows"/>
  </system.web>
</configuration>
```

In this code, the `configSections` node allows the addition of custom configuration sections. The `type` attribute of the `section` node is a pointer to a .NET type that inherits from `System.Configuration` `.ConfigurationSection`. By inheriting from this class, other .NET types are able to parse custom configuration sections, which can be included in Web.config and App.config files. The custom configuration section is implemented in the `WorkflowRuntime` node, which contains a child node that enumerates the runtime services, which should be added automatically. The `ManualWorkflowSchedulerService` is added because this is an ASP.NET application.

Workflow as a Page Flow Engine

You could also use Windows Workflow Foundation and ASP.NET to create a page flow engine. Many web applications have navigation frameworks that drive the order in which various pages are displayed. These frameworks may range from simple and inflexible to somewhat complex and dynamic. Just as Windows Workflow Foundation is provided so that developers aren't reinventing the wheel every time a process engine is needed, the same technology can be used to build a flexible and dynamic ASP.NET page flow engine.

Microsoft has stated that it plans on releasing a set of classes for ASP.NET page flow sitting on Windows Workflow Foundation. However, these plans have not been finalized (as of this book's writing). Therefore, you might want to build your own library of page flow code. Before developing any code, however, you need to understand the characteristics of a good page flow engine.

Model-View-Controller

In GUI-based applications, a common approach to maintaining a flexible code base that is free from ties to the user interface is the Model-View-Controller (MVC) pattern. This pattern prescribes the following three layers:

❑ **The model** — This is the piece of the architecture that represents your business logic. It should know nothing about the front end of your application. The model commonly contains domain-specific entities such as a `Customer` or `Order` class and other supporting types. In addition, any business processes defined in Windows Workflow Foundation is considered part of the model. Finally, data access code, although generally not considered business or domain-specific logic, is part of or below the model.

❑ **The view** — This is the front end. It is the interface the user interacts with and sees on his or her screen. Therefore, in ASP.NET, the ASPX markup is the view. A typical view contains obvious controls, such as text boxes, buttons, and drop-down lists. Although the view contains these data-entry mechanisms, the controller is actually responsible for obtaining the data and passing it to the model.

❑ **The controller** — This is the layer between the model and the view that passes information about events generated in the view to the model. Therefore, the controller, not unlike the view, should generally not contain important business logic. To relate this to ASP.NET, the controller is implemented as code-beside classes, because these classes contain all the event handlers for controls in the ASPX files.

Given this knowledge about the MVC pattern, building a page flow engine with Windows Workflow Foundation tends to be a little more straightforward. As mentioned, any workflow is part of the model because it is the business logic, and the front end is still considered the view. Where it gets interesting is in the controller layer. The controller needs to watch for user interactions with the page and pass that information to the workflow. At that point, the workflow does whatever work it needs to do and then tells the controller it is ready for its next step or piece of information. The controller should then be responsible for taking the response from a workflow and translating it to the page that needs to be displayed to the user next.

This means that each page in an ASP.NET application should have absolutely no knowledge of the order in which it will be displayed. Conversely, the workflow should not directly know that it is controlling an ASP.NET page flow. This type of pattern enables you to swap the front end while using the same back-end logic. For example, consider an organization whose workflow is responsible for enrolling new customers in a rewards program. The workflow should be usable in an ASP.NET web application or a call center's Windows Forms application. Implementing the MVC pattern to create a page flow engine is not necessarily hard. However, you need to take appropriate precautions to ensure application boundaries are not crossed, thereby weakening the flexibility of an application.

Building a Page Flow Application

This section follows the development of a simple ASP.NET application responsible for enrolling employees in various company programs, such as insurance and 401(k). The ASP.NET application needs to include various forms for collecting information about a specific program and then passing the data to the controller. In addition, a workflow needs to be developed for dictating the order in which data is collected from the user. For example, employees will be asked on the first page what type of employee they are (full or part time), how long they have been with the company, and whether they want to enroll in a dental insurance program. Depending on the answers to these questions, the users may or may not see certain forms during their session.

To allow the workflow to communicate with the controller, the application will use the out-of-the-box CallExternalMethod and HandleExternalEvent activities. The instances of these activities in the workflow will point to a page flow service interface developed for this example. Figure 13-1 shows a partial screen shot of the completed workflow. The logic for the retirement plan includes an IfElse activity that checks to see whether the employee is eligible to enroll based on employee type and tenure. If the employee is eligible, a CallExternalMethod activity is executed that tells the web application to forward the user to the retirement plan enrollment page. After user input is collected, a HandleExternalEvent activity captures this event, and the workflow execution is resumed. Next, logic is implemented that checks to see whether the employee opted to enroll in the retirement plan, and if so, code is called that enrolls the user. The workflow proceeds from here to display other enrollment forms, if applicable.

The first step in writing the page flow code for this example is developing the communication plumbing, which includes the local communication service interface, the service class itself, and the event arguments classes. The following code shows the interface:

```
[ExternalDataExchange]
[CorrelationParameter("stepName")]
public interface IPageService
{
    [CorrelationInitializer]
    void AdvancePageFlow(string stepName,
        Dictionary<string, object> dataFromWorkflow);

    [CorrelationAlias("stepName", "e.StepName")]
    event EventHandler<PageFlowEventArgs> StepCompleted;
}
```

The first thing that happens in this interface is that the workflow invokes the `AdvancePageFlow` method, which passes a parameter that represents the name of the next step. (How this determines which page gets called is discussed in the next paragraph.) The second parameter passed to this method holds any parameters that the workflow wants to pass to the outside world. There is also an event called `StepCompleted`, which is raised by the controller when a page is submitted by the end user.

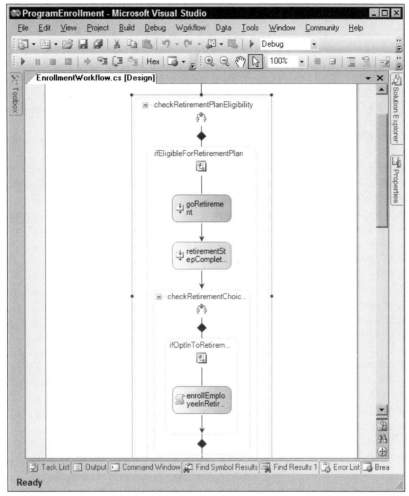

Figure 13-1

Notice the correlation attributes applied to various elements of the interface. The interface itself is decorated with the `CorrelationParameter` attribute, which tells the workflow runtime the field to use so that the correct HandleExternalEvent is called when an event is raised from the controller. The `AdvancePageFlow` method is decorated with the `CorrelationInitializer` attribute. This tells the workflow runtime that when this method is called, the correlation token is initialized, and the value for `stepName` should be noted and used for correlating events. Finally, the event is decorated with the `CorrelationAlias` attribute, which maps the `stepName` parameter to a property in the event's `PageFlowEventArgs` instance.

The following code shows the implementation of the communication service. The interesting piece of code in this class is the `AdvancePageFlow` method. When this method is called from the workflow, any subscribers to the `PageAdvanceCommandReceived` event are notified and passed an instance of the `AdvanceFlowEventArgs` class, which contains any parameters passed from the workflow as well as the next step name.

```
public class PageService : IPageService
{
    public void AdvancePageFlow(string stepName,
        Dictionary<string, object> dataFromWorkflow)
    {
        if (this.PageAdvanceCommandReceived != null)
            this.PageAdvanceCommandReceived(null,
                new AdvanceFlowEventArgs(dataFromWorkflow, stepName));
    }

    public void RaiseStepCompleted(PageFlowEventArgs e)
    {
        if (this.StepCompleted != null)
            this.StepCompleted(null, e);
    }

    public event EventHandler<PageFlowEventArgs> StepCompleted;
    public event EventHandler<AdvanceFlowEventArgs> PageAdvanceCommandReceived;
}
```

That's really about it for the interesting code on the workflow side of things. Now code needs to be written that manipulates the display of ASP.NET web forms (also known as the controller). To serve the purpose of the controller, a class called `WorkflowHelper` is implemented. This class uses the singleton pattern because it is a single-purpose class that does not contain any instance-specific data.

The following code shows the first part of the class, which includes the class constructor and properties:

```
public class WorkflowHelper
{
    // static members
    private static WorkflowHelper instance = null;

    // instance members
    private Dictionary<string, string> pageMappings =
        new Dictionary<string, string>();
    private AutoResetEvent waitHandle = new AutoResetEvent(false);

    // constructors
    private WorkflowHelper()
    {
        // these should be configurable!
        pageMappings.Add("401kEnrollment", "RetirementPlan.aspx");
        pageMappings.Add("DentalEnrollment", "Dental.aspx");
        pageMappings.Add("Done", "ThankYou.aspx");
    }

    // properties
```

```csharp
public static WorkflowHelper Instance
{
    get
    {
        if (instance == null) instance = new WorkflowHelper();
        return instance;
    }
}

public Dictionary<string, object> DataFromWorkflow
{
    get
    {
        return HttpContext.Current.Session["DataFromWorkflow"]
            as Dictionary<string, object>;
    }
}

public WorkflowRuntime WorkflowRuntime
{
    get
    {
        WorkflowRuntime runtime =
            HttpContext.Current.Application["WorkflowRuntime"]
                as WorkflowRuntime;

        if (runtime == null)
        {
            // create the runtime and add the page flow service
            runtime = new WorkflowRuntime();

            ManualWorkflowSchedulerService schedulerService =
                new ManualWorkflowSchedulerService();
            runtime.AddService(schedulerService);

            ExternalDataExchangeService dataExchangeService =
                new ExternalDataExchangeService();
            runtime.AddService(dataExchangeService);
            PageService pageService = new PageService();
            pageService.PageAdvanceCommandReceived += new
                EventHandler<AdvanceFlowEventArgs>(PageAdvanceCommandReceived);
            dataExchangeService.AddService(pageService);

            runtime.StartRuntime();

            // add the workflow runtime instance to the application state
            HttpContext.Current.Application["WorkflowRuntime"] = runtime;
        }

        return runtime;
    }
}

private PageService PageService
```

```
        {
            get
            {
                return this.WorkflowRuntime.GetService(typeof(PageService))
                    as PageService;
            }
        }

        private ManualWorkflowSchedulerService SchedulerService
        {
            get
            {
                return this.WorkflowRuntime.GetService(
                    typeof(ManualWorkflowSchedulerService))
                        as ManualWorkflowSchedulerService;
            }
        }

        private Guid CurrentWorkflowInstanceId
        {
            get
            {
                HttpCookie instanceIdCookie =
                    HttpContext.Current.Request.Cookies["InstanceId"] as HttpCookie;

                if (instanceIdCookie != null)
                    return new Guid(instanceIdCookie.Value);

                throw new ApplicationException("No instance has been started.");
            }
        }
        ...
    }
```

The only thing going on in this constructor is that keys and values are added to a class-level `Dictionary<string, string>` member. This object is responsible for holding mappings of command names to URLs. This mapping allows the workflow and the ASP.NET application to remain loosely coupled. However, in a real-world application, these values should be contained in a configuration file for easy modification later.

The class properties include the singleton instance, a property called `DataFromWorkflow` that holds any parameters passed from the workflow's previous step, properties for runtime services, and a property that retrieves the workflow instance ID from the user's cookies. In addition, there is a property called `WorkflowRuntime` that retrieves a reference to a single instance of the `WorkflowRuntime` class. First, the `get` accessor checks to see whether an instance of the `WorkflowRuntime` class has been stored in the `Application` object. If not, a new instance is created, and the required runtime services are added. Finally, the new `WorkflowRuntime` object is stored in the globally available application state.

Notice that a handler is added to the `PageAdvanceCommandReceived` event of the `PageService`. This is so that when the workflow makes an external method call to the local communication service, this event is raised, and the application's controller knows to redirect the user to a new page. (This event's event-handler method is discussed in more detail later.)

The following code shows the remainder of the `WorkflowHelper` class:

```
public void StartWorkflow(Dictionary<string, object> parms)
{
    this.SubmitData(parms, null);
}

public void SubmitData(string stepName, Dictionary<string, object> parms)
{
    this.SubmitData(parms, stepName);
}

private void SubmitData(Dictionary<string, object> parms, string stepName)
{
    WorkflowInstance instance;
    if (stepName == null)
    {
        instance = this.WorkflowRuntime.CreateWorkflow(
            typeof(Enrollment.EnrollmentWorkflow), parms);
        instance.Start();

        // add the workflow's instance id to the user's cookies
        HttpContext.Current.Response.Cookies.Add(
            new HttpCookie("InstanceId", instance.InstanceId.ToString()));
    }
    else
    {
        instance =
            this.WorkflowRuntime.GetWorkflow(this.CurrentWorkflowInstanceId);
        this.PageService.RaiseStepCompleted(
            new PageFlowEventArgs(instance.InstanceId, stepName, parms));
    }

    // run the workflow on the same thread as the request
    this.SchedulerService.RunWorkflow(instance.InstanceId);
}

private void PageAdvanceCommandReceived(object sender, AdvanceFlowEventArgs e)
{
    HttpContext.Current.Session["DataFromWorkflow"] = e.Parameters;
    string nextUrl = this.pageMappings[e.StepName];
    HttpContext.Current.Response.Redirect(nextUrl, false);
}
```

In this code, the third `SubmitData` overload is responsible for either starting a new workflow instance or obtaining a reference to an existing one and resuming its execution. Whether a new instance is starting or an existing instance is continuing, the `ManualWorkflowSchedulerService` is used because this is an ASP.NET application and the workflow should be executing on the same thread as the web request.

The last method in this class, `PageAdvanceCommandReceived`, is responsible for processing the page flow when the workflow makes an external method call to the local communication class, `PageService`. This event-handler method first grabs a reference to the parameters passed from the workflow and places the object in the user's ASP.NET session. Next, a URL is obtained by using the command-mapping

Dictionary object introduced earlier. This URL is then used to redirect the user to a new page by calling the HttpResponse's Redirect method. It is extremely important that the Redirect method accept a Boolean as its second argument; in this case, it is always passed a value of false. This tells the Redirect method to not end the execution of the current thread before the redirection is performed. If this value is not explicitly passed, the current thread's execution would be terminated, and the workflow would not have a chance to continue. This means that the first page would be correctly shown using a redirection, but after that page was submitted, nothing would happen because the workflow can never progress to the next HandleExternalEvent activity.

At this point, the web forms can be implemented. Remember, each form should have no idea which order it is displayed in except for the initial form that starts the workflow. This makes sense in this example because the data collection screen is always displayed first and starts the workflow. The following is a portion of the code-beside class for the data collection screen. As you can see, there is not much going on here, which is actually good. The majority of the logic is contained in the model, which is where it should be. First, a Person object is created that represents the employee and his or her relevant data. This object is then added to a Dictionary instance. Finally, the parameters object is passed to the WorkflowHelper's StartWorkflow method. The controller and model then decide what happens next.

```csharp
protected void btnSubmit_Click(object sender, EventArgs e)
{
    Person person = new Person(txtFirstName.Text,
        (EmployeeType)Convert.ToInt32(ddlEmployeeType.SelectedValue),
        (Tenure)Convert.ToInt32(ddlTenure.SelectedValue));

    Dictionary<string, object> parms = new Dictionary<string, object>();
    parms.Add("Person", person);

    WorkflowHelper.Instance.StartWorkflow(parms);
}
```

The following block of code is taken from the retirement plan form's code-beside class. This code is similar to the data collection form's code, except that the button event handlers call the SubmitData method of WorkflowHelper, which takes a string parameter that represents the current step's name. This string is eventually passed to the workflow so that the correct HandleExternalEvent activity is executed. There is also a second method that enables the user to opt out of the retirement plan. (The dental-plan code is very similar and thus is not displayed here.)

```csharp
protected void btnSubmit_Click(object sender, EventArgs e)
{
    Dictionary<string, object> parms = new Dictionary<string, object>();
    parms.Add("OptIn", true);
    parms.Add("Amount", txtAmount.Text);
    WorkflowHelper.Instance.SubmitData("401kEnrollment", parms);
}

protected void btnCancel_Click(object sender, EventArgs e)
{
    Dictionary<string, object> parms = new Dictionary<string, object>();
    parms.Add("OptIn", false);
    WorkflowHelper.Instance.SubmitData("401kEnrollment", parms);
}
```

Finally, the following code is found in the last page of the workflow, ThankYou.aspx. This code is interesting because it is finally using the ability to retrieve parameters passed from the workflow to the controller. A BulletedList control is used to display a list of all the programs an employee has enrolled in during the lifecycle of the workflow. Keep in mind that this list could be empty, depending on the employee's eligibility for programs or choices for enrollment.

```
protected void Page_Load(object sender, EventArgs e)
{
    List<string> enrollments =
        WorkflowHelper.Instance.DataFromWorkflow["Enrollments"]
            as List<string>;

    this.BulletedList1.DataSource = enrollments;
    this.BulletedList1.DataBind();
}
```

The page flow application in this example illustrates a great way to use Windows Workflow Foundation to control the UI of an application — more specifically, an ASP.NET application. However, there are a few things that could have been done to make this code more generic and usable for any page flow scenario. The code as shown is not too far from this, but it could benefit from greater configurability. For example, the command-to-URL mapping should decidedly be implemented in a configuration file. In addition, the type of workflow created should be configurable.

Another thing to keep in mind with this type of application is that not only could a sequential workflow be used, but a state-machine workflow would also work just fine. Using a state-machine workflow would allow users to be directed back and forth to different web forms in any order dictated by the workflow logic. This might be useful in a bug tracking or approval scenario when certain steps may be repeated depending on events external to the workflow.

Summary

This chapter covered some of the ways in which ASP.NET and Windows Workflow Foundation can interact. Windows Workflow Foundation is able to sit behind an ASP.NET application just like any other .NET application type. This is useful for wizard-type scenarios, especially one that may be completed over the period of several sessions.

There are also technology-specific issues that you need to consider when determining whether to use a workflow in ASP.NET, the biggest of which concerns the threading model used to execute workflow instances. By default, instances are started on a thread from the thread pool so that the workflow host can continue work while the workflow executes in the background. This may not favorable in a web environment, because a web page may need to wait for some work to be completed before returning control to the user. In addition, IIS and ASP.NET are not meant to have a great deal of their threads used. Therefore, the ManualWorkflowSchedulerService is provided to execute a workflow instance on the same thread as the host.

Finally, this chapter covered the use of Windows Workflow Foundation as a page flow engine in ASP.NET. The MVC pattern was used to ensure that the web forms had no knowledge of the order in which they appear to the users. This approach allows for a great deal of flexibility related to changing the page display order as well as the front-end technology being used. For example, the same workflow could be used to control an ASP.NET application and a Windows Forms application.

Windows Workflow Foundation and Connected Systems

This chapter is about how workflows relates to *connected systems.* Workflows sometimes need to talk to the outside world, and conversely, the outside world may need a way to call in to a workflow. Web services can serve as a great way to provide widespread communications in software; therefore, this chapter includes an in-depth discussion of these services.

In addition, there are architectural issues that you need to consider before applying workflow and web services in your organization. Services-oriented architecture (SOA) has been a very popular buzzword in recent years, and when studied and applied sensibly, it can greatly enhance a company's ability to componentize software and become more agile.

This chapter also covers a new Microsoft technology referred to as Windows Communication Foundation (WCF). WCF encompasses a great deal of functionality related to developing connected systems, and not just around standard web services. You can also use WCF in conjunction with Windows Workflow Foundation to expose workflow functionality outside the bounds of a single application.

Connected Systems and Services-Oriented Architecture

Connected systems and SOA are two often-overloaded terms (connected systems probably more so than SOA). Connected systems can be defined as a concept that has software applications communicating through services. Although these services are commonly XML web services, they do not have to be. E-mail and FTP are other ways in which applications can communicate with one another as well as people. For example, the software system at a company that sits there and waits for orders from the outside world can be considered a connected system.

SOA is a bit easier to define. However, the concept of SOA is still discussed with great passion today, and there are different ideas about what it means. As its name implies, SOA is a way of building systems using services. Although services are commonly implemented with web services, it's not a requirement. Services generally do a single thing well while having no knowledge of other tasks. This concept of having many individual services allows a building-block approach to developing software.

If an organization has a suite of dozens of services that all do different tasks related to the business, building new software applications can become a matter of grabbing one service from here and another service from there. Services can also be exposed by parties outside the organization. The beauty is that no matter what the service is, what its interface is, or where it originates, it can be brought together with other services to provide something useful.

The technology community has generally accepted the following four tenets to describe what SOA is and how SOA services should behave:

❑   Service boundaries are explicit.

❑   Services are autonomous.

❑   Services share a schema and contract.

❑   Service compatibility is based on policy.

Workflow and Web Services

Web services are very important in the concept of connected systems. As such, web services play a large role in Windows Workflow Foundation. There are hooks into the workflow platform that allow external web services to be called as well as allow clients to call workflows as web services. The following sections cover these concepts and the relevant pieces of the workflow platform.

Web Service Activities

This section discusses the web-services-related activities with which you should become familiar.

The InvokeWebService Activity

This activity enables a workflow to call external web services. An instance of the InvokeWebService activity must be associated with one particular web service and one particular method on that web service. Parameters that need to be passed to the web service can be bound to properties on the activity. In addition, any values returned by the web service can be bound to specified properties in the workflow.

The WebServiceInput and WebServiceOutput Activities

These two activities are always found together in a workflow. The WebServiceInput and WebServiceOutput activities are used to facilitate exposing workflows as web services. The WebServiceInput activity is generally found at the top of the workflow and defines the entry point of the web service. Conversely, the WebServiceOutput activity defines the exit point of the web service. Any values that are to be returned to the client are configured on this activity.

The WebServiceFault Activity

The WebServiceFault activity is used when the workflow is acting as a web service. If you need to raise an exception to the client in the form of a SOAP fault, the WebServiceFault activity is the solution. This activity does not behave like a `throw` statement in code, in that the workflow's execution can continue after a WebServiceFault activity is executed. However, the execution of this type of activity produces the same result on the client as if you called a `throw` statement in an ASMX web service.

Calling Web Services inside a Workflow

Before learning how to call a web service from a workflow, you need a web service to call. This section describes an example web service and workflow scenario for admitting a patient to a hospital. The simple web service will have a method called `AdmitPatient` that will be passed basic patient data. This method will also return an instance of a class called `PatientRecord`. The web service will have a method called `GetPatientStatus` that would, in a fully implemented application, return a string representing a patient's status in his or her hospital stay. However, in this example, it will simply return a dummy string.

To create the web service, open Visual Studio 2005 and select File ➪ New ➪ Web Site. In the New Web Site dialog box, select the ASP.NET Web Service option from the project templates. After the web site project has been created, change the web service's name to PatientService.asmx. Finally, add the following code to implement the desired functionality:

```
[WebService(Namespace = "http://tempuri.org/")]
[WebServiceBinding(ConformsTo = WsiProfiles.BasicProfile1_1)]
public class PatientService : WebService
{
    public PatientService()
    {
    }


    [WebMethod]
    public PatientRecord AdmitPatient(string patientId, string name,
        string reasonForVisit)
    {
        Console.WriteLine("Patient {0} was admitted.", name);
        return new PatientRecord(patientId, name, reasonForVisit);
    }


    [WebMethod]
    public string GetPatientStatus(string patientId)
    {
        if (String.IsNullOrEmpty(patientId))
            throw new ArgumentException("Patient ID was null or empty.",
                "patientId");

        return "Dummy status";
    }
}
```

Next, create the `PatientRecord` class by using the following code:

```
public class PatientRecord
{
    public string PatientId;
    public string Name;
    public string ReasonForVisit;
    public DateTime TimeAdmitted;

    public PatientRecord()
        : this(String.Empty, String.Empty, String.Empty)
    {
    }

    public PatientRecord(string patientId, string name, string reasonForVisit)
    {
        this.PatientId = patientId;
        this.Name = name;
        this.ReasonForVisit = reasonForVisit;
        this.TimeAdmitted = DateTime.Now;
    }
}
```

Now that the patient web service has been created, it's time to implement the workflow that will use it. First, create a new Sequential Workflow Console Application project, and name it `CallWebService`. After your project has been created, change the name of the default workflow from `Workflow1` to `PatientWorkflow`. Now you're ready to modify the workflow to call the previously created web service.

The first web service call in this workflow should be to the `AdmitPatient` method. To call the web service, the workflow needs an instance of the InvokeWebService activity, so drag this activity from the Toolbox onto the workflow designer. The Add Web Reference dialog box appears, prompting you to enter the necessary information about the web service you want to call (see Figure 14-1).

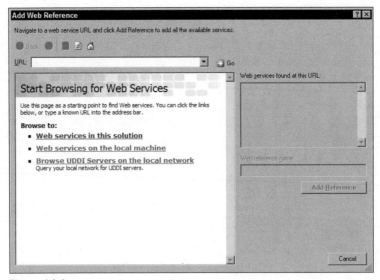

Figure 14-1

Because the web service you created uses the filesystem Web Site type, it is easier to select the Web services in this solution link (shown in Figure 14-1) rather than start the web service and then point to the URL. After clicking the link, you are presented with a list of web services found in the current solution. Select PatientService from this list. You are presented with a list of web methods exposed by the service (which should be AdmitPatient and GetPatientStatus), and you can give a new name to the web reference you are about to create. Enter **PatientWebReference** in the text box, and click the Add Reference button.

When you add a web reference to your workflow project, a web service proxy class is created. You can see this class by first clicking the Show All Files button in the Solution Explorer and then expanding the Web References folder under the workflow project. Next, expand PatientWebReference and then Reference.map. Under Reference.map is a file called Reference.cs. This is the proxy class that makes the call to the patient web service. You don't need to make any changes to this file — it already contains everything it needs to make the call to your web service.

Next, you need to configure the InvokeWebService activity that you placed in the workflow. The first thing you should do is give the activity instance a more meaningful name. Change the name property to callAdmitPatient. Notice that the activity has the red exclamation icon attached to it, indicating that it is not configured fully or correctly. However, the configuration is already partly there because you ran the web reference wizard, as validated by the ProxyClass and URL properties already being set on this screen. Currently, the only property with an error is the MethodName property, which should point to a method on the configured web service. Because this activity needs to call the AdmitPatient method, try selecting that option from the drop-down list of the property.

As you can see, setting the MethodName property made things worse. Now there are four properties with errors: (ReturnValue), name, patientId, and reasonForVisit. These are the parameters and the return value associated with the AdmitPatient method. To correct the configuration errors, you need to bind each property to a field in the workflow class. One option is to manually create fields and properties in the code-beside class and then select them in the Properties Explorer. Another option, and the one chosen for this example, is to let the binding dialog box create the appropriate members and bind to them automatically. To do this, click the ellipsis button on each property that has an error. This displays a binding dialog box where you add the property members. Figure 14-2 shows what this dialog box looks like after you click the ellipsis in the (ReturnValue) property, click the Bind to a new member tab, enter **patientRecord** in the text box, click the Create Field radio button, and then click the OK button. As you can see, a new field in the code-beside class is generated, called patientRecord. In addition, the (ReturnValue) property is automatically bound to the new field.

So far, the return value of the web service method has been accounted for. However, the values to be passed to the method have not yet been set. These can be created and bound the same way in which the return value was created and bound. For name, patientId, and reasonForVisit, create new fields that will be bound to. Your code-beside class should look like the following:

```
public sealed partial class PatientWorkflow : SequentialWorkflowActivity
{
    public PatientWorkflow()
    {
        InitializeComponent();
    }

    public PatientRecord patientRecord = new PatientRecord();
```

```
    public String name = default(System.String);
    public String patientId = default(System.String);
    public String reasonForVisit = default(System.String);
}
```

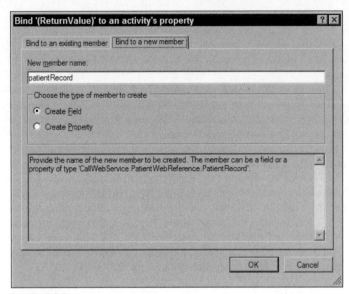

Figure 14-2

Even though the InvokeWebService activity is now correctly configured, the workflow doesn't do any-thing meaningful because all the parameters have a default value of an empty string. To remedy this, add a Code activity to the top of the workflow, and add the following code to its ExecuteCode event handler:

```
private void setValues_ExecuteCode(object sender, EventArgs e)
{
    this.name = "Joe Blow";
    this.patientId = "123";
    this.reasonForVisit = "Broken leg";
}
```

Now when the workflow is executed, the values set with the Code activity are passed to the web service. In addition, when the web service method returns, the patientRecord class field is set. Give it a try.

Now, to make the workflow a little more interesting, add another InvokeWebService activity below the first one, and name it callGetPatientStatus. However, this time when the Add Web Reference dialog box appears, simply cancel it before pointing to a web service. You don't need to add another web refer-ence because you can reuse the proxy generated previously. To do this, select the PatientService class from the ProxyClass property of the activity. Next, you need to configure the activity to point to the GetPatientStatus method and bind the patientId parameter and the return value. Bind the patientId parameter to the PatientId property of the patientRecord class field. Figure 14-3 shows the binding dialog box that is accessed from the patientId property in the properties window. Finally, for the (ReturnValue) property, bind to a new class field called patientStatus.

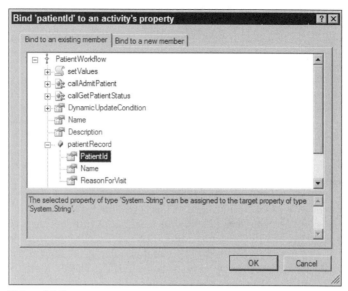

Figure 14-3

To round out this tutorial, add a new Code activity to the end of the workflow, and use the following code in the `ExecuteCode` event handler:

```
private void printStatus_ExecuteCode(object sender, EventArgs e)
{
    Console.WriteLine("The patient's status: " + patientStatus);
}
```

After running the workflow, you should see the message shown in Figure 14-4.

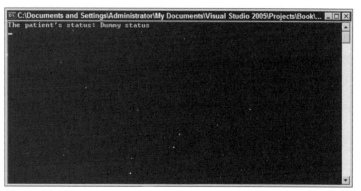

Figure 14-4

Exposing Workflows as Web Services

There are two methods you can use to expose a workflow as a web service. Out of the box, Visual Studio provides you with a wizard of sorts to automatically expose a workflow as a web service, as long as the workflow meets the prerequisites discussed in the following section. Alternatively, you can write custom code that allows your workflow to be called through a web service. The following sections discuss both options.

Using the Wizard

Before getting into the particulars of exposing a workflow as a web service, you need to create a workflow. To keep things focused on the topic at hand, the workflow should simply take a person's name and generate a message.

First, create a Sequential Workflow Library project, and rename the default workflow WebServiceWorkflow.cs. Next, add two fields to the workflow's code-beside class: a string called `name` and a string called `message`. Now add a single Code activity to the workflow and call it `createMessage`. In that activity's `ExecuteCode` event handler, generate a message based on the name field. After you've done all this, the code in the code-beside class should look like the following:

```
public sealed partial class WebServiceWorkflow: SequentialWorkflowActivity
{
    public string name = String.Empty;
    public string message = String.Empty;

    public WebServiceWorkflow()
    {
        InitializeComponent();
    }

    private void createMessage_ExecuteCode(object sender, EventArgs e)
    {
        this.message = "Hello " + this.name;
    }
}
```

Now try running the web service wizard from within Visual Studio. To do this, right-click the project in the Solution Explorer and select the Publish as Web Service option. The error message shown in Figure 14-5 is displayed.

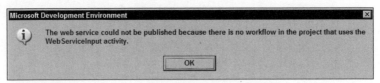

Figure 14-5

The message tells you that the workflow is not yet configured properly to expose it as a web service. You need to add a few activities to the workflow definition before the wizard is able to run. The first thing you need to do is add a WebServiceInput activity to the top of the workflow.

Right off the bat, you can see that the activity is not configured correctly by default. The first property noted as having an error is the IsActivating property. When creating workflows that will be called as external web services, you need to set this property to true. This indicates that the action of the web service being called will create a new instance of the workflow.

After you set IsActivating to true, the InterfaceType property shows that it has an error. As with other activities (such as the HandleExternalEvent and CallExternalMethod activities), the WebServiceInput activity needs an interface to define its public methods. Develop a new interface in the workflow project called IWebService, and make it look like the following code:

```
public interface IWebService
{
    string GetMessage(string name);
}
```

This interface says that the web service will have one method, called GetMessage, that will take a string as a parameter and also return a string. Now you can set the InterfaceType property of the WebServiceInput activity. After doing that, you need to select the GetMessage method for the MethodName property. To fully configure this activity, you also need to bind the name property to the name field of the code-beside class.

Now that you have defined the entry point to the web service, you need to define the exit point as well. This involves adding a WebServiceOutput activity after the initial Code activity. You need to do two things to fully configure this new activity. First, you need to point to the WebServiceInput activity using the InputActivityName property. Doing this links the input and output of the web service to form a cohesive web method. Then you need to bind the (ReturnValue) property to the message field of the code-beside class that will hold the message built by the Code activity.

Now the web service wizard is finally ready to be run without any errors. Right-click the workflow project, and select Publish as Web Service. This automatically creates a new web service project in the same solution as the workflow project. The project includes a new ASMX web service, a Web.config file, and an assembly that can be found in the bin folder. You are also presented with a message indicating that the process was successful.

Take a look at the Web.config file created in the new website project. The following is an excerpt of the markup in that file:

```
<?xml version="1.0"?>
<configuration>
    ...
    <system.web>
        ...
        <httpModules>
            <add
            type="System.Workflow.Runtime.Hosting.WorkflowWebHostingModule,
                System.Workflow.Runtime, Version=3.0.0.0, Culture=neutral,
                PublicKeyToken=31bf3856ad364e35"
            name="WorkflowHost"/>
        </httpModules>
    </system.web>
</configuration>
```

The preceding portion of the Web.config file adds an HTTP module to the ASP.NET runtime. This HTTP module, called WorkflowWebHostingModule, is a class built into the Windows Workflow Foundation API. This class is responsible for managing the session between the web service client and the web service itself. The module simply checks for a cookie from the client upon request. This cookie's value should be a workflow instance ID. If the cookie does not exist in the object representing the client's request, the request is considered a new call to the workflow. After the workflow instance is created, a cookie is added to the response object so that it can be returned to the client. Again, the response cookie contains the created workflow's instance ID. (Obviously, the calling client needs to be able to handle the cookies passed to and from the web service.)

Although the WorkflowWebHostingModule provides an out-of-the-box method for associating client calls to a specific workflow instance, you can develop your own HTTP module to replace this functionality. For example, if you would rather use the query string to associate calls, your module can implement that behavior instead. Take a look at the implementation of WorkflowWebHostingModule in Lutz's Reflector to get an idea of what your custom class needs to provide a full and valid implementation.

Although using the wizard to expose a workflow as a web service has some advantages, such as a quick and easy way to allow a workflow to be called by the outside world, there are some things to consider before going down this path. First, you need to understand what the wizard is doing behind the scenes.

When you run the wizard, the ASMX that is created is very simple. All the magic can be found in the assembly that was generated during the process. This assembly contains a few .NET interfaces and classes, including the web service interface that was defined in the workflow project as well as the workflow class itself.

In addition, the assembly contains a class called Settings that is used to access configuration data during the execution of the workflow. You don't need to worry too much about this class. The interesting code is found in a custom-created class, which follows a <WorkflowClassName>_WebService naming convention. In this example, the class name is WebServiceWorkflow_WebService.

You can inspect the contents of this class by opening the generated assembly in Lutz's Reflector. The custom class inherits from a class called WorkflowWebService, which is defined in System.Workflow .Activities. This class inherits from System.Web.Services.WebService and contains the base functionality common to all workflows exposed as web services. In addition, the derived class contains the code to call the methods on the web service. In this example, there is a method that looks like the following code, which is executed when the web service is called:

```
[WebMethod(Description="GetMessage", EnableSession=false)]
public virtual string GetMessage(string name)
{
    return (string) base.Invoke(typeof(IWebService),
        "GetMessage", true, new object[] { name })[0];
}
```

Because the wizard for exposing a workflow as web service creates this assembly with a compiled version of the workflow, the first limitation of this method is that you must be using a workflow defined with code — workflows defined with XAML will not work. Depending on how your application's workflows are being defined, this may be a deal breaker.

Another limitation of using the web service wizard relates to the `WorkflowWebHostingModule` discussed previously. The out-of-the-box implementation requires cookies to be used on the client to associate individual requests with a specific workflow instance. This can be a disadvantage if you do not have control over the calling client.

Finally, using the web service wizard provides a simple and easy way to expose your workflow to the outside world. However, the flexibility and options provided to you are limited. For example, if you need specific control over things such as the web services metadata or security, the wizard may not meet your exact needs.

Exposing the Workflow Yourself

If the wizard for exposing a workflow as a web service does not provide the exact functionality you are looking for, you can develop a custom ASP.NET web service and host the workflow runtime yourself. The goal of this section is to show you how to integrate Windows Workflow Foundation into a standard ASP.NET web service. The sample workflow shows a scenario that is identical to the workflow scenario used in the previous section covering the web service wizard. A user passes a string representing his or her name, and a personalized message is returned.

As discussed in Chapter 13, there are issues related specifically to ASP.NET that you must consider. Remember that the default workflows scheduler service does not play well with ASP.NET and IIS because it spawns threads freely. Web services are hosted in IIS the same way ASP.NET web forms are, so the same issues apply here. Therefore, you should use the `ManualWorkflowSchedulerService` in your web service-exposed workflows. The Web.config file shown in the following code adds the manual scheduler to the runtime so that this step does not have to take place in code:

```xml
<?xml version="1.0"?>
<configuration>
   <configSections>
      <section
       name="WorkflowRuntime"
       type="System.Workflow.Runtime.Configuration.WorkflowRuntimeSection,
            System.Workflow.Runtime, Version=3.0.00000.0, Culture=neutral,
            PublicKeyToken=31bf3856ad364e35"/>
   </configSections>
   <WorkflowRuntime>
      <Services>
         <add
          type="System.Workflow.Runtime.Hosting.ManualWorkflowSchedulerService,
               System.Workflow.Runtime, Version=3.0.00000.0, Culture=neutral,
               PublicKeyToken=31bf3856ad364e35"
         useActiveTimers="true"/>
      </Services>
   </WorkflowRuntime>
   <system.web>
      ...
   </system.web>
</configuration>
```

The next block of code handles the workflow runtime as well as the task of retrieving messages back from completed workflows:

```
public class Global : HttpApplication
{
    private Dictionary<Guid, string> completedMessages =
        new Dictionary<Guid, string>();

    public void Application_Start(object sender, EventArgs e)
    {
        // create "the" instance of the workflow runtime
        // for this ASP.NET application
        WorkflowRuntime workflowRuntime =
            new WorkflowRuntime("WorkflowRuntime");

        // wire the workflow completed event so we can access the output message
        workflowRuntime.WorkflowCompleted +=
            new EventHandler<WorkflowCompletedEventArgs>(
                workflowRuntime_WorkflowCompleted);

        workflowRuntime.StartRuntime();

        // add the runtime to the application's global state
        Application["WorkflowRuntime"] = workflowRuntime;

        // save the completed messages dictionary collection
        Application["CompletedMessages"] = completedMessages;
    }

    public void Application_End(object sender, EventArgs e)
    {
        WorkflowRuntime workflowRuntime =
            Application["WorkflowRuntime"] as WorkflowRuntime;

        workflowRuntime.StopRuntime();
        workflowRuntime.Dispose();
    }
    ...
}
```

The Global class in this code is the code-behind for the Global.asax file. This class is extremely important to the ASP.NET infrastructure because it handles events related to the ASP.NET application's instance, such as its starting and ending. Because an ASP.NET application needs only one instance of the workflow runtime, the Application_Start method is a perfect place to instantiate the runtime and place it in a globally accessible location.

The Application_Start method also takes care of wiring the WorkflowCompleted event so that messages generated in workflow instances can be accessed and also saved to a globally accessible location. (That method is covered in a moment.) Both the workflow runtime instance and the completedMessages Dictionary<Guid, string> instance are stored in the Application object.

The Application_End method is used to access the single runtime instance and stop it. This ensures that the workflow runtime's resources are cleaned up when the ASP.NET application has ended.

The following code shows the WorkflowCompleted event handler mentioned earlier. This method uses the completedMessages collection to store the message returned using each completed workflow's output parameters. Notice that the collection uses a `Guid` representing a workflow instance's ID as its key. Also remember that the `completedMessages` object was added to the application's global variables.

```
public class Global : HttpApplication
{
    ...
    private void workflowRuntime_WorkflowCompleted(object sender,
        WorkflowCompletedEventArgs e)
    {
        this.completedMessages.Add(e.WorkflowInstance.InstanceId,
            e.OutputParameters["Message"] as string);
    }
    ...
}
```

Finally, the following code shows the implantation of the ASP.NET web service itself. The `Service` class inherits from `System.Web.Services.WebService` and is decorated with the `WebService` attribute. This is the standard way to declare an ASP.NET web service.

```
[WebService(Namespace = "http://tempuri.org/")]
[WebServiceBinding(ConformsTo = WsiProfiles.BasicProfile1_1)]
public class Service : System.Web.Services.WebService
{
    private WorkflowRuntime WorkflowRuntime
    {
        get
        {
            return Application["WorkflowRuntime"] as WorkflowRuntime;
        }
    }

    private Dictionary<Guid, string> CompletedMessages
    {
        get
        {
            return Application["CompletedMessages"] as Dictionary<Guid, string>;
        }
    }

    public Service()
    {
    }

    [WebMethod]
    public string GetMessage(string name)
    {
        WorkflowRuntime runtime = this.WorkflowRuntime;

        // obtain a reference to the manual scheduler service
        // you will need this to start the workflow's execution
        ManualWorkflowSchedulerService scheduler =
            (ManualWorkflowSchedulerService)runtime.GetService(
                typeof(ManualWorkflowSchedulerService));

        // create the parameters to be passed to the workflow
```

```
        Dictionary<string, object> parms = new Dictionary<string, object>();
        parms.Add("Name", name);

        WorkflowInstance instance = runtime.CreateWorkflow(
            typeof(GetMessageWorkflow.GetMessageWorkflow), parms);

        instance.Start();

        // when using the manual workflow scheduler, you must manually
        // tell the workflow to run
        scheduler.RunWorkflow(instance.InstanceId);

        // the workflow is completed; obtain the message through the
        // dictionary object which was populated in the "Global" class
        string message = this.CompletedMessages[instance.InstanceId];

        // now that you have the message it can be discarded
        // from the dictionary
        this.CompletedMessages.Remove(instance.InstanceId);

        return message;
    }
}
```

To make it easier to access the global variables defined in the `Global` class, a couple of properties have been defined at the top of the `Service` class. This allows other methods in this class to access the workflow runtime and the messages returned from completed workflow instances.

This web service has only one web method: `GetMessage`. This method is decorated with the `WebMethod` attribute, which is the standard way to define a web service method in ASP.NET. It is in this method that a new workflow instance is created, executed, and completed. After completion, the returned message is accessed using the `CompletedMessage` property. Remember, this collection is populated in the `WorkflowCompleted` event-handler method of the `Global` class.

The `ManualWorkflowSchedulerService` instance has to be explicitly accessed using the runtime's `GetService` method so that it can be used to tell the workflow instance to run. This is a necessary step when using this service. Because the manual scheduler causes workflow instances to be run synchronously, you know the instance has completed when the `scheduler.RunWorkflow` returns. Therefore, the completed instance's message can be found in the dictionary collection.

Workflow and Windows Communication Foundation

Although you can accomplish a lot by pairing ASP.NET web services and Windows Workflow Foundation, a whole new world of connected systems is being opened up with the release of Windows Communication Foundation (WCF). The following sections cover WCF at a high level and explain how you can use this new technology to enhance the Windows Workflow Foundation functionality to interact with connected systems.

An Introduction to WCF

Simply put, Windows Communication Foundation is the next-generation platform from Microsoft for developing and running connected systems. This technology is also meant to encapsulate other distributed-systems technologies that Microsoft introduced in the past. Technologies such as Microsoft Message Queuing (MSMQ), .NET Remoting, and ASP.NET Web Services (ASMX) all work great with the WCF platform. WCF is meant to be the overriding piece of technology that brings all these legacy technologies together. Furthermore, WCF tries to abstract technology from the implementation of business logic. This means that decisions about which transport your application should use can be delayed until later in the development cycle. Previously, decisions about whether to use .NET Remoting or ASMX would have to be made up front.

A common way to explain the basics of WCF is to discuss the ABCs:

- ❑ Addresses
- ❑ Binding
- ❑ Contracts

Every WCF service has endpoints, which all have addresses, bindings, and contracts. An endpoint's address describes its public location, such as an HTTP URL. The binding describes an endpoint's transport technology, such as HTTP or TCP. A contract describes an endpoint's abilities. For example, an endpoint's contract might dictate that it is able to look up a customer's orders using a unique customer identifier.

As previously mentioned, a service's attributes can be configured after development so that an endpoint's binding can be changed from HTTP to MSMQ at the drop of a hat. The same goes for an endpoint's address. The contact, however, needs to be defined up front. This is rather obvious because you must know what a service is able to do before you build it.

WCF service contracts are defined in a manner quite similar to that of Windows Workflow Foundation data exchange contracts. Standard .NET interfaces, along with WCF-specific attributes, are used to identify a service's behavior. The following is a quick example of a contract for a service that handles a software system's user management capabilities:

```
using System.ServiceModel;

[ServiceContract]
public interface IUserManagement
{
    [OperationContract]
    int CreateUser(string username);

    [OperationContract]
    User GetUserInfo(int userID);

    [OperationContract]
    void DeleteUser(int userID);
}
```

A few things can be determined by studying this code. First, the vital classes relevant to WCF are found in the `System.ServiceModel` namespace. Second, an interface is designated as a service contact by being decorated with the `ServiceContract` attribute. Finally, every method that should be available publicly on the service should be decorated with the `OperationContract` attribute. Other methods that should not be available publicly on the service can be included in the interface — they would just not be decorated with the `OperationContract` attribute.

One of the nice things about WCF is that you can configure almost everything about a service and its respective endpoints. This means that you can change a service's address, binding, and contract by modifying a configuration file. Obviously, this is much more flexible than forcing this information into compiled code.

The following code is an example of an App.config or Web.config file that is hosting a service with a single endpoint:

```xml
<?xml version="1.0" encoding="utf-8" ?>
<configuration>
    <system.serviceModel>
        <services>
            <service
                name="YourNamespace.YourServiceClass"
                behaviorConfiguration="CustomBehaviorName">

                <endpoint
                    address="http://localhost:8080/myService"
                    binding="wsHttpBinding"
                    contract="YourNamespace.IYourServiceContractInterface" />

            </service>
        </services>

        <behaviors>
            <serviceBehaviors>
                <behavior name="CustomBehaviorName">
                    <serviceMetadata
                        httpGetUrl="http://localhost:8080/myService/metadata"
                        httpGetEnabled="true" />
                </behavior>
            </serviceBehaviors>
        </behaviors>
    </system.serviceModel>
</configuration>
```

There are a few things to look for when studying this markup. First, start by looking at the `endpoint` node. The ABCs are represented in here. The endpoint's *address* can be found at `http://localhost:8080/myservice`; its *binding* is using the out-of-the-box `wsHttpBinding` binding; and the *contract* points to an interface that presumably was written by the developer of the service.

`wsHttpBinding` is one of many preconfigured bindings that ship with WCF. These preconfigured bindings have settings that would commonly be needed by developers and are available for ease of use. For example, the `wsHttpBinding` dictates that the messages sent to and from the associated endpoint conform to such standards as WS-Security 1.1 and SOAP 1.2.

Next, notice that the endpoint node lives inside a `service` node that lives inside the `services` node. The `services` node is simply a container for one or more `service` nodes, which contain one or more `endpoint` nodes. The `service` node in this example points to a specific class that will act as the host of the service. It also has a `behaviorConfiguration` attribute that points to a `behavior` node a little lower in the configuration file.

The behavior node can define many fine-grained details related to a service, but in this example, it simply dictates that the service's metadata (or WSDL) will be available for consumption at `http://localhost:8080/myService/metadata`. The Web Service Definition Language (WSDL) informs interested parties (such as client applications) what the web service does and what kind of information it expects and returns.

Because WCF is such a flexible and feature-rich platform, there is a lot more to it than can be explained in this book. If you need to develop a connected system with workflow, you should research WCF. Sites such as `http://msdn.microsoft.com` have tons of resources related to API references as well as technical articles.

Using WCF to Expose a Workflow as a Windows Service

This book has already shown you several ways to host the workflow runtime. Chapter 13 discusses some of the pitfalls associated with hosting in a web environment. Hosting the runtime in a volatile application such a Windows Forms application might have its dangers as well because it is not always guaranteed to be running. An alternative that enables you to have full control over threading considerations and when the application is available is hosting the workflow runtime in a Windows service, sometimes called an *NT service.*

When hosting the workflow runtime in a Windows service, you have to expose the functionality to the outside world. In the past, this was accomplished with technologies such as .NET Remoting. However, with the great functionality and flexibility provided by WCF, a new option is available.

In the following example, a workflow is responsible for adding potential new employees to the system and then converting the potential hires to full-time employees based on an approval status. The software should be able to process information about a candidate and send out a request for approval. Then a hiring manager enters his or her approval status, which dumps the candidate from the system if unapproved or converts him or her to a hired employee if approved.

Remember, this system will be exposed through a Windows service under the guise of a web service. However, to the calling software, this employee service will look no different from a standard XML web service. This is the functionality provided by WCF. Behind the scenes, however, the hosting of the workflow runtime is much different from hosting in a standard ASMX web service.

Before getting to the particulars of the Windows Service and WCF implementation, take a look at some of the workflow-specific code. Figure 14-6 shows the workflow implementation. It consists of a CallExternalMethod activity that sends out a request for employee approval and then a Listen activity that waits for an approval or rejection event to be raised from the host.

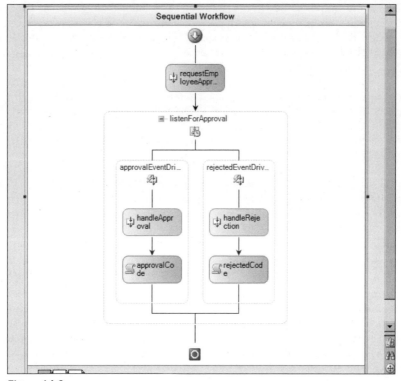

Figure 14-6

The following code shows a standard workflow communication contract decorated with the `ExternalDataExchangeAttribute`. It includes a method that allows the workflow's host to send an external request for the employee service as well as two events that represent either an approval or a rejection coming in from the outside world.

```
[ExternalDataExchange]
public interface IEmployeeService
{
    void RequestApproval();

    event EventHandler<ExternalDataEventArgs> Approved;
    event EventHandler<ExternalDataEventArgs> Rejected;
}
```

The following code is the implementation of the preceding communication contract:

```
public class EmployeeService : IEmployeeService
{
    public event EventHandler<ExternalDataEventArgs> Approved;
    public event EventHandler<ExternalDataEventArgs> Rejected;

    public void RequestApproval()
    {
        // do something to request approval...
```

```
        // perhaps send an email to someone
    }

    public void ApproveEmployee(Guid instanceId)
    {
        if (this.Approved != null)
        {
            this.Approved(null, new ExternalDataEventArgs(instanceId));
        }
    }

    public void RejectEmployee(Guid instanceId)
    {
        if (this.Rejected != null)
        {
            this.Rejected(null, new ExternalDataEventArgs(instanceId));
        }
    }
}
```

Two public methods, `ApproveEmployee` and `RejectEmployee`, are added to raise the `Approved` and `Rejected` events, respectively, when called. Also, the `RequestApproval` method is implemented in order to perform whatever actions are necessary to request an approval for the employee.

Now that the workflow code has been covered, it's time to move on to the WCF and Windows service code. The following block of code shows a communication contract, but this one is for WCF. Like Windows Workflow Foundation, WCF uses .NET interfaces to define the public communication interfaces between services and the outside world. Also like Windows Workflow Foundation, .NET attributes are used to designate the interfaces as important to WCF.

```
[ServiceContract(Namespace = "http://Kitta.Workflow")]
public interface IServiceContract
{
    [OperationContract]
    void CreateEmployee(string name);

    [OperationContract]
    void ApproveEmployee(Guid instanceId);

    [OperationContract]
    void RejectEmployee(Guid instanceId);
}
```

This `IServiceContract` interface is decorated with the `ServiceContract` attribute, which can be found in the `System.ServiceModel`. If you have the .NET Framework 3.0 installed, the WCF classes are available to you just as the Windows Workflow Foundation classes are.

The `ServiceContract` attribute tells the WCF runtime that the designated interface is meant to be just that — a service contract. This attribute also allows you to define a unique namespace for the WCF service. The methods are in turn decorated with an attribute called `OperationContract`. This attribute lets the WCF runtime know that the methods should be exposed as public methods on the service.

The next piece of code is the implementation of the Windows service itself, `WorkflowHostService`:

```
public partial class WorkflowHostService
    : ServiceBase, IServiceContract
{
    private WorkflowRuntime workflowRuntime;
    private EmployeeService employeeService;
    private ServiceHost serviceHost;

    public WorkflowHostService()
    {
        InitializeComponent();

        this.workflowRuntime = new WorkflowRuntime();

        ExternalDataExchangeService dataExchangeService =
            new ExternalDataExchangeService();
        this.workflowRuntime.AddService(dataExchangeService);

        this.employeeService = new EmployeeService();
        dataExchangeService.AddService(this.employeeService);
    }

    protected override void OnStart(string[] args)
    {
        workflowRuntime.StartRuntime();

        Uri baseAddress =
            new Uri("http://localhost:8080/createEmployeeService");

        serviceHost =
            new ServiceHost(typeof(WorkflowHostService), baseAddress);

        // open the host
        // this is what starts the Windows Service listening for requests
        serviceHost.Open();
    }

    protected override void OnStop()
    {
        workflowRuntime.StopRuntime();
        serviceHost.Close();
    }

    public void CreateEmployee(string name)
    {
        Dictionary<string, object> parms = new Dictionary<string, object>();
        parms.Add("EmployeeName", name);

        WorkflowInstance instance =
            this.workflowRuntime.CreateWorkflow(typeof(EmployeeService), parms);

        instance.Start();
    }

    public void ApproveEmployee(Guid instanceId)
```

```
        {
            this.employeeService.ApproveEmployee(instanceId);
        }

        public void RejectEmployee(Guid instanceId)
        {
            this.employeeService.RejectEmployee(instanceId);
        }
    }
```

To be a Windows service, a class must inherit from the `ServiceBase` class, which is found in the `System.ServiceProcess` namespace. Also, notice that the `WorkflowHostService` class implements the `IServiceContact` interface, which was defined earlier. Therefore, the code that is called by external consumers of the WCF service are implemented in this class.

There are a few points of interest in this class. First, take a look at the constructor. Here, usual code can be found to ready the workflow runtime as well as the `ExternalDataExchangeService`. The custom `EmployeeService` class is also added to the data exchange service.

The `OnStart` method is overridden from the `ServiceBase` class and is called when the Windows service is started. It is here that the workflow runtime is started and the WCF service is configured and started. The code found in this method is all that is needed to run in order to start allowing incoming calls on the service. The `OnStop` method conversely stops the workflow runtime and the WCF service.

The remainder of the methods — `CreateEmployee`, `ApproveEmployee`, and `RejectEmployee` — are all implemented per the service contract interface. The `ApproveEmployee` and `RejectEmployee` methods simply call methods of the same name on the `EmployeeService`, which is the data exchange service between the host and the workflow.

The `CreateEmployee` method off a new workflow instance based on the information passed in from the external service caller. The code in this method should look pretty familiar to you by now.

Although the code looks pretty straightforward, there is a lot going on behind the scenes to allow all this goodness to happen. The WCF code in the `OnStart` method would not work without the settings in the App.config file. Take a look at its contents in the following code:

```
<?xml version="1.0" encoding="utf-8" ?>
<configuration>

  <system.serviceModel>
    <services>
      <service name="Kitta.WorkflowService.WorkflowHostService"
               behaviorConfiguration="EmployeeServiceBehavior">
        <endpoint address="http://localhost:8080/createEmployeeService"
                  binding="wsHttpBinding"
                  contract="Kitta.WorkflowService.IServiceContract" />
      </service>
    </services>

    <behaviors>
      <serviceBehaviors>
```

```
            <behavior name="EmployeeServiceBehavior">
              <serviceMetadata
                  httpGetUrl="http://localhost:8080/workflow/metadata"
                  httpGetEnabled="true" />
            </behavior>
          </serviceBehaviors>
        </behaviors>
      </system.serviceModel>
    </configuration>
```

Almost everything contained in the App.config file is specific to WCF. The `system.serviceModel` node encompasses all the WCF-specific settings. The `services` node contains a definition for the service used in this example and points to the service class `Kitta.WorkflowService.WorkflowHostService`. Within the service node is an `endpoint` node. Remember, endpoints are the public interface that the outside world uses to access a WCF service. In this example, the `endpoint` node specifies that the service should have an HTTP interface, making it a standard web service. In addition, the endpoint's interface is defined with the `IServiceContract` interface, which was covered earlier.

The other interesting piece of the configuration file is in the `behaviors` node. It is here that the behavior for the employee WCF service is defined. In this example, the behavior encompasses allowing web service metadata, or WSDL, to be exposed through the defined URL. By exposing WSDL publicly, utilities such as the Add Web Reference wizard in Visual Studio and the wsdl.exe command-line utility are able to generate proxy classes to abstract the calling of a web service using a .NET class.

Summary

This chapter covered the world of connected systems related to Windows Workflow Foundation. In this chapter, *connected systems* refers to communications across application boundaries. This concept is also commonly associated with another popular acronym: SOA. SOA describes an architecture that provides pluggable, loosely coupled services that perform a single job. There are four tenets that commonly describe SOA: Service boundaries are explicit; services are autonomous; services share a schema and contract; and service compatibility is based upon policy. Although it is not a requirement, SOA is commonly implemented using web services.

Windows Workflow Foundation supports the concept of connected systems in a few ways. First, there are several activities that support communications with web services. The InvokeWebService activity supports calling a web service that is external to a workflow and consuming that service's return values. The WebServiceInput and WebServiceOutput activities support exposing workflows as externally callable web services using the wizard included in Visual Studio.

Finally, this chapter covered WCF, the next-generation connected-systems platform from Microsoft. This platform will enable you to develop, configure, and deploy services. It holds under its umbrella the technologies of yesteryear for easier manageability, including .NET Remoting, ASMX, and other legacy transports. The chapter also introduced the concept of exposing a workflow through a WCF service that is hosted in a Windows service. This method of exposing a workflow to the outside world requires a bit more work than using the wizard for exposing a workflow as a web service, but it offers a great deal of scalability and flexibility in return.

Windows Workflow Foundation and the Microsoft Office System

This chapter introduces the Microsoft Office system and shows how workflow plays into its technologies. With the advent of Microsoft Office 2007, workflow is a large part of the new feature set. Up to this point, this book has covered workflow development in the context of developing solutions from scratch. Although custom solutions definitely have their place in the world, extending and using existing technologies such as the Microsoft Office system, where it makes sense, can provide a great deal of time and cost savings.

This chapter covers the following topics:

- ❑ The components of Microsoft Office
- ❑ Collaboration with Microsoft SharePoint
- ❑ How workflow fits into Office and SharePoint
- ❑ Office and SharePoint development scenarios

The Microsoft Office System

Along with Windows, Office has defined Microsoft for many years. Originally, the components of Office were available for purchase separately; then someone had the bright idea to package these applications together as a productivity suite. This launched one of the most successful software mainstays in the history of computing.

Over the years, Microsoft has continued to improve upon the software by offering feature upgrades and occasionally new components. Because Office has generally met people's needs fairly well, the argument to upgrade to the next version needed to be compelling. Adding a few more fancy features in Word doesn't make it worth the sevcral-hundred-dollars-per-user investment.

The Office 2007 system offers lots of new functionality. The most obvious changes from an end-user perspective are the differences in the user interface. Most of the Office 2007 applications use a replacement for standard menus called the *ribbon*. The ribbon is meant to easily expose common tasks in a context-sensitive manner. For example, if a user is working with tables, the ribbon tries to figure this out and presents the user with a common set of tasks for editing tables.

The Usual Suspects

Before digging into workflow and Office too deeply, it wouldn't hurt to refamiliarize yourself with the standard pieces of the Office system that have made the software so famous over the years. What says "Office" better than Microsoft Word? Figure 15-1 is a screen shot of Word 2007 that showcases a couple of the new features, such as the ribbon and the mini-toolbar for formatting changes inline with text.

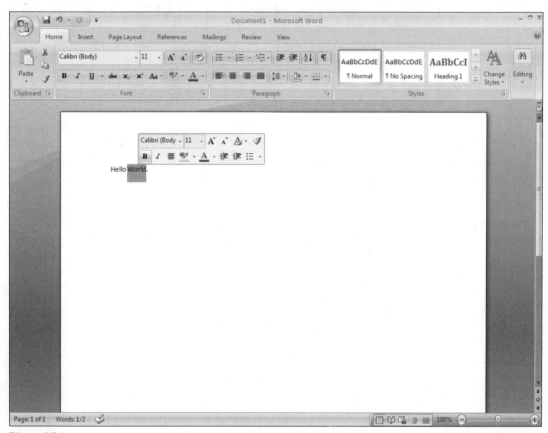

Figure 15-1

Of course, Microsoft Excel is also back with some new features. Along with the new ribbon interface, Excel sports some great new data visualization features. For example, Figure 15-2 showcases a conditional formatting option called *data bars* that displays a cell's numeric value by shading a portion of the cell with a chosen color. Other new features include enhanced connectivity to data sources such as SQL Server databases and SQL Server Analysis Services cubes for live analysis. The charting capabilities in Excel have also been greatly enhanced to allow more professional-looking graphics.

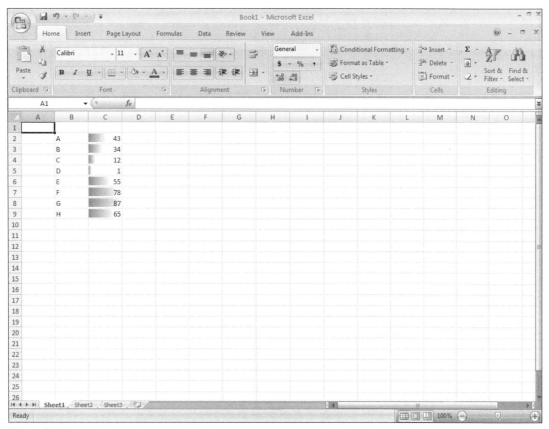

Figure 15-2

The rest of the standard applications — such as Outlook, PowerPoint, Publisher, and Access — are still around in Office 2007, of course. Furthermore, the relatively new, but still updated for 2007, applications such as OneNote and InfoPath can be included in the suite.

New Kids on the Block

Several new applications are included in the Office suite, most of which are on the server. Forms Server greatly expands the possibilities for the InfoPath platform. Although InfoPath is a great tool for creating reusable forms that connect to various back-end systems, it was limited in that users were forced to have the InfoPath client installed on their machines. Forms Server has now gotten rid of this requirement by providing a server-side rendering engine for forms that were authored in the InfoPath client. This allows forms to be viewed and filled out in a standard web browser. Although the number of users that can utilize forms grows with the server-based architecture, it comes with the price of decreased functionality. The browser can be pushed only so far compared with a custom-built client application. (InfoPath and Forms Server are discussed in more detail later in this chapter.)

Excel Services is another server-based product that is related to a client application: Excel, of course. By calculating and rendering spreadsheets on the server, Excel Services provides a few benefits. First, spreadsheets are viewable by users who do not have Excel installed on their workstations. Additionally, when spreadsheets that are important to business processes are stored on the server instead of on multiple users' desktops, there is one version of the truth that can be accessed and modified by different people. Another advantage of the server-based engine is that complex Excel spreadsheets, which may take long to calculate on a workstation, can be offloaded to a more powerful back-end machine.

There are a few other new components in the Office 2007 lineup, including Microsoft Office Groove, which is a virtual-office tool that allows real-time collaboration of distributed teams working on a common project, as well as Microsoft Office SharePoint designer, which is discussed later in this chapter as it relates to workflow development on the Office platform.

SharePoint

SharePoint, Microsoft's answer to the enterprise portal, has quickly grown up since its introduction in 2001. The main selling point for a server-based portal product such as SharePoint is increased collaboration throughout departments and the enterprise. Collaboration is enabled through the use of document libraries, online calendars, announcements, alerts, and many more features. In addition, SharePoint has an extensible programming infrastructure that uses a concept called web parts. *Web parts* are reusable widgets that can be placed in any SharePoint page and configured however the developer specifies.

Pretty much everything in SharePoint is a list. A *list* is what you think it would be: a collection of items. Documents are the items that live in a document library; events live in a calendar; issues live in an issue tracker list; and so on. This architecture makes for a very extensible platform that can handle new types of user-created items.

In Office 2003, SharePoint and Office were integrated to the point that users could open documents directly from SharePoint, and the client applications were aware of the server-based locations of the documents. This allowed users to check in and check out documents from document libraries from within Word, Excel, and other Office applications. Office 2007 enhances this integration, especially as it relates to workflows. The Microsoft Office applications are aware of workflows running against a given document and allow the user to interact with the workflow through context-specific buttons and forms. This functionality is discussed later in this chapter.

There are many new features in SharePoint 2007 compared with SharePoint 2003. A short list includes the following items:

- ❑ ASP.NET 2.0 web part infrastructure
- ❑ Blogs
- ❑ Wikis
- ❑ Recycle Bin
- ❑ Spell check
- ❑ Lists exposed as Really Simple Syndication (RSS)
- ❑ Item-level security
- ❑ Business Data Catalog
- ❑ Enhanced mobile device support
- ❑ PowerPoint slide libraries
- ❑ Forms authentication

SharePoint Flavors

There are two distinctly different versions of SharePoint in the 2007 release: Windows SharePoint Services and Microsoft Office SharePoint Server.

Windows SharePoint Services

Windows SharePoint Services (WSS) version 3 is an updated version of the web-based portal software from 2003. One of the best features of WSS, aside from all the great collaboration tools, is the fact that it is completely free — at least free with the purchase of a Windows Server operating system license. WSS is included with Windows Server as an option, just like IIS or other optional components.

Microsoft Office SharePoint Server

Microsoft Office SharePoint Server (MOSS) is comparable to the nonfree SharePoint Portal Server (SPS) from 2003. It includes many enterprise-level features that are not included in its free counterpart, such as the use of Forms Server.

The SharePoint Web Services

Like SharePoint in 2003, SharePoint in 2007 exposes an API through a set of web services. The API allows interaction with the workflow functionality built into SharePoint. Actions such as obtaining information about running workflows, starting new workflow instances, and completing workflow-related tasks can be performed using the web services.

Workflow and the Office System

One of the greatest new and sought-after features of the Office 2007 system is the addition of workflow. Organizations have long searched for a cohesive answer to the problem of workflow in Office and SharePoint, and with the help of Windows Workflow Foundation, Microsoft has provided a solution. The rest of this chapter is devoted to covering the ways workflow has been baked into this platform.

SharePoint as a Host

Throughout this book, the fact that the workflow runtime needs a host in which to run has been beaten into your head. In Office 2007, SharePoint plays host to the runtime and takes care of all the plumbing you need to architect custom solutions. It handles persistence so that workflow instances are efficiently dehydrated and hydrated at the appropriate times. Because SharePoint needs to be an extremely scalable platform, the workflow persistence service in SharePoint is meticulous about conserving server resources and taking idle workflows out of memory.

Because SharePoint takes care of everything related to hosting Windows Workflow Foundation in SharePoint, there is some abstraction from the workflow runtime. This includes the fact that as a developer, you are not able to specify that workflow runtime services be added to the workflow runtime. This is partly for security reasons and partly because of the scalability issues already mentioned.

Office Applications as a Front End

If SharePoint is the workflow runtime host, the Office applications—such as Word, Excel, and PowerPoint—are the clients. As previously mentioned, these tools are SharePoint and workflowaware. Therefore, the functionality necessary for interacting in workflows is baked into these applications. For example, Word includes the ability to start, modify, and complete workflows without ever leaving the application.

This functionality is enabled by several technologies. First, Forms Server and InfoPath are used to expose workflow task interfaces from within the Office applications. This means that custom-developed forms for interacting with workflows (a topic discussed later in this chapter) are usable inside Word and the other Office applications. In addition, the SharePoint web services can talk to SharePoint to discover the status of a currently running workflow and then expose the appropriate user interface to the user.

Out-of-the-Box Workflows

The following prebuilt workflows are provided with SharePoint out of the box:

- ❑ Approval
- ❑ Collect Feedback
- ❑ Collect Signatures
- ❑ Disposition Approval
- ❑ Translation Management
- ❑ Three-state

Before using these workflows, you must ensure that they are active within SharePoint. To find out if a workflow is active, you can check the Workflows screen by navigating to Site Actions ⇨ Site Settings ⇨ Modify All Site Settings and then clicking the Workflows link under Galleries. You are presented with a screen like the one shown in Figure 15-3.

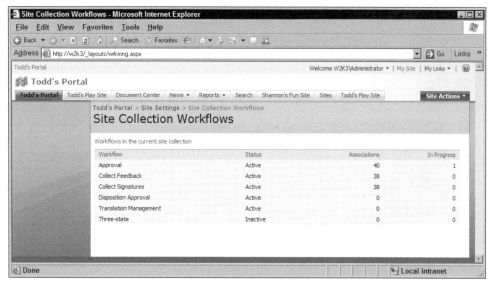

Figure 15-3

Note that the Three-state workflow is marked as Inactive on this screen. To activate a workflow in SharePoint, navigate to the Site Collection Features page from the Site Settings page. From here, you can activate any of the inactive workflows listed. For example, to activate the Three-state workflow (discussed in more detail later), click the Activate button next to the workflow's description in the list. Then if you refresh the page shown in Figure 15-3, the Status column is updated to show the workflow as active.

Approval

The out-of-the-box Approval workflow covers one of the most common workflow scenarios known to man: document approval. This is a natural fit for SharePoint because of its documentcentric nature. By default, the Approval workflow is associated with the Document content type; therefore, additional configuration to associate this workflow with a particular document library is not necessary. However, if you want this workflow to automatically start whenever a document is added or updated, you need to perform further configuration.

This workflow has some basic steps and custom forms. When an Approval workflow is started on a document, a task is created for each designated approver to either approve or reject the document. In addition, the approver can request changes to the document or reassign the task to another person. Figure 15-4 shows what the Approval workflow form looks like. There are buttons and links to perform the desired tasks. In addition, there is a link back to the document on which the workflow is being performed (in this example, it's a document called Project Proposal).

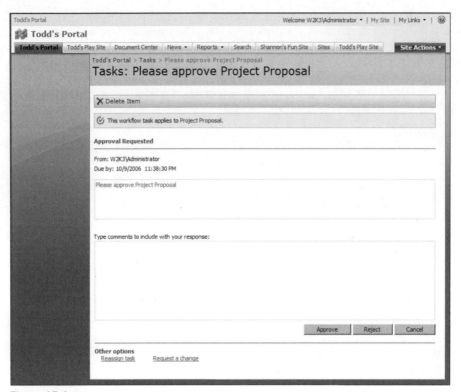

Figure 15-4

When you're configuring this workflow on a specific document library or a new content type, there are a few options that you can set specifically for this workflow. For example, you can have tasks assigned to users serially or in parallel (if there is more than one approver); custom messages can be provided to workflow actors; and you can specify when the workflow should be canceled, among other things. These workflow-specific options are shown on the second page of the wizard that associates the workflow to a document library or content type — the Customize Workflow page.

Collect Feedback

The Collect Feedback workflow supports any process that involves obtaining comments from one or more people related to a document. Like the Approval workflow, the Collect Feedback workflow is associated with the Document content type by default. Therefore, you can manually start it on any document, and it does not need to be associated with a particular document library to be available. However, you can set additional options on the workflow when associating with a new content type or document library.

The additional configurable options of this workflow type are similar to the options on the Approval workflow. When you configure the workflow association, you can control the task assignment order (serial or parallel), whether actors can reassign tasks, default task values, and similar options.

While the workflow is running, the owner can view the feedback that has been provided up until that point in time. This information is available on the Workflow Status screen, which shows the tasks that have been created for a specific workflow instance as well as the associated workflow instance history list. In addition to the text that workflow actors enter in the feedback comments text area of the workflow's form, the commenting system in Word can be used to enhance the value of comments. Figure 15-5 shows the Workflow Status page for a completed Collect Feedback workflow instance. This particular instance involved one actor.

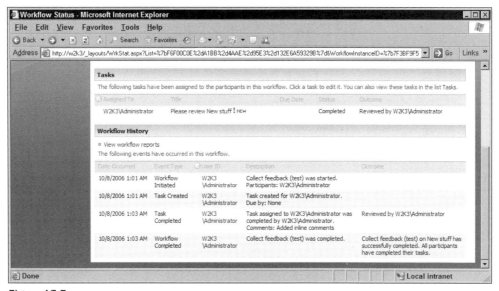

Figure 15-5

Collect Signatures

The Collect Signatures workflow is specific to a feature in Microsoft Office related to digitally signing documents. To use this workflow, a user must first add one or more signature lines to a Word or Excel document from within the application (see Figure 15-6). After the document has been saved to a SharePoint document library, the Collect Signatures workflow can be kicked off from within the client application only.

When the Collect Signatures workflow is initiated from within Word or Excel, the user is prompted to provide an actor for each signature required in the document. Therefore, if three signatures were added to the document, the user is asked to provide three corresponding people who need to digitally sign each line. From here, the behavior is similar to other workflows: Tasks are created ,and e-mails are sent (if the server is configured to send e-mail). After all signatures are collected, the workflow is considered complete.

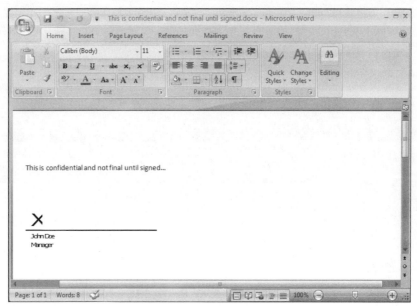

Figure 15-6

Disposition Approval

The out-of-the-box Disposition Approval workflow provides functionality to allow organizations to easily manage expired content. For example, a document library can have a policy that dictates that after a certain amount of time, a document should be expired. This policy can do one of two things when the expiration occurs: delete the document or start a workflow.

The Disposition Approval workflow is a perfect candidate for document expiration policies. Although it can be started manually just like other workflows, it makes perfect sense to start this workflow when a document expires if someone wants to extend the document's lifetime. If the Disposition Approval workflow is started after a document expires, a task is created that allows further action to be taken. Figure 15-7 shows the task form for this workflow.

To associate this workflow with a document library's policy, you must first configure the workflow for the document library. You do this the same way as any other workflow. Next, navigate to the document library's settings and click the Information management policy settings link under the Permissions and Management heading.

On the following page, select Define a Policy and click the OK button. The policy options that include expiration-related items are displayed. If the Enable Expiration box is checked, a few more options appear, such as when document should expire and what should happen when it does. This is where you need to associate the Disposition Approval workflow with the policy to ensure that tasks are created to manage document disposition.

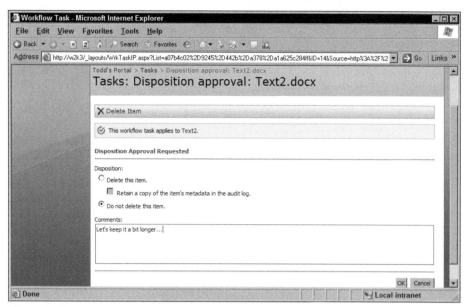

Figure 15-7

Another feature of the Disposition Approval workflow is that it allows bulk editing of the associated workflow tasks. This feature is useful if you have multiple documents in a particular library that expire on a regular basis, which could require an overwhelming number of tasks to complete. Opening up each task individually and setting its corresponding options would be extremely time consuming or even impossible in some situations.

To edit tasks in bulk, navigate to the Task library and select the Process all tasks option from the Actions menu. On the subsequent page, select desired the task type and click OK.. The editing form that is displayed to the user is exactly like the form used for editing a single task. However, when this form is submitted, the information provided in the form is applied to all the tasks you selected on the first screen. This feature can save a great deal of time for end users.

Translation Management

This workflow type facilitates the process of manually translating a document from one language to any number of other languages. It is unique in that it can be associated only with a translation management library. Therefore, to use the Translation Management workflow, you first need to create a translation management library.

To do this, navigate to the main page of the portal and click the View All Site Content link on the Quick Launch bar. Then click the Create button at the top of the subsequent page. This displays a page that allows you to create various SharePoint items, including document libraries and other list types. Translation Management Library is listed under the Libraries heading. Click the link to create a new library for use with the Translation Management workflow. When you're creating a new translation management library, you can automatically create and associate a Translation Management workflow with the new library.

After a translation management library is created and a Translation Management workflow is associated with it, any new documents added to the library are duplicated for each language to be translated to as dictated by the translators list associated with the workflow. You are given an opportunity to create a new list of translators and associated languages when you're configuring the workflow's settings. This list is used when a new document is added to the document library and its language is set. Translators are assigned to source and destination languages.

Three-state

The Three-state workflow is included as a generic state-machine workflow that has three states. Most likely, this workflow type will be associated with an Issue Tracker list because a simple issue tracking process would commonly have three states. For example, if an issue representing a software bug is created, it generally starts out in a state called something like New or Active. After a developer sees and fixes the documented issue, he or she generally changes the issue's status to Fixed or Resolved. The issue's originator then tests the software to make sure the bug was truly taken care of. If everything looks good, the issue transitions to a closed state.

However, the Three-state workflow is not specific to any item or document type. You can configure it to be used for any scenario that requires an item to transition between a beginning, middle, and end state. You can use the choice fields in the document library to customize the workflow's states. When configuring a Three-state workflow, you must specify a choice field to populate the Initial, Middle, and Final states.

For example, in the issue-tracking scenario, you would choose the list's Issue Status field as the workflow's choice field. Then you could set the Initial state to Active, the Middle state to Resolved, and the Final state to Closed. This tells the workflow to change states and create the necessary tasks when these statuses are set during the lifetime of the issue. Applying this workflow to an issue-tracking list in SharePoint adds functionality to an already-useful list in the previous version.

Workflow Features in SharePoint

The following sections cover some of the SharePoint-specific features related to workflows, including tasks, history, reporting, and administration.

Tasks

One of the most important traits of a workflow-enabled system is that it should be able to interact effectively with humans. Generally, workflows communicate most naturally with humans through the use of tasks because tasks provide an artifact that is actionable. Although the concept of tasks in Office and SharePoint is nothing new, workflow-specific tasks were not available in previous versions.

A workflow that has been assigned to a list or content type specifies where tasks for that workflow should be created. For example, an administrator may want all tasks that are created for a feedback collection workflow for a specific document library to appear in one task list and the tasks for all other workflows on the site to appear in another library.

Workflow tasks are unique because they are always associated with specific workflow instances. As a result, they can also be linked back to the originating item, whether it is a Word document or a completed InfoPath form. Workflow tasks can also have distinctly unique interfaces that collect custom data specific to a workflow type. For example, the out-of-the-box Approval workflow needs to collect data specific to that workflow, such as who needs to be involved in the approval process, as well as a description of the approver's notes.

History

History is a very powerful feature of workflows in the SharePoint environment. Basically, there is an architecture that allows workflows to log useful information at certain points during execution. This can be extremely helpful for debugging and troubleshooting scenarios, but the information logged through the history facilities is also useful from a business perspective. For example, the Approval workflow keeps a record of when tasks were created and completed along with text entered by the user so that this history can be later inspected from a "what happened" perspective.

Just like workflow tasks, history items are recorded in a list specified by an administrator. The list in which workflow history items are added does not to be manually separated from other history items. This is because the history items are viewed from the Workflow Status screen, which filters the items according to the instance in question. Figure 15-8 shows a sample Workflow Status screen. The workflow history items are listed at the bottom the screen. There are several other things going on here, including the display of workflow tasks, reporting functions, and administrative functions (discussed next).

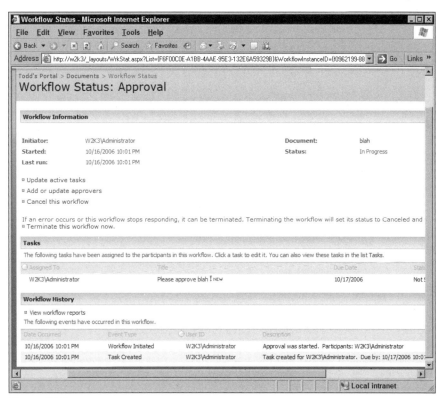

Figure 15-8

Reporting

In SharePoint, reports are generated for each workflow definition associated with a list or content type. The reports are Excel based and provide useful metrics, such as how long it takes an average workflow to complete and any errors that occurred during execution. You access the report page from the Workflow Status screen previously shown in Figure 15-8.

The Activity Duration Report has two tabs. The first tab shows a simple pivot table detailing the duration of each step in all workflow instances as well as a grand total. You can select individual workflows instead of rolling up all instances. The second tab holds the same information that is available in the workflow history list. Having this information in an Excel format makes it easier to read, sort, and filter the data. Figure 15-9 shows an example of this report.

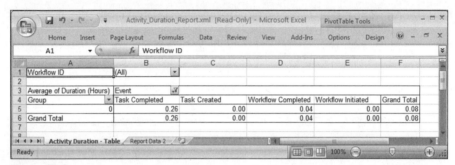

Figure 15-9

The Cancellation & Error Report also has two tabs and is similar to the Activity Duration Report. The first tab contains a pivot table that enables you to view information about how many workflows were cancelled, aborted, and so on. The second tab contains tabular data related to specific errors that occurred during a workflow's execution. This data is extremely useful in troubleshooting scenarios.

Administration

SharePoint provides administrative features that are related to workflows. For example, you can cancel and terminate running workflows from the workflow status screen shown in Figure 15-8. In addition, this screen enables you to modify and delete workflow tasks. Workflow-specific actions are also incited from this screen — for example, the Approval workflow allows you to add or update approvers.

Workflow Associations

Workflow instances in SharePoint are always associated with a specific item. Items can be documents, events, pictures, links, discussions, and so on. Before you can associate a workflow instance with an item, you need to associate the workflow definition with either a list or content type. Content types are the different types of items in SharePoint. After a workflow definition is associated with a library, list, or content type, it is eligible to be run against that entity. For content types, this includes instances of the specific type; for lists, it is any item in that list.

Associating a workflow to a content type is useful when a specific type of item in SharePoint needs to be involved in a process when created or changed as well as when a workflow is manually started on an item regardless of its location. To associate a workflow to a content type, navigate to the Site Settings page and click the Site content types option under the Galleries heading. The resulting page presents all content types for the current site along with some identifying information.

As an example, the creation or modification of Announcements anywhere across the site must be managed by an Approval workflow. This can be easily configured by clicking the Announcement content type link on the Site Content Type Gallery page. Each content type settings page has a link called Workflow Settings, which is where workflow associations are made. From this page, click the Add a Workflow link.

An association of a workflow to a list or content type defines a few important values. First, and most obvious, the type of workflow that should be available to the list or content type is defined. Any deployed and activated workflow type can be used, including out-of-the-box or custom-developed workflows. Figure 15-10 shows an example of a workflow association page that is tying an Approval workflow to the Announcement content type. The main association page for libraries and lists is virtually identical to the one shown in Figure 15-10 except that the Update List and Site Content Types setting does not exist for lists.

This page is standard to all workflow types being associated with a list or type with the exception of the last setting related to content types. (This setting is discussed in a moment.) The first setting at the top enables you to choose the workflow to associate. The second text box, Name, allows you to give the workflow a definitive name according to its purpose. In this case, Announcement Approvals is appropriate.

Because tasks are so important to human workflows in SharePoint, the Task List setting tells the workflow in which SharePoint task list to create new tasks. You can create many different task lists for different workflows or even different workflows associated to individual lists or content types. However, this isn't always necessary or even recommended. As a rule of thumb, unless you have a special need for individual task lists across your site, you should use the same generic task list. You may want to create individual lists if there are special security requirements for a unique set of tasks.

The History List setting points the workflow association to the list in SharePoint in which to create history items. This list is similar to the Task List in that it probably does not need to be a unique workflow association. These lists are simply buckets to hold workflow-related items and can easily hold items from many different workflows.

The Start Options are very important for workflow associations. They define when workflow instances will be started based on several different events. For the Announcement Approvals workflow shown in Figure 15-10, an Approval workflow will be created every time an announcement is created or modified. If desired, you can allow a workflow to be started manually by a user. In addition, the settings can require a user to have the Manage Lists permission before being able to manually start a workflow on an item.

The Update List and Site Content Types setting dictates whether all content types that currently inherit from the selected content type should be updated with the workflow settings. Because the update goes through the site and updates each content type, this option can take a long time to process after you click the Next or OK button.

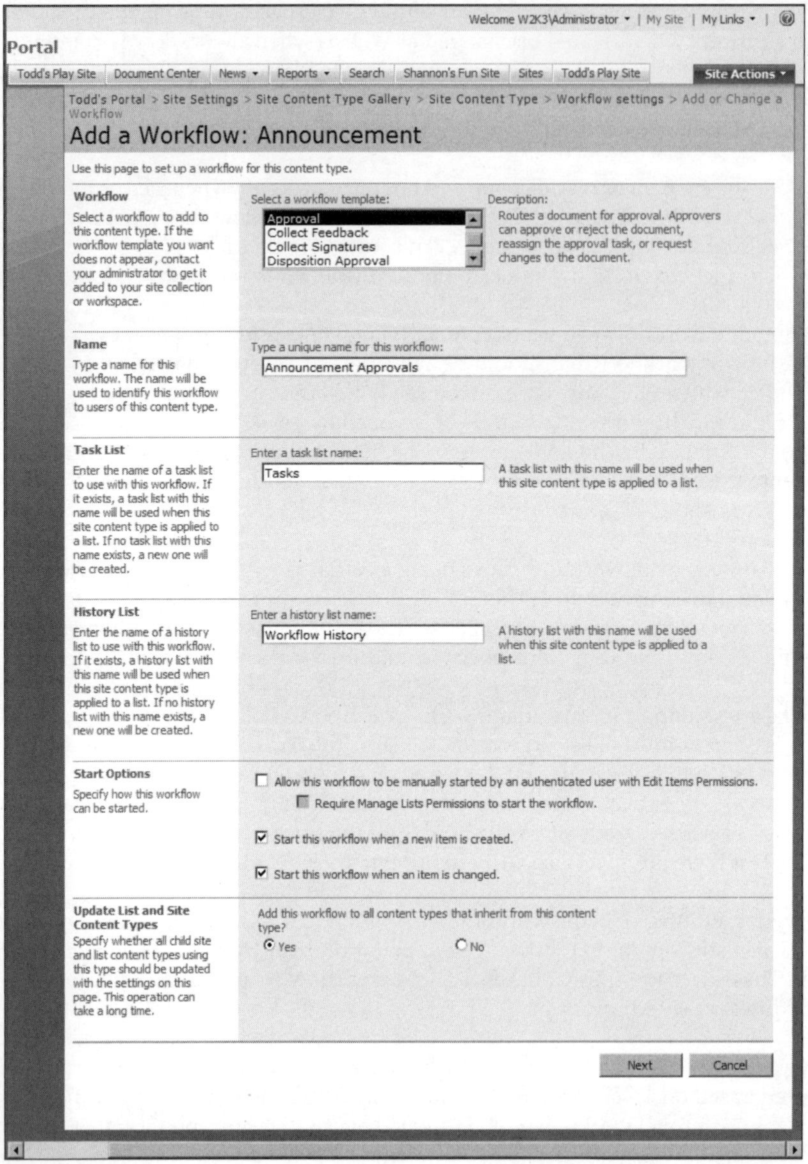

Figure 15-10

Depending on which workflow type you select, there may or may not be another configuration page after this initial page. The button updates itself on the client depending on the item selected in the workflow list box. If the workflow type decrees that further settings are required, the Next button takes you to that workflow's custom association page.

Running Workflows

As you learned in the previous section, there are different ways to start SharePoint workflows. In addition, there are different places where workflows can be initiated. Based on the settings for a workflow, an instance can be started automatically when a new item is added to a list or a new item of a certain content type is created, when an existing item is modified, or when a user chooses to explicitly start a new instance. All three of these options are mutually exclusive and can be turned on and off independently.

Workflow instances can also be kicked off from either the SharePoint interface itself or from inside an Office application. In SharePoint, a workflow is kicked off according to the settings when a new item is added or when an existing item is modified. Also, a user can start a new workflow manually by expanding an item's context menu in a list and choosing the Workflows option. This opens the item's workflow settings page, which has a list of the running workflows associated with the item as well as links at the top of the page to manually start a new instance of whatever workflows are available for that particular item.

You can also interact with SharePoint workflows directly from within Office. Just like uploading a document to SharePoint using the web interface, if an Office document is saved to SharePoint from within Office, any applicable workflow instances are started on the server. In addition, workflows can be manually started from within Office by using the Office button menu. There is a Workflows button in this menu that, when clicked, launches a dialog box (see Figure 15-11), enabling the user to start any workflows allowed for that item depending on the list it is in or its content type.

Figure 15-11

Workflow Forms

Because the out-of-the-box and custom-developed workflows require information specific to each workflow type, you can use custom forms to present and provide data. The out-of-the-box workflows ship with their own custom forms, and you can develop forms for custom workflows using different methods, which are covered later in this chapter. Workflow forms can be classified in different buckets.

Association Forms

Association forms allow the person configuring the workflow to enter initial data for any necessary values in the workflow. A few of the out-of-the-box workflows have association forms. For example, the Approval workflow's association form captures data from the user, such as how to assign tasks to multiple users, how long to give a user to complete his or her task, and when to cancel the workflow, among other things.

Figure 15-12 shows the Three-state workflow's association screen. This page allows you to specify the values for each of the three workflow states as well as actions that should occur when the workflow kicks off.

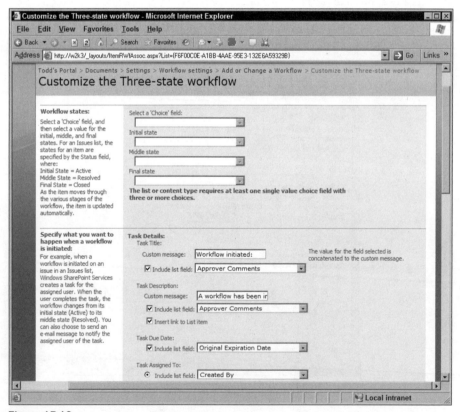

Figure 15-12

Initiation Forms

Initiation forms are the pages that enable users to receive and enter data when a workflow instance is starting. This is useful for selecting which people are to be involved in a workflow or how long to give someone to complete a task. As an example, the initiation form for the out-of-the-box Collect Feedback workflow is shown in Figure 15-13.

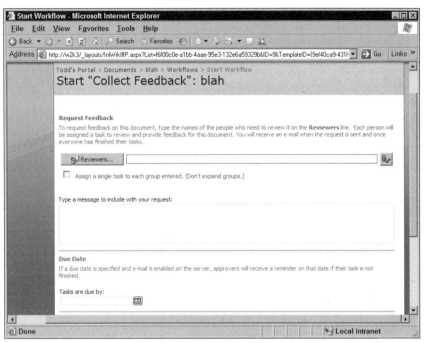

Figure 15-13

Task Completion Forms

Because tasks play such an integral role in workflows in their human interaction, there is a tight integration between tasks and workflow instances. In addition, like the other form types, tasks can expose custom task completion forms that allow users to view and enter relevant data pertaining to the completion of a workflow task.

The completion of a workflow task does not have to be flagged using the traditional method of clicking a check box or changing a status to complete. The logic defined in workflow determines whether a task is complete. For example, a workflow task may be considered complete if the simple condition of text being entered in a text box is met. However, another workflow may not consider a task complete unless several fields are set to no-default values.

Figure 15-14 shows the Collect Feedback workflow's task completion form. In this workflow, the task is considered complete as soon as the Send Feedback button is clicked.

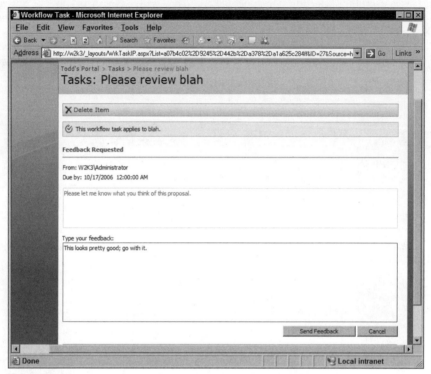

Figure 15-14

Modification Forms

Modification forms provide users with an opportunity to make changes to a live workflow instance. This comes in handy for many scenarios, including reassigning a task or adding another person to a list of active participants, or even a more drastic modification such as skipping steps. Whatever the modification may be, the logic in the workflow determines how the input provided in the form is handled.

Workflow modification forms show up as links on the bottom of a workflow task window. Figure 15-15 shows an example of this for the Approval workflow. Notice the Reassign task link and the Request a change link at the bottom of the page. When the Request a change link is clicked, the user is taken to a page where he or she can request a change from a specific user (likely the originator of the workflow) and enter a description of the change requested.

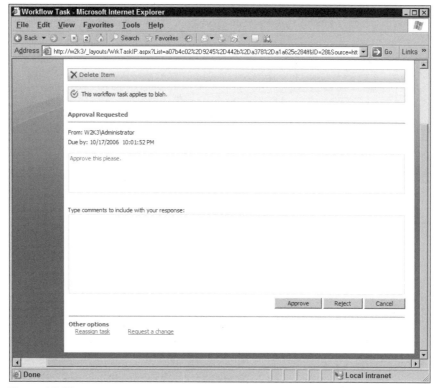

Figure 15-15

Workflow Development in Office

Microsoft never expected the out-of-the-box workflows to meet all possible situations, but it anticipated that users would develop their own custom workflow solutions for the Office platform. There are two methods that you can use to build custom workflows. The new SharePoint Designer application offers a wizard-based approach, and Visual Studio allows you to develop workflows as described throughout this book. The following sections discuss both methods, along with their pros and cons.

Developing in SharePoint Designer

SharePoint Designer 2007 is the replacement for FrontPage, but that description really doesn't do it justice. SharePoint Designer adds functionality that was not available in the past. The new workflow-related tools allow users to build noncode workflows with a wizard-based user interface. The way in which workflows are developed in SharePoint Designer is surprisingly similar to defining rules in Outlook.

To create a new workflow using SharePoint Designer, launch the application and navigate to File ➪ New ➪ Workflow. This displays the initial screen in the Workflow Designer wizard process (see Figure 15-16).

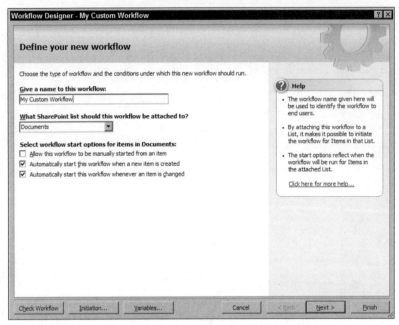

Figure 15-16

There are options on this screen for naming the new workflow, the list that the workflow should be associated with, and when the workflow should start. In addition, there are buttons along the bottom left of the screen that enable the user to validate the workflow as it currently exists, create initiation fields, and create variables that will be used in the workflow. These three buttons are available throughout the workflow development process.

If you click the Initiation button, you are presented with a dialog box that allows the addition or modification of workflow parameters—more specifically, the values that will be set and passed to a new workflow instance when being created. When you create a new field, you must select one of the following field data types:

❑   Single line of text

❑   Multiple lines of text

❑   Number

❑   Date and time

❑   Choice (a list of items to choose among)

❑   Boolean (rendered as a check box)

Additionally, the Variables button presents a dialog box that allows the creation or modification of variables for use in the context of the workflow. Like the initiation fields, the workflow variables have associated data types. The data type options for variables are the following:

- ❑   Boolean

- ❑   Date/Time

- ❑   List Item ID (uniquely references some item in a given list; useful for task IDs)

- ❑   Number

- ❑   String

After you configure the initiation fields and variables, you need to define the workflow logic. To do this, click the Next button on the first screen; an interface like the one shown in Figure 15-17 is displayed. You use this interface to visually define a *branch*, which comprises the *conditions* and *actions* associated with the workflow logic. You can add multiple branches using the hyperlink under the default branch.

Figure 15-17

Conditions are expressions that evaluate to either `true` or `false`, just as with a standard `if` statement in any programming language. The condition does not have to be set if the associated action will always occur.

Conditions can be defined in a number of ways by using the Conditions button. First, an item's fields can be compared with some other value, whether it is a static value, a variable, or the value another item's field. This type of condition can be achieved by selecting Compare *[workflow's list name]* field from the Conditions drop-down menu and then setting the appropriate options for the condition. Options that must be set for a condition or an action are indicated by a hyperlink. Clicking the hyperlink displays the necessary UI for setting the appropriate values.

Other options in the Conditions drop-down menu include prebuilt conditions, such as comparing an items title, its modification or creation date, its type, or size. In addition, the Compare any data source option allows you to set a condition to compare two values from any source, whether it is a field from an item, a variable, or a static value.

You define Actions in the Actions drop-down menu, which contains a list of possible units of work. Multiple actions can be defined for a single condition. Therefore, actions can either run in the sequence in which they are defined or in parallel. This execution option is set using the branch's drop-down menu, which is designated by a down arrow toward the right side of the branch. Table 15-1 is an abbreviated list of available actions.

Table 15-1: Possible Workflow Actions

Action	Description
Collect Data from a User	Allows the user to define a task that will be assigned to the appropriate party. When the workflow is executed, and after the task has been completed, the action is considered executed.
Update List Item	Allows the workflow to set a selected item's field to a value.
Send an Email	Sends an e-mail to a specified user.
Set Workflow Variable	Sets the value of a workflow variable. Variables are defined using the Variables button of the Workflow Designer wizard.
Stop Workflow	Stops the workflow.
Do Calculation	Allows the computation of a simple mathematical expression.

Workflows built in the Workflow Designer also have steps. *Steps* allow the logical grouping of conditions and actions. All the branches of a step must complete before proceeding to a subsequent step.

After you define a workflow, click the Finish button in the Workflow Designer wizard. The workflow definition is saved and deployed to the current site. Several things happen during this save-and-deploy process. If initiation data or custom task fields were defined in the workflow, customer ASPX pages are generated to collect the necessary data from the user. In addition, the workflow definition (.xoml), rules (.rules), and configuration files are created and placed in a new path of the site. A new folder is generally created under the site's Workflow folder. Figure 15-18 shows the SharePoint Designer's Folder List window displaying a custom-developed workflow's folder as well as all the configuration files.

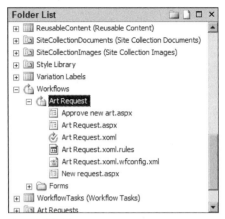

Figure 15-18

After a workflow is deployed and activated, you can easily modify it using SharePoint Designer. To open a workflow's definition, select File ➪ Open Workflow from the main menu. This displays a dialog box that lists all the custom workflows that were developed using SharePoint Designer. After a workflow definition is selected, you are taken to the Workflow Designer wizard UI.

Developing in Visual Studio

The ability to develop custom workflows in Visual Studio and have them execute in a hosted SharePoint environment is a powerful feature. Other parts of this book discussed Windows Workflow Foundation from the perspective that the developer is responsible for everything workflow related: hosting, persistence, and all the other necessary plumbing that comes along with hosting workflows. The ability to develop custom workflows in Visual Studio and then hand them off to SharePoint to handle the plumbing is a pretty big deal.

Developing custom workflows in Visual Studio that are meant to be executed in the SharePoint environment is not necessarily difficult. However, there are prescribed steps that need to be taken to develop, deploy, and properly configure a SharePoint workflow. This section covers these steps in detail. The following is an abbreviated list of the necessary steps that you can use as a quick reference:

1. Create a new SharePoint workflow project.

2. Add SharePoint activities to the toolbox.

3. Develop your workflow with required and optional SharePoint activities as well as standard workflow activities.

4. Sign the assembly.

5. Develop your workflow forms with InfoPath or ASP.NET.

6. Configure the workflow.xml, feature.xml, and install.bat files.

7. Copy everything to the server and run install.bat.

8. Associate the workflow with a list, library, or content type, and configure.

Getting Started

The first thing you need to do to get started is install the SharePoint workflow project templates.

> *As of this book's writing, these templates could be obtained by downloading and installing the Enterprise Content Management Starter Kit from the Microsoft website. The delivery vehicle for these templates may have changed.*

After the templates are installed and associated with Visual Studio, two new project types are available under the SharePoint Server item of the New Project dialog box. Like any other Visual Studio project, you launch this dialog box by navigating to File ➪ New ➪ Project or by pressing Ctrl+Shift+N on the keyboard. Figure 15-19 shows the SharePoint workflow project templates.

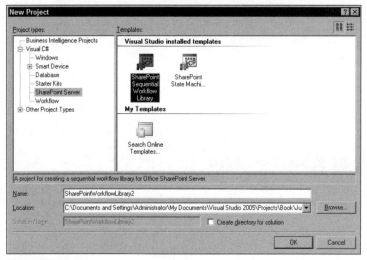

Figure 15-19

The SharePoint templates provide several things. First, necessary references to develop SharePoint work-flows are added. Aside from the standard `System.Workflow.*` assemblies, references are added to `Microsoft.Office.Workflow.Tasks`, `Microsoft.SharePoint`, and `Microsoft.SharePoint.WorkflowActions`. In addition, there are files added to the project that support deployment to SharePoint. These files are workflow.xml, feature.xml, and install.bat.

The feature.xml file is shown in the following code. This file's format is not specific to workflows; rather, it is used for describing all SharePoint features.

```
<?xml version="1.0" encoding="utf-8"?>
<Feature
  Id="{F080F258-164C-44cb-825A-59C85AC09CC2}"
  Title="My Title"
  Description="My description..."
  Version="12.0.0.0"
  Scope="Site"
  ReceiverAssembly="Microsoft.Office.Workflow.Feature, Version=12.0.0.0,
```

```
        Culture=neutral, PublicKeyToken=71e9bce111e9429c"
    ReceiverClass="Microsoft.Office.Workflow.Feature.WorkflowFeatureReceiver"
    xmlns="http://schemas.microsoft.com/sharepoint/">

    <ElementManifests>
      <ElementManifest Location="workflow.xml" />
    </ElementManifests>
    <Properties>
      <Property Key="GloballyAvailable" Value="true" />
      <Property Key="RegisterForms" Value="*.xsn" />
    </Properties>

  </Feature>
```

There are a few interesting workflow-specific parts of this file to check out. First, the `ReceiverClass`
attribute tells SharePoint to use the `WorkflowFeatureReceiver` class when running this feature.
SharePoint essentially hands off control to this class whenever this feature is called. The `ElementManifest`
node points to the workflow.xml file. This node allows additional information not included in the fea-
ture.xml schema to be included. The `Property` node enclosed with the `RegisterForms` key tells the
feature that there are forms to be included. In this example XML, all xsn (InfoPath) files are grabbed
from the same directory as feature.xml.

The following code shows the workflow.xml file, which was referenced in the feature.xml file:

```
<?xml version="1.0" encoding="utf-8" ?>
<Elements xmlns="http://schemas.microsoft.com/sharepoint/">
  <Workflow
    Name="My Workflow"
    Description="This workflow ..."
    Id="{5AAD35C9-5A1E-44ae-B45F-D40A13085D85}"
    CodeBesideClass="MyAssembly.MyProject"
    CodeBesideAssembly="MyAssembly, Version=3.0.0.0,
      Culture=neutral, PublicKeyToken=a7ae913b1faf46ca"
    TaskListContentTypeId="0x01080100C9C9515DE4E24001905074F980F93160"
    AssociationUrl="_layouts/CstWrkflIP.aspx"
    InstantiationUrl="_layouts/IniWrkflIP.aspx"
    ModificationUrl="_layouts/ModWrkflIP.aspx">

    <Categories />

    <MetaData>
      <Association_FormURN>[valid URN]</Association_FormURN>
      <Instantiation_FormURN>[valid URN]</Instantiation_FormURN>
      <Task0_FormURN>[valid URN]</Task0_FormURN>

      <Modification_GUID_FormURN>[valid URN]</Modification_GUID_FormURN>
      <Modification_GUID_Name>My Modification Form</Modification_GUID_Name>

      <StatusPageUrl>_layouts/WrkStat.aspx</StatusPageUrl>
    </MetaData>
  </Workflow>
</Elements>
```

This file defines some of the workflow-specific properties for deployment. At the top are attributes such as `Name` and `Description`. The `Id` attribute is simply a unique GUID, which cannot be the same as the feature's `Id` attribute. The `CodeBesideClass` and `CodeBesideAssembly` attributes tell SharePoint where to find the workflow's code-beside logic. Because the workflow's assembly has to be installed in the Global Assembly Cache (GAC) and strongly signed, it is referenced as such with the public key token.

Three other interesting attributes of the `Workflow` node are `AssociationUrl`, `InstantiationUrl`, and `ModificationUrl`. In this example XML, these are all pointing to default values, which will likely be the same all the time. The paths in these respective attributes are specific to SharePoint and include web parts to handle appropriate actions for a workflow. These attributes are related to the values in the `MetaData` node for forms as well.

Notice that there are child nodes of `MetaData` called `Association_FormURN`, `Instantiation_FormURN`, and `Modification_GUID_FomURN`. These three properties point to InfoPath forms that have been deployed to SharePoint per the feature.xml file. Modification forms are not required for SharePoint work-flows; therefore, the `Modification_GUID_FormURN` and `Modification_GUID_Name` nodes are optional.

Like the `Url` attributes of the `Workflow` node, the `StatusPageUrl` is a standard SharePoint path that can be universally used for different workflows.

The last file that is added to a SharePoint workflow project is install.bat. Although this file is not required, it is a great help when it comes time to deploy custom-developed SharePoint workflows. The following steps are executed in the batch file:

1. Creates a directory for the feature.

2. Copies feature.xml, workflow.xml, and all xsn files to the new directory.

3. Installs the strongly typed assembly (from the Debug folder) to the GAC.

4. Uses the stsadm.exe command-line utility to deactivate and uninstall the feature from SharePoint (if the line is uncommented). This is necessary if the feature had been previously deployed.

5. Uses stsadm.exe to install and activate the feature.

6. Resets IIS so that the changes take effect.

The install.bat file is shown in the following code. Some unnecessary or unused lines were removed from the file that would normally be found in a fresh SharePoint workflow project.

```
echo Copying the feature...

rd /s /q "%CommonProgramFiles%\Microsoft Shared\web server
extensions\12\TEMPLATE\FEATURES\MyFeature"
mkdir "%CommonProgramFiles%\Microsoft Shared\web server
extensions\12\TEMPLATE\FEATURES\MyFeature"

copy /Y feature.xml  "%CommonProgramFiles%\Microsoft Shared\web server
extensions\12\TEMPLATE\FEATURES\MyFeature\"
copy /Y workflow.xml "%CommonProgramFiles%\Microsoft Shared\web server
extensions\12\TEMPLATE\FEATURES\MyFeature\"
```

```
xcopy /s /Y *.xsn "%programfiles%\Common Files\Microsoft Shared\web server
extensions\12\TEMPLATE\FEATURES\MyFeature\"

echo Adding assemblies to the GAC...

"%programfiles%\Microsoft Visual Studio 8\SDK\v2.0\Bin\gacutil.exe" -uf MyFeature
"%programfiles%\Microsoft Visual Studio 8\SDK\v2.0\Bin\gacutil.exe" -if
bin\Debug\MyFeature.dll

echo Activating the feature...

pushd %programfiles%\common files\microsoft shared\web server extensions\12\bin

:: Only have the following 2 lines uncommented if you've previously deployed this
feature
::stsadm -o deactivatefeature -filename MyFeature\feature.xml -url http://localhost
::stsadm -o uninstallfeature -filename MyFeature\feature.xml

stsadm -o installfeature -filename MyFeature\feature.xml -force
stsadm -o activatefeature -filename MyFeature\feature.xml -url http://localhost

echo Doing an iisreset...

popd
iisreset
```

Developing the Workflow

Now that the default files in a workflow project have been inspected, it's time to get down to business. The first thing that needs to be done, if this is the first time a SharePoint workflow has been developed on a workstation, is to add the SharePoint-specific tasks to the Visual Studio Toolbox. Because it is easier to have the SharePoint activities logically grouped together, first create a new Toolbox tab by right-clicking an empty area of the Toolbox and clicking Add Tab. Name it something useful like SharePoint Workflow Activities.

To add the activities to the newly created tab, right-click an empty area of the tab's background and click Choose Items. This displays the Choose Toolbox Items dialog box, which contains a list of the components in referenced assemblies on the .NET Framework Components tab. To find and select the SharePoint activities, sort by the Namespace column and scroll to `Microsoft.SharePoint.WorkflowActions`. Select every item in this namespace and click OK. This adds all of the SharePoint-specific activities to the Toolbox tab that was just created. Now you are ready to develop a custom SharePoint workflow.

To illustrate developing custom SharePoint workflows in Visual Studio, an example of an art request process is used here. Many organizations have an art department that is responsible for creating artwork for products and marketing materials. This example uses an InfoPath form to collect some basic information from a user in need of some art. The user will have the option of specifying whether the request is of high importance — this request will be given greater priority. After the request is generated in a forms library, a task will be created for the user specified in the InfoPath form. That person will then start creating the artwork.

After the art has been created, the artist will set the task to complete, which will then notify the original requestor that the art is available. The requestor will then approve or reject the artwork and provide comments. If the artwork is approved, the workflow will send an e-mail to the person who requested the art as well as the artist, and the workflow will be considered complete. If the artwork is rejected, a new task will be created for the artist, and a loop will continue until the artwork is approved.

The development of the workflow and associated code is covered here first, with the forms development covered in the next section. To get started, rename the default workflow that was added to the project to something more useful, such as ArtRequestWorkflow.cs. Visual Studio asks you whether you want to rename all references of the class name. You should say yes, but not all references to the old class name will be changed. The workflow has an OnWorkflowActivated activity added and configured by default, and its `CorrelationToken` property still points to the old class name. Simply expand the property in the Properties window and change `OwnerActivityName` to the new class name.

The OnWorkflowActivated activity has a property called `WorkflowProperties`, which is already pointing to a class field in the code-beside file. This property is of type `SPWorkflowActivationProperties` and is the workflow's portal to the outside SharePoint environment. This object is used later, when the association and initiation data needs to be accessed. To gain access to the data passed to the workflow from SharePoint you must handle the OnWorkflowActivated activity's `Invoked` event. This workflow's event handler is shown in the following code:

```
private void WorkflowInvoked(object sender, ExternalDataEventArgs e)
{
    Hashtable data = Form.XmlToHashtable(workflowProperties.InitiationData);
    this.artRequestDescription = (string)data["requestDescription"];
    this.thePeople = Contact.ToContacts((string)data["thePeople"],
        workflowProperties.Web);
    this.theRequestor = workflowProperties.OriginatorUser;
}
```

There are a few new things going on here. First, the workflow's initiation data is obtained using the `workflowProperties.InitiationData` property. This property is simply a string representation of XML because InfoPath is being used for the initiation form, and there are a couple of options for accessing its contents. One option would be to use the InfoPath form's XML Schema Definition (XSD) to generate a .NET class and deserialize the initiation data XML. Although this is a perfectly viable technique, this example uses a helper class from the `Microsoft.Office.Workflow.Utility.Form` class. The `XmlToHashtable` method does what its name describes and returns a `Hashtable` instance, named data in the code. The `data` object is then used to gain access to the request description that was entered by the user on the initiation form.

In addition, the `data` object is used to gain access to the people who were assigned to this art request by the originator. As you will see in the next section, which covers the development of the InfoPath form, the list of people is represented by a structured XML schema. Because of this, the Office API exposes a class called `Contact`, which has a helper method called `ToContacts`. This method takes a string representing the XML containing user information as well as an instance of the `SPWeb` class. The return value is set to a class field of type `Contact[`. Finally, the code in the `WorkflowInvoked` event handler obtains a reference to the object representing the user who started the workflow.

The first step in the example workflow is for a task to be created for an artist. However, consider for a moment whether the requestor of the art wants to have more than one artist take a stab at the request. In this case, the initiation form needs to provide a way to enter more than one user. Because a well-designed workflow should be able to account for this situation in an elegant fashion, the Replicator activity from the base activity library is used to design for multiple artists. The Replicator activity takes whatever its children are and replicates them the number of times defined by its InitialChildData property. The thePeople array in the WorkflowInvoked event handler is used for the InitialChildData. The code for the Replicator activity's Initialized event is as follows:

```
private void replicateOnPeople_Initialized(object sender, EventArgs e)
{
    this.childDataForReplicator.AddRange(this.thePeople);
}
```

The workflow logic is defined within the Replicator activity and its required Sequence activity child. This starts with a SharePoint activity called CreateTask. The CreateTask activity is a custom activity developed for SharePoint that inherits from the out-of-the-box CallExternalMethodActivity class to call external code in SharePoint. One of this activity's required properties is CorrelationToken, which allows the workflow runtime to know which activity a particular event from the outside is associated with. This property should be set to a new value, not to workflowToken, which was created with the workflow. You can do this by typing a name in the Properties window. In addition, the TaskId and TaskProperties properties should be bound to new fields in the code-beside class. Finally, the activity's MethodInvoking event should be wired so that the task's necessary properties can be set before the activity is executed. The handler for the MethodInvoking event is shown in the following code:

```
private void createNewTask_MethodInvoking(object sender, EventArgs e)
{
    this.taskGuid = Guid.NewGuid();
    this.taskProperties.AssignedTo = CurrentArtist.LoginName;
    this.taskProperties.Title = "New Art Requested by " +
        this.theRequestor.LoginName;
    this.taskProperties.Description = "Description from user: " +
        this.artRequestDescription;
    this.taskProperties.TaskType = 0;

    int daysToComplete = 21;
    if (this.isHighPriorityRequest)
        daysToComplete = 14;
    this.taskProperties.DueDate = DateTime.Today.AddDays(daysToComplete);
}
```

In this code, a new Guid instance is created and assigned to a class-level member. This is the member that the TaskId properties of the task-related activities are bound to. Also, the task has several of its properties set. The AssignedTo property is set to the current artist's LoginName property. Also, the task type is set to 0. This separates different task types so that each type can have its own task-editing form. The form to task type mapping is defined in the workflow.xml file. Finally, the task's due date is set using logic based on the high-priority flag set in the workflow initiation form.

The next few pieces of logic in the workflow follow what will likely be a very common pattern in task assignment in SharePoint. There is a While activity that loops over an OnTaskChanged activity until a flag tells the loop that the task is completed. After the loop is exited, a CompleteTask activity is used to mark the task in SharePoint as completed. The CreateTask, OnTaskChanged, and CompleteTask activities all point to the same task reference through their respective TaskId properties as well as their CorrelationToken properties.

From here, additional logic is defined in the workflow that implements the art-request algorithm described earlier. In addition to the SharePoint activities introduced thus far, LogToHistoryListActivity is used numerous times to track potentially useful data about the execution of the workflow. Figure 15-20 shows a partial screen shot of the completed workflow.

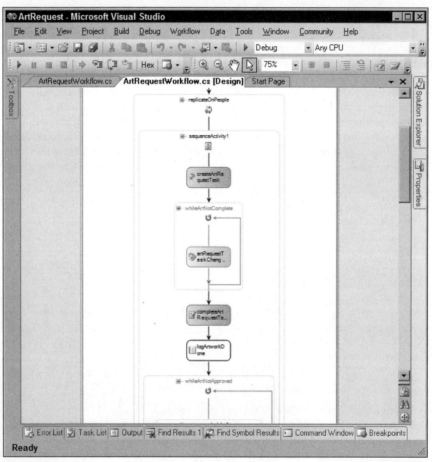

Figure 15-20

Implementing Forms Using InfoPath and Forms Server

So far in this chapter, there has been a lot of talk about the various forms for SharePoint workflows. This section shows you how to develop and use custom forms. To develop custom workflow forms for SharePoint, you use Microsoft Office InfoPath, which includes the InfoPath 2007 client and Forms Server. However, you can use Forms Server only with Microsoft Office SharePoint Server (MOSS), which is not free. If you are developing against WSS, you need to use ASP.NET to develop custom forms.

Although InfoPath forms development is a topic all to itself (it has whole books devoted to it), there are some specific steps you must be take to successfully develop forms for SharePoint workflows. To illustrate these steps, the art-approval example is continued. Developing an InfoPath form for use in a SharePoint workflow is somewhat tedious, as the steps to configure the forms correctly are prescribed.

To get started, launch Microsoft Office InfoPath 2007 and select Design a Form Template from the Getting Started dialog box. In the next screen, choose to design a new form template and make sure that Blank is selected from the list view. Uncheck the Ensure browser-compatible features only check box and then click OK to design the new form.

Another housekeeping task you must do to make sure everything works as it should is to set the forms trust level. To do this, navigate to Tools ➪ Forms Options and then click Security and Trust in the left pane of the options window (see Figure 15-21). To allow the form to access information in SharePoint, which is outside the context of the form, you must select the domain option. Uncheck the Automatically determine security level check box and select the domain-level trust.

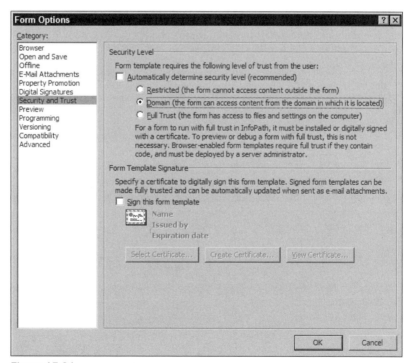

Figure 15-21

The form needs domain-level trust because it has to access information about users in order to create tasks. The way this user information is accessed is through the Contact Selector control that was developed by Microsoft for InfoPath workflow forms. This control works a lot like the check names feature in Microsoft Office Outlook. However, by default the InfoPath controls toolbox does not contain this control. To add it, you need to access the controls panel from InfoPath's Task Pane.

At the bottom of the controls toolbox, click the Add or Remove Custom Controls link. The Add/Remove dialog box is displayed. Click the Add button. The resulting wizard asks whether you want to add a Template Part or an ActiveX control. Because the Contact Selector is an ActiveX control, select that option and click Next. The contact control can be found in the list on the next screen. Next, the wizard asks whether you want to include a cab file. Because this solution needs to be rendered only in the browser, choose to not include a cab file. On the binding screen, select Value and click Next. In the final screen of the wizard, select the Field or group (any data type) option from the field or group type dropdown menu. Click Finish to complete the wizard. The Contact Selector control is now listed in the controls toolbox under the Custom heading.

InfoPath uses XSD to define a form's data. Consequently, some entities need to be defined to hold the data returned by the Contact Selector control. This data structure must be defined in the Data Source section of the Task Pane. Before defining this structure, rename the Contact Selector from `group1` to something useful. To do this, hover over the control and then double-click the tool tip showing the name to display the control's properties. As you may recall from previous workflow code, the artists chosen were obtained by accessing an extended property of the initiation form called `thePeople`. Therefore, this Contact Selector control should be named the same thing.

Now that you have changed the name, you need to modify the form's data source to contain the necessary fields and groups. The Items tab of the Contact Selectors properties shows you the XML structure to which the form must conform. The following code shows the XML. In addition, Figure 15-22 shows the structure of the form's data source.

```
<thePeople>
  <Person>
    <DisplayName />
    <AccountId />
    <AccountType />
  </Person>
</thePeople>
```

Figure 15-22

Now you can use the Data Source section of the Task Pane to define this data structure using a group for the `Person` element and fields for the `DisplayName`, `AccountId`, and `AccountType` nodes. The `requestDescription` and `highPriority` nodes are added automatically when controls are added to the form (do not add them manually).

Next, you need to design the form. In addition to the Contact Selector that is already on the form, it needs a text box for the request description, a check box for the high-priority flag, and a submit button. Add these to the form by dragging them from the Controls section of the Task Pane. Aside from visual modifications, such as sizing, the text box and check box do not need any of their properties changed. The button, however, needs some tweaking before it is ready to be used.

When the button is clicked, it will need to submit the form data to SharePoint, which is an outside environment as far as InfoPath is concerned. To configure the button in this way, double-click it to access its properties. The action needs to be set to Rules and Custom Code, which it is by default. Next, click the Rules button to launch the Rules dialog box and then click the Add button. From here, you need to add two actions: one to submit the form to the outside host and one to close the form.

To add the submit action, click the Add Action button and select the Submit using a data connection option from the drop-down menu. You can either select an existing data connection or create a new one. Click the Add button to create a new data connection, which launches a wizard. Choose the option that enables you to create a new connection to submit data and click Next. In the next screen, choose the destination for the form submission, which is the hosting environment. The next screen enables you to name the new data connection — the Submit default name is fine for this example, so don't change it.

Now the button rule needs a new action to close the form after submission. Click the Add Action button, select the Close the form option from the drop-down menu, and then click OK. Finally, click OK three more times to get back to the form. Now the form is correctly configured and ready to be deployed. Figure 15-23 shows the final form.

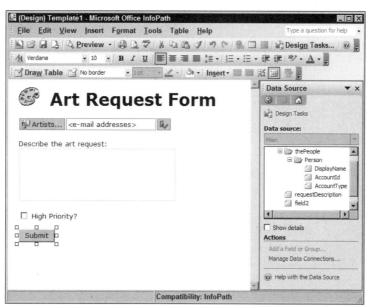

Figure 15-23

All you have left to do with the form is save it and then publish it to a network location. However, for this example, simply publish the form to a local folder on your drive, such as the folder in which your workflow project is located. This will make it easy to deploy everything to the SharePoint server.

Deploying and Configuring Custom Workflows to SharePoint

The install.bat file, which is included in new SharePoint workflow project, was introduced earlier as an easy way to deploy custom SharePoint workflows. Although this is certainly true, and there is nothing wrong with using this method, you need to fully understand what is going on during the deployment process. First, whether or not you are using install.bat, the necessary files need to be copied to the SharePoint front-end server. This includes feature.xml, workflow.xml, and the InfoPath forms developed for the workflow.

After all the necessary files are on the server, they must be installed so that SharePoint is aware of the feature. You do this by using the SharePoint command-line utility called stsadm.exe. This executable not only allows the installation of SharePoint features, but also enables you to perform administrative functions such as adding or deleting users, modifying configuration properties, and managing SharePoint sites. Refer to the preceding install.bat listing for how to install and activate a SharePoint feature.

After the feature is installed and activated, it helps to perform an `iisreset` to ensure that the changes can be seen. At this point, the new workflow feature is visible on the Site Collection Features page in Site Settings. To get to this page, click the Site Actions menu in the upper-right of any page and then select Site Settings, followed by Modify All Site Settings. On the succeeding page, click the Site collection features link under the Site Collection Administration heading. Figure 15-24 shows what this page looks like with a custom feature installed and activated. Now that the workflow is deployed, it can be associated with a list or content type just like any of the workflows covered so far in this chapter.

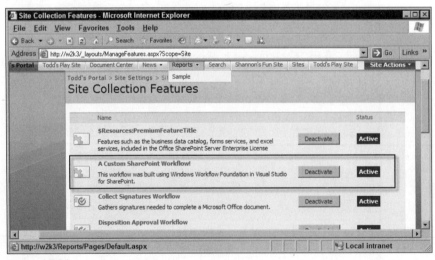

Figure 15-24

After you have deployed a SharePoint workflow to the server, you can make changes by copying the updated assemblies to the server and performing an `iisreset`. However, you can use this method only when you are making changes to the workflow itself, not to any of the workflow forms of the workflow.xml and feature.xml files.

Debugging Custom Workflows in SharePoint

Debugging custom workflows that are deployed and running in a SharePoint site is fairly straightforward. The debugging process involves attaching the Visual Studio debugger to the process that is hosting the workflow. SharePoint is an Internet application, so the process you use is w3wp.exe (World Wide Web Worker Process).

Because debugging workflows involves attaching to a process on the server, and because certain required DLLs are only on the server, you must do all debugging on the server itself. This means that Visual Studio needs to be installed on the server, and physical or remote access to the server (through a Remote Desktop or VNC) is required. Under optimal conditions, remote debugging of workflows may be possible; however, it is likely more trouble than it is worth.

If a workflow needs to be debugged from a SharePoint site, it must be compiled and deployed in Debug mode. After you have a workflow deployed that needs to be monitored, open the project in Visual Studio and select the Attach to Process item from the Debug menu. This opens a dialog box with the w3wp.exe process selected (see Figure 15-25).

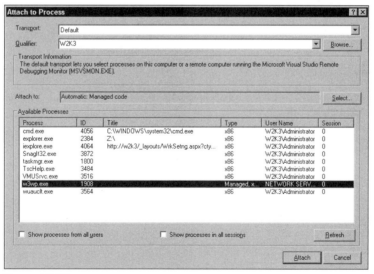

Figure 15-25

Click the Attach button. The debugger is attached, and the required debugging symbols are loaded. Perform the steps required in SharePoint to start the workflow instance that needs to be debugged. After the workflow is loaded and executed, any breakpoints that have been defined in the code windows are monitored, and execution halts when a breakpoint is hit. The debugging process from here is the same as debugging any other type of code in Visual Studio.

Another way to troubleshoot problem workflows is to use the Cancellation & Error Report discussed earlier in this chapter. This Excel report contains two tabs, the second of which holds data related to errors that occur in workflow instances. The columns in this report include the workflow instance's ID, the list and item the workflow instance was associated with, and the date and time the error occurred, among other data points. The last column of the report, labeled Data, includes any error messages received through a .NET exception. This column alone is quite helpful for developing new custom workflows.

Summary

The chapter covered several topics related to workflow and the Microsoft Office system. One of the newer pieces of the Office landscape is SharePoint, which offers a web-based application and content management server. In SharePoint 2007, there is a tight integration between the portal software and workflow. Windows Workflow Foundation provides the foundation for a whole new set of possibilities in SharePoint.

Several out-of-the-box workflows provide functionality such as document approval, signature collection, and translation management. There are also two different ways to develop workflows for SharePoint. You can use SharePoint Designer to develop custom workflows using a wizard-based interface, or for more complex workflows, you can use Visual Studio and custom code.

You use forms to interface with workflows. There are several different classifications of workflow forms, including association forms, initiation forms, and task modification forms. In addition, you can custom-develop forms using InfoPath.

Index

code listings (continued)

Figures (continued)